Mobil
Travel Guide®

NEW ENGLAND

ACKNOWLEDGEMENTS

We gratefully acknowledge the help of our representatives for their efficient and perceptive inspections of the lodging and dining establishments listed, the establishments' proprietors for their cooperation in showing their facilities and providing information about them, and the many users of previous editions who have taken the time to share their experiences. Mobil Travel Guide is also grateful to all the talented writers who contributed entries to this book.

Maps: ©GeoNova. This product contains proprietary property of GeoNova. Unauthorized use, including copying, of this product is expressly prohibited.

Front cover photos:
Signpost in Maine: U.S. Landmarks and Travel/Getty Images
Owl's Head Lighthouse on the Maine Coast: U.S. Landmarks and Travel 2/Getty Images
Massachusetts State House, Capital Building: Copyright © 2007 Corel Corp.
Boston's Faneuil Hall: ©Charles Smith/ Corbis

ISBN: 0-8416-0312-X or 978-0-8416-0312-7
Manufactured in the Canada.
10 9 8 7 6 5 4 3 2 1

CONTENTS

MAPS

NEW ENGLAND

CELEBRATING 50 YEARS

Because time is precious and the travel industry is ever-changing, having accurate, reliable travel information at your has fingertips is essential. Mobil Travel Guide provided invaluable insight to travelers for 50 years, and we are committed to continuing this service into the future.

The Mobil Corporation (known as Exxon Mobil Corporation since a 1999 merger) began producing the Mobil Travel Guide books in 1958 following the introduction of the U.S.-interstate highway system in 1956. The first edition covered only five Southwestern states. Since then, our books have become the premier travel guides in North America, covering all 50 states and Canada.

Since its founding, Mobil Travel Guide has served as an advocate for travelers seeking knowledge about hotels, restaurants and places to visit. Based on an objective process, we make recommendations to our customers that we believe will enhance the quality and value of their travel experiences. Our trusted Mobil One- to Five-Star rating system is the oldest and most respected lodging and restaurant inspection and rating program in North America. Most hoteliers, restaurateurs and industry observers favorably regard the rigor of our inspection program and understand the prestige and benefits that come with receiving a Mobil Star rating.

The Mobil Travel Guide process of rating each establishment includes:

★ Unannouced facility inspections
★ Incognito service evaluations for
★ A review of unsolicited comments from the general public
★ Senior management oversight

For each property, more than 450 attributes, including cleanliness, physical facilities and employee attitude and courtesy, are measured and evaluated to produce a mathematically derived score, which is then blended with the other elements to form an overall score. These scores form the basis that we use to assign our Mobil One- to Five-Star ratings.

This process focuses on guest expectations, guest experience and consistency of service, not just physical facilities and amenities. It's fundamentally a rating system that rewards those properties that continually strive for and achieve excellence each year. The very best properties are consistently raising the bar for those that wish to compete with them.

Only facilities that meet Mobil Travel Guide's standards earn the privilege of being listed in the guide. Deteriorating, poorly managed establishments are deleted. A Mobil Travel Guide listing constitutes a positive quality recommendation. Every listing is an accolade, a recognition of achievement.

★★★★★The Mobil Five-Star Award indicates that a property is one of the very best in the country and consistently provides gracious and courteous service, superlative quality in its facility and a unique ambience. The lodgings and restaurants at the Mobil Five-Star level consistently continues their commitment to excellence, doing so with grace and perseverance.

★★★★The Mobil Four-Star Award honors properties for outstanding achievement in overall facility and for providing very strong service levels in all areas. These award winners provide a distinctive experience for the ever-demanding and sophisticated consumer.

★★★The Mobil Three-Star Award recognizes an excellent property that provides full services and amenities. This category ranges from exceptional hotels with limited services to elegant restaurants with a less-formal atmosphere.

★★The Mobil Two-Star property is a clean and comfortable establishment that has expanded amenities or a distinctive environment. These properties are an excellent place to stay or dine.

★The Mobil One-Star property is limited in its amenities and services but provides a value experience while meeting travelers' expectations. Expect the properties to be clean, comfortable and convenient.

We do not charge establishments for inclusion in our guides. We have no relationship with any of the businesses and attractions we list and act only as a consumer advocate. We do the investigative legwork so that you won't have to.

Restaurants and hotels—particularly small chains and stand-alone establishments—change management or even go out of business with surprising quickness. Although we make every effort to update continuously information, we recommend that you call ahead to make sure the place you've selected is still open.

We hope that your travels are enjoyable and relaxing and that our books help you get the most out of every trip you take. If any aspect of your accommodation, dining, spa or sightseeing experience motivates you to comment, please contact us. Mobil Travel Guide, 200 W. Madison St., Suite 3950, Chicago, IL 60611, or send an e-mail to info@mobiltravelguide.com. Happy travels.

HOW TO USE THIS BOOK

The Mobil Travel Guide Regional Travel Planners are designed for convenience. Each state has its own chapter, beginning with a general introduction that provides a geographical and historical orientation to the state and gives basic statewide tourist information. The remainder of each chapter is devoted to travel destinations within the state—mainly cities and towns, but also national parks and tourist areas—which, like the states, are arranged in alphabetical order.

MAPS

We have provided state maps as well as maps of selected larger cities to help you find your way.

DESTINATION INFORMATION

We list addresses, phone number and web sites for travel information resources—usually the local chamber of commerce or office of tourism—and a brief introduction to the area. Information about airports, ground transportation and suburbs is included for large cities.

DRIVING TOURS AND WALKING TOURS

The driving tours that we include for many states are usually day trips that make for interesting side excursions. They offer you a way to get off the beaten path. These trips frequently cover areas of natural beauty or historical significance.

WHAT TO SEE AND DO

Mobil Travel Guide offers information about thousands of museums, art galleries, amusement parks, historic sites, national and state parks, ski areas and many other attractions.

Following an attraction's description, you'll find the months, days and, in some cases, hours of operation, address, telephone number and web site (if there is one).

SPECIAL EVENTS

Special events are either annual events that last only a short time, such as festivals and fairs or longer, seasonal events such as horse racing, theater and summer concerts. Our Special Events listings also include infrequently occurring occasions that mark certain dates or events, such as a centennial or other commemorative celebration.

LISTINGS

Hotels, restaurants and spas are usually listed under the city or town in which they're located. Make sure to check the nearby cities and towns for additional options, especially if you're traveling to a major metropolitan area that includes many suburbs. If a property is located in a town that doesn't have its own heading, the listing appears under the town nearest it. In large cities, hotels located within 5 miles of major commercial airports may be listed under a separate Airport Area heading that follows the city section.

THE STAR RATINGS
MOBIL RATED HOTELS

Travelers have different needs when it comes to accommodations. To help you pinpoint properties that meet your particular needs, Mobil Travel Guide classifies each lodging by type according to the following characteristics.

★★★★★The Mobil Five-Star hotel provides consistently superlative service in an exceptionally distinctive luxury environment, with expanded services. Attention to detail is evident throughout the hotel, resort or inn, from bed linens to staff uniforms.

★★★★The Mobil Four-Star hotel provides a luxury experience with expanded amenities in a distinctive environment. Services may include automatic turndown service, 24-hour room service and valet parking.

★★★The Mobil Three-Star hotel is well appointed, with a full-service restaurant and expanded amenities, such as a fitness center, golf course, tennis courts, 24-hour room service and optional turndown service.

★★The Mobil Two-Star hotel is considered a clean, comfortable and reliable establishment that has expanded amenities, such as a full-service restaurant on the premises.

★The Mobil One-Star lodging is a limited-service hotel, motel or inn that is considered a clean, comfortable and reliable establishment

For every property, we also provide pricing information. The pricing categories break down as follows:

★ **$** = Up to $150
★ **$$** = $151-$250
★ **$$$** = $251-$350
★ **$$$$** = $351 and up

All prices quoted are accurate at the time of publication, however prices cannot be guaranteed. In some locations, special events, holidays or seasons can affect prices. Some resorts have complicated rate structures that vary with the time of year, so confirm rates when making your plans.

SPECIALITY LODGINGS

A Speciality Lodging is a unique inn, bed and breakfast or guest ranch with limited service, but appealing, attractive facilities that make the property worth a visit.

MOBIL RATED RESTAURANTS

All Mobil Star-rated dining establishments listed in this book have a full kitchen and most offer table service.

★★★★★The Mobil Five-Star restaurant offers one of few flawless dining experiences in the country. These establishments consistently provide their guests with exceptional food, superlative service, elegant décor and exquisite presentations of each detail surrounding a meal.

★★★★The Mobil Four-Star restaurant provides professional service, distinctive presentations and wonderful food.

★★★The Mobil Three-Star restaurant has good food, warm and skillful service and enjoyable décor.

★★The Mobil Two-Star restaurant serves fresh food in a clean setting with efficient service. Value is considered in this category, as is family friendliness.

★The Mobil One-Star restaurant provides a distinctive experience through culinary specialty, local flair or individual atmosphere. about appropriate attire is provided, although it's always a good idea to call ahead and ask if you're unsure; the meaning of "casual" or "business casual" varies widely in different parts of the country. We also indicate whether the restaurant has a bar, whether a children's menu is offered and whether outdoor seating is available. If reservations are recommended, we note that fact in the listing. When valet parking is available, it is noted in the description. Because menu prices can fluctuate, we list a pricing category rather than specific prices. The pricing categories are defined as follows, per diner, and assume that you order an appetizer or dessert, an entrée and one drink:

★ **$** = $15 and under
★ **$$** = $16-$35
★ **$$$** = $36-$85
★ **$$$$** = $86 and up

All prices quoted are accurate at the time of publication, but prices cannot be guaranteed.

MOBIL RATED SPAS

Mobil Travel Guide is pleased to announce its newest category, hotel and resort spas. Until now, hotel and resort spas have not been formally rated or inspected by any organization. Every spa selected for inclusion in this book underwent a rigorous inspection process similar to the one Mobil Travel Guide has been applying to lodgings and restaurants for five decades. After researching more than 300 spas and performing exhaustive incognito inspections of more than 200 properties, we narrowed our list to the best spas in the United States and Canada.

Mobil Travel Guide's spa ratings are based on objective evaluations of more than 450 attributes. Approximately half of these criteria assess basic expectations, such as staff courtesy, the technical proficiency and skill of the employees and whether the facility is maintained properly and hygienically. Several standards address issues that impact a guest's physical comfort and convenience, as well as the staff's ability to impart a sense of personalized service and anticipate clients' needs. Additional criteria measure the spa's ability to create a completely calming ambience.

The Mobil Star ratings focus on much more than the facilities available at a spa and the treatments it offers. Each Mobil Star rating is a cumulative score achieved from multiple inspections that reflects the spa management's attention to detail and commitment to consumers' needs.

★★★★★The Mobil Five-Star spa provides consistently superlative service in an exceptionally distinctive luxury environment

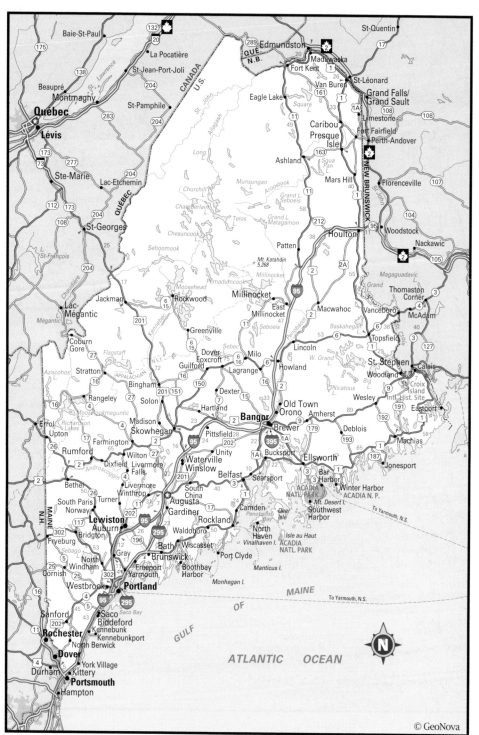

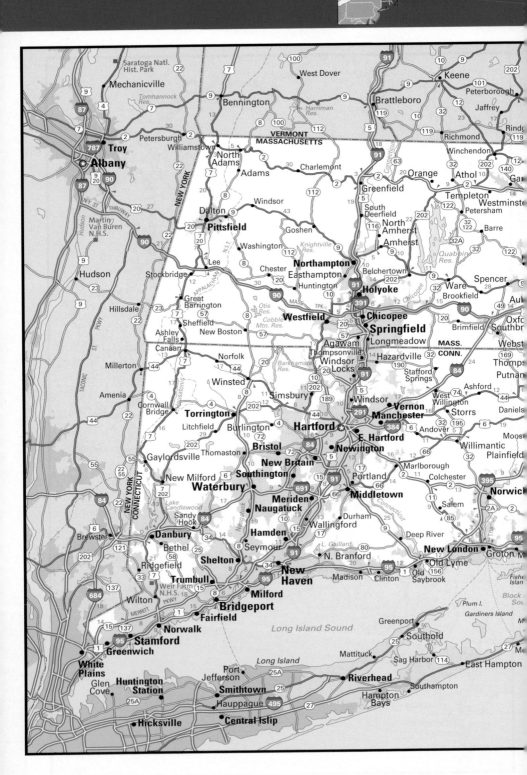

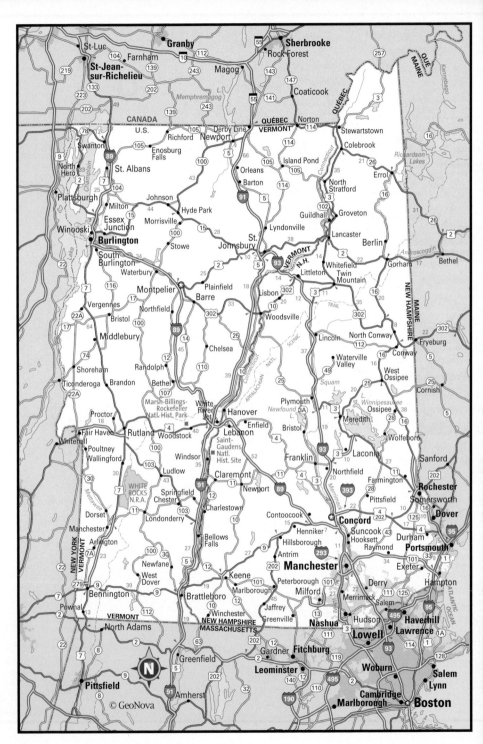

with extensive amenities. The staff at a Mobil Five-Star spa provides extraordinary service beyond the traditional spa experience, allowing guests to achieve the highest level of relaxation and pampering. A Mobil Five-Star spa offers an extensive array of treatments, often incorporating international themes and products. Attention to detail is evident throughout the spa, from arrival to departure.

★★★★The Mobil Four-Star spa provides a luxurious experience with expanded amenities in an elegant and serene environment. Throughout the spa facility, guests experience personalized service. Amenities might include, but are not limited to, single-sex relaxation rooms where guests wait for their treatments, plunge pools and whirlpools in both men's and women's locker rooms, and an array of treatments, including a selection of massages, body therapies, facials and a variety of salon services.

★★★The Mobil Three-Star spa is physically well appointed and has a full complement of staff.

★ CELEBRATING ★
50 YEARS OF MOBIL TRAVEL GUIDE

1962 ——— **1964** ——— **1968** ——— **1971** ⟶

⟵ **1973** ——— **1976** ——— **1978** ——— **1979** ⟶

1986 ——— 1988 ——— 1989 ——— 1992

1994 ——— 1997 ——— 1998 ——— 2003

CONNECTICUT

WHEN SOME PEOPLE THINK OF CONNECTICUT, THEY ENVISION KHAKI-CLAD MILLIONAIRES sipping martinis on manicured Greenwich lawns. Others call to mind the state's manageable capital city, Hartford, home to insurance companies galore and the country's first newspaper. Still others think of charming Mystic and the southeastern coastal area that has been wildly popular ever since Julia Roberts' star performance in *Mystic Pizza*. And some will picture the state's quiet northwestern and northeastern corners, full of rambling old farmhouses and hilly country roads. All, of course, would be correct.

A region of around three million residents, Connecticut has much diversity, and much to offer discerning travelers. For starters, the Constitution State has the mildest climate in New England and historic, leafy towns. It also has an entire southern border on Long Island Sound and an eponymous river. Adriaen Block sailed into the latter in 1614; Connecticut's first colonists soon followed, settling Hartford, Windsor and Wethersfield. The state hosted myriad important Revolutionary and Civil War events, and is home to many famous inventors.

Today, Connecticut's industry revolves around agriculture, manufacturing, and insurance. But most travelers will continue to remember it fondly as a beautiful state full of grand old summer homes, endless green pastures, soft sand beaches and the occasional fleet of mega-yachts.

Information: www.tourism.state.ct.us

★ SPOTLIGHT

★ Connecticut originates from a Mohegan word meaning "place of the long tidal river.".

★ The state song of Connecticut is *Yankee Doodle*.

★ Connecticut has the most million-dollar homes in the Northeast, and the second most in the nation.

★ George W. Bush and Katharine Hepburn were both born in Connecticut.

1

CONNECTICUT

AVON

This town on the Farmington River dates to 1645. The town has historic churches, buildings and even a covered bridge.
Information: Greater Hartford Tourism District, 31 Pratt Street., Hartford, 860-244-8180, 800-793-4480; www.town.avon.ct.us

WHAT TO SEE AND DO
Farmington Valley Arts Center
25 Arts Center Lane, Avon,
860-678-1867;
www.fvac.net

Located in a historic stone explosives plant, these twenty studios are now occupied by artists. The on-site Fisher Gallery features guest-curated exhibits and handmade crafts, gifts and artwork. January-October: Wednesday-Saturday, Sunday afternoons; November-December: daily.

CLASSIC CONNECTICUT

Situated halfway between New York City and Boston, the fabled town of Mystic is one of Connecticut's top tourist destinations. Having read that, you might be imagining swarms of camera-toting day-trippers. And you'd be right, sort of. Mystic in the summer can be tough to navigate, but Mystic in the winter, spring and fall is a charming, uncrowded spot. The ever-popular Seaport Museum and Aquarium are must-visits, as is the nearby Foxwoods Resort, the world's largest gambling casino. But more than anything, Mystic is a great place to start your state exploration. The surrounding seaside, hills, cities and farming communities are, for the most part, picture perfect.

From Mystic, take I-95 to Old Lyme, home of the Florence Griswold Art Museum and Rocky Neck State Park beach. Cross the bridge into Old Saybrook, and follow Highway 9 to Essex, a picturesque village with shops and restaurants. The Connecticut River Museum is located here, as is the departure point for the Valley Railroad, which runs along the river. Follow scenic Highway 154 to Chester, and take the country's oldest continuous ferry—don't worry, it carries cars—across to Gillette Castle in East Haddam. Or continue over the bridge for a great view of the Victorian Goodspeed Opera House, a destination in its own right. You can return via Highway 9, or take the scenic way: Highway 82 to Highway 156 to I-95, back along the eastern side of the river. Continue west on I-95 to Hammonasset Beach State Park in Madison. Then head down Highway 1, past the town's classic historic homes, to Guilford, site of the Henry Whitfield State Museum.

2

CONNECTICUT

★

★

★

★

★

HOTELS

★★★**Avon Old Farms Hotel**
279 Avon Mountain, Avon,
860-677-1651, 800-836-4000;
www.avonoldfarmshotel.com

Avon has many "authentic," rusty (yes, that's rusty, not rustic) B&Bs. Check into the Old Farms Hotel instead. The sweeping 160-room property is low on kitchy charm and high on functionality and service. Twenty landscaped acres, brass chandeliers and white canopied beds save the property from business-retreat banality. A lively outdoor pool scene adds further life to the mountainside hotel.

160 rooms. Complimentary continental breakfast. High-speed Internet access. Restaurant. **$**

RESTAURANTS

★★★**Avon Old Farms Inn**
Rts 10 & 44, Avon,
860-677-2818;
www.avonoldfarmsinn.com

Set in a 1757 stagecoach stop building, this stone-walled eatery is themed accordingly. Old stirrups and bridles hang from the ceiling and the floors and walls are built from smooth stone. Entrees range from hearty (filet mignon, short ribs) to healthy (spinach salad, tomato-basil linguine); the menu also includes a few kosher options. American menu. Lunch, dinner, Sunday brunch. Bar. Children's menu. **$$**

★★**Dakota**
225 W. Main St., Avon,
860-677-4311;
www.dakotarestaurant.com
Seafood, steak menu. Dinner. Bar. Children's menu. **$$**

BRIDGEPORT

Bridgeport is a manufacturing town through and through, but heavy industry doesn't always mean ugly aesthetics. An urban, gritty charm runs through the city's streets and there is a vibrant cultural scene. Settled in 1639, Bridgeport was home to world-famous ringleader P. T. Barnum, founder of the Ringling Brothers and Barnum and Bailey Circus. It wasn't altogether uncommon, way back when, to catch a glimpse of his elephants pulling a plow through the town's fields.

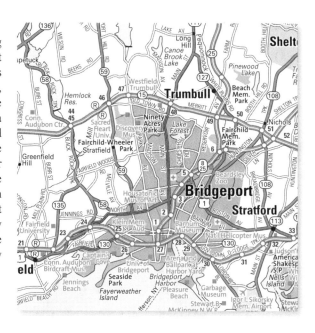

WHAT TO SEE AND DO

Barnum Museum
820 Main St., Bridgeport,
203-331-1104,
www.barnum-museum.org
On display are memorabilia from P. T. Barnum's life and circus career, including artifacts relating to Barnum's General Tom Thumb and Jenny Lind and a scale model of three-ring circus. Tuesday-Sunday.

Connecticut's Beardsley
Beardsley Park, 1875 Noble Ave.,
Bridgeport,
203-394-6565;
www.beardsleyzoo.org
The state's only zoo covers 30 acres and houses more than 200 animals. Daily.

Discovery Museum and Planetarium
4450 Park Ave., Bridgeport,
203-372-3521;
www.discoverymuseum.org
This kid-friendly spot has a planetarium; 120 hands-on science and art exhibits; a children's museum; and the Challenger Learning Center. Tuesday-Sunday.

SPECIAL EVENTS

Barnum Festival
1070 Main St., Bridgeport,
203-367-8495, 866-867-8495;
www.barnumfestival.com
Commemorates the life of P.T. Barnum.
March-September.

HOTELS

★★Holiday Inn
1070 Main St., Bridgeport,
203-334-1234, 888-465-4329;
www.holiday-inn.com
234 rooms. High-speed Internet access. Restaurant, bar. Airport transportation available. $

★★★Trumbull Marriott Merritt Parkway
180 Hawley Lane, Trumbull,
203-378-1400, 800-682-4095;
www.marriott.com
320 rooms. High-speed Internet access. Restaurant, bar. $$

RESTAURANTS

★Black Rock Castle
2895 Fairfield Ave., Bridgeport,
203-336-3990;
www.blackrockcastle.com
Irish menu. Dinner. Children's menu. Valet parking. $$

3

★
★
★
★

CLINTON

This popular beach town, which overlooks Long Island Sound, is equidistant to New York and Boston.
Information: Chamber of Commerce, 50 E. Main St., Clinton,
860-669-3889;
www.clintonct.com

WHAT TO SEE AND DO

Chamard Vineyards
115 Cow Hill Rd., Clinton,
860-664-0299, 800-371-1609;
www.chamard.com
A 15-acre vineyard and winery offers chardonnay, pinot noir, merlot and other varieties. Tours and tastings. Wednesday-Saturday.

Chatfield Hollow State Park
381 Route 80, Killingworth,
860-663-2030
Nearly 550 acres sit in a heavily wooded hollow peppered by natural caves that once provided shelter for Native Americans. On-site pond, swimming, fishing; hiking, ice skating, picnicking.

Stanton House
63 E. Main St., Clinton,
860-669-2131

(1789) This 13-room house connected to a general store is the site of Yale University's first classroom. Exhibits include period furnishings; antique American and Staffordshire dinnerware; a weapon collection; and the bed used by the Marquis de Lafayette during an 1824 visit. (June-September, by appointment)

HOTELS

★Clinton Motel
163 E. Main St., Clinton,
860-669-8850
15 rooms. $

RESTAURANTS

★Log Cabin Restaurant and Lounge
232 Boston Post Rd., Clinton,
860-669-6253
Italian menu. Lunch, dinner. Bar. Children's menu. $

DANBURY

This western Connecticut town's history is replete with patriotic pride. During the American Revolution, it was a supply depot and the site of a Continental Army hospital. Originally settled by eight Norwalk families seeking fertile land, the city was once the hub of the hat industry. Danbury native Zadoc Benedict is credited with opening the first factory in 1790—it made three hats a day. Things have since sped up.
Information: Housatonic Valley Tourism District, 30 Main St., Danbury,
203-743-0546, 800-841-4488;
www.danbury.org

WHAT TO SEE AND DO

Candlewood Lake
35 E. Hayestown Rd., Danbury
Connecticut's largest lake is more than 14 miles long and, with more than 60 miles of shoreline, extends one finger into Danbury. Swimming, fishing, boating; picnicking, concession. Fees for some activities.

SPECIAL EVENTS

Charles Ives Center for the Arts
Mill Plain Rd., Danbury,
203-837-9226
Outdoor classical, country, folk, jazz, and pop concerts on Western Connecticut State University's Westside campus. July-early September: Friday-Sunday.

Taste of Greater Danbury
Danbury Green, Green Ives and
White Streets, Danbury,
203-792-1711;
www.citycenterdanbury.com
Food vendors, live music, and children's games draw crowds together year after year at this outdoor festival. September.

HOTELS
★★Ethan Allen Hotel
21 Lake Ave., Danbury,
203-744-1776, 800-742-1776;
www.ethanallenhotel.com
195 rooms. Restaurant, bar. Airport transportation available. $

★★Holiday Inn
80 Newtown Rd., Danbury,
203-792-4000, 888-465-4329;
www.holiday-inn.com
114 rooms. High-speed Internet access. Restaurant, bar. Airport transportation available. $

★★★Sheraton Danbury Hotel
18 Old Ridgebury Rd., Danbury,
203-794-0600, 800-325-3535;
www.sheraton.com
Conveniently located just three miles from Danbury Airport, this Sheraton has comfort-ably outfitted room, and onsite restaurant and fitness room.
242 rooms. Restaurant, bar. $

SPECIALTY LODGINGS
The Homestead Inn
5 Elm St., New Milford,
860-354-4080;
www.homesteadct.com
14 rooms. Complimentary continental breakfast. $

RESTAURANTS
★★Ciao Cafe and Wine Bar
2B Ives St., Danbury,
203-791-0404;
www.ciaocafetwosteps.com
Italian menu. Lunch, dinner. Bar. Reservations recommended. Outdoor seating. $$

★The Hearth
Route 7, Brookfield,
203-775-3360
Seafood, steak menu. Lunch, dinner. Closed Monday; February. Bar. Children's menu. $$

★★Two Steps Downtown Grille
5 Ives St., Danbury, 203-794-0032;
www.ciaocafetwosteps.com
American, Southwestern menu. Lunch, dinner, Sunday brunch. Bar. Children's menu. Outdoor seating. $$

ESSEX
Twelve years ago, its tree-lined Main Street helped win Essex the honor of "The Best Small Town in America." Not much has changed since then. The peaceful eastern Connecticut village of 6,000 exudes storybook charm in the form of its brick post office, antique shops and 1700s-era ship captain's houses.
Information: Connecticut River Valley & Shoreline Visitors Council, 393 Main St., Middletown, 860-347-0028, 800-486-3346; www.cttourism.org

WHAT TO SEE AND DO
Connecticut River Museum
67 Main St., Essex,
860-767-8269;
www.ctrivermuseum.org
Housed in the last remaining steamboat dock building on the Connecticut River, the museum features exhibits that celebrate the rich cultural heritage and natural resources of the river valley, including the only full-size operating replica of the *Turtle*, America's first successful submarine. Tuesday-Sunday.

Valley Railroad
1 Railroad Ave., Essex,
860-767-0103;
www.essexsteamtrain.com

A scenic 12-mile steam train excursion along the Connecticut River to Chester, with an optional one-hour Connecticut River cruise. Early May-late October, days vary; also Christmas trips.

SPECIAL EVENTS

Deep River Ancient Muster and Parade

Devitt's Field, Main St., Deep River,
860-388-7575

Approximately 60 fife and drum players recall the Revolutionary War period. Third Saturday in July.

HOTELS

★★★Copper Beech Inn

46 Main St., Ivoryton,
860-767-0330, 888-809-2056;
copperbeechinn.com

Travelers looking for a romantic New England getaway should check into this charming 1889 Victorian inn. Once the residence of a prominent ivory importer, the country retreat is set on sprawling wooded grounds.

13 rooms. Children over 12 years only. Complimentary full breakfast. Restaurant. Closed a week in January. **$$**

★★★Griswold Inn

36 Main St., Essex,
860-767-1776;
www.griswoldinn.com

Known to locals as "the Griz," this 1776 inn is known for its lavish English-style Sunday buffet breakfast (don't skip the mimosas). The rooms and suites are full of fresh flowers and antiques.

31 rooms. Complimentary continental breakfast. Restaurant. **$$**

RESTAURANTS

★★★Copper Beech Inn

46 Main St., Ivoryton,
860-767-0330, 888-809-2056;
copperbeechinn.com

Patrons here dine on hearty, French country fare amidst fresh flowers, sparkling silver, and soft candlelight. Much like its namesake inn, the restaurant is all soft elegance and warm romance. American, French menu. Dinner. Bar. Jacket required. Closed Monday. **$$$**

★★Sage American Bar & Grill

129 W. Main St., Chester,
860-526-9898;
www.sageamerican.com

Seafood, steak menu. Dinner. Children's menu. Outdoor seating. **$$**

FARMINGTON

Home to the erstwhile "finishing school" Miss Porter's, Farmington is one of New England's most bucolic towns. During the early 1800s, the small city bustled with silversmiths, tinsmiths, cabinetmakers, clockmakers and carriage builders.

Information: Greater Hartford Tourism District, 234 Murphy Rd., Hartford, 860-244-8181, 800-793-4480; www.farmington-ct.org

WHAT TO SEE AND DO

Hill-Stead Museum

35 Mountain Rd., Farmington,
860-677-4787;
www.hillstead.org

A Colonial Revival-style country house designed by Theodate Pope in collaboration with McKim, Mead, and White contains industrialist A. A. Pope's collection of French impressionist paintings. Tuesday-Sunday.

Stanley-Whitman House

37 High St., Farmington,
860-677-9222;

This 1720 home is one of the finest early 18th-century houses in the United States. May-October: Wednesday-Sunday afternoons; November-April: Saturday-Sunday afternoons, also by appointment.

SPECIAL EVENTS

Farmington Antiques Weekend

Polo Grounds, Farmington,
860-677-7862;
www.farmington-antiques.com
More than 600 dealers descend on the town for one of the largest annual antique events in the state. Mid-June and early September.

HOTELS

★★Centennial Inn Suites

5 Spring Lane, Farmington,
860-677-4647, 800-852-2052;
www.centennialinn.com
112 rooms, all suites. Complimentary continental breakfast. **$$**

★★★Hartford Marriott Farmington

15 Farm Springs Rd., Farmington,
860-678-1000, 800-228-9190;
www.marriott.com
Close enough to downtown to be convenient, yet far enough away from the city center to be peaceful, this modern Marriott pampers business travelers and leisure guests alike with a full range of amenities, including two swimming pools and a tennis court. 380 rooms. High-speed Internet access. Restaurant. Bar. **$$**

★★★The Farmington Inn of Greater Hartford

827 Farmington Ave., Farmington,
860-677-2821, 800-648-9804;
www.farmingtoninn.com
72 rooms. Complimentary continental breakfast. Wireless Internet access. Restaurant, bar. **$**

RESTAURANTS

★★Apricot's

1593 Farmington Ave., Farmington,
860-673-5405
American menu. Lunch, dinner, brunch. Bar. Casual attire. Reservations recommended. Outdoor seating. **$$**

★Stonewell

354 Colt Hwy., Farmington,
860-677-8855;
www.thestonewell.com
American menu. Lunch, dinner. Bar. Children's menu. Casual attire. **$$**

GREENWICH

Possibly the state's most talked about town, Greenwich has long been home to hedge fund barons, ladies who lunch and other well-moneyed folk. Its proximity to New York City— 28 miles from Times Square—and the sea —oceanfront mega-mansions dot the coastline—has made this settlement of 58,000 one of the most coveted places to live, anywhere. Even those without an "it" address can stroll Greenwich's leafy, photo-friendly 18th-century streets, shop in its Manhattan-worthy boutiques and maybe even catch a glimpse of a millionaire.

Information: Chamber of Commerce, 21 W. Putnam Ave., Greenwich, 203-869-3500; www.greenwichchamber.com

WHAT TO SEE AND DO

Audubon Center

613 Riversville Rd., Greenwich,
203-869-5272
This 522-acre sanctuary includes a self-guided nature trail. Daily.

Bruce Museum

1 Museum Dr., Greenwich,
203-869-0376
The arts and sciences museum features exhibits, lectures, concerts and educational programs. Tuesday-Sunday.

Bush-Holley House

39 Strickland Rd., Cos Cob,
203-869-6899
This former residence of a successful 18th-century farmer became the site of the Cos Cob art colony at the turn of the century. Current exhibits include late 18th-century Connecticut furniture; paintings by Childe Hassam, Elmer Livingston MacRae and John Henry Twachtman; sculptures by John Rogers; and pottery by Leon Volkmar. Tuesday-Sunday, afternoons.

Putnam Cottage/Knapp Tavern

243 E. Putnam Ave., Greenwich,
203-869-9697;
www.putnamcottage.org
Near this tavern, Revolutionary General Israel Putnam made a daring escape from the Redcoats in 1779. The on-site museum now has an herb garden and a restored barn April-December: Sunday afternoon; also by appointment.

HOTELS

★★★De La Mar

500 Steamboat Rd., Greenwich,
203-661-9800;
www.thedelamar.com
The award-winning De La Mar looks more like a Lake Como mansion than an old Connecticut retreat. Its sprawling cream-colored façade hides an interior rich with original artwork, sparkling chandeliers, ornate sconces and a plethora of marble. Overlooking the Greenwich Marina, the property has 82 rooms filled with up-to-date electronics, luxe Italian linens and cast-iron tubs. Even pooches get pampered here—the resort's "sophisticated pet" program includes a doggie bed, a personalized ID tag, food and water bowls, and a Pet Services Menu.
82 rooms. Children over 12 years only. Restaurant, bar. **$$$**

★★★Homestead Inn

420 Field Point Rd., Greenwich,
203-869-7500;
www.homesteadinn.com
The rooms at the Homestead Inn aren't called rooms—they're called "chambers." And the lodging at this renovated 1799 inn is anything but average: second and third floor suites have imported furniture, Frette linens and original artwork. Heated bathroom floors. Renovated by Greenwich hoteliers Thomas and Theresa Henkelmann, the inn—and its accompanying three-star restaurant—is a study in old-school sumptuous elegance.
18 rooms. Closed two weeks in March. Children over 12 years only. Restaurant, bar. **$$$$$**

★★★Hyatt Regency Greenwich

1800 E. Putnam Ave.,
Old Greenwich,
203-637-1234, 800-633-7313;
www.greenwich.hyatt.com
Before magazine giant Conde Nast moved to Manhattan, the *Vogue* and *Glamour* publisher was headquartered at 1800 East Putnam. Now a Hyatt, the building has retained much of its early glamour, in the form of an elegant atrium-style lobby with ponds, stone walls and an impressive array of trees, plants and flowers. Guest rooms are spacious and feature Internet access, bath robes and plush pillows.
373 rooms. Wireless Internet access. Restaurant. Bar. **$$$**

SPECIALTY LODGINGS

Harbor House Inn

165 Shore Rd., Old Greenwich,
203-637-0145; www.hhinn.com
22 rooms. Complimentary continental breakfast. **$**

Stanton House Inn

76 Maple Ave., Greenwich, 203-869-2110;
www.shinngreenwich.com
24 rooms. Complimentary continental breakfast. **$$**

RESTAURANTS

★★★Jean-Louis

61 Lewis St., Greenwich,
203-622-8450;
www.restaurantjeanlouis.com

Sophisticated and elegant with professional service to match, this cozy restaurant has a menu grounded in the precision of French classicism. Its decor is decidedly Parisian as well—the serving china and candle lamps were all custom made in France. The chef works directly with local farmers for the freshest ingredients and in addition to the a la carte menu, the restaurant offers tastings, petit tastings and vegetarian and vegan menus.

French menu. Lunch, dinner. Closed Sunday; also first two weeks of August. Business casual attire. Reservations recommended. **$$$**

★★★L'Escale
500 Steamboat Rd., Greenwich,
203-661-4600;
www.lescalerestaurant.com
This French-Mediterranean restaurant earns its stars by re-creating the Mediterranean on the North Atlantic shore, importing a stone fireplace and terra-cotta floors to warm the dining room, and setting up light-filtering thatched bamboo to shade the patio. The menu from Francois Kwaku-Dongo includes a salad of caramelized leeks and chanterelles; apple- and prune-paired foie gras; and crispy duck breast. The eatery has become quite a gathering place for locals and travelers, and it's no wonder why—L'Escale allows guests to sail to dinner and tie up their yachts at its waterfront dock.

French, Mediterranean menu. Breakfast, lunch, dinner, Sunday brunch. Bar. Business casual attire. Reservations recommended. Valet parking. Outdoor seating. **$$$**

★★Terra Ristorante Italiano
156 Greenwich Ave., Greenwich,
203-629-5222;
www.terraofgreenwich.com
Italian menu. Lunch, dinner. Bar. Business casual attire. Reservations recommended. Outdoor seating. **$$$**

★★That Little Italian Restaurant
228-230 Mill St., Greenwich,
203-531-7500;
www.tlirgreenwich.com
Italian menu. Lunch, dinner. Closed Monday. Casual attire. Outdoor seating. **$$**

★★★Thomas Henkelmann
420 Field Point Rd., Greenwich,
203-869-7500,
www.thomashenkelmann.com
German-born, French-trained chef Thomas Henkelmann's eatery proffers clever takes on traditional French fare. The formal spot's lobster bisque is Henkelmann's specialty—a rich, creamy concoction full of sweet and savory flavors. Service is discreet and attentive, and well-cared-for gardens are ideal for an after dinner stroll.

French menu. Breakfast, lunch, dinner. Closed Sunday; also two weeks in March. Bar. Jacket required. Reservations recommended. Valet parking. **$$$$**

GROTON

To the military minded, the town of Groton is synonymous with the submarine. It was here, in 1912, that the General Dynamics Corporation built the world's first diesel-powered sub. The first nuclear-powered one appeared here some four decades later. Today, the town hosts a U.S. naval base and several scientific research plants.

Information: Connecticut's Mystic & More, 470 Bank St., New London,
860-444-2206 800-863-6569;
www.town.groton.ct.us

WHAT TO SEE AND DO

Fort Griswold Battlefield State Park
57 Fort St., Groton,
860-445-1729
The park includes a 135-foot monument to 88 Revolutionary soldiers slain by British troops under the command of Benedict Arnold. Park (daily). Monument and museum Memorial Day-Labor Day: daily; Labor Day-Columbus Day: Saturday-Sunday.

Historic Ship *Nautilus* and Submarine *Force* Museum
Naval Submarine Base New London,
1 Crystal Lake Rd., Groton,
860-694-3174, 800-343-0079
The permanent home of the *Nautilus*, the world's first nuclear-powered submarine. Self-guided and audio tours are available, as well as museum exhibits depicting history of the US Submarine *Force*. Spring-fall: daily; Winter: Monday, Wednesday-Sunday; closed the first two weeks in May and the last two weeks in October.

HOTELS

★★★Mystic Marriott Hotel and Spa
625 North Rd., Groton,
860-446-2600, 800-228-9290;
www.marriott.com
Just outside the historic seafaring town of Mystic, this full-service hotel is a perfect base for exploring the Mystic Aquarium or the nearby Foxwoods and Mohegan Sun casinos. The guest rooms and suites are sophisticated and show off a continental flair. The centerpiece of the hotel is the Elizabeth Arden Red Door Spa, favored for its superior treatments and fine service.
285 rooms. High-speed Internet access. Two restaurants, bar. Airport transportation available. **$$**

RESTAURANTS

★★★Octagon
625 North Rd., Groton,
860-326-0360
www.waterfordgrouprestaurants.com/octagon
Located in the Mystic Marriott Hotel & Spa, this upscale steak house serves prime cuts in sleek surroundings. Filet mignon, New York strip steak and Kobe sirloin are on the menu as well as lighter choices like sesame-crusted tuna, seared salmon with Maryland lump crab and grilled swordfish. The wine list, winner of Wine Spectator's Award of Excellence, features more than 200 varietals.
Steak menu. Breakfast, dinner. Bar. Children's menu. Business casual attire. Reservations recommended. Valet parking. **$$$**

★★Vines
625 North Rd., Groton,
860-446-2600
American menu. Lunch, dinner. Bar. Children's menu. Casual attire. Valet parking. **$$**

★

★

★

★

★

GUILFORD
Guilford was settled by a group of Puritans who followed the Reverend Henry Whitfield here from England. After repeated runs for political office, one of the residents, Samuel Hill, gave rise to the expression "run like Sam Hill."
Information: Chamber of Commerce, 63 Whitfield St., Guilford,
203-453-9677; www.guilfordct.com

WHAT TO SEE AND DO

Henry Whitfield State Museum
248 Old Whitfield St., Guilford,
203-453-2457
This 1639 house is the oldest in the state. April-mid-December: Wednesday-Sunday.

Hyland House
84 Boston St., Guilford,
203-453-9477
Restored and furnished in 17th-century period, this 1660 house has an herb gar-

den and guided tours. Early June-October: Tuesday-Sunday.

Thomas Griswold House Museum
171 Boston St., Guilford,
203-453-3176
A fine example of a saltbox house, this 1775 home has period gardens and a restored working blacksmith shop. Early June-October: Tuesday-Sunday; winter by appointment.

HOTELS
★Tower Suites Motel
320 Boston Post Rd., Guilford,
203-453-9069
14 rooms, all suites. **$**

RESTAURANTS
★★Sachem Country House
111 Goose Lane, Guilford,
203-453-5261
Seafood menu. Dinner, Sunday brunch. Children's menu. Reservations recommended. **$$**

HARTFORD
Connecticut's capital city falls, appropriately enough, in the center of the state. Settled in 1633 on the region's eponymous river, Hartford has deep democratic roots. When Brit Sir Edmund Andros tried to seize the state's own declaration of independence, loyal citizen Joseph Wadsworth hid the charter in a hollow tree. The secret stashing place is still known as the Charter Oak, and Hartford still exhibits creative spirit. The Hartford Courant, founded in 1764, is the oldest continuously published newspaper in the United States. The daily regularly covers the city's booming insurance and education industries.

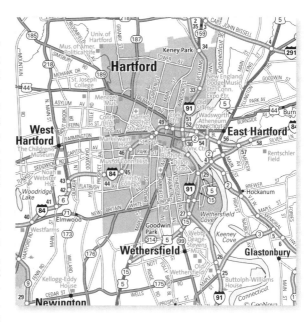

Information: Greater Hartford Convention & Visitors Bureau,
One Civic Center Plaza, Hartford, 860-728-6789, 800-446-7811; www.enjoyhartford.com

11

CONNECTICUT

WHAT TO SEE AND DO
Butler-McCook Homestead and Main Street History Center
396 Main St., Hartford,
860-522-1806

This preserved house, occupied by four generations of one family (1782-1971), has possessions dating back 200 years, a collection of Victorian toys, Japanese armor and a Victorian garden. Wednesday-Sunday.

Harriet Beecher Stowe Center
77 Forest St., Hartford,
860-522-9258;
www.harrietbeecherstowecenter.org
The restored Victorian cottage of the author of *Uncle Tom's Cabin* contains original furniture and memorabilia. Tours. Monday-Saturday 9:30 a.m.-4:30 p.m., Sunday noon-4:30 p.m.

Mark Twain House
351 Farmington Ave., Hartford,
860-247-0998
Tom Sawyer, Huckleberry Finn and other books were published while Samuel Clemens (Mark Twain) lived in this three-story Victorian mansion featuring the decorative work of Charles Comfort Tiffany and the Associated Artists. Tours. May-October and December: daily; rest of year: Monday, Wednesday-Sunday.

12

Museum of Connecticut History
Connecticut State Library,
231 Capitol Ave., Hartford,
860-737-6535
Exhibits include the Colt Collection of Firearms; Connecticut artifacts, including the original 1662 Royal Charter; and portraits of Connecticut's governors. The library features law, social sciences, history, genealogy collections and official state archives. Monday-Saturday.

Noah Webster Foundation and Historical Society
227 S. Main St., West Hartford,
860-521-5362;
www.noahwebsterhouse.org
This 18th-century homestead was the birthplace of America's first lexicographer, writer of the *Blue-Backed Speller* and the *American Dictionary*. Thursday-Monday 1-4 p.m.

Old State House
800 Main St., Hartford,

860-522-6766
The oldest state house in the nation was designed by Charles Bulfinch. The restored Senate chamber has a Gilbert Stuart portrait of George Washington. Monday-Saturday.

State Capitol
210 Capitol Ave., Hartford,
860-240-0222
Take guided one-hour tours of the restored, gold-domed capitol building and the contemporary legislative office building. Monday-Friday.

University of Hartford
200 Bloomfield Ave., West Hartford,
860-768-4100; www.hartford.edu
An independent institution with 6,844 students on a 320-acre campus. Many free concerts, operas, lectures and art exhibits.

Wadsworth Atheneum Museum of Art
600 Main St., Hartford,
860-278-2670
This is one of the nation's oldest continuously operating public art museums with more than 40,000 works of art spanning 5,000 years. Exhibits include 15th-to 20th-century paintings; American furniture; sculpture, porcelains; English and American silver, the Amistad Collection of African-American art; and changing contemporary exhibits. Wednesday-Sunday. Free admission Thursday and Saturday mornings.

HOTELS
★★Crowne Plaza
50 Morgan St., Hartford,
860-549-2400; 877-227-6963
www.crowneplaza.com
350 rooms. Restaurant, bar. Airport transportation available. **$**

★★★Goodwin Hotel
1 Haynes St., Hartford,
860-246-7500, 800-922-5006;
www.goodwinhotel.com

This luxury hotel is among Hartford's best, and its downtown location across from the Civic Center makes it a popular choice with business travelers. Built in 1881 for business tycoon J. P. Morgan, the red brick Queen Anne–style building has rooms and suites with a masculine, clubby decor. The boys club appeal extends to the Goodwin's two eateries.
124 rooms. Restaurant, bar. **$$**

★★Holiday Inn
363 Roberts St., East Hartford,
860-528-9611, 888-465-4329;
www.holiday-inn.com
130 rooms. Wireless Internet access. Restaurant, bar. **$**

★★★Sheraton Hartford Hotel
100 E. River Dr., East Hartford,
860-528-9703, 888-530-9703;
www.sheraton.com
199 rooms. Restaurant, bar. **$$**

RESTAURANTS
★★Butterfly
831 Farmington Ave., West Hartford,
860-236-2816
Chinese menu. Lunch, dinner. Sunday brunch. Bar. **$$**

★★★Carbone's
588 Franklin Ave., Hartford,
860-296-9646.
www.carbonesct.com
Hearty Italian dishes and friendly service have kept Carbone's a longtime Hartford favorite. Need evidence? Take a look at the entrance walls, plastered with many autographed pictures of politicians, sports figures and other satisfied customers. Italian

menu. Lunch, dinner. Closed Sunday. Bar. Casual attire. Reservations recommended. **$$$**

★Hot Tomatoes
1 Union Place, Hartford,
860-249-5100
American menu. Lunch, dinner, late-night, late-night. Bar. Casual attire. Outdoor seating. **$$**

★★★Max Downtown
185 Asylum St., Hartford,
860-522-2530;
www.maxrestaurantgroup.com
Lively and central, Max Downtown is a hit with staffers from the nearby Capitol Building. Many other city dwellers make the pilgrimage to the New American spot as well, eager to partake in its upscale atmosphere, extensive wine list and inventive cuisine.
American menu. Lunch, dinner, late-night. Bar. Business casual attire. Reservations recommended. Valet parking. **$$$**

★★Peppercorn's Grill
357 Main St., Hartford, 860-547-1714;
www.peppercornsrestaurant.com
Italian menu. Lunch, dinner, late-night. Closed Sunday; also one week in summer. Bar. Business casual attire. Reservations recommended. Valet parking. Outdoor seating. **$$$**

★Restaurant Bricco
78 LaSalle Rd., West Hartford,
860-233-0220;
www.restaurantbricco.com
Italian, Mediterranean menu. Lunch, dinner. Children's menu. Outdoor seating. **$$**

LAKEVILLE
Like many of its New England neighbors, Lakeville played a key part in the American Revolution. The town's blast furnace—once owned by Ethan Allen—cast scores of guns used by soldiers to fight the British. In 1843, the furnace was torn down and the first knife manufacturing plant took its place. The Hotchkiss School is nearby.
Information: www.lakevillect.com

CONNECTICUT

★
★
★
★

WHAT TO SEE AND DO
Holley-Williams House
15 Millerton Rd., Lakeville,
860-435-3878
The museum is full of 18th- and 19th-century history, including a 1768 iron-master's home and a Holley Manufacturing Company pocketknife exhibit from 1876. Mid-June-Labor Day: Saturday-Sunday, and holiday afternoons; also by appointment.

SPECIAL EVENTS
Music Mountain Summer Music Festival
Music Mountain Rd., Falls Village,
860-824-7126
www.musicmountain.org
Performances by well-known ensembles and guest artists; jazz series. Mid-June-early September: Saturday-Sunday.

Road Racing Classic
497 Lime Rock Rd., Lakeville,
800-722-3577; www.limerock.com
The Mohegan Sun Grand Prix and NASCAR Busch North 200 events are held the same weekend. Memorial Day weekend.

HOTELS
★★Inn at Iron Masters
229 N. Main St., Lakeville,
860-435-9844;
www.innatironmasters.com
28 rooms. Restaurant, bar. **$**

★★★Interlaken Inn
74 Interlaken Rd., Lakeville,
860-435-9878, 800-222-2909;
www.interlakeninn.com
This century-old inn has rooms furnished with antiques. There's an onsite spa and restaurant. Activities include tennis, ping-pong and an outdoor heated pool.
80 rooms. Restaurant. **$**

SPECIALTY LODGINGS
Wake Robin Inn
106 Sharon Rd., Lakeville,
860-435-2000;
www.wakerobininn.com
This stately inn has been in operation since 1914. Rooms are traditionally decorated, some with canopied beds.
39 rooms. **$$**

LITCHFIELD
Home to the country's first law school, Litchfield sits on a plateau above the Naugatuck Valley. For the most part, the industrial revolution bypassed the quiet hamlet; its most famous citizens include the Reverend Henry Ward Beecher and his sister, Harriet Beecher Stowe, author of *Uncle Tom's Cabin*.
Information: Litchfield Hills Visitors Bureau, Litchfield, 860-567-4506;
www.litchfieldhills.com

WHAT TO SEE AND DO
Haight -Brown Vineyard and Winery
29 Chestnut Hill Rd., Litchfield,
860-567-4045
One of the few vineyards to grow vinifera-grapes in New England, Haight is Connecticut's first winery. Tours, tastings. Daily.

Litchfield History Museum
7 South St., Litchfield,
860-567-4501
Onsite is an outstanding collection of American art and artifacts from the 18th-21st centuries. Mid-April-November: Tuesday-Sunday.

Tapping Reeve House
82 South St., Litchfield,
860-567-4501
A retrospective of 19th-century Litchfield through the lives of the students who attended the Litchfield Law School and the Litchfield Female Academy; graduates include Aaron Burr and John C. Calhoun. Mid-April-November: Tuesday-Sunday.

Topsmead State Forest
46 Chase Rd., Litchfield,
860-567-5694
This 511-acre forest includes an English Tudor mansion overlooking a 40-acre wild-

life preserve. (Second and fourth weekends of June-October)

HOTELS

★★★Litchfield Inn

432 Bantam Rd., Litchfield, 860-567-4503, 800-499-3444; www.litchfieldinnct.com

32 rooms. Complimentary continental breakfast. Restaurant, bar. **$**

RESTAURANTS

★Senor Panchos

7 Village Green Dr., Litchfield, 860-567-3663; www.senor-panchos.com

Mexican menu. Lunch, dinner. Casual attire. **$$**

★★Village Restaurant

25 West St., Litchfield, 860-567-8307

American menu. Lunch, dinner, Sunday brunch. Bar. Children's menu. **$$**

★★★West Street Grill

43 West St., Litchfield, 860-567-3885

Owner James O'Shea has created the improbable: a trendy hotspot that appeals to both second-home New Yorkers and local residents.

American menu. Lunch, dinner. Bar. Children's menu. Reservations recommended. **$$$**

MADISON

This beachfront central Connecticut town has a quaint main street lined with boutiques, coffee shops and bed and breakfasts.

Information: Chamber of Commerce, 22 Scotland Ave., Madison, 203-245-7394
Tourism Office, 12 School St., Madison, 203-245-5659; www.madisonct.com

WHAT TO SEE AND DO

Allis-Bushnell House and Museum

853 Boston Post Rd., Madison, 203-245-4567

Period rooms with four-corner fireplaces, doctor's office and equipment, costume exhibits and shipbuilding tools are all inside this 1785 house. May-October: Wednesday, Friday-Saturday, limited hours; other times by appointment.

Hammonasset Beach State Park

1288 Boston Post Rd., Madison, 203-245-2785

This beach covers more than 900 acres and has a two-mile-long stretch on Long Island Sound. Saltwater swimming, scuba diving, fishing, boating, hiking, picnicking and camping are available.

HOTELS

★★Madison Beach Hotel

94 W. Wharf Rd., Madison, 203-245-1404; www.madisonbeachhotel.com

35 rooms. Closed January-February. Complimentary continental breakfast. Restaurant, bar. **$**

RESTAURANTS

★★★Cafe Allegre

725 Boston Post Rd., Madison, 203-245-7773; www.allegrecafe.com

Italian menu. Lunch, dinner. Closed Monday. Bar. Children's menu. Outdoor seating. **$$**

★★Friends and Company

11 Boston Post Rd., Madison, 203-245-0462

Seafood, steak menu. Lunch, dinner. Sunday brunch. Closed last Monday in June. Bar. Children's menu. **$$**

15

CONNECTICUT

MANCHESTER

Locals brag their town is like a "city of village charm." They might be right: Manchester's 50,000 citizens live on streets out of another era, ones filled with leafy trees and restored 18th-century homes. The spot was once the silk capital of the Western world and is still a major manufacturing center.

Information: Greater Manchester Chamber of Commerce, 20 Hartford Rd., Manchester, 860-646-2223;
www.manchesterchamber.com

WHAT TO SEE AND DO

Cheney Homestead
106 Hartford Rd., Manchester,
860-647-9983
This is the birthplace of the brothers who launched the state's once-promising silk industry. Friday-Sunday.

Connecticut Firemen's Historical Society Fire Museum
230 Pine St., Manchester, 860-649-9436
Located in a 1901 firehouse, this museum has antique firefighting equipment and memorabilia, leather fire buckets, hoses, helmets, hand-pulled engines, a horse-drawn hose wagon,and old prints and lithographs. Mid-April-mid-November: Friday-Sunday.

HOTELS

★**Best Value Inn-Manchester**
400 Tolland Tpke, Manchester,
860-643-1555, 888-315-2378;
www.bestvalueinn.com
31 rooms. **$**

★**Clarion Hotel**
191 Spencer St., Manchester,
860-643-5811, 800-992-4004;
www.clarionsuites.com
104 rooms, all suites. Complimentary full breakfast. Airport transportation available. **$**

RESTAURANTS

★★★**Black Swan**
4384 Main St., Manchester, 802-362-3807;
www.blackswanrestaurant.com
International menu. Dinner. Bar. Closed Thanksgiving. **$$**

★★★**Cavey's French Restaurant**
45 E. Center St., Manchester,
860-643-2751
This family-run restaurant has been a Connecticut landmark since the 1930s. On the lower level of a two-story building (the upstairs holds the same family's Italian restaurant), Cavey's serves seasonal, contemporary French cuisine in a charming atmosphere. French menu. Dinner. Closed Sunday-Monday. Bar. **$$$**

★★★**Cavey's Italian Restaurant**
45 E. Center St., Manchester,
860-643-2751
The Italian counterpart to Cavey's French, this upstairs Italian eatery offers a menu of Northern Italian food. Dishes like veal piccata and chicken tetrazzini are served in an elegant dining room with the same personalized and friendly service you'll find downstairs. Italian menu. Dinner. Closed Sunday-Monday. Bar. **$$**

MYSTIC

The town of Mystic, a shipbuilding and whaling center from the 17th to 19th centuries, sits on both sides of its eponymous river. Its name is derived from the Pequot, "Mistuket."
Information: Tourist Information Center, Olde Mystic Village, 860-536-1641;
Connecticut's Mystic & More, 470 Bank St., New London, 860-444-2206, 800-863-6569;
www.mysticcountry.com

WHAT TO SEE AND DO

Denison Homestead

120 Pequotsepos Rd., Mystic,
860-536-9248

This1717 home is full of heirlooms from 11 generations of a single family. Guided tour. Mid-May-mid-October: Thursday-Monday afternoons; rest of year, by appointment.

Mystic Aquarium

55 Coogan Blvd., Mystic,
860-572-5955;
www.mysticaquarium.org

The exhibits here feature more than 6,000 live specimens from around the world. Demonstrations with dolphins, sea lions, and the only whales in New England delight young and old alike, as does Seal Island, an outdoor exhibit of seals and sea lions in natural settings, and the penguin pavilion. The facility also includes Dr. Robert Ballard's Institute for Exploration, which is dedicated to searching the deep seas for lost ships. The museum's Challenge of the Deep exhibit allows patrons to use state-of-the-art technology to re-create the search for the *Titanic* or explore the biology of undersea ocean vents. Daily; hours vary by season.

Mystic Seaport

75 Greenmanville Ave., Mystic,
860-572-5315;
www.visitmysticseaport.org

This 17-acre complex is the nation's largest maritime museum, dedicated to preservation of 19th-century oceanic history. Visitors may board the 1841 wooden whale ship *Charles W. Morgan*, square-rigged ship *Joseph Conrad*, or fishing schooner *L.A. Dunton*. The collections also include some 400 smaller vessels; a representative seaport community with historic homes and waterfront industries; a working shipyard, children's museum and planetarium. May-October: daily.

HOTELS

★Comfort Inn

48 Whitehall Ave., Mystic,
860-572-8531, 800-572-9339;
www.comfortinn.com

120 rooms. Complimentary continental breakfast. Wireless Internet access. **$$**

★★★Hilton Mystic

20 Coogan Blvd., Mystic,
860-572-0731, 800-774-1500;
www.hilton.com

On a quiet side road near the noisy Olde Mystic Village, and just one block from I-95, this business-oriented hotel is all about location. Shopping outlets, the Seaport Museum, and the aquarium are all nearby. Not into fighting through the tourist hoards? Stay inside and mellow out at the hotel pool.

183 rooms. Wireless Internet access. Restaurant, bar. Children's activity center. **$$**

★★★Inn at Mystic

3 Williams Ave., Mystic,
860-536-9604, 800-237-2415;
www.innatmystic.com

This five-building property is the only Connecticut inn that overlooks both Mystic Harbor and Long Island Sound. Its five buildings are spread over 15 manicured acres, in the center of which sits the 1904 Classical Revival mansion where Lauren Bacall and Humphrey Bogart honeymooned. Inside, the rooms come with period furnishings, whirlpools, orchard views, and—sorry, kids—are for adults only.

68 rooms Restaurant, bar. **$$**

★★★Whaler's Inn

20 E. Main St., Mystic,
860-536-1506, 800-243-2588;
www.whalersinnmystic.com

Homey, comfortable and located in the heart of historic Mystic, the Whalers Inn is ideal for those seeking a very upscale New England bed-and-breakfast experience. The 1865 Colonial clapboard comes complete with a wide front porch and rocking chairs, and rooms outfitted with Waverly wall coverings, four-poster beds and wing-back chairs. The large bathrooms host pedestal sinks and whirlpool tubs and each guest room has a breathtaking view of the scenic Mystic River. Lucky guests will snag suites with private verandas.

49 rooms. Complimentary continental breakfast. Restaurant, bar. **$$**

SPECIALTY LODGINGS
The Old Mystic Inn

52 Main St., Old Mystic, 860-572-9422; www.oldmysticinn.com

Built in 1784, the Old Inn is set in a serene neighborhood a few miles from downtown Mystic. The rooms in the main house feature Early American decor, antiques, private baths and fireplaces. The carriage house has four guest rooms with private entrances.

8 rooms. Children over 15 years only. Complimentary full breakfast. **$$**

RESTAURANTS
★★★Bravo Bravo

20 E. Main St., Mystic, 860-536-3228; www.whalersinnmystic.com

This local favorite, located at the seaside Whaler's Inn, serves creative gourmet dishes. Thanks to floor-to-ceiling windows, the spacious dining room is bright and inviting.

Italian menu. Lunch, dinner. Bar. Casual attire. Reservations recommended. **$$**

★★★Flood Tide

3 Williams Avenue, Mystic, 860-536-8140, 800-237-2415; www.mysticinns.com

Complimentary hors d'oeuvres are served in the piano lounge at this waterfront restaurant. The gourmet dishes, Sunday brunch and harbor views are all worth the trip.

American, Continental menu. Breakfast, lunch, dinner, Sunday brunch. Bar. Children's menu. Casual attire. Reservations recommended. Outdoor seating. **$$$**

★★Go Fish

Olde Mistick Village, Mystic, 860-536-2662
Seafood menu. Lunch, dinner. Bar. Casual attire. Reservations recommended. **$$**

★Mystic Pizza

56 W. Main St., Mystic, 860-536-3700; www.mysticpizza.com
Pizza. Lunch, dinner. Casual attire. **$**

★★Seamen's Inne

105 Greenmanville Ave., Mystic, 860-572-5303; www.seamensinne.com
American, seafood menu. Lunch, dinner. Bar. Children's menu. Casual attire. Reservations recommended. Outdoor seating. **$$**

NEW HAVEN

New Haven is an unlikely cultural center. Part gritty metropolis of 130,000, part educational Mecca, the city has long struggled with its split personality. Much of the action revolves around Yale University, which hosts some 10,000 students and countless more employees. No doubt every Yalie knows the historical importance of his adopted city: it was here that Eli Whitney worked out the principles of mass production, and where Revolutionary War hero Nathan Hale studied. Just 75 miles from New York City, New Haven is a park-filled industrial city on the rise.

Information: Greater New Haven Convention & Visitors Bureau, 169 Orange St., New Haven, 203-777-8550 800-332-7829; www.visitnewhaven.com or www.cityofnewhaven.com

SPOT LIGHT

★YALE UNIVERSITY (THEN YALE COLLEGE) OPENED IN NEW HAVEN IN 1718.

★YALE GRAD ELI WHITNEY DEVELOPED THE COTTON GIN IN 1794.

★NEW HAVEN CLAIMS TO BE THE BIRTHPLACE OF PIZZA IN AMERICA.

18

CONNECTICUT

WHAT TO SEE AND DO

Amistad Memorial

165 Church St., New Haven

This 14-foot bronze relief sculpture is a unique three-sided form that depicts a trio of significant episodes in the life of Joseph Cinque, one of 50 Africans kidnapped in Sierra Leone and slated for sale in Cuba in 1839. His ship was secretly rerouted to Long Island Sound, after which a fierce battle for the would-be slaves' freedom ensued in New Haven. Two years later, their victory was won.

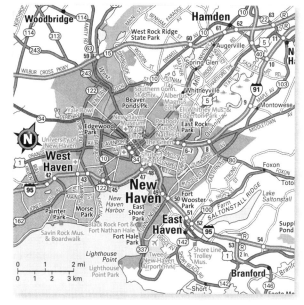

East Rock Park

Orange and Cold Spring Streets, New Haven, 203-946-6086

The city's largest park includes the Pardee Rose Gardens, a bird sanctuary, hiking trails, athletic fields, tennis courts and picnic grounds. April-November: daily; rest of year: Saturday-Sunday, and holidays.

Fort Nathan Hale Park and Black Rock Fort

36 Woodward Ave., New Haven, 203-946-8790

Federal guns kept British warships out of the harbor in 1812. Since then, Black Rock Fort has been restored and archaeological excavations are in progress. The Civil War–era Fort Nathan Hale has also been reconstructed. Both offer spectacular views of the harbor. Memorial Day-Labor Day: daily.

Grove Street Cemetery

227 Grove St., New Haven,

This was the first cemetery in the United States to be divided into family plots. Noah Webster, Charles Goodyear, Eli Whitney and many early settlers of the area are buried here.

Lighthouse Point Park

2 Lighthouse Point Rd., New Haven, 203-946-8005

The 82-acre park on Long Island Sound has an 1840 lighthouse, restored antique carousel, bird sanctuary, bathhouse, boat ramp and beach. Daily.

Pardee-Morris House

325 Lighthouse Rd., New Haven, 203-772-7060

Built in 1750, burned by the British in 1779 and rebuilt in 1780, this house has American period furnishings and a kitchen garden. June-August: Saturday-Sunday.

The Green

Church and Elm Streets, New Haven

In 1638, these 16 acres were laid out, making New Haven the first planned city in America. On the town common are three churches: United, Trinity Episcopal and Center Congregational. The latter is a masterpiece of American Georgian architecture.

Yale University

149 Elm St., New Haven, 203-432-2300; www.yale.edu

Founded by 10 Connecticut ministers and named for Elihu Yale, an early donor to the school, Yale is widely recognized as one of the best universities in the country. Walking

19

CONNECTICUT

★

★

★

★

★

tours are conducted daily by undergraduate students. Weekdays 10:30 a.m., 2 p.m.; Saturday-Sunday 1:30 p.m.

Peabody Museum of Natural History
170 Whitney Ave., New Haven, 203-432-5050
The museum has exhibits of mammals, invertebrate life, Plains and Connecticut Native Americans, meteorites, minerals, birds of Connecticut and several life-size dinosaurs, including a 60-foot-long brontosaurus reconstructed from original fossil material. Daily.

SPECIAL EVENTS
New Haven Symphony Orchestra
Woolsey Hall, College and Grove Streets, New Haven, 203-776-1444
A series of concerts by leading artists. October-May.

Yale Repertory Theater
1120 Chapel St., New Haven, 203-432-1234, 800-833-8134; www.yale.edu/yalerep
The Yale Repertory Theater prides itself on creating bold and passionate theatrical productions. The troupe often includes artistic leaders; four of the productions have won the Pulitzer Prize. Early October-mid-May.

HOTELS
★★The Colony
1157 Chapel St., New Haven, 203-776-1234, 800-458-8810; www.colonyatyale.com
86 rooms. Closed for renovation until spring 2008. Restaurant. Airport transportation available. $

★★Courtyard By Marriott
30 Whalley Ave., New Haven, 203-777-6221, 800-228-9290; www.courtyard.com
160 rooms. Restaurant, bar. $

★★★Omni New Haven Hotel
155 Temple St., New Haven, 203-772-6664, 800-843-6664; www.omnihotels.com
306 rooms. Restaurant, bar. $$

SPECIALTY LODGINGS
Three Chimneys
1201 Chapel St., New Haven, 203-789-1201, 800-443-1554; www.threechimneysinn.com
This lovely historic inn, built in the 1870s, is one block from Yale University. Guest rooms feature canopy beds with Edwardian bed drapes.
11 rooms. Complimentary full breakfast. $$

RESTAURANTS
★Indochine Pavilion
1180 Chapel St., New Haven, 203-865-5033
Vietnamese menu. Lunch, dinner. Closed Monday. Bar. $$

★
★
★
★
★

NEW LONDON

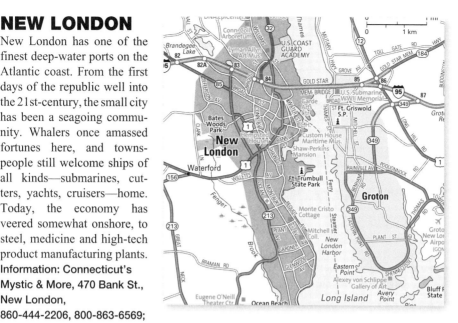

New London has one of the finest deep-water ports on the Atlantic coast. From the first days of the republic well into the 21st-century, the small city has been a seagoing community. Whalers once amassed fortunes here, and townspeople still welcome ships of all kinds—submarines, cutters, yachts, cruisers—home. Today, the economy has veered somewhat onshore, to steel, medicine and high-tech product manufacturing plants. Information: Connecticut's Mystic & More, 470 Bank St., New London, 860-444-2206, 800-863-6569; www.mysticcountry.com

WHAT TO SEE AND DO

Eugene O'Neill Theater Center
305 Great Neck Rd., Waterford, 860-443-5378; www.oneilltheatercenter.org
The complex includes the O'Neill Playwrights Conference, O'Neill Critics Institute, O'Neill Music Theater Conference, O'Neill Puppetry Conference, and the National Theater Institute. There are staged readings of new plays and musicals during summer at the Barn Theater, Amphitheater, and Instant Theater. (June-August)

Joshua Hempsted House
11 Hempstead Court, New London, 860-443-7949.
This is the oldest house in the city. The Hempsted family diary details life in the house during colonial times. Mid-May-mid-October: Thursday-Sunday afternoons.

Nathaniel Hempsted House
11 Hempstead Court, New London, 860-443-7949.
One of the state's two surviving examples of mid-18th-century cut-stone architecture. Mid-May-mid-October: Thursday-Sunday afternoons.

Lyman Allyn Art Museum
625 Williams St., New London, 860-443-2545; www.lymanallyn.org
More than 15,000 works are on display; the collection includes Contemporary, Modern, and Early American fine arts. Tuesday-Saturday 10 a.m.-5 p.m., Sunday 1-5 p.m.

Monte Cristo Cottage
325 Pequot Ave., New London, 860-443-5378
The restored boyhood home of playwright and Nobel prize winner Eugene O'Neill. Mid-June-Labor Day: Tuesday-Saturday.

Ocean Beach Park
1225 Ocean Ave., New London, 800-510-7263
Swim in the ocean or an Olympic-size pool (with a waterslide). There's also a boardwalk, amusement arcade, and mini golf. Saturday before Memorial Day-Labor Day: daily.

Shaw Perkins Mansion
11 Blinman St., New London, 860-443-1209

★
★
★
★

The Naval headquarters for the state during the Revolution is now a genealogical and historical library.

US Coast Guard Academy
31 Mohegan Ave., New London, 860-444-8444
The school houses 800 active cadets. The Visitors' Pavilion has a multimedia show (May-October: daily); the museum includes the 295-foot-long ship *Eagle*. Friday-Sunday, when in port; limited hours.

SPECIAL EVENTS
Connecticut Storytelling Festival
Connecticut College, 270 Mohegan Ave., New London, 860-439-2764; www.connstorycenter.org/festival.html
Nationally acclaimed artists lead readings, workshops and concerts. Late April.

Sailfest
New London City Pier, Bank St., New London, 860-443-1879; www.sailfest.org
Arts and crafts and food vendors line the streets downtown while people of all ages browse, eat and enjoy the three stages of entertainment. The largest fireworks show on the East Coast takes place on Saturday night. One weekend in early July.

HOTELS
★★Radisson Hotel New London
35 Governor Winthrop Blvd., New London, 860-443-7000, 888-201-1718; www.radisson.com
120 rooms. Restaurant, bar. Airport transportation available. $

NORWALK
Norwalk's growth was heavily influenced by Long Island Sound. The city evolved rapidly from an agricultural community to a major seaport, then to a manufacturing center known for high-fashion hats, corsets and clocks. The Sound still plays an important part in Norwalk's development, providing beauty, recreation and, of course, oysters.
Information: Coastal Fairfield County Convention & Visitors Bureau, 297 West Ave., Norwalk, 203-853-7770, 800-866-7925; www.coastalct.com

WHAT TO SEE AND DO
Historic South Norwalk (SoNo)
Washington and Water Streets, South Norwalk, 800-866-7925; www.southnorwalk.com
The 19th-century waterfront neighborhood has historical buildings, unique shops art galleries, and restaurants.

Lockwood-Mathews Mansion Museum
295 West Ave., Norwalk, 203-838-9799; www.lockwoodmathewsmansion.org
This 60-room Victorian mansion was built by financier LeGrand Lockwood and features a 42-foot-tall skylit rotunda, ornamented doors, carved marble and inlaid woodwork, period furnishings and a mechanical music exhibit. Mid-March-December:

Wednesday-Sunday noon-4 p.m.; rest of year: by appointment only.

Maritime Aquarium at Norwalk
10 N. Water St., Norwalk, 203-852-0700; www.maritimeaquarium.org
A hands-on maritime museum with a shark touch tank and a harbor seal pool, plus 125 species and an IMAX screen. Daily.

Mill Hill Historic Park
2 E. Wall St., Norwalk, 203-846-0525; www.geocities.com/Heartland/Trail/8030
The complex of historic Early American buildings includes the Town House Museum (circa 1835), Fitch House Law Office (circa 1740) and a schoolhouse (circa 1826). Memorial Day-Labor Day: Sunday 1-4 p.m.

SPECIAL EVENTS

International In-Water Boat Show

Norwalk Cove Marina, 48 Calf Pasture
Beach Rd., Norwalk, 212-984-7000;
www.boatshownorwalk.com
The show features more than 750 of the
newest and most innovative performance
boats, sailboats and sailing yachts. Guests at
this waterside boat show can also try scuba
diving, view a restored classic boat, or grab
a drink at the Sand Bar. Third weekend in
September.

Oyster Festival

Veteran's Park, Seaview Ave.,
East Norwalk, 800-866-7925;
www.seaport.org
Featuring appearances from tall ships and
vintage oyster boats, this festival has regu-
larly drawn 60,000 visitors a year since it
began in 1978. More than 3,000 volunteers
make the festival possible each year and
many local nonprofit groups benefit. Weekend after Labor Day.

Round Hill Highland Games

Cranbury Park, Kensett Rd.,
Norwalk, 800-866-7925;
www.roundhill.org
A heritage celebration with Highland dancing, pipe bands, caber tossing, clan tents,
and Scottish and American food. Late June
or early July.

SoNo Arts Celebration

Washington and S. Main Streets,
South Norwalk, 203-866-7916;
www.sonoarts.org
Juried crafts, kinetic sculpture race, entertainment, concessions and a block party
make up this celebration in historic South
Norwalk. First weekend in August.

HOTELS

★★Doubletree Club Hotel

789 Connecticut Ave., Norwalk,.
203-853-3477, 800-222-8733;
www.doubletree.com
268 rooms. Wireless Internet access.
Restaurant, bar. $

★★Four Points by Sheraton

426 Main Ave., Norwalk,
203-849-9828, 800-329-7466;
www.fourpoints.com
127 rooms. Restaurant, bar. $$

★★★The Silvermine Tavern

194 Perry Ave., Norwalk, 203-847-4558;
www.silverminetavern.com
10 rooms. Closed Tuesday, September-May.
Complimentary continental breakfast. Res-
taurant, bar. $$

RESTAURANTS

★★★Pasta Nostra

116 Washington St., South Norwalk,
203-854-9700
www.pastanostra.com
Italian menu. Dinner. Closed Sunday-
Tuesday. Casual attire. Reservations rec-
ommended. $$$

★★Silvermine Tavern

194 Perry Ave., Norwalk,
203-847-4558, 888-693-9967;
www.silverminetavern.com
American menu. Lunch, dinner, late-night,
Sunday brunch. Closed Tuesday; also Mon-
day in January-April. Bar. Children's menu.
Casual attire. Reservations recommended.
Outdoor seating. $$$

NORWICH

Norwich was one of the first chartered cities in Connecticut and since the end of the 18th
century, it has been a leader in area industrial development. The colony's first paper mill
was opened here in 1766, and the first cut nails in America were Norwich-made in 1772.
The city of nearly 40,000 is divided into three distinct sections: Norwichtown to the north-

west; a business section near the Thames docks; and a central residential area that showcases many 19th-century homes.

Information: Connecticut's Mystic and More, 470 Bank St., New London, 860-444-2206, 800-863-6569; www.mysticcountry.com

WHAT TO SEE AND DO

Indian Leap
Yantic and Sachem Streets,
Norwich, 860-886-4683

These falls were a favorite resort and outpost of the Mohegan. Legend has it that a band of Narragansetts, during the 1643 Battle of Great Plains, came upon the falls while fleeing the Mohegans (more popularly known as the Mohicans). Many were forced to jump off the cliffs and into the chasm below.

Royal Mohegan Burial Grounds
Sachem and Washington Streets, Norwich,
860-862-6390;
www.mohegan.nsn.us

The resting place of Uncas, chief of the Mohicans.

Tantaquidgeon Indian Museum
1819 Norwich-New London Tpke.,
Uncasville,
860-848-9145

Works of Mohegan and other New England tribes, past and present. May-November: Monday-Friday 10 a.m.-3 p.m.

SPECIAL EVENTS

Blue Grass Festival
Strawberry Park, 42 Pierce Rd.,
Preston, 860-886-1944, 888-794-7944;

www.strawberrypark.net/bluegrass.html

You can either come for the day or make reservations for a campsite and enjoy four days of bluegrass music. Past performers have included Rhonda Vincent, the Tim O'Brien Band and the Waybacks. Late May-early June.

HOTELS

★★★The Spa at Norwich Inn
607 W. Thames St., Norwich,
860-886-2401, 800-275-4772;
www.thespaatnorwichinn.com

From the outside, this property looks just like any other posh New England country inn. Step across the Norwich Inn's threshold, though, and you'll be transported to a very bucolic paradise. The property has 42 acres of grounds to roam, plus a 32-treatment-room spa. Offerings include the requisite massage and facials, but also more cutting-edge treatments like hydrotherapy and energy work.

65 rooms. Restaurant, bar. $

RESTAURANTS

★★Kensington
607 W Thames St., Norwich,
860-886-2401

American menu. Breakfast, lunch, dinner, Sunday brunch. Bar. Outdoor seating. $$$

OLD LYME

Lore has it that sea captains, flush from their huge hauls, once owned and occupied every Old Lyme house. The town's modern inhabitants are a more sophisticated (though no less loaded) lot. The sleepy village, with its restored manors and safe, tree-lined streets, has become a classier mini-Greenwich for summering New Yorkers. Artsy types come here for the local design scene; tourists flock here for the seaside vistas. Only a privileged few get to stay year-round.

Information: Connecticut's Mystic and More, 470 Bank St., New London, 860-444-2206, 800-863-6569; www.mysticcountry.com

WHAT TO SEE AND DO

Florence Griswold Museum

96 Lyme St., Old Lyme,
860-434-5542; www.flogris.org
This stately late-Georgian mansion housed America's most celebrated art colony at the turn of the century. Paintings by Willard Metcalf, Childe Hassam and other artists are on display. Krieble Gallery: Tuesday-Saturday 10 a.m.-5 p.m., Sunday 1-5 p.m.; Chadwick Studio: mid-May-October.

HOTELS

★★★Bee and Thistle Inn

100 Lyme St., Old Lyme,
860-434-1667, 800-622-4946;
www.beeandthistleinn.com
This 1756 inn is widely recognized by savvy travelers as one of the state's most romantic getaways. The antique-decorated rooms are cozy and clean, and the service is precise but never fawning.
11 rooms. Closed two weeks in January. Children over 12 years only. Restaurant, bar. **$**

★★★Old Lyme Inn

85 Lyme St., Old Lyme,
860-434-2600, 800-434-5352;
www.oldlymeinn.com
Located in the town's historic district, this classic bed-and-breakfast is close to Essex, Mystic Seaport, Mystic Aquarium, and several local art galleries. Most guests, however, choose to stay put in their sumptuous rooms, or watch the sunset from a deep Adirondack chair on the sweeping front lawn.
13 rooms. Complimentary continental breakfast. Restaurant, bar. **$$**

RESTAURANTS

★★★Bee and Thistle Inn

100 Lyme St., Old Lyme,
860-434-1667, 800-622-4046;
www.beeandthistleinn.com
Romance is alive and well in the Bee and Thistle's white-table-clothed main dining room. The formal, candlelit scene looks like something out of an Austen novel, but the food is all 21st-century. Chef Kristofer Rowe blends fresh produce with first-rate seafood and steak for hearty but arty meals. American menu. Breakfast, lunch, dinner, Sunday brunch. Bar. Closed two weeks in January. **$$$**

★★★Old Lyme Inn

85 Lyme St, Old Lyme,
860-434-2600, 800-434-5352;
www.oldlymeinn.com
The meat-heavy menu and clubhouse-like décor of the inn's grill room gives way to the dining room's more sophisticated appeal. The real draw here, though, are the mouth-watering homemade desserts like triple chocolate silk tower and "meltaway" chocolate cake.
American menu. Lunch, dinner. Bar. **$$$**

OLD SAYBROOK

This shabby chic town at the mouth of the Connecticut River is full of magnificent second homes. Originally the site of Yale College, it's the third-oldest named community in the state.
Information: Chamber of Commerce, 146 Main St., Old Saybrook, 860-388-3266; Connecticut Valley Tourism Commission, 393 Main St., Middletown, 860-347-0028; www.oldsaybrookct.com

WHAT TO SEE AND DO

Fort Saybrook Monument Park

Hwy 154, Saybrook Point,
Old Saybrook, 860-395-3152
An 18-acre park with remains of Fort Saybrook, the state's first military fortification. Daily.

25

CONNECTICUT

★
★
★
★

General William Hart House
350 Main St., Old Saybrook, 860-388-2622
The 1767 Georgian-style residence of well-to-do New England merchant and politician William Hart features eight corner fireplaces, one of which is decorated with Sadler and Green transfer-print tiles illustrating *Aesop's Fables*. Mid-June-Labor Day: Friday-Sunday 1-4 p.m.

SPECIAL EVENTS
Arts and Crafts Show
Town Green, Main St.,
Old Saybrook, 860-388-3266;
www.oldsaybrookct.com
More than 200 artists and craftspersons. Last full weekend in July.

Christmas Torchlight Parade
Main St., Old Saybrook, 860-388-3266;
www.connecticutblues.com
Forty fife and drum corps march down Main Street on the second Saturday in December.

HOTELS
★★★Saybrook Point Inn and Spa
2 Bridge St., Old Saybrook,
860-395-2828, 800-243-0212
Water views of Long Island Sound and the Connecticut River provide a postcard-perfect backdrop to this seaside getaway. Like many area inns, guest rooms here are replete with 18th-century period-style furnishings and accessories. Unlike the others, though, the Point has a state-of-the-art fitness center, full service spa and the fine-dining eatery Terra Mar Grille.
62 rooms. Restaurant, bar. **$$**

★★★Water's Edge Resort And Conference Center
1525 Boston Post Rd., Westbrook,
860-399-5901, 800-222-5901;
www.watersedge-resort.com
It's fun for the whole family at the Water's Edge, located on Long Island Sound. Kids have their own activity center, but adults can also partake in myriad activities including softball, face painting, scavenger hunts, kite flying, football, horseshoes and volleyball. 32 rooms. Restaurant, bar. Children's activity center. Beach. **$$**

RESTAURANTS
★★Dock and Dine
College St., Old Saybrook, 860-388-4665
Seafood, steak menu. Lunch, dinner. Closed Monday-Tuesday Mid-October-mid-April. Bar. Children's menu. **$$**

RIDGEFIELD
It's not exactly Paris, but this southwestern Connecticut town *does* have a rare Champs Elysées-style boulevard. Ninety-nine feet wide, the street is lined with trees and stately houses. It was here that, in 1777, a pre-traitorous Benedict Arnold set up barricades and fought the Battle of Ridgefield.
Information: Chamber of Commerce, 9 Bailey Ave., Ridgefield, 203-438-5992, 800-386-1708
Housatonic Valley Tourism Commission, 30 Main St., Danbury, 203-743-0546, 800-841-4488; www.ridgefieldchamber.org

WHAT TO SEE AND DO
Aldrich Contemporary Art Museum
258 Main St., Ridgefield,
203-438-4519; www.aldrichart.org
The museum has changing exhibits and a sculpture garden. Tuesday-Sunday noon-5 p.m.

Keeler Tavern Museum
132 Main St., Ridgefield,
203-438-5485;
www.keelertavernmuseum.org
A restored 18th-century tavern, stagecoach stop and home that was once revolutionary patriot headquarters. A British cannonball

is still embedded in the wall. Wednesday, Saturday-Sunday 1-4 p.m.

HOTELS

★★★The Elms Inn
500 Main St., Ridgefield,
203-438-2541;
www.elmsinn.com
Established in 1799, this is the oldest continuously run inn in the state. But don't expect creaky stairs and peeling paint—the property has been lovingly restored and now boasts historic appeal (antique furnishings, old-world charm) and modern conveniences (wireless Internet, dry cleaning). 23 rooms. Complimentary continental breakfast. Restaurant, bar. **$$$**

★★★Stonehenge Inn
35 Stonehenge Rd., Ridgefield,
203-438-6511; www.stonehengeinn-ct.com
Set on a swan-filled lake, Stonehenge looks like an old white rambling farmhouse. Inside are elegant rooms and top-notch service. 16 rooms. Complimentary continental breakfast. Restaurant, bar. **$$**

★★★West Lane Inn
22 West Lane, Ridgefield,
203-438-7323;
www.westlaneinn.com
This country inn has comfortably decorated rooms with televisions, Vcrs and refrigerators. Breakfast is served each morning in the breakfast room or on the terrace.

18 rooms. Complimentary continental breakfast. Restaurant. **$$**

RESTAURANTS

★★★The Elms
500 Main St., Ridgefield, 203-438-9206;
www.elmsinn.com
A roaring fireplace sets the tone at the Elms, where award-wining savory dishes are created under the watchful eye of head chef Brendan Walsh. His "Yankee Cuisine" includes standout dishes such as pulled wild boar and lobster Shepherd's pie.
American menu. Lunch, dinner. Closed Monday-Tuesday. Reservations recommended. Outdoor seating. **$$**

★★★Stonehenge
35 Stonehenge Rd., Ridgefield,
203-438-6511;
www.stonehengeinn-ct.com
The restaurant's tranquil scenery and attentive service make it popular among locals and tourists alike. Menu highlights include pan seared scallops and shrimp, and a buttery fresh steamed lobster.
French menu. Dinner. Reservations recommended. Valet parking. **$$$**

★Venice Restaurant
3 Cops Hill Rd., Ridgefield,
203-438-3333.
Italian menu. Lunch, dinner. Bar. Children's menu. Casual attire. Outdoor seating. **$$**

STAMFORD
Stamford is so close to New York, some label the growing city an out-of-state suburb. But while it does have several resident commuters, not all its professionals travel to Manhattan. More than 20 *Fortune* 500 companies are headquartered here, making Stamford a booming business town in its own right with pretty marinas and beaches on Long Island Sound.
Information: Chamber of Commerce, 733 Summer St., Stamford, 203-359-4761; www.stamfordchamber.com

WHAT TO SEE AND DO
Bartlett Arboretum and Gardens
151 Brookdale Rd., Stamford,
203-322-6971;
www.bartlett.arboretum.uconn.edu

Collections of dwarf conifers, rhododendrons, azaleas, wildflowers, perennials and witches brooms are open to the public, as are ecology trails and the natural woodlands surrounding the gardens. Gardens daily, 8:30 a.m.-sunset; Visitors center Monday-

Friday 8:30 a.m.-4:30 p.m.;
Greenhouse Monday-Friday
9:30 a.m.-11 a.m.

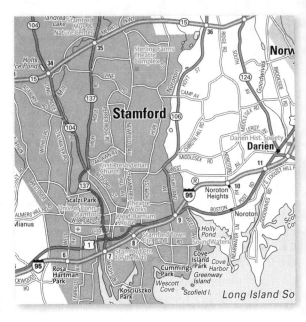

HOTELS

★★Holiday Inn
700 E. Main St., Stamford,
203-358-8400, 888-465-4329;
www.holiday-inn.com
383 rooms. Wireless Internet
access. Restaurant, bar. **$**

★★★Stamford Marriott Hotel & Spa
243 Tresser Blvd., Stamford,
203-357-9555, 800-732-9689;
www.marriott.com
This hotel's biggest draw
might be its prime location—
right across the street from the
Stamford Town Center Mall.
If you can't find anything you like in those
130 stores, you're in luck: The Marriott is
also close to the Palace Theater, Playland
Amusement Park, or Whitney Museum.
Still not enticed? Pack your pooch and
check in to the on-site spa (canines get their
own Pet Travel Kits).
506 rooms. High-speed Internet access.
Two restaurants, bar. Airport transportation
available. **$$$**

★★★Sheraton Stamford Hotel
2701 Summer St., Stamford,
203-359-1300, 800-325-3535;
www.sheraton.com/stamford
The Sheraton is 45 minutes from
Manhattan, but most guests never make
it into the city, preferring to explore
Connecticut's fabled Gold Coast instead.
Cream-colored walls, blue and white fur-
nishings, and lots of plants lend a coastal
theme to the hotel. Pets are welcome here
as well, thanks to the resort's "Love that
Dog" program.
448 rooms. Wireless Internet access.
Restaurant, bar. Airport transportation
available. **$$$**

★★★The Westin Stamford
1 Stamford Place, Stamford,
203-967-2222, 888-627-7154;
www.westinstamford.com
The Westin's quick, efficient service and
central downtown location make it a hit with
business travelers. New York culture vultures
often stop in on their way to soak in some
New England charm.
462 rooms. Wireless Internet access. Restau-
rant, bar. **$$**

RESTAURANTS

★Crab Shell
46 Southfield Ave., Stamford,
203-967-7229; www.crabshell.com
American, seafood menu. Lunch, dinner.
Bar. Casual attire. Outdoor seating. **$$**

★★Fio's Ristorante
299 Long Ridge Rd., Stamford,
203-964-9802; www.fiosristorante.com
Italian menu. Lunch, dinner. Bar. Casual
attire. Reservations recommended. Outdoor
seating. **$$$**

★★Il Falco
59 Broad St., Stamford,
203-327-0002; www.ilfalco.com
Italian menu. Lunch, dinner. Closed Sunday.
Bar. Casual attire. Valet parking. **$$$**

28

CONNECTICUT

★

★

★

★

★

★★La Bretagne
2010 W. Main St., Stamford,
203-324-9539
Continental, French menu. Lunch, dinner.
Closed Sunday. Bar. Business casual attire.
Reservations recommended. $$$

★★La Hacienda
222 Summer St., Stamford, 203-324-0577
Mexican menu. Lunch, dinner. Bar. Children's menu. Casual attire. Reservations recommended. Outdoor seating. $$

WASHINGTON
With its prime location in posh Litchfield County, Washington is a favorite destination for antiquing. Quaint churches and historic buildings dot the rolling landscape.
Information: www.washingtonct.org

WHAT TO SEE AND DO
Historical Museum of Gunn Memorial Library
5 Wykeham Rd., Washington,
860-868-7756; www.gunnlibrary.org
This house, built in 1781, contains collections and exhibits on area history, paintings, furnishings, gowns, dolls, dollhouses and tools. Thursday-Saturday 10 a.m.-4 p.m.; otherwise by appointment.

Institute for American Indian Studies
38 Curtis Rd., Washington,
860-868-0518; www.birdstone.org
A museum of Northeastern Woodland Indian artifacts with a permanent exhibit hall. Exhibits include changing Native American art displays, a replicated indoor longhouse, an outdoor replicated Algonkian village and a simulated archaeological site. Monday-Saturday 10 a.m.-5 p.m., Sunday noon-5 p.m.

HOTELS
★★★★★The Mayflower Inn
118 Woodbury Rd., Washington,
860-868-9466;
www.mayflowerinn.com
This country inn, located less than two hours from New York City, evokes the feeling and quiet elegance of an English countryside hotel. It's set on 28 acres of rolling hills, streams and lush gardens.

Guest rooms and suites are swathed in luxurious fabrics and feature four-poster, canopied beds, 18th- and 19th-century art, and modern touches like flat-screen TVs. The inn's dining room has a seasonal menu that makes good use of fresh, local ingredients with dishes such as organic Atlantic salmon with fresh veggies. The tap room has a more casual menu of Vermont cheddar-topped burgers and lemon-rosemary chicken. The sprawling spa is superlative. 24 rooms. Children over 12 years only. Wireless Internet access. Restaurant, bar. $$$$

SPAS
★★★★The Mayflower Spa
118 Woodbury Rd., Washington,
860-868-9466; www.mayflowerinn.com
The 20,000-square-foot Mayflower Spa, opened in 2006, features the same classic design, elegant furnishing and quiet luxury of its namesake inn. Those who come for the full spa experience receive a pre-arrival consultation to create a schedule of pampering services and fitness and nutrition classes. Guests are provided with everything from yoga mats to MP3 players to loungewear to rain boots. The spa has an indoor heated pool and mosaic-domes whirlpool, as well as private yoga and Pilates studios. Classes include everything from kickboxing to ballet.

29

CONNECTICUT

WESTPORT

Much like neighboring Greenwich, Westport is home to several uber-successful corporate warriors. It's also full of thriving small businesses and notable actors and illustrators. The town is surrounded by wooded hills and Long Island Sound beaches, making it a pretty, if pricey, place to live.

Information: Westport/Weston Chamber of Commerce, 60 Church Lane, Westport, 203-227-9234; www.westportchamber.com

SPECIAL EVENTS

Levitt Pavilion for the Performing Arts

Jesup Green, 260 Compo Rd. S., Westport, 203-226-7600; www.levittpavilion.com

Nightly free outdoor performances of jazz, pop, rock, dance, and children's music. Late June-early August.

HOTELS

★★★Inn at National Hall

2 Post Rd. W, Westport, 203-221-1351, 800-628-4255; www.innatnationalhall.com

This distinctive inn sits along the banks of the Saugatuck River, and is walking distance to shops, galleries, and the beach. Slightly quirky with an *Alice in Wonderland* feel, the 1873 Italianate property has just 15 individually designed rooms decorated in vibrant themes (the watermelon room, the equestrian suite). River views add an enchanting touch to the accommodations, and several chambers boast soaring two-story ceilings and crystal chandeliers.

15 rooms. Complimentary continental breakfast. Restaurant. $$$

★★Westport Inn

1595 Post Rd. E, Westport, 203-259-5236, 800-446-8997; www.westportinn.com

116 rooms. Restaurant, bar. $

SPECIALTY LODGINGS

The Inn at Longshore

260 Compo Rd. S., Westport, 203-226-3316; www.innatlongshore.com

Rooms at this sprawling country inn are simply decorated with antique furnishings. 12 rooms. Complimentary continental breakfast. Restaurant. $

RESTAURANTS

★★★Cobb's Mill Inn

12 Old Mill Rd., Weston, 203-227-7221; www.cobbsmillinn.com

At the Cobb's Mill Inn, excellent service merges with an elegant, historic ambience. The cuisine is beautifully presented, and the setting is a rustic, cozy barn.

Seafood, steak menu. Lunch, dinner. Bar. Valet parking. $$$

★★Nistico's Red Barn

292 Wilton Rd., Westport, 203-222-9549; www.redbarnrestaurant.com

American menu. Lunch, dinner, brunch. Children's menu. Valet parking. Outdoor seating. $$$

WETHERSFIELD

Wethersfield, "the most ancient towne in Connecticut," has a rich heritage. Settled by a group of Massachusetts colonists, it became the commercial center of the Connecticut River communities, and an important post in the American colonies-West Indies trade route. Agriculture, especially corn, rye and red onion, was Wethersfield's main industry. During the American Revolution, notable figures such as George Washington and Count de Rochambeau came to Wethersfield to craft war plans.

Information: Wethersfield Historical Society, 150 Main St., Wethersfield, 860-529-7656; www.wethhist.org

WHAT TO SEE AND DO

Buttolph-Williams House
249 Broad St., Wethersfield,
860-529-0460

This restored 1700 building contains a fine collection of pewter, delft, fabrics, period furniture. May-October: Wednesday-Monday, limited hours.

Dinosaur State Park
400 West St., Rocky Hill,
860-529-8423;
www.dinosaurstatepark.org

While excavating the site of a new building, construction crews discovered a stone slab bearing three-toed tracks of dinosaurs; eventually, more than 2,000 prints were unearthed. The building project was cancelled and the 65-acre area was designated a state park. Visitors can examine the crisscrossing tracks and view a skeletal cast and life-size models of the area's prehistoric inhabitants. Tuesday-Sunday.

Hurlburt-Dunham House
200 Main St., Wethersfield,
860-529-7656

A Georgian house updated in Italianate style. Rich in decoration, it includes original Rococo Revival wallpapers, painted ceilings and a varied collection of furniture. Mid-March-mid-May and mid-October-December 25: Saturday-Sunday.

Webb-Deane-Stevens Museum
211 Main St., Wethersfield,
860-529-0612

The museum consists of three 18th-century houses that stand at the center of old Wethersfield: the Joseph Webb house (1752), the Silas Deane house (1766), and the Isaac Stevens house (1789). They have been restored and reflect the different lives of their owners—a merchant, a diplomat, and a tradesman. May-October: Wednesday-Monday; rest of year: Saturday-Sunday.

HOTELS

★Best Western Camelot Inn
1330 Silas Deane Hwy, Wethersfield,
860-563-2311, 888-563-3930;
www.bestwestern.com

112 rooms. Complimentary continental breakfast. Bar. $

WINDSOR LOCKS

Located on the Connecticut River, this town is home to Bradley International Airport.
Information: Chamber of Commerce, Windsor Locks, 860-623-9319; www.wmch.com

WHAT TO SEE AND DO

New England Air Museum
36 Perimeter Rd., Windsor Locks, 860-623-3305

One of the largest and most comprehensive collections of aircraft and aeronautical memorabilia in the world is located right next to Bradley International Airport. More than 80 aircraft, including bombers, fighters, helicopters and gliders, are on display; some date back to 1909. There's also a jet fighter cockpit simulator. Daily.

Noden-Reed House & Barn
58 West St., Windsor Locks,
860-627-9212

Housed in an 1840 house and an 1825 barn are an antique sleigh bed, 1871 taffeta evening dress, 1884 wedding dress, antique quilts, kitchen utensils, and 1880s newspapers and periodicals. May-October: Sunday afternoons.

Old Newgate Prison
115 Newgate Rd., East Granby,
860-653-3563

Here, a 1707 copper mine was converted to a Revolutionary prison for Tories. It then became a state prison. Check out self-guided tour of underground caverns where the prisoners once lived. Mid-May-October: Wednesday-Sunday.

HOTELS

★★Doubletree Hotel
16 Ella Grasso Tpke.,
Windsor Locks,
860-627-5171, 800-222-8733;
www.doubletree.com
200 rooms. Restaurant, bar. Airport transportation available. **$**

★Homewood Suites
65 Ella Grasso Tpke., Windsor Locks,
860-627-8463, 800-225-5466;
www.homewoodsuites.com
132 rooms, all suites. Complimentary continental breakfast. Airport transportation available. **$**

★★★Sheraton Bradley Airport Hotel
1 Bradley International Airport,
Windsor Locks,
860-627-5311, 877-422-5311;
www.sheraton.com/bradleyairport
237 rooms. Restaurant, bar. **$**

32

CONNECTICUT

MAINE

MAYBE IT'S THE FLAT YANKEE TWANG OR THE SALTY SEA AIR. WHATEVER IT IS, THERE IS something about Maine. With the highest tides in the country and a temperature that ranges from –46 to 105 degrees Fahrenheit, Maine is a popular state to visit year-round. There are 6,000 lakes and ponds and 3,500 miles of seacoast (though the water can be a bit chilly, with temperatures steady in summer in the 50s).

In 1604, St. Croix Island became Maine's first settlement, but it only lasted one winter. Another early settlement was established near Pemaquid Point, but it was the short-lived Popham Colony, at the mouth of the Kennebec River, that built America's first transatlantic trader in 1607, called the *Virginia*. Maine was a part of Massachusetts until 1820, when it was officially admitted to the Union.

Today, Maine is a vast playground of natural beauty, populated (in some places sparsely) by hearty Mainers who earn their stripes by surviving the long, dark winters. Most of Maine's 17.6 million acres of forest are open for public recreational use, including more than 580,000 acres owned by the state. Acadia National Park is one of the nation's wildest and most beautiful areas, now filled with a resurgent bald eagle population. Other wildlife can easily be seen in Maine, from the large numbers of seals and porpoises that swim in the waters off Penobscot Bay in summer, to the pods of migratory whales that pass through each year.

In summer, the state swells with vistors who come to feast on lobster, sail the rugged, rocky coast, poke through antique shops in achingly quaint towns or even take a plunge in the constantly chilly coastal waters. Celebrities and the merely shockingly wealthy—including Martha Stewart, the Bush family, Stockard Channing, John Travolta and Stephen King—keep compounds here in places like Kennebunkport and Bar Harbor, and occasionally add a dash of glamour to what is typically a humble, down-to-earth population.

Of course, fall rivals summer for the most popular time to visit New England's largest state, and that's because of the resplendant display of autumn leaves the landscape produces each year. Tourists who come (in droves) during this time are called "leafpeepers." The state's inns, restaurants and roads are usually packed to capacity in September and October.

Local residents muddle through the summer and autumn crowds and dream of quiet, snowy winters, when they have the charms of this great state (mostly) to themselves again. Information: www.visitmaine.com

 SPOTLIGHT

★ Nearly 90 percent of the nation's lobster supply is caught off the coast of Maine.

★ Maine has more than 5,000 miles of coastline—more than California.

★ The state has 63 lighthouses.

★ Maine grows more blueberries than any other state.

ACADIA NATIONAL PARK

The rocky coastline and thick woodlands filled with wildlife make Acadia National Park a favorite spot to visit in Maine. The park takes up almost half of Mount Desert Island and has smaller areas on Isle au Haut, Little Cranberry Island, Baker Island, Little Moose Island and part of the mainland at Schoodic Point. Created by the force of glaciers, the coastal area has countless valleys, lakes and mountains.

Although small compared to other national parks, Acadia is one of the most visited parks in the country and the only national park in the northeastern United States. A 27-mile-loop road connects the park's eastern sights on Mount Desert Island, and ferry services take travelers to some of the smaller islands. Visitors can explore 1,530-foot Cadillac Mountain, the highest point on the Atlantic Coast of the United States, watch waves crash against Thunder Hole, or swim in the ocean at various coastal beaches. A road to the summit of Cadillac provides views of Frenchman, Blue Hill and Penobscot bays.

Mount Desert Island was founded by the French explorer Samuel de Champlain in 1604. Shortly thereafter, French Jesuit missionaries settled there until driven off by an armed vessel from Virginia. This was the first act of overt warfare between France and England for control of North America. Until 1713, the island was a part of French Acadia and it wasn't until after the Revolutionary War that it was officially settled. In 1916, a portion of the area was proclaimed Sieur de Monts National Monument. It was changed to Lafayette National Park in 1919, and finally, in 1929, it was enlarged and renamed Acadia National Park.

Like all national parks, Acadia is a wildlife sanctuary, where bald eagles are thriving. Fir, pine, spruce, many hardwoods and hundreds of varieties of wildflowers flourish. There are more than 120 miles of trails, and park rangers take visitors on various walks and cruises, pointing out and explaining the natural, cultural and historical features of the park. Forty-five miles of carriage roads offer bicyclists scenic rides through Acadia. Copies of ranger-led programs and trail maps are available at the visitor center.

There is saltwater swimming at Sand Beach and freshwater swimming at Echo Lake. Snowmobiles are allowed in some areas, and cross-country skiing is available. Most facilities are open Memorial Day-September. Portions of the park are open year-round, and the picnic grounds are open May-October. Limited camping is available at two park campgrounds: Blackwoods, open year-round, requires reservations from mid-June to mid-September; and Seawall, open late-May to late-September, is on a first-come, first-served basis. The park headquarters, 2 1/2 miles west of Bar Harbor on Highway 233, provides visitor information.

MAINE

AUGUSTA

Augusta, the capital of Maine, was settled in 1628 when settlers from Plymouth established a trading post on the site of Cushnoc, a Native American village. Soon after, in 1754, Fort Western was built to protect settlers against Native American raids, and from that, the settlement grew. Located 39 miles from the sea, Augusta is at the head of navigation on the Kennebec River.

Information: Kennebec Valley Chamber of Commerce, 21 University Dr., 207-623-4559; www.augustamaine.com

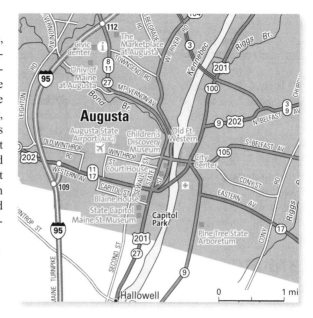

WHAT TO SEE AND DO

Old Fort Western
City Center Plaza, 16 Cony St., Augusta, 207-626-2385; www.oldfortwestern.org
Fort complex built in 1754 by Boston merchants; main house and reproduction blockhouse, watchboxes and palisade. Costumed staff interprets 18th-century life on the Kennebec River. Memorial Day-Labor Day: daily; after Labor Day-Columbus Day: Saturday-Sunday, limited hours.

State House
83 State House Station, Augusta, 207-287-2301
(1829-1832) The original design for this impressive building was by Charles Bulfinch (architect of the Massachusetts State House). Remodeled and enlarged (1909-1910), it rises majestically above Capitol Park and the Kennebec River. On its 185-foot dome is a statue, designed by W. Clark Noble, of a classically robed woman bearing a pine bough torch. Monday-Friday.

Blaine House
State and Capitol Streets, Augusta, 207-287-2301
This is the 1833 house of James G. Blaine, Speaker of the U.S. House of Representatives and an 1884 presidential candidate. Since 1919, this 28-room house has been the official residence of Maine's governors. Originally built in Federal-style, it was remodeled several times and today appears semi-colonial. Tours. Tuesday-Thursday, limited hours.

Maine State Museum
83 State House Station, Augusta, 207-287-2301
Exhibits of Maine's natural environment, prehistory, social history and manufacturing heritage. Daily.

HOTELS

★Best Inn
65 Whitten Rd., Augusta, 207-622-3776, 800-237-8466; www.bestinn.com
58 rooms. Complimentary continental breakfast. Outdoor pool. $

35

MAINE

★
★
★
★

★Comfort Inn
281 Civic Center Dr., Augusta,
207-623-1000, 800-808-1188;
www.comfortinn.com
99 rooms. Pets accepted. Complimentary continental breakfast. Restaurant. Bar. Fitness room. Indoor pool. **$**

★★★Best Western Senator Inn & Spa
284 Western Ave., Augusta,
207-622-5804, 877-772-2224;
www.senatorinn.com
124 rooms. Pets accepted, some restrictions; fee. Complimentary full breakfast. High-speed Internet access, wireless Internet access. Restaurant, bar. Children's activity center. Fitness room, fitness classes available, spa. Indoor pool, outdoor pool, whirlpool. **$$**

SPECIALTY LODGINGS
Wings Hill Inn
9 Dry Point Drive, Rome,
207-495-2400, 866-495-2400;
www.wingshillinn.com
Renovated farmhouse built in 1800; antique quilts.
8 rooms. Complimentary full breakfast. **$**

BAILEY ISLAND
Located at the end of Highway 24, along the northern shore of Casco Bay, Bailey Island is the most popular of the 365 Calendar Islands. Together with Orr's Island—to which it's connected by a cribstone bridge—Bailey is a resort and fishing center. Originally called Newwaggin by an early trader from Kittery, Bailey Island was renamed after Deacon Timothy Bailey of Massachusetts, who banished early settlers and claimed the land for himself. Bailey Island and Orr's Island partially enclose an arm of Casco Bay called Harpswell Sound—the locale of John Whittier's poem "The Dead Ship of Harpswell" and of Harriet Beecher Stowe's "Pearl of Orr's Island."

36

Information: Chamber of Commerce of the Bath-Brunswick Region, 59 Pleasant St., Brunswick, 207-725-8797; www.midcoastmaine.com

MAINE

WHAT TO SEE AND DO
Giant Staircase
Washington Street
Natural rock formation dropping 200 feet in steps to ocean. Scenic overlook area.

SPECIALTY LODGINGS
Log Cabin Island Inn
5 Log Cabin Lane, Bailey Island,
207-833-5546; www.logcabin-maine.com
Log cabin; panoramic view of bay.
8 rooms. Closed November-March. Complimentary full breakfast. Restaurant. **$**

RESTAURANTS
★Cook's Lobster House
Garrison Cove Rd., Bailey Island,
207-833-2818;
www.cookslobsterhouse.com
Dockage. Seafood menu. Lunch, dinner. Bar. Children's menu. Outdoor seating. **$$$**

BANGOR

In 1604, Samuel de Champlain sailed up the Penobscot River to what is now Bangor and reported that the area was "most pleasant and agreeable," the hunting good and the oak trees impressive. Started as a harbor town, Bangor turned to lumber when the railroads picked up much of the shipping business. In 1842, it became the second-largest lumber port in the country.

Bangor received its name by mistake. An early settler, Reverend Seth Noble, was sent to register the new town under its chosen name of Sunbury. When officials asked Noble for the name, he thought they were asking him for the name of a tune he was humming and he replied "Bangor". Today, the city is the third largest in Maine and is a trading and distribution center.

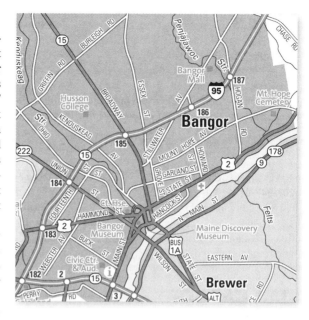

Information: Bangor Convention and Visitors Bureau, 207-947-5205; www.bangorcvb.org

★AUTHOR STEPHEN KING LIVES IN BANGOR.

★BANGOR WAS ATTACKED BY THE BRITISH DURING THE WAR OF 1812.

★THE CITY IS THE THIRD LARGEST IN MAINE.

WHAT TO SEE AND DO

Bangor Museum and Center for History
25 Broad St., Bangor,
207-942-1900
Features exhibits of regional artifacts and the Quipus collection of historic clothing. Tuesday-Saturday.

Cole Land Transportation Museum
405 Perry Rd., Bangor,
207-990-3600;
www.colemuseum.org
The Cole Museum showcases the history of transportation in the American Northeast. The museum houses one of the largest collections of snow removal equipment found in one place anywhere in the country, as well as a cache of military vehicles. A great place to take children, this museum has more than 20,000 visitors go through its turnstiles each year to see the permanent collection of local railroad pieces and cars and trucks, uniquely designed to traverse the streets of Bangor. Historic photographs of Maine are also on display. May-mid-November: daily 9 a.m.-5 p.m.

Monument to Paul Bunyan
Bass Park, Main St., Bangor
A 31-foot-tall statue commemorating the legendary lumberjack.

HOTELS
★Fairfield Inn
300 Odlin Rd., Bangor,
207-990-0001, 800-228-2800;
www.fairfieldinn.com
153 rooms. Complimentary continental breakfast. Fitness room. Indoor pool, whirlpool. **$**

★★Holiday Inn
404 Odlin Rd., Bangor,
207-947-0101, 800-799-8651;
www.holiday-inn.com
123 rooms. Pets accepted, some restrictions. Restaurant. Bar. Outdoor pool. Airport transportation available. **$**

SPECIALTY LODGINGS
The Lucerne Inn
2517 Main Rd., Dedham,
207-843-5123, 800-325-5123;
www.lucerneinn.com
Colonial-style farmhouse and connecting stable, established as an inn in 1814. 31 rooms. Complimentary continental breakfast. Restaurant. Outdoor pool. **$$**

RESTAURANTS
★Captain Nick's Seafood House
1165 Union St., Bangor, 207-942-6444
Seafood menu. Lunch, dinner. Bar. Children's menu. Casual attire. **$$**

BAR HARBOR
Bar Harbor, the largest village on Mount Desert Island, has a summer population of more than 20,000 and is headquarters for the surrounding summer resort area. The island, which includes most of Acadia National Park, is mainly rugged granite, with many bays and inlets for sailing. In the mid-1800s, socially prominent figures, including publisher Joseph Pulitzer, had elaborate summer cottages built on the island. However, prosperity ended with the Great Depression, World War II and the great fire of 1947, which destroyed many of the estates and scorched more than 17,000 acres. As a result, instead of just evergreens, the forests in the area now have younger, more varied trees bearing red, yellow and orange leaves in fall.
Information: Chamber of Commerce, 93, Cottage St., 207-288-5103; www.barharborinfo.com

WHAT TO SEE AND DO
Abbe Museum
★
26 Mount Desert St., Bar Harbor,
207-288-3519;
★
www.abbemuseum.org
This museum holds an extensive collection
★
of Native American artifacts. Daily 9
a.m.-5 p.m.; closed January. The original
★
location in Acadia National Park (open
Memorial Day-mid-October) now houses
★
exhibits on the archaeology of Maine and
the history of the Abbe.

Bar Harbor Historical Society Museum
33 Ledgelawn Ave.,
Bar Harbor, 207-288-0000;
www.barharborhistorical.org
Collection of early photographs of hotels, summer cottages and Green Mountain cog

railroad; hotel registers from the early to late 1800s; maps, scrapbook of the 1947 fire. Mid-June-October, Monday-Saturday 1-4p.m.

Bar Harbor Whale Watch Company
1 West St., Bar Harbor,
207-288-2386, 888-533-9253;
www.barharborwhales. com
Offers a variety of cruises aboard catamarans *Friendship V* or *Helen H* to view whales, seal, puffin, osprey and more. Also nature cruises and lobster and seal-watching. Cruises vary in length and destination. May-October: daily. Depart from Bluenose Ferry Terminal.

Ferry Service to Yarmouth, Nova Scotia
121 Edens St., Bar Harbor,

207-288-3395; www.catferry.com
Passenger and car carrier *Cat Ferry* makes three-hour trips.

The Jackson Laboratory
600 Main St., Bar Harbor,
207-288-6049; www.jax.org
An internationally known mammalian genetics laboratory conducting research relevant to cancer, diabetes, AIDS, heart disease, blood disorders, birth defects, aging and normal growth and development. Audiovisual and lecture programs. Early June-late August: Wednesday afternoons

Lobster Hatchery
Route 3, Bar Harbor, 207-288-5005
Young lobsters are hatched from eggs to 1/2 inch in length, then returned to the ocean to supplement the supply; guides narrate process. Mid-May-late October: Monday-Saturday.

HOTELS

★Acadia Inn
98 Eden St., Bar Harbor,
207-288-3500, 800-638-3636;
www.acadiainn.com
95 rooms. Closed mid-November-March. Complimentary continental breakfast. Outdoor pool, whirlpool. $$

★★Bar Harbor Inn
Newport Dr., Bar Harbor,
207-288-3351, 800-248-3351;
www.barharborinn.com
153 rooms. Pets accepted, some restrictions; fee. Complimentary continental breakfast. Restaurant. Bar. Fitness room. Outdoor pool. Beach. $$

★Bar Harbor Motel
100 Eden St., Bar Harbor,
207-288-3453, 800-388-3453;
www.barharbormotel.com
70 rooms. Closed mid-October-mid-May. Outdoor pool. $

★Best Western Inn
452 Route 3, Bar Harbor,
207-288-5823, 800-937-8376;
www.bestwesterninn.com
70 rooms. Closed November-April. Pets accepted, some restrictions. Complimentary continental breakfast. Outdoor pool. $$

★★Harborside Hotel & Marina
55 West St., Bar Harbor,
207-288-5033, 800-328-5033;
www.theharborsidehotel.com
88 rooms. Closed November-March. Complimentary continental breakfast. Restaurant. Bar. Whirlpool. $$

★★Holiday Inn
123 Eden St., Bar Harbor,
207-288-9723, 800-234-6835;
www.barharborregency.com
280 rooms. Closed November-April. High-speed Internet access, wireless Internet access. Three restaurants, two bars. Fitness room. Outdoor pool, whirlpool. Tennis. $$

★★Quality Inn
40 Kebo St., Bar Harbor,
207-288-5403, 800-282-5403;
www.qualityinn.com
77 rooms. Closed November-mid-April. Outdoor pool, whirlpool. $$

★Wonder View Inn
50 Eden St., Bar Harbor,
207-288-3358, 888-439-8439;
www.wonderviewinn.com
79 rooms. Closed November-April. Pets accepted, some restrictions; fee. Restaurant. Bar. Outdoor pool. $$

★★★Bar Harbor Hotel - Bluenose Inn
90 Eden St., Bar Harbor,
207-288-3348, 800-445-4077;
www.bluenoseinn.com
From its hilltop location on Mount Desert Island, this hotel offers scenic views of Frenchman Bay. Explore nearby Acadia National Park or walk down to the dock and catch the *Cat Ferry* for a day trip to Yarmouth, Nova Scotia. The guest rooms feature traditional four-poster beds and balconies and include mini-refrigerators, CD and DVD players and bathrobes. Enjoy gourmet dining in the Rose Garden Restaurant.

39

MAINE

★
★
★
★

98 rooms. Closed November-mid-April. High-speed Internet access, wireless Internet access. Restaurant. Bar. Fitness room. Indoor pool, outdoor pool, whirlpool. Business center. **$$**

★★★The Bayview
111 Eden St., Bar Harbor,
207-288-5861, 800-356-3585;
www.barharbor.com/bayview
Located directly on the water, this 8-acre inn is within five minutes of the town's center, but still offers a private setting. There are three buildings, including condos for guests on longer stays. Guest rooms are spacious and feature French doors which lead to wide, private decks overlooking the water. Furnishings, including four-poster beds, inlaid wood tables and armoires, are luxurious and provide a residential feel.
33 rooms. Complimentary full breakfast. Wireless Internet access. Fitness room. Tennis. Airport transportation available. Business center. Closed November-mid-May. **$$**

40   SPECIALTY LODGINGS

Balance Rock Inn
21 Albert Meadow, Bar Harbor,
207-288-2610, 800-753-0494;
www.balancerockinn.com
23 rooms. Closed late October-early May. Pets accepted; fee. Complimentary full breakfast. **$$**

Bar Harbor Grand Hotel
269 Main St., Bar Harbor,
207-288-5226, 888-766-2529;
www.barharborgrand.com
70 rooms. Complimentary continental breakfast. Closed December-April. **$$**

Black Friar Inn
10 Summer St., Bar Harbor,
207-288-5091; www.blackfriarinn.com
This inn is decorated with Victorian style furniture and fabrics.
7 rooms. Children over 12 years only. Complimentary full breakfast. **$**

Castelmaine
39 Holland Ave., Bar Harbor,
207-288-4563, 800-338-4563;

www.castlemaineinn.com
Tucked away on a quiet side street, this inn is a Victorian-style house (1886) located one mile from Acadia National Park and within walking distance of the ocean. It was once the summer residence of the Austro-Hungarian ambassador.
17 rooms. Closed November-April. Complimentary continental breakfast. **$**

Cleftstone Manor
92 Eden St., Bar Harbor,
207-288-8086, 888-288-4951;
www.cleftstone.com
This Victorian inn (1894) is set on terraced grounds and is located less than one mile from downtown Bar Harbor. The inn was once owned by the Blair family of Washington D.C.
16 rooms. Children over 10 years only. Complimentary full breakfast. Closed November-April. **$**

Inn At Bay Ledge
150 Sand Point Rd., Bar Harbor,
207-288-4204;
www.innatbayledge.com
This inn (built in 1907) is located at the top of an 80-foot cliff on Mount Desert Island near Acadia National Park.
10 rooms. Children over 16 years only. Complimentary full breakfast. Closed late October-April. **$$$**

Manor House Inn
106 West St., Bar Harbor,
207-288-3759, 800-437-0088;
www.barharbormanorhouse.com
This is a restored historic Victorian mansion (1887).
18 rooms. Children over 12 years only. Complimentary full breakfast. **$$**

Mira Monte Inn & Suites
69 Mount Desert St.,
Bar Harbor, 207-288-4263, 800-553-5109;
www.miramonte.com
This is a restored Victorian home (1864) on 2 1/2 acres with wraparound porch and period furnishings.

16 rooms. Closed mid-October-April. Complimentary full breakfast. **$$**

Thornhedge Inn
47 Mount Desert St., Bar Harbor,
207-288-5398, 877-288-5398;
www.thornhedgeinn.com
This Queen Anne-style inn is located in the Historic Corridor District of Bar Harbor, close to many shops, galleries and restaurants. It was built by the publisher of Louisa May Alcott's *Little Women* as a summer cottage (1900).
13 rooms. **$**

RESTAURANTS
★124 Cottage Street
124 Cottage St., Bar Harbor,
207-288-4383
American menu. Dinner. Closed November-May. Bar. Children's menu. Outdoor seating. **$$**

★★Maggie's
6 Summer St., Bar Harbor,
207-288-9007;
www.maggiesbarharbor.com
International menu. Dinner. Casual attire. Reservations recommended. Outdoor seating. Closed Sunday; late October-mid-June. **$$**

★★★Reading Room
Newport Dr., Bar Harbor,
207-288-3351; 800-248-3351.
www.barharborinn.com
Located on the oceanfront, this restaurant offers a panoramic view of the harbor and docks through large windows. Seafood is the star of the menu, with everything from lobster pie to local diver sea scallops available. American menu. Breakfast, lunch, dinner, Sunday brunch. Bar. Children's menu. Casual attire. Reservations recommended. Valet parking. Closed December-March. **$$$**

★Route 66
21 Cottage St., Bar Harbor, 207-288-3708
American menu. Lunch, dinner. Bar. Children's menu. Casual attire. Reservations recommended. Outdoor seating. Closed mid-October to mid-May. **$$**

★★Seasons
51 Rodick St., Bar Harbor,
207-288-5117; www.seasonsbarharbor.com
American menu. Dinner. Bar. Children's menu. Casual attire. Outdoor seating. Closed mid-November to late-March. **$$**

BATH
For more than two centuries, Bath has been a shipbuilding center on the west bank of the Kennebec River. The Bath Iron Works, which dates to 1833, began building ships in 1889. It has produced destroyers, cruisers, a battleship, pleasure craft and steamers, and now also produces patrol frigates. Altogether, Bath has launched more than 4,000 ships from its shores. Several mansions, built when Bath was a great seaport, still stand. A restored 19th-century business district, waterfront park and public landing are also part of the city.
Information: Chamber of Commerce of the Bath-Brunswick Region, 45 Front St., 207-443-9751; www.midcoastmaine.com

WHAT TO SEE AND DO
Fort Popham Memorial
Popham Beach. Hwy 209., 207-389-1335
Construction of the fort began in 1861. Never finished, it was garrisoned in 1865-1866 and remains an impressive masonry structure with gun emplacements. Picnic tables. May-November: daily.

Maine Maritime Museum
243 Washington St., Bath, 207-443-1316;
www.mainemaritimemuseum.org

Maritime History Building has exhibits of maritime art and artifacts, ship models and paintings. Tours of original shipyard buildings, demonstrations of sea-faring techniques (seasonal); waterfront picnic area and playground. Museum store. Daily.

Popham Colony
Hwy. 209 on Sabino Head

In 1607, the first American vessel, the *Virginia*, was built here by colonists who shortly thereafter returned to England. On the hilltop nearby is Fort Baldwin, built during World War I. A 70-foot tower offers a panoramic view of the coast and the Kennebec River.

HOTELS

★★Holiday Inn
139 Richardson St., Bath,
207-443-9741, 800-465-4329;
www.holiday-inn.com

141 rooms. Pets accepted, some restrictions. Restaurant. Bar. Fitness room. Outdoor pool, whirlpool. $

SPECIALTY LODGINGS

Galen C. Moses House
1009 Washington St., Bath,
207-442-8771, 888-442-8771;
www.galenmoses.com

This inn, built in 1874, is on the National Register of Historic Houses. It features a Victorian interior and stained-glass win-

BAXTER STATE PARK

While serving as a legislator and as governor of Maine, Percival P. Baxter wanted to create a wilderness park around Mount Katahdin—Maine's highest peak (5,267 feet). Rebuffed by voters but not deterred, Baxter bought the land with his own money and deeded to the state of Maine a 201,018-acre park "to be forever left in its natural, wild state." The park can be reached from Greenville via paper company roads, from Millinocket via Highway 157, or from Patten via Highway 159.

The Park Authority operates the following campgrounds: Katahdin Stream, Abol and Nesowadnehunk, Roaring Brook (Roaring Brook Road), Chimney Pond (by trail 3.3 miles beyond Roaring Brook), Russell Pond (Wassataquoik Valley, seven miles by trail beyond Roaring Brook), South Branch Pond (at outlet of Lower South Branch Pond), Trout Brook Farm (Trout Brook Crossing). There are cabins ($17/person/night) at Daicey Pond off Nesowadnehunk Road and at Kidney Pond. All areas except Chimney, Kidney and Daicey ponds have tent space, and all areas except Trout Brook Farm, Kidney and Daicey ponds have lean-tos ($6/person/night), water (unprotected, should be purified), and primitive facilities (no indoor plumbing, no running water; some springs); bunkhouses ($7/night) at some campgrounds. Under age 7 free throughout the park.

Reservations should be made by mail (and paid in full) in advance. For detailed information, contact the Reservation Clerk, Baxter State Park, 64 Balsam Drive, Millinocket, Maine 04462. Swimming, fishing, canoes for rent at Russell Pond, South Branch Pond, Daicey Pond, Kidney Pond and Trout Brook farm.

The park is open for camping mid-May to mid-October. No pets or motorcycles are permitted. Vehicles exceeding 7 feet wide, 9 feet high, or 22 feet long will not be admitted.

Information: 18 miles N.W. of Millinocket, 207-723-5140

dows. All the rooms are decorated with antiques.

6 rooms. Children over 12 years only. Complimentary full breakfast. **$$**

RESTAURANTS
★Mae's Café and Bakery
160 Centre St., Bath,
207-442-8577

American menu. Breakfast, lunch, dinner. Casual attire. Outdoor seating. **$$**

★Taste of Maine
Highway 1, Woolwich,
207-443-4554; www.tasteofmaine.com

Seafood, steak menu. Lunch, dinner. Children's menu. Outdoor seating. Closed late December-mid-March. **$$**

BELFAST

Belfast, named for the city in Northern Ireland, was settled in 1770 by Irish and Scottish immigrants. An old seaport on the west shore of Penobscot Bay, Belfast is also a hub of small boat traffic to the bay islands. It is the seat of Waldo County.

Information: Chamber of Commerce, 17 Main St., 207-338-5900; www.belfastmaine.org

WHAT TO SEE AND DO
Lake St. George State Park
278 Belfast Augusta Rd., Liberty,
207-589-4255

More than 360 acres. Swimming, bathhouse, lifeguard, fishing, boating (ramp, rentals); snowmobiling permitted, picnicking, camping. Mid-May to mid-October.

HOTELS
★Belfast Harbor Inn
91 Searsport Ave., Belfast,
207-338-2740, 800-545-8576;
www.belfastharborinn.com

61 rooms. Pets accepted, some restrictions; fee. Complimentary continental breakfast. Restaurant. Outdoor pool. **$**

SPECIALTY LODGINGS
Penobscot Bay Inn
192 Northport Ave., Belfast,

207-338-5715, 800-335-2370;
www.penobscotbayinn.com

This turn-of-the-century country inn overlooks the bay.

19 rooms. Pets accepted, some restrictions; fee. Complimentary full breakfast. **$$**

RESTAURANTS
★★Darby's
155 High St., Belfast,
207-338-2339

International menu. Lunch, dinner. Bar. Children's menu. Casual attire. Reservations recommended. **$$**

★Young's Lobster Pound
2 Fairview St., Belfast, 207-338-1160

Seafood menu. Breakfast, lunch, dinner. Outdoor seating. Casual attire. Reservations recommended. **$$**

★
★
★
★
★

BETHEL

Bethel, on both banks of the winding Androscoggin River, is built on Oxford Hills and is backed by the rough foothills of the White Mountains. In addition to being a year-round resort, it's an educational and wood products center. One of Maine's leading preparatory schools, Gould Academy (founded in 1836), is located here, as is Sunday River ski resort, one of New England's snowiest ski areas.

Information: Chamber of Commerce, 207-824-2282, 800-442-5826; www.bethelmaine.com

WHAT TO SEE AND DO

Carter's X-Country Ski Center
420 Main St., Bethel,
207-539-4848; www.cartersxcski.com
One thousand acres with 55 kilometers of groomed cross-country trails. Rentals, lessons, lounge, shop, two lodges. December-March.

Dr. Moses Mason House Museum
14 Broad St., Bethel, 207-824-2908;
www.bethelhistorical.org/museum.html
Restored 1813 home of prominent congressman who served during Andrew Jackson's administration. Antique furnishings, Early American murals. July-Labor Day: Tuesday-Sunday afternoons; rest of year: by appointment.

Grafton Notch State Park
Hwy. 2., 207-824-2912
The Appalachian Trail passes through the notch; interpretive displays, scenic view, picnicking; fishing. Mid-May to mid-October.

Sunday River Ski Resort
Sunday River Rd., Bethel,
207-824-3000, 800-543-2754;
www.sundayriver.com
Nine quad, four triple, two double chairlifts (including four high-speed detachables and one surface lift); patrol, school, rentals, ski shop; snowmaking; cafeterias, restaurants; bars. 127 runs; longest run is three miles; vertical drop 2,340 feet. Mid-November to mid-April, daily. 100 cross-country trails adjacent. Mountain biking May-Labor Day: daily; Labor Day-late October: weekends.

HOTELS

★Norseman Inn
134 Mayville Rd., Bethel, 207-824-2002;
www.norsemaninn.com
31 rooms. Complimentary continental breakfast. $$

★★★Bethel Inn & Country Club
On the Common, Bethel,
207-824-2175, 800-654-0125;
www.bethelinn.com
This hotel features rooms in a three traditional colonial buildings as well as a series of luxury townhouses, perfect for families visiting the nearby slopes. In summer, there is a championship golf course designed by architect Geoffrey Cornish.
60 rooms. Pets accepted, some restrictions; fee. Restaurant. Bar. Children's activity center. Fitness room. Outdoor pool, whirlpool. Golf. Tennis. $$

★★★The Briar Lea Inn and Restaurant
150 Mayville Rd., Bethel,
207-824-4717, 877-311-1299;
www.briarleainn.com
Built in the 1850s, this inn has a farmhouse atmosphere, with rooms decorated in vintage prints and antiques. The onsite pub and restaurant, the Jolly Drayman, is modeled after similar pubs in England and serves a wide selection of English, Irish and local beers.
6 rooms. Pets accepted, some restrictions; fee. Complimentary full breakfast. Restaurant. $

RESTAURANTS

★S. S. Milton
43 Main St., Bethel, 207-824-2589
Seafood, steak menu. Lunch (May-October), dinner. Closed Tuesday. Children's menu. Casual attire. Reservations recommended. Outdoor seating. $$

44

MAINE

BLUE HILL

Named for a nearby hill that delivers a beautiful view of Mount Desert Island, Blue Hill evolved from a thriving seaport to a summer colony known for its crafts and antiques. Mary Ellen Chase, born here in 1887, wrote about Blue Hill in *A Goodly Heritage* and *Mary Peters*.

Information: Blue Hill Peninsula Chamber of Commerce, 207-374-3242; www.bluehillme.com

WHAT TO SEE AND DO

Holt House

Water St., Blue Hill, 207-326-8250

One of the oldest houses in Blue Hill; now home of the Blue Hill Historical Society. Memorabilia. July-September 1: Tuesday, Friday-Saturday afternoons.

Rackliffe Pottery

132 Elsworth Rd., Blue Hill, 207-374-2297; www.rackliffepottery.com Family manufactures wheel-thrown dinnerware from native red-firing clay. Open workshop. July-August: daily; rest of year: Monday-Saturday.

Rowantrees Pottery

84 Union St., Union, 207-374-5535 Manufactures functional pottery and wheel-thrown handcrafted dinnerware. (June-September, Monday-Saturday: closed holidays)

HOTELS

★★★Blue Hill Inn

40 Union St., Blue Hill, 207-374-2844, 800-826-7415; www.bluehillinn.com This federal-style house at the tip of the bay has operated as a bed-and-breakfast since 1840 and is on the National Register of Historic Houses. Choose one of the quaint guest rooms or the adjacent Cape House suite for a more private retreat.

12 rooms. Restaurant. Airport transportation available. $$

45

MAINE

★
★
★
★
★

BOOTHBAY HARBOR

Native Americans were paid 20 beaver pelts for the area encompassing Boothbay Harbor. Today, it's a protected harbor, a haven for boatmen and the scene of well-attended regattas several times a summer. Boothbay Harbor, on the peninsula between the Sheepscot and Damariscotta rivers, shares the peninsula and adjacent islands with a dozen other communities, including Boothbay (settled 1630), of which it was once a part.

Information: Boothbay Harbor Region Chamber of Commerce, 207-633-2353, 800-266-8422; www.boothbayharbor.com

WHAT TO SEE AND DO

Boothbay Railway Village

586 Wiscasset Rd., Highway 27, Boothbay, 207-633-4727; www.railwayvillage.org Historical Maine exhibits of rural life, railroads and antique autos and trucks. Rides on a coal-fired, narrow-gauge steam train to an antique vehicle display. Also on exhibit are displays of early fire equipment, a general store, a one-room schoolhouse and two restored railroad stations. Mid-June to mid-October: daily.

Boothbay Region Historical Society Museum

72 Oak St., Boothbay Harbor, 207-633-0820; www.boothbayhistorical. org Artifacts of Boothbay Region. July-Labor Day: Wednesday, Friday-Saturday; rest of year: Friday-Saturday.

SPECIAL EVENTS

Windjammer Days

192 Townsend Ave., Boothbay Harbor, 207-633-2353

Old schooners that previously sailed the trade routes and now cruise the Maine coast sail en masse into harbor. Waterfront food court, entertainment, street parade, children's activities. Late June.

HOTELS

★★Brown's Wharf Motel
121 Atlantic Ave., Boothbay Harbor, 207-633-5440, 800-334-8110; www.brownswharfinn.com
70 rooms. Pets accepted, some restrictions. Restaurant. Bar. Closed November-April. $

★★Fisherman's Wharf Inn
22 Commercial St., Boothbay Harbor, 207-633-5090, 800-628-6872; www.fishermanswharfinn.com
54 rooms. Complimentary full breakfast. Wireless Internet access. Restaurant. Bar. Closed November-May. $$

★Tugboat Inn
80 Commercial St., Boothbay Harbor, 207-633-4434, 800-248-2628; www.tugboatinn.com
64 rooms. Restaurant. Bar. Closed December to mid-March. $

★★★Spruce Point Inn
88 Grandview Ave., Boothbay Harbor, 207-633-4152, 800-553-0289; www.sprucepointinn.com
Located on a quiet peninsula on the east side of Boothbay Harbor, this retreat is the perfect getaway for families, groups and couples. Activities include swimming in salt and freshwater pools, kayaking, bicycling, fishing and hiking trails.
85 rooms. Pets accepted. Closed mid-October-mid-May. High-speed Internet access, wireless Internet access. Two restaurants, bar. Children's activity center. Fitness room, fitness classes available, spa. Two outdoor pools, whirlpool. Tennis. Business center. $$

SPECIALTY LODGINGS

1830 Admiral's Quarters Inn
71 Commercial St., Boothbay Harbor, 207-633-2474, 800-644-1878;
www.admiralsquartersinn.com
Built in 1830, this sprawling inn has ocean views.
7 rooms. Children over 12 years only. Complimentary full breakfast. Closed mid-December to mid-February. $$

Anchor Watch Bed & Breakfast
9 Eames Rd., Boothbay Harbor, 207-633-7565; www.anchorwatch.com
This inn is located on Boothbay Harbor and has its own private pier.
5 rooms. Children over 9 years only. Complimentary full breakfast. $$

Five Gables Inn
107 Murray Hill Rd., East Boothbay, 207-633-4551, 800-451-5048; www.fivegablesinn.com
This inn, built in 1890, features Victorian decor.
15 rooms. Children over 12 years only. Complimentary full breakfast. November to mid-May, $

Harbour Towne Inn on the Waterfront
71 Townsend Ave., Boothbay Harbor, 207-633-3934, 800-722-4240; www.harbourtowneinn.com
Located in a historic Victorian house, this bed and breakfast has views of the ocean.
12 rooms. Complimentary continental breakfast. $$

Howard House Lodge
347 Townsend Ave., Boothbay Harbor, 207-633-3933, 800-466-6697; www.howardhouselodge.com
This country, chalet-style building is set in a wooded area.
14 rooms. Complimentary full breakfast. $

Kenniston Hill Inn
Wiscasset Rd., Boothbay, 207-633-2159, 800-992-2915; www.kennistonhillinn.com
This restored Colonial-style farmhouse (1786) is decorated with antiques.
10 rooms. Children over 10 years only. Complimentary full breakfast. $$

MAINE

RESTAURANTS

★★★88 Grandview

88 Grandview, Boothbay Harbor,
207-633-4152, 800-553-0289;
www.sprucepointinn.com

This restaurant, located inside the Spruce Point Inn, overlooks the Atlantic Ocean. Tables are covered with crisp white linens and are set with fine china. Seating is also provided on the enclosed sun-porch and outdoor deck with umbrella-topped tables. Dishes include candied duck breast and beef with Bordelaise sauce. A pianist performs nightly.
Continental menu. Dinner. Bar. Business casual attire. Reservations recommended. Outdoor seating. Closed late October to mid-May. $$$

★Andrew's Harborside Restaurant

12 Bridge St., Boothbay Harbor,
207-633-4074

American, seafood menu. Breakfast, lunch, dinner. Bar. Children's menu. Casual attire. Reservations recommended. Closed mid-October to Mother's Day. $$

★Blue Moon Café

54 Commercial St., Boothbay Harbor,
207-633-2349

American menu. Breakfast, lunch. Casual attire. Outdoor seating. Closed November-March. $

★★China by the Sea

96 Townsend Ave., Boothbay Harbor,
207-633-4449;
www.chinabythesea.com

Chinese menu. Lunch, dinner. Bar. Children's menu. Casual attire. Reservations recommended. $$

★★Chowder House

22 Granary Way, Boothbay Harbor,
207-633-5761

Seafood, barbecue menu. Lunch, dinner. Bar. Casual attire. Outdoor seating. Closed October-May. $

★★Fisherman's Wharf Inn

22 Commercial St., Boothbay Harbor,
207-633-5090, 800-628-6872;
www.fishermanswharfinn.com

American, seafood menu. Lunch, dinner. Bar. Children's menu. Casual attire. Reservations recommended. Valet parking. Outdoor seating. Closed mid-October to mid-May. $$

BRIDGTON

This community between Long and Highland lakes is within easy reach of Pleasant Mountain (2,007 feet), a recreational area that offers skiing as well as a magnificent view of 50 lakes. Bridgton also has many unique craft and antiques shops located within a 2-mile radius of the town center.
Information: Bridgton Lakes Region Chamber of Commerce, 207-647-3472; www.mainelakeschamber.com

WHAT TO SEE AND DO

Gibbs Avenue Museum

44 Gibbs Ave., Bridgton, 207-647-3699

Headquarters of Bridgton Historical Society. Permanent exhibits include narrow-gauge railroad memorabilia; Civil War artifacts; Sears "horseless carriage" (1911). Special summer exhibits. Genealogy research facility includes Bridgton and Saw River railroad documents. September-June: by appointment; rest of year: Monday-Friday afternoons.

Shawnee Peak Ski Area

119 Mountain Rd., Bridgton, 207-647-8444;
www.shawneepeak.com

Quad, two triple, double chairlift; snowmaking, school, rentals, patrol; nursery; restaurant, cafeteria, bar. Longest run 1 1/2 miles; vertical drop 1,350 feet. Night skiing. December-March: daily.

HOTELS
★★★The Inn at Long Lake
Lake House Rd., Naples,
207-693-6226, 800-437-0328;
www.innatlonglake.com
The colonial style of this Lakes Region inn (1906) fits right in with the ambience of historic Naples Village. Amenities include country breakfasts, cozy common rooms and a landscaped backyard.
16 rooms. Complimentary continental breakfast. Closed January-March. **$$**

RESTAURANTS
★Black Horse Tavern
8 Portland St., Bridgton,
207-647-5300
Seafood, steak menu. Lunch, dinner, Sunday brunch. Bar. Children's menu. **$$**

BRUNSWICK
Once a lumbering center and later a mill town, Brunswick is now mainly concerned with trade, health care and education. It is the home of Bowdoin College and Brunswick Naval Air Station. The city lies northeast of a summer resort area on the shores and islands of Casco Bay. Federalist mansions along Federal Street and Park Row recall Brunswick's past.
Information: Chamber of Commerce of the Bath-Brunswick Region, 59 Pleasant St., 207-725-8797; www.midcoastmaine.com

WHAT TO SEE AND DO
Bowdoin College
1 College St., Brunswick,
207-725-3000;
www.bowdoin.edu
(1794) (1,500 students) Nathaniel Hawthorne, Henry Wadsworth Longfellow, Robert Peary, Franklin Pierce and Joan Benoit Samuelson graduated from this small liberal arts college.

Peary-MacMillan Arctic Museum
Hubbard Hall, Bowdoin College,
9500 College Station,
Brunswick, 207-725-3416
Exhibits relating to Arctic exploration, ecology and Inuit (Eskimo) culture. Tuesday-Sunday.

Pejepscot Historical Society Museum
159 Park Row, Brunswick, 207-729-6606;
www.curtislibrary.com/pejepscot.htm
Regional historical museum housed in an 1858 sea captain's home; changing exhibits, research facilities. Tuesday-Saturday.

Joshua L. Chamberlain Museum
226 Maine St., Brunswick,
207-719-6606
Former residence of Maine's greatest Civil War hero, four-term Governor of Maine and president of Bowdoin College. Guided tours. May-October: Tuesday-Sunday.

Skolfield-Whittier House
161 Park Row, Brunswick,
207-729-6606
An 18-room Victorian structure last occupied in 1925; furnishings and housewares of three generations. Guided tours. Memorial Day-Columbus Day, Tuesday-Saturday.

Thomas Point Beach
29 Meadow Rd., Brunswick,
207-725-6009
Swimming, lifeguard. Picnicking, tables, fireplaces. Snack bar; gift shop, arcade, playground; camping (fee). Memorial Day-Labor Day: daily.

HOTELS
★Comfort Inn
199 Pleasant St., Brunswick,
207-729-1129, 877-424-6423;
www.comfortinn.com
77 rooms. Complimentary continental breakfast. High-speed Internet access, wireless Internet access. Fitness room. **$**

★★★Captain Daniel Stone Inn
10 Water St., Brunswick,
207-725-9898, 877-573-5151;
www.captaindanielstoneinn.com
This 1819 Federal style inn, housed in a sea captain's home, has been elegantly restored to include modern amenities. The onsite restaurant is a local favorite for its seafood dishes (including plenty of fresh lobster.)

34 rooms. Complimentary continental breakfast. Restaurant. Bar. **$$**

RESTAURANTS
★Great Impasta
42 Maine St., Brunswick,
207-729-5858; www.thegreatimpasta.com
Italian menu. Lunch, dinner. **$$**

BUCKSPORT
Although originally settled in 1762, the Penobscot Valley town of Bucksport was so thoroughly burned by the British in 1779 that it was not resettled until 1812. On the east bank of the Penobscot River, Bucksport is a shopping center for the area, but is primarily an industrial town with an emphasis on paper manufacturing. The Waldo Hancock Bridge crosses the Penobscot to Verona Island. Nearby Castine is home to the Maine Maritime Academy, and is one of the oldest settlements in New England.
Information: Bucksport Chamber of Commerce, 207-469-6818; www.allmaine.com/bucksport

WHAT TO SEE AND DO
Accursed Tombstone
Buck Cemetery, Main and Hinks Streets, Bucksport, Near Verona Island Bridge
Granite obelisk over grave of founder Jonathan Buck bears an indelible mark in the shape of a woman's leg—said to have been put there by a witch whom he had hanged.

Wilson Museum
107 Perkins St., Castine,
207-326-9247; www.wilsonmuseum.org
Prehistoric, historic, geologic and art exhibits Late May-September: Tuesday-Sunday. On grounds is John Perkins House (1763-1783), Hearse House, Blacksmith Shop. Memorial Day-September: Tuesday-Sunday afternoons.

SPECIALTY LODGINGS
Castine Inn
33 Main St., Castine, 207-326-4365;
www.castineinn.com
Built in 1898, this elegant inn has 17 rooms decorated in a simple, crisp style. Gourmet breakfasts are served in the inn's dining room each morning.
17 rooms. Children over 8 years only. Complimentary full breakfast. Restaurant. Bar. Closed November-April. **$$**

Pentagoet Inn
26 Main St., Castine,
207-326-8616, 800-845-1701;
www.pentagoet.com
Victorian main building (1894) with smaller, colonial annex (circa 1770); library and sitting room, antiques, period furnishings.
16 rooms. Pets accepted, some restrictions; fee. Complimentary full breakfast. Restaurant. Bar. Closed November-April. **$**

MAINE

CALAIS
This town, nestled on the border of Maine and New Brunswick, has a unique distinction—it is located exactly halfway between the North Pole and the equator. The 45th Parallel passes a few miles south of town. A marker on Highway 1 near Perry indicates the spot.
Information: Calais Regional Chamber of Commerce, 16 Swan St., 207-454-2308, 888-422-3112; www.visitcalais.com

WHAT TO SEE AND DO

Moosehorn National Wildlife Refuge

Charlotte Rd., Calais, 207-454-7161;
www.moosehorn.fws.gov
Glacial terrain with forests, valleys, lakes, bogs and marshes. Abundant wildlife. Fishing, hiking, hunting, cross-country skiing, bird-watching. Daily.

St. Croix Island International Historic Site

Hwy. 1, St. Croix River;
accessible only by boat,
207-288-3338; www.nps.gov/sacr
In 1604, French explorers Pierre Duguaf and Samuel de Champlain, leading a group of approximately 75 men, selected this as the site of the first attempted European settlement on the Atlantic Coast north of Florida. Information shelter; no facilities. Daily.

SPECIAL EVENTS

International Festival Week

207-454-2308, 888-422-3112
Celebration of friendship between Calais and St. Stephen, New Brunswick; entertainment, concessions, contests, fireworks, parade. Early August.

RESTAURANTS

★Wickachee

282 Main St., Calais, 207-454-3400
American menu. Breakfast, lunch, dinner. Children's menu. Casual attire. Closed Sunday. $

CAMDEN

Used as the backdrop for the 1950s movie *Peyton Place*, Camden is the quintessential New England coastal town. Its unique setting makes it a popular four-season resort area. Activities include sailing, kayaking, swimming, camping, hiking and in winter, skiing on a mountain with views of the ocean. The poet Edna St. Vincent Millay began her career in Camden.
Information: Camden-Rockport-Lincolnville Chamber of Commerce, 207-236-4404. www. camdenme.org

WHAT TO SEE AND DO

Camden Hills State Park

280 Belfast, Camden, 207-236-3109
Maine's third-largest state park, surrounding 1,380-foot Mount Megunticook. Road leads to Mount Battie (800 feet). Spectacular view of coast. Hiking, picnic facilities, camping. Memorial Day-Columbus Day.

Camden Opera House

29 Elm St., Camden, 207-236-7963
www.camdenoperahouse.com
Elm Street Theater with musical and theatrical performances and concerts.

Camden Snow Bowl

Hosmer Pond Rd., Camden, 207-236-3438;
www.camdensnowbowl.com
Double chairlift, two T-bars; patrol, school, rentals; toboggan chute and rentals; snowboarding; snowmaking; snack bar, lodge. Views of the ocean from the top of the mountain. Late December to mid-March, daily.

Conway Homestead-Cramer Museum

Hwy. 1 and Conway Rd., Camden,
207-236-2257
Authentically restored 18th-century farmhouse. Collection of carriages, sleighs and farm implements in old barn; blacksmith shop, privy and herb garden. Mary Meeker Cramer Museum contains paintings, ship models, quilts; costumes, documents and other memorabilia; changing exhibits. July-August, Monday-Thursday.

Maine State Ferry Service

McKay St., and Hwy. 1, Lincolnville Beach, 207-789-5611
Twenty minute trip to Islesboro (Dark Harbor) on *Margaret Chase Smith*. Mid-May to late October: weekdays, nine trips; Sunday, eight trips; rest of year: six trips daily.

Windjammer Sailing

Camden Harbor, 800-807-9463;
www.sailmainecoast.com

Old-time schooners leave from Camden and Rockport Harbors for half-to six-day trips along the coast of Maine. May-October. For further information, rates, schedules or reservations, contact the Maine Windjammer Association.

SPECIAL EVENTS

Bay Chamber Concerts

Rockport Opera House, Central St.,
Rockport, 207-236-2823;
www.baychamberconcerts.org

Classical music performances by Vermeer Quartet and guest artists. July-August, Thursday-Friday evenings. Jazz musicians perform September-June (one show each month).

Windjammer Weekend

Camden Harbor, 207-236-4404;
www.windjammerweekend.com

Celebration of Maine's windjammer fleet; fireworks. Labor Day weekend.

HOTELS

★Best Western Camden Riverhouse Hotel

11 Tannery Lane, Camden,
207-236-0500, 800-755-7483;
www.camdenmaine.com

35 rooms. Pets accepted, some restrictions; fee. Complimentary continental breakfast. Fitness room. Indoor pool, whirlpool. **$$**

★★Cedar Crest Motel

115 Elm St., Camden,
207-236-4839, 800-422-4964;
www.cedarcrestmotel.com

37 rooms. Check-out 11 a.m. Restaurant. Outdoor pool. Closed November-April. **$**

★★★Blue Harbor House, A Village Inn

67 Elm St., Camden,
207-236-3196, 800-248-3196;
www.blueharborhouse.com

Built in 1768 as the home of the first Camden settler, James Richards, this property now offers guest rooms filled with quilts and antiques. Enjoy a hearty breakfast

before hiking Camden Hills State Park or taking a Penobscot Bay boat ride.

11 rooms. Complimentary full breakfast. **$$**

★★★Dark Harbor House

117 Jetty Rd., Islesboro, 207-734-6669;
www.darkharborhouse.com

Built in 1896, this island inn represents Georgian Revival architecture and is listed on the National Register of Historic Places. Visitors will be impressed by the grand double staircase in the entrance foyer and hilltop location overlooking Dark Harbor.

11 rooms. No children under 12. Complimentary full breakfast. Restaurant. Bar. Closed November-April. **$$**

SPECIALTY LODGINGS

Camden Windward House

6 High St., Camden, 207-236-9656,
877-492-9656; www.windwardhouse.com

This 1854 inn is located in the center of Camden's historic district, walking distance to many restaurants, shops and Camden Harbor. Mount Battie and Camden Hills State Park are nearby.

8 rooms. Children over 12 years only. Complimentary full breakfast. **$$**

Elms Bed & Breakfast

84 Elm St., Camden,
207-236-6250, 800-388-6000;
www.elmsinn.net

This Federal-style home, built in 1806, features a lighthouse theme.

7 rooms. Children over five years only. Complimentary full breakfast. **$$**

Hawthorn Inn

9 High St., Camden,
207-236-8842, 866-381-3647;
www.camdenhawthorn.com

This 1894 Victorian inn is conveniently located near Camden's downtown area. The rooms all have private baths, and some have fireplaces, whirlpools and private decks with harbor views.

10 rooms. Children over 12 years only. Complimentary full breakfast. Closed January. **$$**

★
★
★
★
★

Inn at Ocean's Edge

Hwy. 1, Camden, 207-236-0945;
www.innatoceansedge.com

This contemporary inn overlooks Penobscot Bay. Spacious rooms feature four-poster king beds. Most rooms have an ocean view.

30 rooms. No children under 14. Complimentary full breakfast. Fitness room. **$$**

Inn At Sunrise Point

Hwy. 1, Camden, 207-236-7716,
800-435-6278; www.sunrisepoint.com

This oceanfront hideaway is just minutes from Camden Harbor. Guests can choose to stay in a restored 1920s Maine-style cottage or in the main house. Breakfast is served in the conservatory and hors d'oeuvres are available in the library in the afternoons.

13 rooms. Children over 12 years only. Complimentary full breakfast. Whirlpool. **$$$**

The Lodge and Cottages at Camden Hills

Hwy. 1, Camden, 207-236-8478,
800-832-7058;
www.thelodgeatcamdenhills.com

This inn is located near Camden Hills State Park. Some rooms have fireplaces, Jacuzzi tubs or kitchens.

14 rooms. Pets accepted, some restrictions; fee. **$$**

Maine Stay Bed & Breakfast

22 High St., Camden, 207-236-9636;
www.mainestay.com

Farmhouse built in 1802; barn and carriage house. Antiques include a 17th-century samurai chest.

8 rooms. Children over 12 years only. Complimentary full breakfast. **$$**

Norumbega Inn

63 High St., Camden, 207-236-4646;
www.norumbegainn.com

This stone castle-by-the-sea was designed and built by the inventor of duplex telegraphy and is located near Penobscot Bay.

Offering panoramic views of the ocean, the property has been fully restored and is furnished with modern conveniences. Each room has a king bed, private bath and evening turndown service is provided.

13 rooms. Children over 7 years only. Complimentary full breakfast. **$$**

The Victorian By The Sea

Sea View Dr., Lincolnville,
207-236-3785, 800-382-9817;
www.victorianbythesea.com

This Victorian summer cottage was built in 1881.

7 rooms. Children over 12 years only. Complimentary full breakfast. **$$**

Whitehall Inn

52 High St., Camden,
207-236-3391, 800-789-6565;
www.whitehall-inn.com

Spacious old resort inn (1834); poet Edna St. Vincent Millay gave a reading here in 1912.

50 rooms. Restaurant. Bar. Tennis. Closed mid-October to mid-May. **$$**

RESTAURANTS

★★Atlantica

1 Bayview Landing, Camden,
207-236-6011;
www.atlanticarestaurant.com

Seafood menu. Dinner. Bar. Business casual attire. Reservations recommended. Outdoor seating. Closed Tuesday in winter; also month of January or March. **$$$**

★The Helm

Camden Rd., Rockport, 207-236-4337

American, French menu. Lunch, dinner. Bar. Children's menu. Closed mid-December to early-April. **$$**

★★The Lobster Pound

Hwy. 1, Lincolnville Beach,
207-789-5550;
www.lobsterpoundmaine.com

American, seafood menu. Lunch, dinner. Children's menu. Casual attire. Reservations recommended. Closed November-April. **$$**

★★Peter Ott's
16 Bayview St., Camden, 207-236-4032
Seafood, steak menu. Dinner. Bar. Children's menu. Casual attire. Closed major holidays. **$$**

★★★Vincent's
52 High St., Camden, 207-236-3391,
800-789-6565; www.whitehall-inn.com
Located in the quaint Whitehall Inn, this restaurant not only attracts overnight guests, but also local residents. The cuisine is New American, with a healthy focus on seafood. Guests can dine in the main dining room, the glass-enclosed dining porch, the seasonal side patio or order bar food in the adjacent lounge.
American, seafood, steak menu. Breakfast, dinner. Bar. Business casual attire.

Reservations recommended. Outdoor seating. Closed late October to late May. **$$**

★★Waterfront
40 Bayview St., Camden, 207-236-3747;
www.waterfrontcamden.com
For more than 25 years, the Waterfront has specialized in presenting fresh regional seafood in both traditional and adventurous ways. Originally a boat shed, this restaurant is located on Camden Harbor with docking and access for boaters. The outdoor deck is the place to be for an exceptional harbor view and the decor includes open beamed ceilings, hanging lanterns and a double fireplace.
Seafood, steak menu. Lunch, dinner. Bar. Children's menu. Casual attire. Outdoor seating. **$$**

CARIBOU

Caribou, the nation's most northeastern city, is primarily an agricultural area, but has become a center for manufacturing. The area's many lakes are perfect for swimming, fishing, boating and camping.
Information: Chamber of Commerce, 24 Sweden St., 800-722-7648; www.cariboumaine.net

WHAT TO SEE AND DO
Caribou Historical Center
Highway 1, Caribou, 207-498-2556
Museum devoted to history of northern Maine. June-August: Thursday-Saturday; rest of year: by appointment.

Nylander Museum
657 Main St., Caribou, 207-493-4209;
www.nylandermuseum.org
Fossils, rocks, minerals, butterflies and shells collected by Olof Nylander, Swedish-born geologist and naturalist; early man artifacts; changing exhibits. Gift shop. Memorial Day-Labor Day: Tuesday-Saturday; rest of year: by appointment.

HOTELS
★★Caribou Inn & Convention Center
19 Main St., Caribou, 207-498-3733,
800-235-0466; www.caribouinn.com
73 rooms. Restaurant. Bar. Indoor pool, whirlpool. Airport transportation available. **$**

RESTAURANTS
★Jade Palace
Skyway Plaza, Caribou, 207-498-3648
American, Chinese menu. lunch, dinner. Bar. **$$**

★Reno's
117 Sweden St., Caribou, 207-496-5331
American, Italian menu. Breakfast, lunch, dinner. Children's menu. **$**

CENTER LOVELL

This community on Kezar Lake is close to the New Hampshire border and the White Mountain National Forest. The surrounding region is rich in gems and minerals.

HOTELS

★★Quisisana Lodge
Pleasant Point Rd., Center Lovell, 207-925-3500;
www.quisisanaresort.com
16 rooms. Restaurant. Private sand beaches. Tennis. Closed September-May. $$$

SPECIALTY LODGINGS

Admiral Peary House
27 Elm St., Fryeburg, 207-935-3365, 877-423-6779;
www.admiralpearyhouse.com
Located in the oldest village in the White Mountains of western Maine, this bed-and-breakfast—named after the discoverer of the North Pole—sits on 10 acres of landscaped lawns and gardens.
7 rooms. Complimentary full breakfast. Whirlpool. Tennis. Airport transportation available. $

Oxford House Inn
548 Main St., Fryeburg, 207-935-3442, 800-261-7206;
www.oxfordhouseinn.com
This turn-of-the-century mission style house is now a bed and breakfast with comfortably furnished rooms. A full gourmet breakfast is prepared for guests each morning.
4 rooms. Complimentary full breakfast.

RESTAURANTS

★★Oxford House Inn
548 Main St., Fryeburg, 207-935-3442, 800-261-7206;
www.oxfordhouseinn.com
Seafood, steak menu. Dinner. Bar. Children's menu. Reservations recommended. Outdoor seating. Closed Monday-Wednesday in winter and spring. $$

54

CHEBEAGUE ISLANDS

Little Chebeague and Great Chebeague islands, off the coast of Portland in Casco Bay, were once a favorite camping spot of various tribes. The Native Americans had a penchant for clams and the first European settlers found heaps of clamshells scattered across the land. Those shells were later used to pave many of the islands' roads, some of which still exist today.

Great Chebeague, six miles long and approximately three miles wide, is connected to Little Chebeague at low tide by a sandbar. There are various locations for swimming. Additionally, both islands are easy to explore on foot or bicycle. At one time, Great Chebeague was home to a prosperous fishing and shipbuilding community, and it was a quarrying center in the late 1700s. Today, it receives hundreds of visitors every summer.

WHAT TO SEE AND DO

Casco Bay Lines
56 Commercial St., Portland, 207-774-7871; www.cascobaylines.com
From Portland, Commercial and Franklin streets; one-hour crossing. Daily.

Chebeague Transportation
207-846-3700; www.chebeaguetrans.com
From Cousins Island, near Yarmouth; 15-minute crossing. Daily. Off-site parking with shuttle to ferry.

CRANBERRY ISLES

The Cranberry Isles, named because of the rich, red cranberry bogs that once covered Great Cranberry Isle, lie off the southeast coast of Mount Desert Island. There are five islands in the group: Little and Great Cranberry, Sutton, Bear and Baker. Great Cranberry, the largest, covers about 900 acres. Baker Island is part of Acadia National Park, and Sutton is privately owned. In 1830, the islands petitioned the state to separate from Mount Desert Island.

WHAT TO SEE AND DO
Islesford Historical Museum
Main St., and Sand Beach Rd., Cranberry Isles, 207-244-9224

Exhibits on local island history from 1604. Mid-June-September, daily.

DAMARISCOTTA

Damariscotta, whose name is an Abenaki word meaning "river of many fishes," has a number of colonial, Greek Revival and pre-Civil War houses. With the neighboring city of Newcastle across the Damariscotta River, this is a trading center for a seaside resort region extending to Pemaquid Point and Christmas Cove.

Information: Chamber of Commerce, 207-563-8340; www.damariscottaregion.com

WHAT TO SEE AND DO
Chapman-Hall House
Main and Church Streets, Damariscotta,
Restored 1754 house with original white-wash kitchen, period furniture; local ship-building exhibition. July-early September: Monday-Saturday.

Colonial Pemaquid State Park
Colonial Pemaquid Rd., New Harbor, 207-677-2423
Excavations have uncovered foundations of a jail, tavern and private homes. Fishing, boat ramp; picnicking; free parking. Memorial Day-Labor Day, daily.

Fort William Henry State Memorial
New Harbor, 207-677-2423
This reconstructed 1692 fort tower; museum contains relics, portraits, maps and copies of Native American deeds. Memorial Day-September: daily.

Pemaquid Point Lighthouse Park
Pemaquid Lighthouse, New Harbor, 207-677-2494
Includes an 1827 lighthouse that towers above the pounding surf (not open to public); Fishermen's Museum housed in old lightkeeper's dwelling; art gallery; recreational facilities. Fishermen's Museum. Memorial Day-Columbus Day: daily; rest of year: by appointment.

HOTELS
★★★The Bradley Inn
3063 Bristol Rd., New Harbor, 207-677-2105, 800-942-5560; www.bradleyinn.com
This inn, built by a sea captain for his bride in 1880, is located at the tip of Pemaquid Peninsula, near John's Bay and the Pemaquid Lighthouse. Nearby activities include golfing, fishing, boating, walks on the beach, a winery, nature area and fine restaurants.
16 rooms. Complimentary full breakfast. Restaurant. $$$

★★★Newcastle Inn
60 River Rd., Newcastle, 207-563-5685, 800-832-8669; www.newcastleinn.com
Overlooking gardens and the Damariscotta River, this Federal-style inn (1850) offers some rooms and suites with four-poster or canopy beds, while others have sitting areas or fireplaces. A four-course dinner preceded by complimentary hors d'oeuvres is served in one of the two dining rooms.
15 rooms. Children over 12 years only. Restaurant. Bar. $$

SPECIALTY LODGINGS
The Brannon Bunker Inn
349 Highway 129, Walpole, 207-563-5941, 800-563-9225; www.brannonbunkerinn.com

★
★
★
★

The area's first bed and breakfast, this inn features rooms simply furnished with quilts and antique furniture.

8 rooms. Pets accepted, some restrictions; fee. Complimentary continental breakfast. **$$**

Down Easter Inn
220 Bristol Rd., Damariscotta,
207-563-5332, 207-563-1134;
www.downeasterinn.com
This Greek Revival farmhouse (1785) was built by a ship chandler whose ancestors were among the first settlers of Bristol.
22 rooms. Complimentary continental breakfast. Restaurant. Closed Columbus Day-Memorial Day. **$**

DEER ISLE

A bridge over Eggemoggin Reach connects these islands to the mainland. There are two major villages here—Deer Isle (the older) and Stonington. Lobster fishing and tourism are the backbone of the economy and fishing, sailing, tennis and golf are available in the area.

Information: Deer Isle/Stonington Chamber of Commerce, Stonington, 207-348-6124 (in season); www.deerisle.com

WHAT TO SEE AND DO

Isle au Haut
Reached by ferry from Stonington. Much of this island—with hills more than 500 feet tall, forested shores and cobblestone beaches—is in Acadia National Park.

Isle au Haut Boat Services
Seabreeze Ave., Stonington,
207-367-6516, www.isleauhaut.com.
Service to the island and excursion trips available.

HOTELS

★★Goose Cove Lodge
300 Goose Cove Rd., Sunset,
207-348-2508, 800-728-1963;
www.goosecovelodge.com
23 rooms. Children's activity center. Closed mid-October to April. **$**

★★★Pilgrims Inn
20 Main St., Deer Isle,
207-348-6615; www.pilgrimsinn.com
This restored, historic wood frame building was built in 1793 and has eight-foot-wide fireplaces. Nearby are art galleries and a famous art school. The chef prepares meals from local seafood, produce and fresh-grown ingredients from the garden.
16 rooms. Pets accepted, some restrictions; fee. Restaurant. Closed November to mid-May, **$$**

EASTPORT

At the southern end of Passamaquoddy Bay, Eastport is a community with 150-year-old houses and ancient elms. The average tide at Eastport is approximately 18 feet, although tides up to 25 feet have been recorded here. Eastport was the site of one of the country's first tide-powered electric generating projects, and though never completed, it resulted in the construction of two tidal dams. The city is also the nation's aquaculture capital, where millions of salmon and trout are raised in pens in the chilly off-shore waters.

Information: 207-853-4644; www.eastport.net

WHAT TO SEE AND DO

Barracks Museum
74 Washington St., Eastport
This 1822 building once served as the officers' barracks for a nearby fort, which was held by British troops during the War of

1812. Memorial Day-Labor Day, Wednes-day-Saturday afternoons.

Old Sow Whirlpool
Between Moose and Deer Islands;
www.oldsowwhirlpool.com
One of the largest in the Western Hemisphere; most active three hours before high tide.

Passamaquoddy Indian Reservation
Highway 190, Perry, 207-853-2551
In 1604, Samuel de Champlain was the first European to encounter members of this Algonquin tribe. Festivals and ceremonies throughout the year.

SPECIALTY LODGINGS
Todd House
1 Capen Ave., Eastport,

207-853-2328
This authentic New England Cape once housed soldiers during the War of 1812. It is near the ocean and has views of the bay. 8 rooms. Pets accepted; fee. Complimentary continental breakfast. **$**

Weston House Bed & Breakfast
26 Boyton St., Eastport,
207-853-2907, 800-853-2907;
www.westonhouse-maine.com
This restored 19th-century residence has a sitting room with an authentic tin ceiling. Rooms are comfortably decorated with antiques.
4 rooms. No children allowed. Complimentary full breakfast. **$**

ELLSWORTH
This is the shire town and trading center for Hancock County—which includes some of the country's choicest resort territory, including Bar Harbor. In the beginning of the 19th century, Ellsworth was the second-largest lumber shipping port in the world.
Information: Chamber of Commerce, 163 High St., Ellsworth, 207-667-5584;
www.ellsworthchamber.org

WHAT TO SEE AND DO
Lamoine State Park
23 State Park Rd., Ellsworth,
207-667-4778
A 55-acre recreation area around beach on Frenchman Bay. Fishing; boating; picnicking, camping. Memorial Day to mid-October, daily. Standard fees.

Stanwood Sanctuary (Birdsacre) and Homestead Museum
289 High St., Ellsworth, 207-667-8460
Trails, ponds and picnic areas on 130-acre site. Collections include mounted birds, nests and eggs. Wildlife rehabilitation center with shelters for injured birds,

including hawks and owls. Museum was home of pioneer ornithologist, photographer and writer Cordelia Stanwood (1865-1958). Sanctuary and rehabilitation center daily; museum mid-June to mid-October.

HOTELS
★★**Holiday Inn**
215 High St., Ellsworth,
207-667-9341, 888-465-4329;
www.holidayinnellsworth.com
103 rooms. Pets accepted, some restrictions; fee. Restaurant. Bar. Fitness room. Indoor pool, whirlpool. Tennis. **$**

FORT KENT
Fort Kent, at the northern end of famous Highway 1 (the other end is at Key West, Florida), is the chief community of Maine's "far north." A bridge across the St. John River leads to Clair, New Brunswick. The town is a lumbering, farming, hunting and fishing center.

Canoeing, downhill and cross-country skiing, as well as snowmobiling are popular here. A campus for the University of Maine is located here.
Information: Fort Kent Chamber of Commerce, 291 W. Main St., 207-834-5354, 800-733-3563; www.fortkentchamber.com

WHAT TO SEE AND DO

Fort Kent Block House
North edge of town, 207-834-3866
Built in 1839, during the Aroostook Bloodless War with Britain, and used as a guard post. Restored; antique hand tools in museum; interpretive displays. Picnicking. Memorial Day-Labor Day, daily.

Fort Kent Historical Society Museum and Gardens
54 W. Main St., Fort Kent, 207-834-5121
Former Bangor and Aroostook railroad station, built in early 1900s, now houses historical museum. Usually last two weeks in June-August, Tuesday-Friday.

Lonesome Pine Trails
Forest Ave., Fort Kent, 207-834-5202
Thirteen trails, 2,300-foot slope with 500-foot drop; beginners slope and tow; rope tow, T-bar; school, patrol, rentals; lodge, concession. (December-April)

SPECIAL EVENTS

Can Am Crown Sled Dog Races
W. Main St., Fort Kent, 207-834-3312, 800-733-3563; www.can-am.sjv.net
Three races (30, 60 and 250-mile) begin on Main Street and finish at the Lonesome Pine Ski Lodge. Late February-early March.

58 FREEPORT

Freeport is an historic seaside town that played a part in Maine's early history—papers were signed here separating the state from Massachusetts in 1820. Today the town is known as a shopping mecca. It's home to dozens of outlets and the renowned L. L. Bean clothing and sporting goods store, which stays open 24 hours a day, selling everything from kayaks to bikes, thermal underwear to colorful fleece jackets.
Information: Freeport Merchants Association, 23 Depot St., 207-865-1212, 800-865-1994; www.freeportusa.com

WHAT TO SEE AND DO

Atlantic Seal Cruises
South Freeport. Depart from Town Wharf, 207-865-6112
Cruises aboard 40-foot, 28-passenger vessel on Casco Bay to Eagle Island and Robert E. Peary house museum; also seal and bird-watching trips, fall foliage sightseeing cruises. Schedules vary. Tickets can be purchased at Main Street office.

Factory Outlet Stores
42-28 Main St., Freeport, 800-865-1994; www.freeportusa.com
Freeport is home to more than 170 outlet stores and centers that offer brand-name merchandise at discounted prices, including the famous L. L. Bean clothing and sporting goods store, which stays open 24 hours a day.

Mast Landing Sanctuary
20 Gilsland Farm Rd., Falmouth, 207-781-2330
A 140-acre area maintained by the Maine Audubon Society. Hiking, cross-country skiing. Daily.

HOTELS

★★Best Western Freeport Inn
31 Highway 1, Freeport, 207-865-3106, 800-780-7234;

www.bestwestern.com
80 rooms. Pets accepted, some restrictions. Restaurant. Two outdoor pools. **$$**

★Casco Bay Inn
107 Highway 1, Freeport,
207-865-4925, 800-570-4970;
www.cascobayinn.com
45 rooms. Closed mid-December to mid-April. **$**

★★★Harraseeket Inn
162 Main St., Freeport,
207-865-9377, 800-342-6423;
www.harraseeketinn.com
This inn is located just two blocks from the L.L. Bean flagship store and the town's more than 170 shopping outlets. Three structures make up the inn: the Federalist House (1798), the Early Victorian House (1850) and a modern, colonial-style inn. Guest rooms are spacious, filled with antiques and feature mahogany furnishings, fireplaces and quarter canopy beds with heirloom bedspreads. Each afternoon, complimentary tea is served in the paneled drawing room, as is a complimentary breakfast buffet each morning.
84 rooms. Pets accepted, some restrictions; fee. Complimentary full breakfast. Restaurant. Bar. Indoor pool. Airport transportation available. **$$**

SPECIALTY LODGINGS

Brewster House Bed & Breakfast
180 Main St., Freeport,
207-865-4121, 800-865-0822;
www.brewsterhouse.com
Built in 1888, this waterfront inn has rooms decorated with fresh floral prints and antique furniture.
7 rooms. Children over 8 years only. Complimentary full breakfast. **$$$**

Freeport Clipper Inn
181 Main St., Freeport,
207-865-9623, 866-866-4002;
www.freeportclipperinn.com
This restored Greek Revival Cape home (circa 1840) features colonial furnishings.
7 rooms. Children over 12 years only.

Complimentary full breakfast. Outdoor pool. **$**

Kendall Tavern B&B
213 Main St., Freeport,
207-865-1338, 800-341-9572;
www.kendalltavern.com
This bed-and-breakfast is located at the north end of Freeport. Built in 1832, the first floor was opened as a tavern, and a second story was added years later. Guest rooms feature antiques and hand-made quilts. Each morning, a country-style breakfast is served in the dining room
7 rooms. Children over 8 only. Complimentary full breakfast. **$$**

Royalsborough Inn at Bagley House
1290 Royalsborough Rd., Durham,
207-865-6566, 800-765-1772;
www.royalsboroughinn.com
Restored country inn (1772); wood beams, wide pine floors, original beehive oven.
8 rooms. Complimentary full breakfast. **$$**

White Cedar Inn
178 Main St., Freeport,
207-865-9099, 800-853-1269;
www.whitecedarinn.com
Former home of Arctic explorer Donald MacMillan.
7 rooms. Pets accepted, some restrictions; fee, Children over 8 years only. Complimentary full breakfast. **$**

RESTAURANTS

★Corsican
9 Mechanic St., Freeport, 207-865-9421;
www.corsicanrestaurant.com
Italian, seafood menu. Lunch, dinner. Closed holidays. Children's menu. Casual attire. Reservations recommended. **$$**

★Gritty McDuff's
187 Lower Main St., Freeport,
207-865-4321; www.grittys.com
American, seafood menu. Lunch, dinner, late-night. Bar. Children's menu. Casual attire. Outdoor seating. **$$**

★★Jameson Tavern
115 Main St., Freeport, 207-865-4196
www.jamesontavern.com
Seafood, steak menu. Lunch, dinner. Bar.
Children's menu. Casual attire. Reservations
recommended. Outdoor seating. **$$**

★Lobster Cooker
39 Main St., Freeport, 207-865-4349;
www.lobstercooker.com
Seafood menu. Lunch, dinner. Children's
menu. Casual attire. Outdoor seating. **$$**

★★★The Maine Dining Room
162 Main St., Freeport,
207-865-9377, 800-342-6423;
www.harraseeketinn.com
This restaurant, located in the Harraseeket
Inn, offers a cozy atmosphere, enhanced
by two wood-burning fireplaces and windows overlooking the gardens. The menu
consists of organic, homegrown foods and
the wine selection is one of the largest in
Maine.
American menu. Breakfast, dinner, brunch.
Bar. Business casual attire. Reservations rec-
ommended. **$$$**

GREENVILLE

Greenville is a starting point for trips into the Moosehead Lake region. Until it was incor-
porated in 1836, it was known as Haskell, in honor of its founder Nathaniel Haskell.
Information: Moosehead Lake Region Chamber of Commerce, 207-695-2702, 888-876-
2778; www.mooseheadlake.org

WHAT TO SEE AND DO
Moosehead Marine Museum
N. Main St., Greenville, 207-695-2716
Located on the steamboat *Katahdin*, berthed
in East Cove. Exhibits of the steamboat era
and the Kineo Hotel; cruises available.
July-Columbus Day.

HOTELS
★Chalet Moosehead Lakefront Motel
Birch St., Greenville,
207-695-2950, 800-290-3645;
www.mooseheadlodging.com
27 rooms. Pets accepted, some restrictions;
fee. **$**

★Indian Hill Motel
127 Moosehead Lake Rd., Greenville,
207-695-2623, 800-771-4620;
www.mooseheadlodging.com/ihm.html
15 rooms. **$**

SPECIALTY LODGINGS
Greenville Inn
40 Norris St., Greenville
207-695-2206, 888-695-6000,
www.greenvilleinn.com
13 rooms. Complimentary continental
breakfast. Restaurant. Bar. **$$**

The Lodge at Moosehead Lake
368 Lily Bay Rd., Greenville,
207-695-4400, 800-825-6977;
www.lodgeatmooseheadlake.com
This romantic retreat offers lodge rooms
and adjacent carriage house suites, each
with charming rustic interiors including
hand-carved poster beds. Most guest rooms
feature sunset views over the water and
Squaw Mountain. Explore nearby Lily Bay
State Park or take part in the year-round
recreations of the lake and surrounding
wilderness.
5 rooms. Children over 14 years only. Complimentary full breakfast. **$$$$**

MAINE

KENNEBUNK

The inland sister to tony beach town Kennebunkport, this village is equally visually appealing and quaint. At one time, the original settlement that was to become Kennebunk used to be a part of Wells. When Maine separated from Massachusetts in 1820, Kennebunk separated from Wells. Once a shipbuilding community on the Mousam and Kennebunk Rivers, today Kennebunk is the business center for the summer resort area that includes Kennebunkport and Kennebunk Beach.

Information: Chamber of Commerce, 17 Western Ave., 207-967-0857; www.kkcc.maine.org

WHAT TO SEE AND DO

Brick Store Museum

117 Main St., Kennebunk, 207-985-4802; www.brickstoremuseum.org

A block of restored 19th-century buildings including William Lord's Brick Store (1825); exhibits of fine and decorative arts, historical and maritime collections. Tuesday-Saturday.

HOTELS

★The Seasons Inn of the Kennebunk

55 York St., Kennebunk, 207-985-6100; 800-336-5634; www.theseasonsinnofthekennebunks.com

44 rooms. Complimentary continental breakfast. Outdoor pool. $

SPECIALTY LODGINGS

Arundel Meadows Inn

1024 Portland Rd., Kennebunk, 207-985-3770; www.arundelmeadowsinn.com

This restored farmhouse (built in1827) is decorated with antiques and features expansive gardens.

7 rooms. Children over 12 years only. Complimentary full breakfast. Outdoor pool. $

The Beach House

211 Beach Ave., Kennebunk Beach, 207-967-3850; www.beachhseinn.com

This inn (circa 1890) is located on Kennebunk Beach, just two miles from Kennebunkport. Rooms are crisp and contemporary, with plush duvet topped beds. Afternoon tea is served in the sitting room, which has a view of the ocean.

34 rooms. Complimentary continental breakfast. $$$$

The Kennebunk Inn

45 Main St., Kennebunk, 207-985-3351; www.thekennebunkinn.com

Built in 1799, this cozy inn features turn-of-the-century decor.

22 rooms. Pets accepted, some restrictions; fee. Complimentary continental breakfast. Restaurant. $

RESTAURANTS

★Federal Jack's Restaurant and Brew Pub

8 Western Ave., Kennebunk, 207-967-4322; www.federaljacks.com

American, seafood menu. Lunch, dinner, late-night. Bar. Children's menu. Casual attire. Outdoor seating. $$

★★★Grissini

27 Western Ave., Kennebunk, 207-967-2211; www.restaurantgrissini.com

Grissini offers Tuscan cooking in an airy, loft-like setting. The restaurant features a large stone fireplace, an open kitchen and an outdoor garden dining area.

Italian menu. Dinner. Bar. Casual attire. Reservations recommended. Outdoor seating. $$

★★The Kennebunk Inn

45 Main St., Kennebunk, 207-985-3351; www.thekennebunkinn.com

American, seafood menu. Lunch, dinner, brunch. Bar. Children's menu. Casual attire. Reservations recommended. Outdoor seating. $$$

★★★Windows on the Water

12 Chase Hill Rd., Kennebunk, 207-967-3313, 800-773-3313; www.windowsonthewater.com

This local favorite opened in 1985 and is family owned and operated. The menu features plenty of meat dishes (filet mignon and parmesan crusted rack of lamb), but the specialty here is fresh, sustainable fish and seafood, from native striped bass to day boat sea scallops.

American menu. Lunch, dinner. Children's menu. Casual attire. Reservations recommended. Outdoor seating. **$$$**

KENNEBUNKPORT

At the mouth of the Kennebunk River, this quaint coastal town is a favorite summer destination of well-heeled New Englanders. The Bush family has its warm-weather compound here, and generations of blue bloods have checked into the historic Colony Hotel and walked along the beach to Walker's Point. In fall and winter, the town is equally appealing, with its many boutiques, restaurants and charming inns as diversions.

Information: Chamber of Commerce, 17 Western Ave., Kennebunk, 207-967-0857; www.kkcc.maine.org

WHAT TO SEE AND DO

School House
135 North St., Kennebunkport, 207-967-2751
(1899) Headquarters of the Kennebunkport Historical Society. Houses collections of genealogy, photographs, maritime history and many artifacts and documents on Kennebunkport's history. Tuesday-Friday.

HOTELS

★★The Breakwater Inn and Hotel
127-131 Ocean Ave., Kennebunkport, 207-967-5333; www.thebreakwaterinn.com
37 rooms. Complimentary continental breakfast. Restaurant. **$$$**

★Rhumb Line Motor Lodge
Ocean Ave., Kennebunkport, 207-967-5457, 800-337-4862; www.rhumblinemaine.com
59 rooms. Complimentary continental breakfast. Bar. Fitness room. In-door pool, outdoor pool, whirlpool. **$**

★★★The Colony Hotel
140 Ocean Ave., Kennebunkport, 207-967-3331, 800-552-2363; www.thecolonyhotel.com/maine
Located on a rock promontory overlooking the Atlantic Ocean and the mouth of the Kennebec River, this hotel features a heated saltwater pool, beach and gardens. Other nearby activities include golf, tennis, kayaking, bicycling, boating, shopping and touring art galleries. Maine lobster and local seafood are the focus at the hotel's restaurant.
125 rooms. Pets accepted; fee. Restaurant. Bar. Beach. Outdoor pool. Closed November-mid-May. **$$**

★★★Kennebunkport Inn
1 Dock Square, Kennebunkport, 207-967-2621, 800-248-2621; www.kennebunkportinn.com
Conveniently located in the heart of the historic seaport of Kennebunkport, this inn is an easy walk to the harbor and all the shops and galleries of Dock Square. Built by a wealthy tea and coffee merchant, the Victorian mansion (1899) was renovated to be an inn in 1926. Guest rooms feature period antiques and reproductions, elegant fabrics and floral carpeting. Many of the beds are high four-posters.
48 rooms. Complimentary continental breakfast. High-speed Internet access, wireless Internet access. Restaurant. Bar. Spa. Outdoor pool. **$$$**

★★★Nonantum Resort
95 Ocean Ave., Kennebunkport, 207-967-4050, 800-552-5651; www.nonantumresort.com
The guest rooms at this hotel all have air-conditioning, cable and private baths. The beach is nearby, as is the Bush family compound for those hoping for a glimpse of the 41st or 43rd presidents. Maine seafood is

the specialty at the onsite restaurant. This is one of the oldest operating inns in the state.

115 rooms. Restaurant. Bar. Outdoor pool. Closed mid-November-April. **$**

★★★★The White Barn Inn

37 Beach Ave., Kennebunkport,
207-967-2321;
www.whitebarninn.com

This cluster of cottages, restored barns, and a circa-1860s house make up the White Barn Inn, a quaint spot that delivers quiet luxury on the coast of Maine. The charming rooms and suites are decorated with antiques and feature wood-burning fireplaces, whirlpool tubs, and flat screen TVs with DVDs, CD players. Simple pleasures here include relaxing by the stone swimming pool, riding a bike along the coast, experiencing a spa treatment, and having afternoon tea by the fire in the comfortable sitting room. The inn has one of the region's most acclaimed restaurants, which serves New England cuisine in a rustic, candlelit setting.

25 rooms. Complimentary full breakfast. High-speed Internet access, wireless Internet access. Restaurant. Bar. Spa. Outdoor pool. Business center. **$$$$**

SPECIALTY LODGINGS

Bufflehead Cove

Bufflehead Cove Lane, Kennebunkport,
207-967-3879; www.buffleheadcove.com

This secluded Victorian inn is spacious, old-fashioned, and close to downtown Kennebunkport. Guests can leisurely explore the local beaches or visit the numerous restaurants, art galleries, antique shops and old bookstores.

6 rooms. Children over 11 years only. Complimentary full breakfast. **$$$**

Cape Arundel Inn

208 Ocean Ave., Kennebunkport,
207-967-2125; www.capearundelinn.com

This Victorian-style inn (1890) features turn-of-the-century decor and overlooks the seacoast.

14 rooms. Complimentary continental breakfast. Restaurant. Closed mid-December to mid-April. **$$**

Captain Fairfield Inn

8 Pleasant St., Kennebunkport,
207-967-4454, 800-322-1928;
www.captainfairfield.com

This Federal-style historic bed-and-breakfast (1813) is in the heart of the seaport resort of Kennebunkport. It is surrounded by towering trees, gardens and overlooks the river and harbor. It is within walking distance to shops and art galleries, as well as the ocean and a variety of restaurants. Guest rooms are decorated with antique and period furniture and each has its own private bath and sitting area.

9 rooms. Children over 6 years only. Complimentary full breakfast. **$$**

The Captain Jefferds Inn

5 Pearl St., Kennebunkport,
207-967-2311, 800-839-6844;
www.captainjefferdsinn.com

This historic inn, built in 1804, has been fully restored and is furnished with antiques and period reproductions. All rooms have private baths, fresh flowers, down-filled comforters, fireplaces and CD players. A complimentary three-course breakfast is included as are afternoon refreshments.

15 rooms. Pets accepted, some restrictions; fee. Children over 8 years only. Complimentary full breakfast. Closed last two weeks in December. **$$$**

The Captain Lord Mansion

6 Pleasant St., Kennebunkport,
207-967-3141, 800-522-3141;
www.captainlord.com

Set on an acre of gardens, this inn is decorated with a worldly mix of period furnishings and different themes. Repeat visitors are rewarded with an engraved stone in the Memory Garden after their tenth stay.

17 rooms. Children over 12 years only. Complimentary full breakfast. **$**

English Meadows Inn

141 Port Rd., Kennebunkport,

63

MAINE

207-967-5766, 800-272-0698;
www.englishmeadowsinn.com
Victorian farmhouse (1860) and attached
carriage house.
12 rooms. Pets accepted, some restrictions;
fee. Complimentary full breakfast. Closed
January. **$**

**Maine Stay Inn & Cottages at the Melville
Walker House**
34 Maine St., Kennebunkport,
207-967-2117, 800-950-2117;
www.mainestayinn.com
This 19th-century bed-and-breakfast (1860)
is located in the residential area of Kennebunkport's historic district. It is near the
harbor and beach.
17 rooms. Complimentary full breakfast.
$$$

Old Fort Inn
8 Old Fort Ave., Kennebunkport,
207-967-5353, 800-828-3678;
www.oldfortinn.com
This inn, located just one block from the Atlan-
tic Ocean, has guest rooms in a turn-of-the-
century carriage house built of red brick and
local stone. There is a tennis court and heated
freshwater pool on site, and guests can explore
nearby beaches, boutiques and art galleries.
16 rooms. Complimentary full breakfast.
Outdoor pool. Tennis. Closed mid-Decem-
ber to mid-April. **$$$$**

Tides Inn by the Sea
252 Kings Hwy., Kennebunkport,
207-967-3757; www.tidesinnbythesea.com
Built as an inn in 1899. Original guest book
on display; signatures include Theodore
Roosevelt and Arthur Conan Doyle.
22 rooms. Complimentary continental
breakfast. Restaurant. Closed mid-October
to mid-May. **$$$**

Yachtsman Lodge & Marina
57 Ocean Ave., Kennebunkport,
207-967-2511; www.yachtsmanlodge.com
30 rooms. Pets accepted, some restrictions;
fee. Complimentary continental breakfast.
Closed December-April. **$**

RESTAURANTS
★Alisson's
11 Dock Square, Kennebunkport,
207-967-4841; www.alissons.com
Seafood menu. Lunch, dinner. Bar.
Children's menu. Casual attire. **$$**

★Bartley's Dockside
Western Ave., Kennebunkport,
207-967-5050;
www.bartleys-dockside.com
Seafood menu. Lunch, dinner. Children's
menu. Casual attire. Outdoor seating. **$$**

★★The Belvidere Room
252 Kings Highway, Kennebunkport,
207-967-3757; www.tidesinnbythesea.com
American menu. Dinner. Closed Tuesday;
also mid-October to mid-May. Bar.
Children's menu. Casual attire. Reserva-
tions recommended. **$$**

★★The Landing Hotel & Restaurant
21 Ocean Ave., Kennebunkport,
207-967-4221, 866-967-4221;
www.thelandinghotelandrestaurant.com
American, Seafood menu. Lunch, dinner.
Closed late October-early May. Bar.
Children's menu. Casual attire. Outdoor
seating. **$$**

★Mabel's Lobster Claw
124 Ocean Ave., Kennebunkport,
207-967-2562
Seafood menu. Lunch, dinner. Children's
menu. Casual attire. Reservations recommended. Outdoor seating. Closed Novem-
ber-early April. **$$**

★Nunan's Lobster Hut
9 Mills Rd., Kennebunkport,
207-967-4362
Seafood menu. Dinner. Casual attire. Closed
Columbus Day-May. **$$**

★★★Stripers
131-133 Ocean Ave., Kennebunkport,
207-967-5333; www.thebreakwaterinn.com
Located within the Breakwater Inn and Spa,
Stripers is close to Dock Square's shops
and galleries. Inside the restaurant feels like

64

MAINE

a modern seaside cottage, with a soft green banquette, steel-rimmed tabletops and a see-through aquarium wall that divides the entry from the main dining room. The menu includes options such as local Kennebunkport oysters, farm-raised striped bass, halibut and scallops.

Seafood menu. Dinner, brunch. Bar. Business casual attire. Reservations recommended. Valet parking. Outdoor seating. Closed late October-early April. $$$

★★★★★The White Barn Inn Restaurant
37 Beach Ave., Kennebunkport,
207-967-2321; www.whitebarninn.com
A New England classic, this charming candlelit space inside the White Barn Inn is filled with fresh flowers and white linen-topped tables. Chef Jonathan Cartwright creates delicious regional dishes expertly accented with a European flair. The four-course prix fixe menu changes weekly, highlighting seafood from Maine's waters as well as native game and poultry. The

vast wine selection perfectly complements the cuisine, and a rolling cheese cart offers some of the best local artisans' products. American menu. Bar. Jacket required. Reservations recommended. Valet parking. No Disabled Facilities. Dinner. Closed three weeks in January. $$$$

SPAS
★★★★Spa at White Barn Inn
37 Beach Ave., Kennebunkport,
207-967-2321; www.whitebarninn.com
Though located in a traditional New England country inn, the décor at the Spa at White Barn Inn delivers a dash of minimalism without compromising on luxury. Guests can request a light-of-the-moon plunge, which is a fizz of marine pebbles infused with mandarin orange and lemon essential oils, or an aroma sea bath. The nearby Kennebunk River provides the materials used in the spa's signature stone massage, while natural marine algae and Maine sea salts are incorporated into the body wraps.

KINGFIELD
Located in the valley of the Carrabassett River, Kingfield once had several lumber mills. The town was named after William King, Maine's first governor, and was the birthplace of F. E. and F. O. Stanley, the twins who developed the Stanley Steamer. Canoeing, hiking, and downhill skiing are available in nearby areas.

WHAT TO SEE AND DO
Carrabassett Valley Ski Area
Sugarloaf Access Rd., Kingfield,
207-237-2000; www.sugarloaf.com
Approximately 50 miles of ski touring trails. Center offers lunch (daily); school, rentals; skating rink (fee), rentals; trail information area; shop. Half-day rates. Early December to late April, daily.

Sugarloaf/USA Ski Area
Sugarloaf Access Rd., Kingfield,
207-237-2000, 800-843-5623.
Two quad, triple, eight double chairlifts; T-bar; school, patrol, rentals; snowmaking; lodge; restaurants, coffee shop, cafeteria, bars; nursery; bank, health club, shops. Six Olympic runs, 45 miles of trails; longest run 3 1/2 miles; vertical drop 2,820 feet. 65

miles of cross-country trails. Early November-May, daily.

HOTELS
★★The Herbert Grand Hotel
Main St., Kingfield,
207-265-2000, 800-843-4372;
www.herbertgrandhotel.com
33 rooms. Pets accepted; fee. Complimentary continental breakfast. Restaurant. $

★★Sugarloaf Inn
Highway 27, Kingfield,
207-237-6814, 800-843-5623;
www.sugarloaf.com
42 rooms. Restaurant. Bar. Indoor pool, outdoor pool, whirlpool. Golf. Tennis. Ski in/ski out. $

★★★Grand Summit Resort Hotel
5091 Access Rd., Kingfield,
207-237-2222, 800-843-5623;
www.sugarloaf.com
Each room in this hotel has a view of the mountains and features oak furniture and brass fixtures, television with a VCR and a coffee maker. Skiing and golfing are nearby. The hotel is located at the base of the slopes.

120 rooms. Restaurant. Bar. Fitness room. Whirlpool. Golf, 18 holes. Tennis. Ski in/ski out. **$**

RESTAURANTS
★★Longfellow's
247 Main Street, Kingfield, 207-265-4394
American, seafood menu. Lunch, dinner. Children's menu. Outdoor seating. **$**

KITTERY

This old sea community has built ships since its early days. Kittery men built the *Ranger*, which sailed to France under John Paul Jones with the news of Burgoyne's surrender. Across the Piscataqua River from Portsmouth, New Hampshire, Kittery is the home of the Portsmouth Naval Shipyard.

Information: Greater York Region Chamber of Commerce, 1 Stonewall Lane, Kittery, 207-363-4422; www.yorkme.org

WHAT TO SEE AND DO
Fort Foster Park
Northeast via Highway 103 to Gerrish Island., 207-439-3800
A 92-acre park with picnicking, pavilion; beach; baseball field; fishing pier. Cross-country skiing in winter. Entrance fee per individual and per vehicle. June-August: daily; May and September: Saturday-Sunday.

Hamilton House
40 Vaughan Lanes, South Berwick, 207-384-2454
This Georgian house, overlooking the Salmon Falls River, was redecorated at the turn of the century with a mixture of antiques, painted murals and country furnishings to emulate America's colonial past. Perennial garden, flowering trees and shrubs and garden cottage. Tours. June-mid-October, Wednesday-Sunday afternoons.

Kittery Historical and Naval Museum
Highway 1 and Rogers Rd., Kittery, 207-439-3080
Exhibits portray history of U.S. Navy and Kittery—Maine's oldest incorporated town—as well as southern Maine's maritime heritage. June-October, Tuesday-Saturday.

Sarah Orne Jewett House
5 Portland St., South Berwick, 207-384-2454
Novelist Sarah Orne Jewett spent most of her life in this 1774 Georgian residence. Interior restored to re-create the appearance of the house during her time (1849-1909). Contains some original 18th-and 19th-century wallpaper; fine paneling. Her own bedroom-study has been left as she arranged it. June-mid-October, Friday-Sunday.

HOTELS
★Coachman Inn
380 Highway 1, Kittery, 207-439-4434, 800-824-6183; www.coachmaninn.net
43 rooms. Complimentary continental breakfast. Outdoor pool. **$**

RESTAURANTS
★Cap'n Simeon's Gallery
90 Pepperell Rd., Kittery Point, 207-439-3655; www.capnsimeons.com
Located in a 17th-century boathouse, this restaurant features nautical décor. There are views of the pier and lighthouses, and entertainment is offered on weekends. Seafood menu. Lunch, dinner, Sunday brunch. Bar. Children's menu. Casual attire. **$$**

★★Warren's Lobster House
11 Water St., Kittery, 207-439-1630;
www.lobsterhouse.com

Seafood menu. Lunch, dinner. Bar. Children's menu. Casual attire. Valet parking. Outdoor seating. **$$**

LEWISTON

Maine's second-largest city is 30 miles up the Androscoggin River from the sea, directly across the river from its sister city of Auburn. Known as the Twin Cities, both are strong manufacturing communities. Lewiston was the first of the two cities to harness the water power of the Androscoggin Falls but both cities make good use of the river.
Information: Androscoggin County Chamber of Commerce,
179 Lisbon St., 207-783-2249;
www.androscoggincounty.com

WHAT TO SEE AND DO

Bates College
56 Campus Ave., Lewiston,
207-786-6255; www.bates.edu
(1855) New England's oldest and the nation's second-oldest co-educational institution of higher learning; originally the Maine State Seminary, it was renamed after a prominent Boston investor. Liberal arts and sciences. On its well-landscaped campus are the Edmund S. Muskie Archives (1936 alumnus and former Senator and U.S. Secretary of State) and a beautiful chapel containing a hand-crafted tracker-action organ.

SPECIAL EVENTS

Festival de Joie
190 Birch St., Lewiston,

207-782-6231; www.festivaldejoie.org
Celebration of Lewiston and Auburn's Franco-American heritage. Features ethnic song, dance, cultural activities and traditional foods. Late July-early August.

HOTELS

★★Ramada Inn
490 Pleasant St., Lewiston,
207-784-2331, 800-272-6232;
www.ramadamaine.com
117 rooms. Complimentary continental breakfast. Restaurant. Bar. Fitness room. Indoor pool, whirlpool. Business center. **$**

LUBEC

Quoddy Head State Park, the easternmost point in the United States, is located in Lubec. There is a lighthouse here, as well as the Franklin D. Roosevelt Memorial Bridge, which stretches over Lubec Narrows to Campobello Island. Roosevelt summered here throughout much of his childhood and into his adult years.

★
★
★
★

WHAT TO SEE AND DO

Roosevelt Campobello International Park

459 Highway 774, New Brunswick,
506-752-2922; www.nps.gov/roca
Canadian property jointly maintained by
Canada and the United States. Approximately 2,800 acres includes the 11-acre
estate where Franklin D. Roosevelt had
his summer home and was stricken with
poliomyelitis. Self-guided tours of 34-room
house, interpretive guides available, films
shown in visitor center, picnic sites in natural area, observation platforms and interpretive panels at Friar's Head. No camping.
Saturday before Memorial Day-October 31,
daily.

MILLINOCKET

Maine's tallest peak, Mount Katahdin rises over Baxter State Park, the origin point of the
Appalachian Trail. Millinocket provides the closest base for exploring this outdoor wilderness area, where sightings of moose and even the northern lights are common.
**Information: Katahdin Area Chamber of Commerce, 1029 Central St., 207-723-4443;
www.katahdinmaine.com**

HOTELS

**★★Best Value Heritage Motor
Inn-Millinocket**

935 Central St., Millinocket,
207-723-9777; www.hertiageinnmaine.com
49 rooms. Pets accepted. Complimentary
continental breakfast. Restaurant. Bar. Fitness room. **$**

★★Katahdin Inn

740 Central St., Millinocket,
207-723-4555, 877-902-4555;
www.katahdininn.com

82 rooms. Pets accepted, some restrictions.
Complimentary continental breakfast. Bar.
Fitness room. Indoor pool, children's pool,
whirlpool. **$**

★★Pamola Motor Lodge

973 Central St., Millinocket,
207-723-9746;
www.pamolamotorlodge.com
29 rooms. Complimentary continental
breakfast. Restaurant. Bar. Outdoor pool,
whirlpool. **$**

MONHEGAN ISLAND

Monhegan Plantation, nine miles out to sea, approximately two miles long and one
mile wide, is devoted to lobsters and summer visitors. Rockwell Kent and Milton Burns
were among the first of many artists to summer here. Today, the warm-weather population is about 20 times the year-round number. There is more work in winter—by
special law, lobsters may be trapped in Monhegan waters only from January to June.
This gives them the other six months to fatten. Monhegan lobsters thus command the
highest prices.

Leif Ericson may have landed on Monhegan Island in AD 1000. In its early years,
Monhegan Island was a landmark for sailors, and by 1611 it was well known as a general

headquarters for European fishermen, traders and explorers. For a time, the island was a pirate den. Small compared to other Maine islands, Monhegan is a land of contrasts. On one side of the island, sheer cliffs drop 150 feet to the ocean below, while on the other side, Cathedral Woods offers visitors a quiet forest to explore.

WHAT TO SEE AND DO
Monhegan Lighthouse/Museum
1 Lighthouse Hill, Monhegan Island
207-596-7003
Historic lighthouse has been in operation since 1824; automated since 1959.

NORTHEAST HARBOR
This coastal village is located on Mount Desert Island, a land of rocky coastlines, forests and lakes. The island is reached from the mainland by a short bridge.

WHAT TO SEE AND DO
Ferry Service
33 Main St., Cranberry Isles, 207-244-3575
Connects Northeast Harbor with the Cranberry Isles; three-mile, 30-minute crossing. Summer: daily; rest of year: schedule varies.

Woodlawn Museum (The Black House)
172 Surrey Rd., Northeast Harbor,
207-667-8671;
www.woodlawnmuseum.com
(Circa 1820) Federal house built by a local landowner; antiques. Garden; carriage house with old carriages and sleighs. May-October, Tuesday-Sunday; rest of year, by appointment.

HOTELS
★★★Asticou Inn
15 Peabody Dr., Northeast Harbor,
207-276-3344, 800-258-3373;
www.asticou.com
Rooms at this sprawling Victorian inn are decorated with oriental rugs and traditional furniture. The grounds include beautifully landscaped gardens as well as clay tennis courts and an outdoor heated pool.
31 rooms. Restaurant. Bar. Outdoor pool. Tennis. Closed mid-September to mid-June. $$$

SPECIALTY LODGINGS
Maison Suisse Inn
Kimball Lane and Main St.,
Northeast Harbor,
207-276-5223, 800-624-7668;
www.maisonsuisse.com
This restored, single-style summer cottage (1892) was once a speakeasy during Prohibition.
15 rooms. Pets accepted, some restrictions. Complimentary full breakfast. Closed November-April. $$$

RESTAURANTS
★Docksider
14 Sea St., Northeast Harbor,
207-276-3965
Seafood menu. Lunch, dinner. Children's menu. Casual attire. Outdoor seating. Closed Columbus Day-mid-May. $$

NORWAY
Norway was founded by English settlers in the late 1700s. This tiny hamlet is known for its picturesque, rolling hills.
Information: Oxford Hills Chamber of Commerce, 213 Main St., South Paris, 207-743-2281; www.oxfordhillsmaine.com

MAINE

WHAT TO SEE AND DO
Pennesseewassee Lake
This seven-mile-long lake, covering 922 acres, received its name from the Native American words meaning "sweet water." Swimming, beaches, water-skiing; fishing for brown trout, bass and perch; boating (marina, rentals, launch). Ice skating. Contact Chamber of Commerce.

HOTELS
★★★Waterford Inne
258 Chadbourne Rd., Waterford,
207-583-4037; www.waterfordinn.com
This 19th-century eight-room farmhouse (1825) is surrounded by fields and woods. The rooms here are decorated in fresh country prints and simple farmhouse style furniture, while the restaurant is a cozy welcoming spot that serves hearty, satisfying dishes like crab and leek bisque, and pork chops with apples.
8 rooms. Pets accepted; fee. Complimentary full breakfast. Restaurant. $

RESTAURANTS
★★Maurice Restaurant Francais
109 Main St., South Paris,
207-743-2532;
www.mauricerestaurant.com
French menu. Lunch, dinner. Bar. $$

OGUNQUIT
Maine's "stern and rockbound coast" becomes a sunny strand here with a great white beach that stretches for three miles. The Ogunquit public beach is one of the finest on the Atlantic offering marine views of Perkins Cove and attracting a substantial art colony.
Information: Chamber of Commerce, 207-646-2939; www.ogunquit.org

WHAT TO SEE AND DO
Ogunquit Museum of American Art
543 Shore Rd., Ogunquit,
207-646-4909;
www.ogunquitmuseum.org
Twentieth-century American sculpture and painting. Museum overlooks the ocean and sculpture gardens. (July-mid-October, daily)

SPECIAL EVENTS
Ogunquit Playhouse
10 Highway 1, Northeast Harbor,
207-646-2402;
www.ogunquitplayhouse.org
Established in the early 1930s. Top plays and musicals with professional actors. Late June-Labor Day weekend.

HOTELS
★The Beachmere Inn
62 Beachmere Place, Ogunquit,
207-646-2021, 800-336-3983;
www.beachmereinn.com
53 rooms. Complimentary continental breakfast. Closed mid-December to April. $$

★★Gorges Grant Hotel
449 Main St., Ogunquit,
207-646-7003, 800-646-5001;
www.ogunquit.com
81 rooms. Restaurant. Fitness room. Indoor pool, outdoor pool, whirlpool. Closed mid-December to March $

★★The Grand Hotel
276 Shore Rd., Ogunquit,
207-646-1231, 800-806-1231;
www.thegrandhotel.com
28 rooms. Complimentary continental breakfast. Indoor pool.Closed September-March. $

★Juniper Hill Inn
336 Main St., Ogunquit,
207-646-4501, 800-646-4544;
www.ogunquit.com
100 rooms. Fitness room. One indoor pool, two outdoor pools, two whirlpools. $

★★Meadowmere
Hwy. 1, Ogunquit,

207-646-9661, 800-633-8718;
www.meadowmere.com
145 rooms. Complimentary continental breakfast. Restaurant. Fitness room. Indoor pool, outdoor pool, whirlpool. **$$**

★**The Milestone**
687 Main St., Ogunquit,
207-646-4562, 800-646-6453;
www.ogunquit.com
70 rooms. Fitness room. Outdoor pool, whirlpool. Closed November-March. **$**

★**Riverside**
159 Shore Rd., Ogunquit, 207-646-2741;
www.riversidemotel.com
38 rooms. Complimentary continental breakfast. Closed November to mid-April. **$**

★★★**Anchorage By The Sea**
125 Shore Rd., Ogunquit, 207-646-9384;
www.anchoragebythesea.com
This property has a prime location directly on the ocean. Rooms are comfortable and have views of the sea.
212 rooms. Complimentary continental breakfast. Restaurant. Indoor pool, outdoor pool, children's pool, whirlpool. **$**

★**The Terrace By The Sea**
23 Wharf Lane, Ogunquit, 207-646-3232;
www.terracebythesea.com
36 rooms. Complimentary continental breakfast. Outdoor pool. Closed January-February. **$**

SPECIALTY LODGINGS

Hartwell House
312 Shore Rd., Ogunquit,
207-646-7210, 800-235-8883;
www.hartwellhouseinn.com
Located in the countryside of Maine, this bed-and-breakfast is only minutes from a summer resort. Most rooms have French doors leading to terraces or balconies that overlook the gardens. A full gourmet breakfast and afternoon tea are served daily.
16 rooms. Children over 14 years only. Complimentary full breakfast. **$$**

The Pine Hill Inn
14 Pine Hill Rd. S., Ogunquit,
207-361-1004; www.pinehillinn.com
Turn-of-the-century cottage with sun porch. 6 rooms. Children over 12 years only. Complimentary full breakfast. **$**

RESTAURANTS

★★★**98 Provence**
262 Shore Rd., Ogunquit,
207-646-9898; www.98provence.com
This welcoming country French restaurant offers an appealing menu in a small clapboard house. The cottage-like setting provides a warm, comfortable atmosphere. Classics like fisherman soup or escargot often make an appearance on the menu. French menu. Dinner. Bar. Casual attire. Closed Tuesday; mid-December to mid-April. **$$**

★★★**Arrows**
Berwick Rd., Ogunquit, 207-361-1100;
www.arrowsrestaurant.com
Co-owners and co-chefs Clark Frasier and Mark Gaier have made this idyllic restaurant, which is housed in an 18th-century farmhouse, a seasonal dining destination. They bake their own breads, grow their own organic vegetables and offer a creative and elegant menu. American menu. Dinner. Bar. Business casual attire. Reservations recommended. Closed Monday; also December-early April. **$$$**

★**Barnacle Billy's**
Perkins Cove, Ogunquit,
207-646-5575, 800-866-5575;
www.barnbilly.com
Lobster tank. Seafood menu. Lunch, dinner. Casual attire. Valet parking. Outdoor seating. **$$**

★★**Billy's Etc.**
Oarweed Cove Rd., Ogunquit,
207-646-4711; www.barnbilly.com
American, seafood menu. Lunch, dinner. Closed November-mid-April. Bar. Valet parking. Outdoor seating. **$$**

71

MAINE

★
★
★
★

★★Blue Elephant
309 Shore Rd., Ogunquit, 207-641-2028
Thai menu. Dinner. Bar. Casual attire. Reservations recommended. Outdoor seating. **$$**

★★★Clay Hill Farm
220 Clay Hill Rd., Cape Neddick,
207-361-2272; www.clayhillfarm.com
This restaurant, housed in a historic farmhouse (1780), is located on 30 acres of protected woodlands and is certified by the National Wildlife Association as a wildlife habitat and bird sanctuary. The menu features fresh and season dishes, such as basil roasted haddock with tomato, cured olives and artichoke hearts.
Seafood menu. Dinner. Bar. Valet parking. Closed Monday-Wednesday November-April. **$$$**

★★Gypsy Sweethearts
30 Shore Rd., Ogunquit, 207-646-7021;
www.gypsysweethearts.com
International menu. Dinner. Bar. Casual attire. Reservations recommended. Outdoor seating. Closed Monday. **$$**

★★★Jonathan's
92 Bourne Lane, Ogunquit, 207-646-4777;
www.jonathansrestaurant.com
This restaurant is located in a house surrounded by gardens that was once the home of the owner's parents. This rustic, simple restaurant serves dishes created with fresh, seasonal ingredients (many of the fruits and vegetables come from the restaurant's own farm, as does the lamb.)
American menu. Dinner. Bar. Casual attire. Closed Monday. **$$**

★★No. Five-O
50 Shore Rd., Ogunquit, 207-646-5001;
www.five-oshoreroad.com
American menu. Dinner. Bar. Casual attire. Reservations recommended. Outdoor seating. Closed December 24-28, late February-late March. **$$**

★Oarweed Cove
Oarweed Rd., Ogunquit, 207-646-4022;
www.oarweed.com
American, seafood menu. Lunch, dinner. Bar. Children's menu. Casual attire. Valet parking. Outdoor seating. Closed mid-October to early May. **$$**

★Ogunquit Lobster Pound
504 Main St., Ogunquit, 207-646-2516
Seafood menu. Dinner. Closed mid-November to mid-February. Bar. Children's menu. Casual attire. Outdoor seating. **$$**

★★Old Village Inn
250 Main St., Ogunquit, 207-646-7088;
www.theoldvillageinn.com
This cozy and romantic restaurant features Victorian decor and is located in a mid-19th-century inn. American menu. Dinner. Bar. Children's menu. **$$**

★★S. W. Swan Bistro
309 Shore Rd., Ogunquit, 207-646-7210;
www.swanbistro.com
American, French menu. Dinner. Bar. Casual attire. Reservations recommended. Outdoor seating. **$$$**

OLD ORCHARD BEACH
This popular beach resort, 12 miles south of Portland, is a long-time favorite on the Maine Coast. It has a crescent beach seven miles long and about 700 feet wide.
Information: Chamber of Commerce, 207-934-2500, 800-365-9386; www.oldorchardbeachmaine.com

WHAT TO SEE AND DO

The Pier

Old Orchard Beach

Extends 475 feet into the harbor; features shops, boutiques, restaurant. May-September, daily.

HOTELS

★**The Edgewater**

57 W. Grand Ave., Old Orchard Beach, 207-934-2221, 800-203-2034; www.janelle.com

35 rooms. Closed mid-November to mid-March. Outdoor pool. **$**

★**The Gull Motel Inn & Cottages**

89 W. Grand Ave., Old Orchard Beach, 207-934-4321, 877-662-4855; www.gullmotel.com

25 rooms. Outdoor pool. Closed mid-October to April. **$**

★**Horizon**

2 Atlantic Ave., Old Orchard Beach, 207-934-2323, 888-550-1745; www.horizonmotel.com

14 rooms, all suites. Closed mid-October to April. **$**

★**Royal Anchor Resort**

203 E. Grand Ave., Old Orchard Beach, 207-934-4521, 800-934-4521; www.royalanchor.com

40 rooms. Complimentary continental breakfast. Outdoor pool. Tennis. Closed mid-October to April. **$**

SPECIALTY LODGINGS

Atlantic Birches Inn

20 Portland Ave., Old Orchard Beach, 207-934-5295, 888-934-5295; www.atlanticbirches.com

Restored Victorian house.

10 rooms. Complimentary continental breakfast. Outdoor pool. **$**

RESTAURANTS

★★**Bell Buoy Restaurant**

24 Old Orchard St., Old Orchard Beach, 207-934-2745

American, seafood menu. Breakfast, dinner. Bar. Children's menu. Casual attire. Reservations recommended. **$$**

★★**Captain's Galley Restaurant**

168 Saco Ave., Old Orchard Beach, 207-934-1336

Seafood, steak menu. Breakfast, lunch, dinner. Bar. Children's menu. Casual attire. **$$**

★★★**Joseph's by the Sea**

55 W. Grand Ave., Old Orchard Beach, 207-934-5044; www.josephsbythesea.com

American, seafood menu. Breakfast, dinner. Bar. Casual attire. Reservations recommended. Outdoor seating. Closed December 25-April; hours vary in May, November-December. **$$**

★★**Oceanside Grille at the Brunswick**

39 W. Grand Ave., Old Orchard Beach, 207-934-4873; www.thebrunswick.com

American, seafood menu. Lunch, dinner, late-night. Bar. Casual attire. Reservations recommended. Outdoor seating. **$$**

73

MAINE

★
★
★
★

ORONO

The Penobscot River flows through this valley town, which is named after Native American chief Joseph Orono. The "Maine Stein Song" was popularized here in the 1930s by Rudy Vallee.

Information: Bangor Region Chamber of Commerce, 519 Main St., Bangor, 207-947-0307; www.bangorregion.com

WHAT TO SEE AND DO

University of Maine-Orono

5703 Alumni Hall, Orono,
207-581-1110; www.umaine.edu
This is the largest of seven campuses of the University of Maine system. On campus is Jordan Planetarium (207-581-1341).

RESTAURANTS

★★Margarita's

15 Mill St., Orono, 207-866-4863;
www.margs.com
American, Mexican menu. Lunch, dinner. Bar. Children's menu. Casual attire. **$$**

PORTLAND

Maine's largest city is located on Casco Bay and dotted with islands that are popular with summer visitors. Because of its size, affordable housing and free-spirited feel, Portland is increasingly popular as an alternative to the nation's biggest cities (and absorbs Boston refugees annually). It's a city of fine elms, stately old homes, historic churches and charming streets. Portland was raided by Native Americans several times before the Revolution. In 1775, it was bombarded by the British, who afterward burned the town. Another fire, in 1866, wiped out large sections of the city. Henry Wadsworth Longfellow, the famed poet who lived in Portland, remarked that the ruins reminded him of Pompeii.

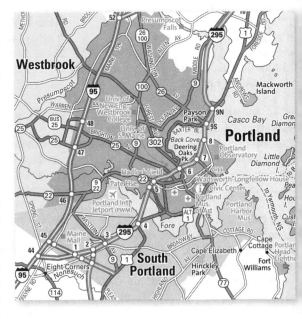

Information: Convention & Visitors Bureau of Greater Portland, 305 Commercial St., 207-772-5800; www.visitportland.com

SPOT★ LIGHT

★PORTLAND IS MAINE'S LARGEST CITY WITH A POPULATION OF MORE THAN 63,000.

★THE CITY HAS BEEN DEVASTATED BY FIRE FOUR TIMES IN ITS HISTORY.

★POET HENRY WADSWORTH LONGFELLOW WAS BORN IN PORTLAND.

WHAT TO SEE AND DO

Children's Museum of Maine

142 Free St., Portland, 207-828-1234;
www.childrensmuseumofme.org
Hands-on museum where interactive exhibits allow children to become a Maine lobsterman, storekeeper, computer expert or astronaut. Memorial Day-Labor Day, daily; rest of year, Tuesday-Sunday.

Maine History Gallery

489 Congress St., Portland, 207-774-1822
Features Museum's Collection with more than 2,000 paintings, prints and other original works of art, and approximately 8,000 artifacts. Collection includes costume and textiles, decorative arts, Native American artifacts and archaeological material, political items and military artifacts. Changing programs and exhibits trace the history of

life in Maine. Gallery talks and hands-on workshops also offered. (Daily)

Portland Head Lighthouse Museum
1000 Shore Rd., Cape Elizabeth,
207-799-2661,
www.portlandheadlight.com
(1791) Said to be first lighthouse authorized by the United States and oldest lighthouse in continuous use; erected on orders from George Washington. June-October: daily. November-December and April-May: weekends.

Portland Museum of Art
7 Congress Square, Portland,
207-775-6148; www.portlandmuseum.org
Collections of American and European painting, sculpture, prints and decorative art; State of Maine Collection with works by artists from and associated with Maine; John Whitney Payson Collection (Renoir, Monet, Picasso and others). Free admission Friday evenings. May-October: daily; November-April: Tuesday-Sunday.

Portland Observatory
138 Congress St., Portland,
207-774-5561
(1807) This octagonal, shingled landmark is the last surviving 19th-century signal tower on the Atlantic. There are 102 steps to the top. Memorial Day-Columbus Day, daily.

Tate House
1270 Westbrook St., Portland,
207-774-6177; www.tatehouse.org
(1755) Georgian structure built by George Tate, mast agent for the British Navy. Furnished and decorated in the period of Tate's residence, 1755-1800; 18th-century herb gardens. Mid-June-mid-October: Tuesday-Sunday; weekends through Oct. 31.

Victoria Mansion
109 Danforth St., Portland,
207-772-4841;
www.victoriamansion.org
(1858) One of the finest examples of 19th-century architecture surviving in the United States. Opulent Victorian interior includes frescoes, carved woodwork and stained and etched glass. May-October, Tuesday-Sunday.

Wadsworth-Longfellow House
489 Congress St., Portland,
207-772-1807
(1785) Boyhood home of Henry Wadsworth Longfellow. Built by the poet's grandfather, General Peleg Wadsworth, it is maintained by the Maine Historical Society. Contains furnishings, portraits and personal possessions of the family. June to mid-October, daily.

SPECIAL EVENTS
New Year's Eve Portland
582 Congress St., Portland, 207-772-5800
Fifteen indoor and many outdoor locations. More than 90 performances, mid-afternoon to midnight; a citywide, non-alcoholic celebration with parade and fireworks. December 31.

Old Port Festival
400 Congress St., Portland, 207-772-6828
Celebration of Portland's restored waterfront district between Commercial Street and Congress Street. This one-day event features a parade, entertainment and food. Early June.

Sidewalk Art Show
1 Congress Square, Portland,
207-772-5800
Exhibits extend along Congress Street from Congress Square to Monument Square. Third Saturday in August.

HOTELS
★★Best Western Merry Manor Inn
700 Main St., South Portland,
207-774-6151, 800-780-7234;
www.merrymanorinn.com
153 rooms. Pets accepted. High-speed Internet access, wireless Internet access. Restaurant. Fitness room. Outdoor pool, children's pool, whirlpool. Airport transportation available. Business center. $

★

★

★

★

★★★Eastland Park Hotel
157 High St., Portland,
207-775-5411, 888-671-8008;
www.eastlandparkhotel.com
202 rooms. Pets accepted; fee. High-speed Internet access, wireless Internet access. Restaurant. Bar. Fitness room. Airport transportation available. Business center. $$

★★Embassy Suites
1050 Westbrook St., Portland,
207-775-2200, 800-753-8767;
www.embassysuitesportland.com
This hotel is located close to the Portland International Jetport and the Maine Mall (complimentary shuttle service is provided to both). Guest rooms feature a separate sitting area and sleeping room, plush beds, two small desks and a wet bar with microwave. An evening manager's reception (with a three-piece band) is offered on Thursdays.
119 rooms, all suites. Pets accepted. Complimentary full breakfast. High-speed Internet access, wireless Internet access. Restaurant. Bar. Fitness room. Indoor pool, whirlpool. Airport transportation available. Business center. $$

★Hampton Inn
171 Philbrook Ave., South Portland,
207-773-4400, 800-426-7866;
www.portlandhamptoninn.com
117 rooms. Pets accepted; fee. Complimentary continental breakfast. High-speed Internet access. Airport transportation available. $

★★Holiday Inn
88 Spring St., Portland,
207-775-2311, 800-345-5050;
www.innbythebay.com
239 rooms. High-speed Internet access, wireless Internet access. Restaurant. Bar. Fitness room. Indoor pool. Airport transportation available. Business center. $$

★★★Portland Marriott at Sable Oaks
200 Sable Oaks Dr., South Portland,
207-871-8000, 800-752-8810;

www.marriott.com
Just a few miles from the Portland International Jetport and close to historic downtown Portland, this hotel is situated on a hill in a surprisingly rural setting. A small pond with a fountain and covered portico welcomes guests at the hotel entry. Guest rooms feature a spacious work desk, two-line phone, speaker phone, voice mail and data ports. Nearby activities include golf, jogging, tennis, a spa and the beach.
227 rooms. Pets accepted, some restrictions; fee. High-speed Internet access, wireless Internet access. Two restaurants, bar. Fitness room. Indoor pool, whirlpool. Golf, 18 holes. Airport transportation available. Business center. $$

★★★Portland Harbor Hotel
468 Fore St., Portland,
207-775-9090, 888-798-9090;
www.portlandharborhotel.com
This hotel is located in the Old Port district of downtown Portland, a fully restored area of Victorian buildings that are now restaurants, shops and galleries, just one block from the waterfront. A boutique hotel, it exudes European style and charm. An enclosed garden patio with a fountain is just off the lobby dining room. Guest rooms feature toile spreads, custom mattresses with fine linens, feather pillows and duvets and a two-level desk with a leather chair.
97 rooms. Pets accepted, some restrictions; fee. Wireless Internet access. Restaurant. Bar. Fitness room. Airport transportation available. Business center. $$

★★★Portland Regency Hotel & Spa
20 Milk St., Portland,
207-774-4200, 800-727-3436;
www.theregency.com
This small European-style hotel is located in Portland's Old Port waterfront district, surrounded by galleries, shops and restaurants. A circular brick driveway leads guests to the historic red brick building, which was built in 1895. The lobby and public rooms hold true to the hotel's heritage, with mahogany woodwork, Victorian

furnishings and a "map room" with burgundy leather chairs. The period decor in the guest rooms includes two or four-poster beds and antique or reproduction dressers, tables and desks. The spa offers a complete selection of treatments.
95 rooms. Wireless Internet access. Restaurant. Bar. Fitness room, spa. Whirlpool. Airport transportation available. Business center. **$$**

★★★Inn By The Sea
40 Bowery Beach Rd., Cape Elizabeth, 207-799-3134, 800-888-4287; www.innbythesea.com
This all-suite resort property is located close to the historic city of Portland on the coast. Every guest room has a porch or deck with a view of the ocean. Recreational activities include an outdoor pool, tennis, shuffleboard, walking or jogging and volleyball. Amenities for guests include terry robes and turndown service with a 24-hour business and concierge service.
43 rooms, all suites. Pets accepted, some restrictions. Restaurant. Outdoor pool. Tennis. **$$**

★★★Black Point Inn
510 Black Point Rd., Scarborough, 207-883-2500, 800-258-0003; www.blackpointinn.com
This seaside resort is located on a hill at the tip of Prout's Neck with the natural rugged beauty of the Maine coast on three sides. There are numerous rooms and many cottages, which were former sea captains' homes. Each room has period wallpaper and both porcelain and crystal lamps.
65 rooms. Pets accepted, some restrictions; fee. Restaurant. Bar. Fitness room. Beach. Indoor pool, outdoor pool, whirlpool. Airport transportation available. Closed December-April. **$$$**

SPECIALTY LODGINGS

Inn at Saint John
939 Congress St., Portland, 207-773-6481, 800-636-9127; www.innatstjohn.com

Built in 1896; European motif, antiques. 39 rooms. Pets accepted, some restrictions. Complimentary continental breakfast. Airport transportation available. **$**

Inn on Carleton
46 Carleton St., Portland, 207-775-1910, 800-639-1779; www.innoncarleton.com
This brick townhouse was built in 1869. 6 rooms. Children over 9 years only. Complimentary full breakfast. **$$**

Pomegranate Inn
49 Neal St., Portland, 207-772-1006, 800-356-0408; www.pomegranateinn.com
This inn (built in 1884) is small, yet sophisticated and located in the Western Promende historic neighborhood. There are antiques and art throughout the property, as well as an urban garden for guests to enjoy. It is a short walk to the midtown arts district and there are museums, art galleries, boat rides, fine restaurants and recreational activities nearby.
8 rooms. Children over 16 years only. Complimentary full breakfast. **$$**

RESTAURANTS

★★★Back Bay Grill
65 Portland St., Portland, 207-772-8833; www.backbaygrill.com
Located in downtown Portland in a restored pharmacy (1888), this local favorite offers innovative cuisine and an intimate dining room. The pressed-tin ceiling adds to the ambience of the cozy rooms. The daily menu features the freshest locally sourced foods (the restaurant is a member of the Maine Organic Farmers Growers Association) and emphasizes fresh, high-quality ingredients. Special dinners are offered with a prix fixe menu (wine tastings, wine dinners, lobster evenings).
American menu. Dinner. Closed Sunday. Bar. Business casual attire. Reservations recommended. **$$$**

★★Di Millo's Floating Restaurant
25 Long Wharf, Portland,

★

★

★

★

207-772-2216; www.dimillos.com
American, seafood menu. Lunch, dinner, late-night. Bar. Children's menu. Casual attire. Reservations recommended. Outdoor seating. **$$**

★★Eggspectation
125 Western Ave., South Portland,
207-871-7000;
www.eggspectationusa.com
American menu. Breakfast, lunch, dinner. Bar. Children's menu. Casual attire. Reservations recommended. Outdoor seating. **$$**

★★Fore Street
288 Fore St., Portland, 207-775-2717
Seafood, steak menu. Dinner. Bar. Casual attire. Reservations recommended. **$$**

★★★Natasha
82 Exchange St., Portland, 207-774-4004
Natasha is located in downtown Portland, on the edge of the historic waterfront district. The decor is sophisticated, with modern art, brick walls, cushioned banquette seating and inlaid tabletops. The menu is influenced by the flavors of the Mediterranean, with dishes such as garlicky chicken marinated in herbs de provence.
International menu. Lunch, dinner. Bar. Business casual attire. Reservations recommended. Outdoor seating. Closed Sunday. **$$**

★Newick's Seafood
740 Broadway, South Portland,
207-799-3090, 877-439-0255;
www.newicks.com
Seafood menu. Lunch, dinner. Bar. Children's menu. Casual attire. Closed Monday (off-season). **$**

★★★Park Kitchen
422 N.W. Eighth Ave., Portland,
503-223-7275; www.parkkitchen.com
Wines and microbrews are recommended for each entrée that chef Scott Dolich creates at this welcoming restaurant, which features an open kitchen. Located in a historic building along the North Park blocks, the food here is influenced by the seasons, with dishes such as lamb cassoulet mak-

ing an appearance in winter, while salmon with cucumber and caraway is a summer specialty.
American menu, other. Lunch, dinner. Brunch. Bar. Children's menu. Casual attire. Reservations recommended. Outdoor seating. Closed Monday. **$$**

★★Ribolita
41 Middle St., Portland, 207-774-2972
Italian menu. Dinner. Children's menu. Casual attire. Reservations recommended. Outdoor seating. Closed Sunday-Monday. **$$**

★★★The Roma Café
769 Congress St., Portland,
207-773-9873; www.theromacafe.com
Located in a Victorian mansion (circa 1887), this restaurant features small dining rooms with fireplaces, a beautiful carved wood staircase and beveled glass windows in a charming atmosphere. Menu offerings include seafood, lobster and Italian dishes.
Italian, seafood menu. Lunch, dinner. Bar. Casual attire. Reservations recommended. Closed Sunday-Monday. **$$**

★★★Street & Co.
33 Wharf St., Portland, 207-775-0887
Located in the Old Port District on a cobblestone street, this 19th-century building was formerly a fish warehouse. The decor is upscale rustic, with exposed bricks, original plank hardwood flooring and beamed ceilings. Tables are heavy black stone slabs with rough-hewn wood legs. A fully open kitchen is opposite the center dining room, which offers large windows that open to the street. Only seafood is served, along with the freshest seasonal organic produce.
American, seafood menu. Dinner. Bar. Casual attire. Reservations recommended. **$$$**

★★Typhoon! On Broadway
410 S.W. Broadway, Portland,
503-243-7577;
www.typhoonrestaurants.com

78

MAINE

Thai menu. Lunch, dinner. Casual attire. Reservations recommended. Outdoor seating. **$$**

★★Village Café
112 Newbury St., Portland,
207-772-5320, 800-866-5320;
www.villagecafemaine.com
American, Italian menu. Lunch, dinner. Bar. Children's menu. Casual attire. Res-ervations recommended. Outdoor seating. **$$**

★★Walter's Café
15 Exchange St., Portland,
207-871-9258; www.walterscafe.com
International menu. Lunch, dinner. Bar. Business casual attire. Reservations recommended. **$$**

RANGELEY

There are 40 lakes and ponds within 10 miles of Rangeley. The six lakes that form the Rangeley chain—Rangeley, Cupsuptic, Mooselookmeguntic, Aziscoos, Upper Richardson and Lower Richardson—spread over a wide area and give rise to the Androscoggin River. Some of Maine's highest mountains rise beside the lakes. The development of ski and snowmobiling areas has turned this summer vacation spot into a year-round resort.
Information: Rangeley Lakes Chamber of Commerce,
207-864-5364, 800-685-2537; www.rangeleymaine.com

WHAT TO SEE AND DO
Rangeley Lake State Park
S. Shore Dr., Rangeley, 207-864-3858
More than 690 acres on Rangeley Lake. Swimming, fishing, boating (ramp, floating docks); snowmobiling permitted; picnicking, camping. Standard fees. May-October.

Wilhelm Reich Museum
19 Dodge Pond Rd., Rangeley,
207-864-3443;
www.wilhelmreichmuseum.org
Unusual stone building housing scientific equipment, paintings and other memorabilia of this physician-scientist; slide presentation, nature trail, discovery room. July-August: Wednesday-Sunday; September: Sunday only; rest of year: by appointment.

HOTELS
★★Country Club Inn
1 Country Club Dr., Rangeley,
207-864-3831;
www.countryclubinnrangeley.com
19 rooms. Pets accepted, some restrictions; fee. Restaurant. Bar. Outdoor pool. Airport transportation available. Closed April, November. **$$**

★★★Rangeley Inn
2443 Main St., Rangeley,
207-864-3341, 800-666-3687;
www.rangeleyinn.com
This restored inn is located within the mountain lake wilderness of the Longfellow mountains of western Maine. The year-round resort offers skiing and snowmobiling in the winter and swimming and boating in the summer. Moose can be spotted here, and loons can be both seen and heard.
50 rooms. Pets accepted, some restrictions; fee. Restaurant. Bar. **$**

RESTAURANTS
★★★Rangeley Inn
51 Main St., Rangeley, 207-864-3341;
www.rangeleyinn.com
This romantic inn has been open for more than 90 years, and the dining room still showcases an ornate tin ceiling and chandeliers. Enjoy an elegant dinner in the main dining room and then retire to the pub that has a crackling fire in the fireplace and local microbrews on tap.
American, seafood menu. Breakfast, dinner. Bar. Children's menu. Outdoor seating. Closed Sunday-Thursday; also April-May. **$**

ROCKLAND

This town on Penobscot Bay is the banking and commercial center of the region and the seat of Knox County. It is also the birthplace of the poet Edna St. Vincent Millay. Its economy is geared to the resort trade, but there is commercial fishing and light industry. It is the railhead for the whole bay. Supplies for boats, public landing and guest moorings are here.

Information: Rockland-Thomaston Area Chamber of Commerce, 207-596-0376, 800-562-2529; www.therealmaine.com

WHAT TO SEE AND DO

Farnsworth Art Museum and Wyeth Center

16 Museum St., Rockland, 207-596-6457; www.farnsworthmuseum.org

Cultural and educational center for the region. Collection of more than 10,000 works of 18th- to 20th-century American art. Center houses personal collection of Wyeth family (N.C., Andrew and Jamie) art and archival material. Memorial Day-Columbus Day: daily; rest of year: Tuesday-Sunday.

Maine Lighthouse Museum

1 Park Dr., Rockland, 207-594-3301; www.mainelighthousemuseum.com

A large collection of lighthouse lenses and artifacts; Civil War collection. Museum shop. Daily.

Maine State Ferry Service

517A Main St., Rockland, 207-596-2202

Ferries make a 15-mile (1 hour, 15 minute) trip to Vinalhaven and a 12 1/2-mile (1 hour, 10 minute) trip to North Haven. (All year, two to three trips daily.) Also a 23-mile (2 hour, 15 minute) trip to Matinicus Island once a month.

Windjammers

Maine Windjammer Association, 800-807-9463; www.sailmainecoast.com

Twelve old-time schooners sail out for three to six days following the same basic route through Penobscot Bay into Blue Hill and Frenchman's Bay, stopping at small villages and islands along the way. Each ship carries an average of 30 passengers. For further information, rates, schedules or reservations, contact the Maine Windjammer Association. Memorial Day-Columbus Day.

SPECIAL EVENTS

Maine Lobster Festival

Harbor Park, or at the public landing, Rockland, 207-596-0376, 800-562-2529

A five-day event centered on Maine's chief marine creature, with a huge tent cafeteria serving lobster and other seafood. Parade, harbor cruises, maritime displays, bands, entertainment. First weekend in August.

Schooner Days & North Atlantic Blues Festival

Rockland Harbor, 207-596-0376

Three-day festival celebrating Maine's maritime heritage, featuring a parade of the area's fleet of historic schooners, arts, entertainment, concessions, fireworks, blues bands and club crawl. Weekend after July 4.

HOTELS

★Glen Cove Motel

Highway 1, Glen Cove, 207-594-4062, 800-453-6268; www.glencovemotel.com

36 rooms. Outdoor pool. Closed February. $

★★★Samoset Resort

220 Warrenton St., Rockport, 207-594-2511, 800-341-1650; www.samoset.com

Named for the chief of the Pemaquid Indians who greeted the Pilgrims, this inn has welcomed guests since 1889. It is a year-round resort set on 230 ocean-side acres of the rugged coast of Maine.

80

MAINE

178 rooms. Restaurant. Bar. Children's activity center. Fitness room. Indoor pool, outdoor pool, whirlpool. Tennis. **$$**

★★★Captain Lindsey House Inn
5 Lindsey St., Rockland,
207-596-7950, 800-523-2145;
www.lindseyhouse.com

This inn (built in 1830) is located in downtown Rockland, close to galleries, shops and the waterfront. The guest rooms have furnishings from around the world. 10 rooms. Children over 10 years only. Complimentary continental breakfast. Restaurant. **$$**

SPECIALTY LODGINGS
Craignair Inn
5 Third St., Spruce Head,
207-594-7644, 800-320-9997;
www.craignair.com

Built in 1930; boarding house converted to an inn in 1947.
21 rooms. Pets accepted, some restrictions; fee. Complimentary full breakfast. Restaurant. **$**

Lakeshore Inn
184 Lakeview Dr., Rockland,
207-594-4209, 866-540-8800;
www.lakeshorebb.com

This Colonial New England farmhouse was built in 1767.
4 rooms. Children over 12 years only. Complimentary full breakfast. Whirlpool. **$$**

RESTAURANTS
★Harbor View
Thomaston Landing, Thomaston,
207-354-8173

Seafood, steak menu. Lunch, dinner. Bar. Outdoor seating. Closed Sunday-Monday (November-April). **$$**

★★★Primo
2 S. Main St., Rockland, 207-596-0770;
www.primorestaurant.com

An ardent supporter of sustainable agriculture, chef Melissa Kelly uses mostly local, organic produce (much of it grown on the restaurant's farm) and makes vegetables present, even in meat dishes. The menu, which changes weekly, draws from coastal Italy and France, and features everything from asparagus soup with goat cheese to olive oil–poached salmon with bitter greens and beets to wood-roasted oysters. Co-owner and pastry chef Price Kushner contributes equally savory desserts.
American menu. Dinner. Bar. Casual attire. Reservations recommended. Closed Tuesday. **$$$**

81

MAINE

ROCKWOOD
This town is located on the shores of Moosehead Lake, the state's largest lake. Though the area is rustic and largely unspoiled, it's a favorite of hikers, campers and tourists.

WHAT TO SEE AND DO
Northern Outdoors, Inc.
Martins Pond and Hwy. 201, Rockwood,
207-663-4466, 800-765-7238;
www.northernoutdoors.com

Specializes in outdoor adventures including whitewater rafting on Maine's Kennebec, Penobscot and Dead rivers (May-October). Also snowmobiling (rentals), hunting, and resort facilities, rock climbing and freshwater kayak touring.

Wilderness Expeditions, Inc.
207-534-2242, 800-825-9453;
www.birches.com

Whitewater rafting on the Kennebec, Penobscot and Dead rivers; also canoe trips and ski tours. May-September: daily.

HOTELS
★★Moosehead Motel
16 Moosehead Motel Lane, Rockwood,
207-534-7787;
www.maineguide.com/moosehead/motel
14 rooms. Restaurant. **$**

★

★

★

★

RUMFORD

This papermill town is located in the valley of the Oxford Hills, where the Ellis, Swift and Concord rivers flow into the Androscoggin. The spectacular Penacook Falls of the Androscoggin are right in town. Rumford serves as a year-round resort area.

Information: River Valley Chamber of Commerce, 34 River St., 207-364-3241; www.rivervalleychamber.com

WHAT TO SEE AND DO

Mount Blue State Park

Hwy. 142, Weld, 207-585-2347

Recreation areas on Lake Webb include swimming, bathhouse, lifeguard, fishing, boating (ramp, rentals); hiking trail to Mount Blue, cross-country skiing, snowmobiling permitted, picnicking, camping. Memorial Day-Labor Day.

HOTELS

★Blue Iris Motor Inn

1405 U.S. Route 2, Rumford,

207-364-4495, 800-601-1515; www.blueiris.50megs.com 13 rooms. Outdoor pool. $

★★Madison Resort Inn

Highway 2, Rumford, 207-364-7973, 800-258-6234; www.madisoninn.com 38 rooms. Pets accepted. Restaurant. Bar. Fitness room. Outdoor pool, whirlpool. $

SACO

Saco, on the east bank of the Saco River, was originally called Pepperellboro, until its name was changed in 1805. Saco is only four miles from the ocean.

Information: Biddeford/Saco Chamber of Commerce, 110 Main St., 207-282-1567; www.biddefordsacochamber.com

WHAT TO SEE AND DO

Dyer Library & Saco Museum

371 Main St., Saco, 207-283-3861

Public library has arts and cultural programs. Museum features local history, decorative and fine art; American paintings, ceramics, glass, clocks and furniture; changing exhibits. Tuesday-Friday.

Ferry Beach State Park

Highway 9, Saco, 207-283-0067

Beach, swimming, picnicking, nature and cross-country trails. Standard fees. Memorial Day-Labor Day: daily.

RESTAURANTS

★★Cascade Inn

941 Portland Rd., Saco, 207-283-3271

American, seafood menu. Lunch, dinner. Bar. Children's menu. Reservations recommended. $$

SCARBOROUGH

Scarborough contains some industry, but it is primarily a farming community and has been for more than 300 years. It is also a bustling tourist town during the summer months as vacationers descend upon nearby beaches and resorts. The first Anglican church in Maine is here, as is painter Winslow Homer's studio, now a national landmark.

Information: Convention & Visitors Bureau of Greater Portland, 305 Commercial St., Portland, 207-772-5800; www.visitportland.com

MAINE

WHAT TO SEE AND DO

Scarborough Marsh Audubon Center

Pine Point Rd., Scarborough,
207-883-5100; www.maineaudubon.org
Miles of nature and waterway trails through
marshland area; canoe tours, special programs. Mid-June-Labor Day: daily.

HOTELS

★Fairfield Inn

2 Cummings Rd., Scarborough,
207-883-0300, 800-228-2800;
www.fairfieldinn.com
120 rooms. Complimentary continental
breakfast. Check-in 3 p.m., check-out noon.
Outdoor pool. **$**

**★Towneplace Suites By Marriott Portland
Scarborough**

700 Roundwood Dr., Scarborough,
207-883-6800, 800-491-2268;
www.towneplacesuites.com
95 rooms. Pets accepted; fee. Fitness room.
Outdoor pool. **$**

SEARSPORT

On the quiet upper reaches of Penobscot Bay, this is an old seafaring town. In the 1870s, at
least 10 percent of the captains of the U.S. Merchant Marines lived here. The village abounds
with antiques shops and is sometimes referred to as the "antique capital of Maine."
Information: Chamber of Commerce, Main St., 207-548-6510

WHAT TO SEE AND DO

Penobscot Marine Museum

5 Church St., Searsport, 207-548-2529;
www.penobscotmarinemuseum.org
Old Town Hall (1845), Merithew House
(circa 1860), Fowler-True-Ross House
(1825), Phillips Library and Carver Memorial Gallery. Ship models, marine paintings,
American and Asian furnishings. Memorial
Day weekend-mid-October: daily; rest of
year, Monday-Saturday.

SPECIALTY LODGINGS

Inn Britannia

132 W. Main St., Searsport,
207-548-2007, 866-466-2748;
www.innbritannia.com
This former captain's house was built in
1850.
8 rooms. Pets accepted, some restrictions;
fee, Children over 11 years only. Compli-
mentary full breakfast. **$$**

SEBAGO LAKE

The second-largest of Maine's lakes, this is perhaps the most popular, partly because of its
proximity to Portland. About 12 miles long and 8 miles wide, it lies among wooded hills.
Boats can travel a total of more than 40 miles from the south end of Sebago Lake, through
the Songo River to the north end of Long Lake. Numerous resort communities are hidden
in the trees along the shores. Sebago, home of the landlocked salmon (*Salmo sebago*), is
also stocked with lake trout.

WHAT TO SEE AND DO

Marrett House and Garden

Highway 25, Standish, 207-642-3032
Built in 1789 in Georgian style, but later
enlarged and remodeled in the Greek
Revival fashion; period furnishings; farm
implements. Coin from Portland banks was
stored here during the War of 1812, when
it was thought that the British would take
Portland. Perennial and herb garden. Tours
June-October, first Saturday of the month.

HOTELS

★★★Migis Lodge

Hwy. 302, South Casco, 207-655-4524;
www.migis.com
This property is set on more than 100 acres
of wooded land on the shore of a lake.
A gift shop sells crafts from Maine. Wood

83

MAINE

for the fireplace in each guest room is delivered daily and there are handmade quilts on every bed and fresh flowers in the room.
58 rooms. Restaurant. Bar. Children's activity center. Fitness room. Beach. Tennis. Airport transportation available. Closed mid-October-May. $$$

SKOWHEGAN

Skowhegan, on the Kennebec River, is surrounded by beautiful lakes. Shoes, paper pulp and other wood products are made here. In the village's center, there is a 12-ton, 62-foot-high Native American carved of native pine by Bernard Langlais. Skowhegan is the birthplace of Margaret Chase Smith, who served three terms in the U.S. House of Representatives and four terms in the Senate.
Information: Chamber of Commerce, 23 Commercial St., 207-474-3621, 888-772-4392; www.skoweganchamber.com

WHAT TO SEE AND DO
History House
2 Coburn Ave., Skowhegan, 207-474-6632
(1839) Old household furnishings; museum contains books, china, dolls and documents. Mid-June to mid-September: Tuesday-Friday afternoons.

SPECIAL EVENTS
Skowhegan State Fair
Madison Ave., Fairgrounds, Skowhegan, 207-474-2947;

www.skoweganstatefair.com
One of the oldest in the country (1818). One-mile-long midway, stage shows, harness racing; contests, exhibits. August.

RESTAURANTS
★★Heritage House
182 Madison Ave., Skowhegan, 207-474-5100
Seafood, steak menu. Lunch, dinner. Bar. Casual attire. $$

RESTAURANTS
★★Barnhouse Tavern Restaurant
61 Highway 35, Windham, 207-892-2221; www.barnhousetavern.com
Seafood, steak menu. Lunch, dinner. Bar. Outdoor seating. Closed Monday. $$

SOUTHWEST HARBOR

This is a prosperous, working seacoast village on Mount Desert Island. There are lobster wharves, where visitors can watch about 70 fishermen bring in their catch, and many shops where boats are constructed. Visitors can also rent sailboats and power boats in Southwest Harbor to explore the coves and islands; hiking trails and quiet harbors offer relaxation.
Information: Chamber of Commerce, 207-244-9264, 800-423-9264; www.acadia.net/swhtrcoc

WHAT TO SEE AND DO
Cranberry Cove Boating Company
207-244-5882
Cruise to Cranberry Islands. See native wildlife and learn island history. Six departures daily. Departs from Upper Town Dock. Mid-June-mid-September: daily.

Maine State Ferry Service
Grandville Rd., Bass Harbor, 207-244-3254
Ferry makes six-mile (40-minute) trip to Swans Island and 8 1/4-mile (50-minute) trip to Frenchboro (limited schedule). Swans Island (all-year, one to six trips daily).

Mount Desert Oceanarium
172 Clark Point Rd., Southwest Harbor,

MAINE

207-244-7330; www.theoceanarium.com
More than 20 tanks with Gulf of Maine marine creatures. Touch tank permits animals to be picked up. Exhibits on tides, seawater, plankton, fishing gear, weather. Inquire for information on special events. Mid-May-mid-October: Monday-Saturday.

Wendell Gilley Museum
4 Herrick Rd., Southwest Harbor,
207-244-7555;
www.wendellgilleymuseum.org
Art and natural history museum featuring a collection of bird carvings by local artist Wendell Gilley; changing exhibits of local and historical art; films. June-October: Tuesday-Sunday; May and November-December: Friday-Sunday.

SPECIALTY LODGINGS
The Clark Point Inn
109 Clark Point Rd., Southwest Harbor,

207-244-9828, 888-775-5953;
www.clarkpointinn.com
Captain's house (1857); deck with harbor view.
5 rooms. Children over 8 years only. Complimentary full breakfast. Closed mid-October to April. **$$**

Kingsleigh Inn
373 Main St., Southwest Harbor,
207-244-5302; www.kingsleighinn.com
Built in 1904, wraparound porch.
8 rooms. Children over 10 years only. Complimentary full breakfast. **$**

RESTAURANTS
★Beal's Lobster Pier
182 Clark Point Rd., Southwest Harbor,
207-244-3202
Seafood menu. Lunch, dinner. Casual attire. Outdoor seating. **$$**

WATERVILLE

A large Native American village once occupied the west bank of the Kennebec River where many of Waterville's factories now stand. An important industrial town, Waterville is the center of the Belgrade and China lakes resort area. Manufactured goods include men's and women's shirts, paper and molded pulp products and woolens.
Information: Mid-Maine Chamber of Commerce, One Post Office Square, 207-873-3315; www.mid-mainechamber.com

WHAT TO SEE AND DO
Colby College
4601 Mayflower Hill Dr., Waterville,
207-872-3000; www.colby.edu
(1813) (1,700 students) This 714-acre campus includes an art museum in the Bixler Art and Music Center (daily; free); a Walcker organ designed by Albert Schweitzer in Lorimer Chapel; and books, manuscripts and letters of Maine authors Edwin Arlington Robinson and Sarah Jewett in the Miller Library. Monday-Friday; free.

Redington Museum
62 Silver St., Waterville, 207-872-9439
(1814) Waterville Historical Society collection includes 18th-and 19th-century furnishings, manuscripts, Civil War and Native American relics; historical library;

children's room; apothecary museum. Mid-May-Labor Day: Tuesday-Saturday.

Two-Cent Footbridge
Front St., Waterville
One of the few remaining former toll footbridges in the United States.

HOTELS
★★Best Western Waterville Inn
356 Main St., Waterville,
207-873-3335, 800-780-7234;
www.bestwestern.com
86 rooms. Pets accepted. Restaurant. Bar. Outdoor pool. **$**

★★Holiday Inn
375 Upper Main St., Waterville,
207-873-0111, 888-465-4329;

www.holiday-inn.com
139 rooms. Pets accepted, some restrictions. Restaurant. Bar. Fitness room. Indoor pool, whirlpool. **$**

RESTAURANTS

★Big G's Deli
581 Benton Ave., Winslow, 207-873-7808
Deli menu. Breakfast, lunch, dinner. Children's menu. **$**

★★John Martin's Manor
54 College Ave., Waterville, 207-873-5676;
www.johnmartinsmanor.com
American, seafood menu. Lunch, dinner. Bar. Children's menu. Casual attire. Reservations recommended. **$**

★Weathervane
470 Kennedy Memorial Dr., Waterville, 207-873-4522; 800-654-4369; www.weathervaneseafoods.com
Seafood menu. Lunch, dinner. Children's menu. Casual attire. Reservations recommended. **$$**

WELLS

One of the oldest English settlements in Maine, Wells includes Moody, Wells Beach and Drake's Island. It was largely a farming center, with some commercial fishing, until the resort trade began in the 20th century. Charter boats, surfcasting and pier fishing attract anglers; there are also seven miles of beaches for swimming.

Information: Chamber of Commerce, 207-646-2451; www.wellschamber.org

WHAT TO SEE AND DO

Rachel Carson National Wildlife Refuge
Hwy. 9, Wells, 207-646-9226; www.fws.gov/rachelcarson
Approximately 5,000 acres of salt marsh and coastal edge habitat; more than 250 species of birds may be observed during the year. Visitor center; one-mile interpretive nature trail. All year, sunrise-sunset.

Wells Natural Estuarine Research Reserve
342 Laudholm Farm Rd., Wells, 207-646-1555; www.wellsreserve.org
Approximately 1,600 acres of fields, forest, wetlands and beach. Laudholm Farm serves as visitor center. Programs on coastal ecology and stewardship, exhibits and tours. Reserve (daily). Visitor center. May-October: daily; rest of year: Monday-Friday.

HOTELS

★Garrison Suites
1099 Post Rd., Wells, 207-646-3497, 800-646-3497; www.garrisonsuites.com
47 rooms. Pets accepted, some restrictions. Outdoor pool, whirlpool. Closed mid-October-April. **$**

★★Village By The Sea
1373 Post Road., Wells, 207-646-1100, 800-444-8862; www.vbts.com
73 rooms, all suites. Indoor pool, outdoor pool. **$$**

RESTAURANTS

★★Grey Gull
475 Webhannet Dr., Wells, 207-646-7501; www.thegreygullinn.com
American menu. Dinner. Bar. Children's menu. Casual attire. Reservations recommended. **$$**

★Hayloft
Hwy. 1, Moody, 207-646-4400
American, seafood menu. Breakfast, lunch, dinner, brunch. Children's menu. Casual attire. **$$**

★Litchfield's
2135 Post Rd., Wells, 207-646-5711; www.litchfields-restaurant.com

86

MAINE

★
★
★
★
★

American menu. Lunch, dinner. Bar. Children's menu. Casual attire. **$$**

★★Lord's Harborside
352 Harbor Rd., Wells, 207-646-2651.
www.lordsharborside.com
Seafood menu. Lunch, dinner. Bar. Children's menu. Casual attire. Closed Tuesday.
$$

★Maine Diner
2265 Post Rd., Wells, 207-646-4441;
www.mainediner.com
American menu. Breakfast, lunch, dinner, brunch. Children's menu. Casual attire. **$$**

★★Steakhouse
1205 Post Rd., Wells, 207-646-4200
Steak menu. Dinner. Bar. Children's menu. Casual attire. Reservations recommended. Closed Monday. **$$**

WISCASSET

Many artists and writers live here in beautiful old houses put up in the golden days of clipper ship barons and sea captains. Chiefly a summer resort area built around its harbor, Wiscasset is half as populous as it was in 1850. Wiscasset is home to the remains of two ancient wooden schooners, which were hauled into the harbor in 1932.

WHAT TO SEE AND DO
Lincoln County Museum and Old Jail
133 Federal St., Wiscasset, 207-882-6817
First penitentiary built in the District of Maine (1809-1811). Jailer's house has changing exhibits, relics of Lincoln County. June and September: Saturday-Sunday; July-August, Tuesday-Sunday.

Nickels-Sortwell House
121 Main St., Wiscasset,
(1807) Classic Federal-style elegance. Built for a shipmaster in the lumber trade, William Nickels, it was used as a hotel between 1820 and 1900. The mansion was then bought by Mayor Alvin Sortwell of Cambridge, Massachusetts, as a private home. Graceful elliptical stairway; many Sortwell family furnishings; restored garden. June-mid-October: Friday-Sunday.

Pownalborough Courthouse
Dresden, 207-882-6817
(1761) Oldest pre-Revolutionary courthouse in Maine. Three-story building houses furnished courtroom, spinning room, tavern, bedrooms, parlor and kitchen. Nature trails along river; picnic areas; Revolutionary cemetery. June and September: Saturday-Sunday; July-August: Tuesday-Sunday.

SPECIALTY LODGINGS
Cod Cove Inn
22 Cross Rd., Edgecomb,
207-882-9586, 800-882-9586;
www.codcoveinn.com
Located high on a hill, this New England-style inn overlooks the Sheepscott River and the harbor. The grounds include a flowering garden with gazebo and outdoor swimming pool and whirlpool. Area activities include lighthouse touring, antique shopping, whale-watching or dining on lobster.
30 rooms. Complimentary continental breakfast. Outdoor pool, whirlpool.

Squire Tarbox Inn
1181 Main Rd., Westport Island,
207-882-7693; 800-818-0626;
www.squiretarboxinn.com
Restored 18th-century farmhouse situated on working dairy goat farm.
11 rooms. Pets accepted, some restrictions. Complimentary full breakfast. Restaurant. Closed January-March. **$$**

RESTAURANTS
★★Le Garage
Water St., Wiscasset,
207-882-5409
Seafood, steak menu. Lunch, dinner. Bar. **$$**

87

MAINE

★
★
★
★

YARMOUTH

Yarmouth is a quaint New England village 10 miles north of Portland. There are many well-maintained older homes and specialty shops. It is linked by a bridge to Cousins Island in the bay.

Information: Chamber of Commerce, 158 Main St., 207-846-3984; www.yarmouthmaine.org

WHAT TO SEE AND DO

Eartha
2 DeLorme Dr., Yarmouth, 207-846-7000; www.delorme.com
World's largest globe. Three stories high, Eartha is the largest printed image of the Earth ever created and spins in the lobby of the DeLorme Map Company. Daily.

Yarmouth Historical Society Museum
215 Main St., Yarmouth, 207-846-6259
Two galleries with changing exhibits of local and maritime history, fine and decorative arts. Local history research room; historical lecture series. July-August: Monday-Friday afternoons; rest of year: Tuesday-Saturday.

SPECIAL EVENTS

Clam Festival
158 Main St., Yarmouth, 207-846-3984; www.clamfestival.com
Celebration of soft-shelled clams. Arts and crafts, entertainment, parade, fireworks. Third weekend in July.

RESTAURANTS

★★Royal River Grillhouse
106 Lafayette St., Yarmouth, 207-846-1226; www.royalrivergrillhouse.com
American menu. Lunch, dinner, Sunday brunch. Bar. Children's menu. Outdoor seating. $$

88

MAINE

YORK

Originally named Agamenticus by the Plymouth Company, the area was settled in 1624 and chartered as a city—the first in America—in 1641 and renamed Gorgeanna. Following a re-organization in 1652, the "city" in the wilderness took the name York. The present-day York area includes York Village, York Harbor, York Beach and Cape Neddick.

Information: Greater York Region Chamber of Commerce, 1 Stonewall Lane, 207-363-4422; www.yorkme.org

WHAT TO SEE AND DO

Old York Historical Society
140 Lindsay Rd., York, 207-363-4974
Tours of seven buildings dating to the early 1700s. (Mid-June-September) Visitor orientation and tickets at Jefferds Tavern. Administration Office houses museum offices (Monday-Friday) and historical and research library.

Emerson-Wilcox House
York and Lindsey Roads, York
Built in 1742, with later additions. Served at various times as a general store, tavern and post office, as well as the home of two of the town's prominent early families. Now contains a series of period rooms dating to 1750; antique furnishings.

John Hancock Warehouse
York and Lindsey Rds., York, 207-363-4974
Owned by John Hancock until 1794, this is one of the earliest surviving customs houses in Maine. Used now to interpret the maritime history of this coastal village. Mid-June-mid-October: Tuesday-Saturday afternoons.

Old Gaol
Lindsay Rd., York
Built in 1719 with 18th-century additions.

One of the oldest English public buildings in the United States, it was used as a jail until 1860. Dungeons and cells for felons and debtors, as well as galleries of local historical artifacts, and late 1800s photography exhibit.

Sayward-Wheeler House

9 Barrell Lane, York Harbor, 207-384-2454 (1718) Home of the 18th-century merchant and civic leader Tory Jonathan Sayward. Tours. June-October: first Saturday of the month.

HOTELS

★★Anchorage Motor Inn

265 Long Beach Ave., York Beach, 207-363-5112; www.anchorageinn.com
179 rooms. Bar. Fitness room. Two indoor pools, outdoor pool, whirlpool. $

★★★Stage Neck Inn

8 Stage Neck Rd., York Harbor, 207-363-3850, 800-340-1130; www.stageneck.com
This inn is located on an ocean-bound peninsula in York Harbor. The resort offers a beach and is also close to the Kittery outlet malls, antiques shops, art galleries and historic attractions of York.
58 rooms. Restaurant. Bar. Fitness room. Beach. Indoor pool, outdoor pool, whirlpool. Tennis. $$

SPECIALTY LODGINGS

Dockside Guest Quarters

22 Harris Island Rd., York, 207-363-2868, 888-860-7428; www.docksidegq.com
25 rooms. Restaurant. Closed weekdays late October-December, March-Memorial Day, December-February. $$

Edwards Harborside Inn

Stage Neck Rd., York Harbor, 207-363-3037; www.edwardsharborside.com
Turn-of-the-century house with period furnishings.
9 rooms. Complimentary continental breakfast. $$$

York Harbor Inn

Coastal Highway 1A, York Harbor, 207-363-5119, 800-343-3869; www.yorkharborinn.com
54 rooms. Complimentary continental breakfast. Restaurant. Whirlpool. $$

RESTAURANTS

★★Dockside

22 Harris Island Rd., York, 207-363-2722; www.docksidegq.com
Seafood, steak menu. Lunch, dinner. Bar. Casual attire. Reservations recommended. Outdoor seating. Closed Monday; day after Columbus Day-late May $$

★★Fazio's Italian

38 Woodbridge Rd., York, 207-363-7019; www.fazios.com
Italian menu. Dinner. Bar. Children's menu. Casual attire. Reservations recommended. $$

★★★York Harbor Inn

Highway 1A, York Harbor, 207-363-5119; www.yorkharborinn.com
The menu at this seaside inn features local seafood, much of it caught close to the restaurant. Antique furnishings, floral wallpaper and lace curtains add to the ambience of this quaint, colonial inn.
Seafood menu. Dinner, Sunday brunch. Children's menu. Casual attire. Reservations recommended. Closed Monday-Thursday (fall-spring). $$

89

MAINE

★
★
★
★

MASSACHUSETTS

★
★
★
★
★

MASSACHUSETTS

TO SOME, "NEW ENGLAND" MEANS ONE THING: MASSACHUSETTS. OVER FIVE CENTURIES, the Bay State has become the region's emblematic poster child—one rich in historical personality and modern diversions. Case in point: explorer John Cabot (his ancestors would become the ultimate Boston Brahmins) landed on these shores in 1497, just 5 years after Columbus' famed cross-Atlantic trip. The legendary Mayflower soon followed, establishing roots in what would become an area of American greats. Paul Revere, John Hancock, Sam Adams and, of course, the Kennedys all hailed from Massachusetts. So did literary giants like Ralph Waldo Emerson, Henry David Thoreau and Emily Dickenson. But for all its historical heft—it was local patriots who jump-started the American Revolution—the Bay State is not stuck in the past.

Boston, the biggest city in New England, is a lively metropolis, home to booming businesses and the fiercely followed Red Sox. Its residents live in a cross-section of neighborhoods along the (newly clean!) Charles River. The North End, the city's Little Italy, bursts with gelaterias and red sauce–heavy trattorias; the South End, by contrast, is awash in chic clothing boutiques and avant-garde eateries. To the west, north and south of the city stretch verdant, upscale suburbs and quiet, laid-back beach towns. Farther west, along the Massachusetts-New York border is the Berkshires, a county so steeped in arts, culture and culinary experiences, it has become a go-to destination for people several states over.

And then there's Cape Cod and the Islands—Nantucket and Martha's Vineyard—a few of America's most sought-after summer spots. The area's hundreds of miles of coastline and soft, white-sand beaches are a vacationers' paradise. Locals live in gray-shingled homes in small beach hamlets and for the most part, welcome visitors to their postcard-perfect Main Streets. The vibe is Puritan modern, slightly conservative but fun loving.

It is often said that every town in Massachusetts has a small part in the American story. A statewide trip takes travelers from Plymouth Rock, where it all began, to the battle of Bunker Hill, to the philosopher favorite Walden Pond, to the academic powerhouse Cambridge, to the industrial savvy Lowell, to the constantly innovating Boston. Indeed, the whole state is a melting pot of old traditions and modern ideas, lived out along a breathtaking coastline and myriad quiet hill villages.

91

MASSACHUSETTS

★ SPOTLIGHT

★ The first computer was developed in 1928 at the Massachusetts Institute of Technology (M.I.T.)

★ Cranberry juice is the state beverage of Massachusetts.

★ The Boston terrier, a cross between an English bulldog and an English terrier, was the first purebred dog to be developed in the U.S.

★ Ruth Wakefield invented the chocolate chip cookie at the Tollhouse Inn in Whitman, Massachusetts.

AMHERST

This storied Central Mass town exudes academia. More than half its citizens are students (the other half might be professors), and its former natives include such scholarly types as Eugene Field, Emily Dickinson, Robert Frost and Noah Webster. The seat of Amherst College and the crown jewel of the University of Massachusetts system, this is a town filled with life, culture and ideas.

Information: Chamber of Commerce, 409 Main St., Amherst, 413-253-0700; www.amherstchamber.com

WHAT TO SEE AND DO

Amherst College
100 Boltwood Ave., Amherst, 413-542-2000; www.amherst.edu
One of the best liberal arts colleges in the country, Amherst enrolls some 1,550 students. On a tree-shaded green in the middle of town, its Robert Frost Library owns approximately half of Emily Dickinson's poems, as well as materials by Wordsworth, Eugene O'Neill and others.

Emily Dickinson Museum: the Homestead and the Evergreens
280 Main St., Amherst, 413-542-8161; www.emilydickinsonmuseum.org
The Homestead was the birthplace and home of poet Emily Dickinson; the Evergreens housed her brother and his family. Selected rooms are open for tours on a first-come, first-served basis. March-May, September-October: Wednesday-Saturday 1-5 p.m.; June-August: Wednesday-Saturday 10 a.m.-5 p.m., Sunday 1-5 p.m.; November-mid-December: Wednesday, Saturday 1-5 p.m.

Eric Carle Museum of Picture Book Art
125 W. Bay Rd., Amherst, 413-658-1100; www.picturebookart.org
This 40,000-square-foot facility opened in 2002 as the first museum in the United States exclusively devoted to children's picture book art. Its founder, Eric Carle, has illustrated more than 70 picture books, including *The Very Hungry Caterpillar* which has been published in more than 30 languages and has sold more than 18 million copies. Tuesday-Saturday 10 a.m.-4 p.m., Sunday noon-4 p.m.

University of Massachusetts
Massachusetts Ave. and N. Pleasant St., Amherst, 413-545-0111; www.umass.edu
Founded in 1863, and with 24,000 students, UMass-Amherst is the state's major facility of public higher education. It has more than 150 buildings on a 1,450-acre campus. Tours. Daily.

HOTELS

★Howard Johnson
401 Russell St., Hadley, 413-586-0114; www.hojo.com
100 rooms. Complimentary full breakfast. $

SPECIALTY LODGINGS

Allen House Victorian Inn
599 Main St., Amherst, 413-253-5000; www.allenhouse.com
7 rooms. Children over 10 years only. Complimentary full breakfast. $

Lord Jeffery Inn
30 Boltwood Ave., Amherst, 01002. 413-253-2576; 800-742-0358. www.lordjefferyinn.com
48 rooms. Two restaurants, Bar. $

MASSACHUSETTS

★
★
★
★
★

ANDOVER

The seat of Boston's northern suburbs is a picturesque small city bursting with brick homes and quiet charm. Many of its residents commute to jobs in Boston. Many others are connected to the legendary Phillips Andover Academy—known simply as Andover—the posh prep school which is also the oldest incorporated school in the country.
Information: Merrimack Valley Chamber of Commerce, 264 Essex St., Lawrence, 978-686-0900; www.merrimackvalleychamber.com

WHAT TO SEE AND DO

Phillips Academy
180 Main St., Andover,
978-749-4000; www.andover.edu
Nearly 1,100 students make up this coed boarding school for grades 9-12. Notable alumni include photographer Walker Evans, poet Oliver Wendell Holmes, child-rearing expert Benjamin Spock and actor Humphrey Bogart. The campus sits on 450 acres with 170 buildings. The Cochran Sanctuary, a 65-acre landscaped area, has walking trails, a brook and two ponds. Daily.

Peabody Museum
175 Main St., Andover, 978-749-4490
This Native American archaeological museum has exhibits on the physical and cultural evolution of man and the prehistoric archaeology of New England, the Southwest, Mexico and the Arctic. Monday-Friday 9 a.m.-5 p.m., by appointment only.

HOTELS

★★★Andover Inn
4 Chapel Ave., Andover,
978-475-5903, 800-242-5903;
www.andoverinn.com
Located on the campus of Phillips Andover Academy, this neo-Georgian country inn was built in 1930 to provide lodging for visiting parents and alumni.
29 rooms. Restaurant. Bar. $

★★Andover Wyndham Hotel
123 Old River Rd., Andover,
978-975-3600, www.wyndham.com
293 rooms. Restaurant. Bar. Airport transportation available. $$

★★La Quinta Inn & Suites Andover
131 River Rd., Andover, 978-685-6200
185 rooms. Complimentary continental breakfast. Restaurant. $

RESTAURANTS

★China Blossom
946 Osgood St., North Andover,
978-682-2242
Chinese menu. Lunch, dinner. Bar. $$

93

BOSTON

With the culture of Chicago, the beauty of San Francisco and the diversity of Paris, Boston is the social, financial, educational, historical, culinary and sports center of New England. It should be no surprise that its nickname is "the Hub," and most state happenings revolve around what's going on in this port city of some 600,000 citizens. America's early settlers moved here in the mid-1600s; their legacy is still very much alive in the old Colonials of Charlestown and narrow, winding streets of the North End. Paul Revere's fabled ride, and indeed the Revolution itself, started here, giving Boston bragging rights over nearly every other American city.

Visitors can retrace Revere and other early patriots' steps along the Freedom Trail, a three-hour walking route that encapsulates much of the area's history. Current citizens, though, leave the past to tourists and obsess instead over the Boston Red Sox and New England Patriots, two championship teams known as much for their die-hard fans as for their athletic prowess. Fenway Park, the oldest U.S. baseball stadium and home to the legendary Green Monster, hosts the Red Sox—visitors would do well to take in a game here while in town. Afterward, they can explore the city's neighborhoods, from the upscale Beacon Hill to the bursting-with-life North End to the formerly Irish, rapidly gentrifying South Boston (i.e. the "Southie" so well portrayed in local son Matt Damon's *Good Will Hunting.*)

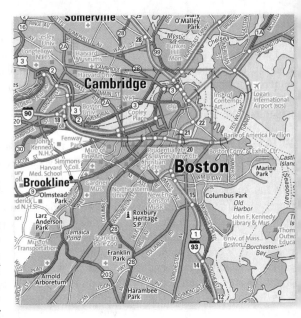

Boston is perhaps best known for its top-tier universities—a whopping 100 in all—the most famous of which include Harvard, M.I.T., Boston University and the Berklee School of Music. During the academic year, students canvas Commonwealth Avenue and the Back Bay's Newbury Street shopping district, lending the whole city a youthful, energetic vibe (though older residents love to complain about the youngsters' rowdiness).

Students, locals and tourists alike love strolling through this walking city—possibly because of Boston drivers' rightful reputation as the worst in the world—especially along the landscaped Charles River Esplanade. The 18-mile-long waterside stretch has walking, running, and biking trails, boathouses, tennis courts, and myriad shaded benches. On a summer day, the spot is packed with Bostonians getting exercise and checking out the evolving city skyline.

Information: Greater Boston Convention & Visitors Bureau, 2 Copley Place, 617-536-4100, 888-733-2678; www.bostonusa.com

WHAT TO SEE AND DO

Boston African American National Historic Site

46 Joy St., Boston,
617-742-5415;
www.nps.gov/boaf

Built by free black Bostonians in 1806, the building was an educational and religious center and site of the founding of the New England Anti-Slavery Society in 1832. May-September: daily; rest of year: Monday-Saturday. The Meeting house is the starting point for the Black Heritage Trail, a walking tour conducted by the National Park Service that takes guests past black history–related sites.

Boston Ballet

270 Tremont St., Boston, 617-695-6955; www.bostonballet.com

The Boston Ballet offers classic and more contemporary performances by a company of some of the finest dancers in the world. If you're visiting in late November or

December, don't miss *The Nutcracker,* performed annually before more than 140,000 people—that's the largest ballet audience in the world. Performances held October-May.

Boston Bruins

TD Banknorth Garden, 1 Legends Way, Boston, 617-624-1000; www.bostonbruins.com

One of the great hockey traditions in the NHL, the Bruins were one of the league's founding six teams.

Boston Celtics

TD Banknorth Garden, 1 Legends Way, Boston, 617-624-1000; www.nba.com/celtics

With 16 championships notched in its belt, Boston's pro basketball team has won more NBA titles than any other franchise. October-June.

Boston College

140 Commonwealth Ave., Chestnut Hill, 617-552-8000; www.bc.edu

This huge Catholic college of 14,500 students has a major presence in the city, thanks in part to its top ranked basketball, hockey and football teams. The school's main campus in Chestnut Hill is full of old stone manors with stained glass windows.

Boston Common

Beacon and Tremont Streets, Boston

The oldest public park in the United States, the Boston Common is steeped in history. In the 1640s, farmers used the Common as a cattle pasture; later, the colonial militia used it to train soldiers. Colonists gathered here to hear speeches, witness public hangings and watch spirited fencing duels. Today, the Common's 45 acres are still a vibrant city center—an ideal place to stroll, in-line skate, play Frisbee, catch a free concert or enjoy a picnic. In the winter, the park's famous Frog Pond freezes over into a public ice skating rink. Daily.

Boston Public Garden

Arlington, Boylston, Charles and Beacon Streets, Boston, 617-522-1966

Adjacent to the Boston Common, this is the first botanical garden in the United States, with 24 acres featuring a splendid variety of flowers and ornamental shrubs. It's also home to the city's famous Swan Boats, which visitors can rent for a 15-minute paddled ride around the garden's lagoon.

Boston Harbor Islands National Recreation Area

349 Lincoln St., Hingham, 781-740-1605; www.bostonharborislands.areaparks.com

This national park is actually several Boston Harbor islands, some open to the public, some private. Take the ferry to Georges Island; from there, a free water taxi sails you to Lovells, Peddocks, Gallops, Grape and Bumpkin islands. Each is unique, with features such as sand dunes, freshwater ponds and native wildlife. Camp on Lovells and Peddocks islands with a permit from the Metropolitan District Commission. May-mid-October.

Boston Public Library

700 Boylston St., Boston, 617-536-5400; www.bpl.org

The stunning Italian Renaissance building by Charles McKim includes a central courtyard and fountain. Other highlights include mural decorations, bronze doors, sculptures and several reading rooms, including the Bates Room, where visitors study and surf the Internet in silence. Monday-Thursday 9 a.m.-9 p.m.; Friday-Saturday 9 a.m.-5 p.m.

Boston Red Sox

Fenway Park, 4 Yawkey Way, Boston, 617-482-4769; www.redsox.mlb.com

Going to Fenway isn't just about watching the Red Sox, it's about steeping yourself in the tradition. Built in 1901, the park is home to the Green Monster, the infamous 37-foot, left-field wall. Cy Young pitched a perfect game at Fenway in 1904, and in 1914, young Babe Ruth joined the home team. Today's 2004 *and* 2007 World Series Champs are no less impressive. Regular tours. March-October.

95

MASSACHUSETTS

Boston Symphony Orchestra/Boston Pops
**301 Massachusetts Ave., Boston,
617-266-1492; www.bso.org**
Symphony Hall is said to have perfect acoustics, a draw that packs the house despite lofty ticket prices. Both the old-school Boston Symphony Orchestra and the livelier Boston Pops perform here, when they're not giving free outdoor concerts on the Charles River Esplanade. BSO performances October-April; Pops performances May-early July, mid- to late-December.

Boston Tea Party Ship and Museum
**300 Congress St., Boston, 617-338-1773;
www.bostonteapartyship.com**
The museum ship is a replica of one of the three famous boats docked in the harbor the night of the Boston Tea Party. In 2001, the museum was badly damaged by a fire and closed for renovations. It's scheduled to reopen in the fall of 2008.

Boston University
**595 Commonwealth Ave., Boston,
617-353-2300; www.bu.edu**
A college of more than 28,000 students, B.U. encompasses an entire area of the city (not the least of which is the "B.U. Beach," a riverside strip of grassy lawn typically littered with sunbathing coeds). The Mugar Memorial Library houses the papers of Dr. Martin Luther King Jr., Robert Frost, Isaac Asimov and other writers and artists.

Charles River Esplanade
This flat, smooth asphalt path runs for 18 miles along the Charles River, from Boston to Cambridge to Watertown. During the summer months, active types stroll, jog, bike or blade the Esplanade; lazier locals picnic or sunbathe along both sides of the river. On a clear day, the river and skyline views are magnificent—some of the best in Boston. Rent a bike at Back Bay Bikes & Boards, 336 Commonwealth Ave., Boston, 617-247-2336, www.backbaybicycles.com; Community Bicycle Supply, 496 Tremont St., Boston, 617-542-8623, www.communitybicycle.com; Cambridge Bicycle, 259 Massachusetts Ave., Cambridge, 617-876-6555; or

Ata Cycle, 1773 Massachusetts Ave., Cambridge, 617-354-0907, www.atabike.com; Rent rollerblades at Beacon Hill Skate Shop, 135 Charles St., Boston, 617-482-7400; or Blades Board & Skate, Boston and Cambridge, 617-437-6300, www.blades.com

Children's Museum of Boston
**300 Congress St., Boston, 617-426-8855;
www.bostonkids.org**
With interactive exhibits on science, technology, art and culture, the Childrens Museum lives up to its billing as "Boston's best place for kids 0-10." A kid-size construction site includes a mini artist studio, real loom and weaving area, full-size wigwam and rock climbing area. Saturday-Thursday 10 a.m.-5 p.m., Friday 10 a.m.-9 p.m.

Community Boating
**21 David Mugar Way, Boston,
617-523-7406;
www.community-boating.org**
Community Boating runs the largest and oldest public sailing program in the country. Purchasing a two-day membership means unlimited use of boats, plus sailing, windsurfing or kayaking instruction. April-November: daily; closed December-March.

Copley Place
**100 Huntington Ave., Boston,
617-369-5000;
www.shopcopleyplace.com**
With more than 100 stores and a central glass atrium, Copley Place is all about upscale shopping and dining. Stores include Barneys, Neiman Marcus, Louis Vuitton, Christian Dior and Gucci. Daily.

Duck Tours
**790 Boylston St., Boston, 800-226-7442;
www.bostonducktours.com**
This long-standing Boston tradition takes you from land to sea in a World War II half-boat, half-truck vehicle known as a Duck. Your conDUCKtor starts the 80-minute tour near the Boston Common and drives through the city before diving into the Charles River. April-November:

on the hour from 9 a.m. to one hour before sunset.

Franklin Park Golf Course (William J. Devine Golf Course)

1 Circuit Dr., Dorchester, 617-265-4084; www.sterlinggolf.com

This 6,009-yard, par-70 golf course is the second-oldest public golf course in the country. Rates are reasonable, especially for kids under 18, and club rentals are just $10. The course is wide open but demanding, with some steep hills. Daily dawn-dusk; closed for snow and inclement weather.

Franklin Park Zoo

1 Franklin Park Rd., Dorchester, 617-541-5466; www.zoonewengland.org

The medium-sized zoo has "Bird's World," an indoor/outdoor aviary complex with natural habitats; an African tropical forest; a hilltop range with camels, antelopes, and zebras; and a children's zoo. Daily.

Freedom Trail

617-242-5642; www.thefreedomtrail.org

This two- to three-hour walking tour takes visitors past some of Boston's most famous historical sites. It begins at the Boston Common and ends at the Bunker Hill Monument in Charlestown. Red bricks or red paint mark the trail, which you can follow on your own (free brochures are available) or with guided assistance.

Bunker Hill Monument

Monument Square, Charlestown, 617-242-5641

Standing 221 feet high (that's 294 steps, with no elevator), the Bunker Hill Monument marks the site of the first major battle of the Revolutionary War. It was here that American Colonel William Prescott ordered his troops not to fire until "you see the whites of their eyes," so that no bullets would be wasted. Daily.

Copp's Hill Burying Ground

Hull and Snow Hill Streets, Boston,

617-635-4505

This is the second-oldest burying ground in Boston. Robert Newman, who hung the lanterns in the steeple of Old North Church, is buried here, as is the Puritan Mather family and African Americans from the nearby New Guinea Community, who lie in unmarked graves. Daily.

Faneuil Hall Marketplace

4 S. Market Bldg., Boston, 617-523-1300

Faneuil Hall is more than just a shopping center: it has operated as a local marketplace since 1742, when wealthy merchant Peter Faneuil built and donated the area to the city. Today, it buzzes with tourists catching street performances or snacking on treats from indoor food mall Quincy Market. Daily.

Granary Burying Ground

Tremont and Bromfield Streets, Boston, 617-635-4505

Revolutionary War patriots Paul Revere, John Hancock, Samuel Adams, and Peter Faneuil (whose headstone is typoed Peter Funal) all lie here. The name stems from a grain storage building (called a granary) that used to sit nearby. Daily 9 a.m.-7 p.m.

King's Chapel and Burying Ground

58 Tremont St., Boston, 617-227-2155

Kings Chapel, started by the Massachusetts Royal Governor, has held church services at its location longer than any other church in the United States. When the congregation outgrew the church in 1754, a new building was erected around the old, which was then dismantled. The Burying Ground next door is the oldest cemetery in Boston. Daily; closed Sunday-Friday in winter.

Old North Church

193 Salem St., Boston, 617-523-6676

Old North Church is the oldest church in Boston. On April 18, 1775, church sexton Robert Newman hung two lanterns in the steeple to signal that the British Army was heading up the Charles River. When Paul Revere saw the signal, he jumped on his horse and rode to Lexington to warn the militia. The next day, the shot heard round the world was fired on Lexington Green, officially beginning the Revolutionary War. Daily.

Old South Meeting House
310 Washington St., Boston, 617-482-6439
The most important date in Old South's history is December 16, 1773, when 5,000 colonists gathered at the church to protest the British tax on tea and decide on a course of action. From there, the men dressed as Native Americans, snuck onto three ships laden with tea, and dumped the cargo overboard. Daily.

Old State House/Site of Boston Massacre
206 Washington St., Boston, 617-720-1713
The Old State House was originally built as the headquarters of the British government in Boston. It is now the city's oldest surviving public building. Inside, a museum exhibits the prominent role the building played in the American Revolution. In 1770, British troops shot into a crowd that had gathered here to hear a proclamation; the fallen are memorialized by a small circle of paving stones (it now sits under dense city traffic). Daily 9 a.m.-5 p.m.

Park Street Church
1 Park St., Boston, 617-523-3383
William Lloyd Garrison delivered his first antislavery address here in 1829. The church is often called "Brimstone Corner" because brimstone for gunpowder was stored here during the War of 1812. mid-June-August: limited hours; Sunday services all year.

Paul Revere House
19 North Square, Boston, 617-523-2338
Built in 1680, the well-preserved Paul Revere House is Boston's oldest building. It still includes authentic furnishings and offers a rare glimpse of colonial life. Here, Paul Revere plied his silversmith trade and sold his wares, often in exchange for food or livestock. His successful ride to Lexington on April 18, 1775, was immortalized by Henry Wadsworth Longfellow in "The Mid-

night Ride of Paul Revere." Mid-April-late October: daily 9:30 a.m.-5:15 p.m.; early November-mid-April: daily 9:30 a.m.-4:15 p.m.; closed Monday in January-March.

State House
24 Beacon St., Boston, 617-727-3676
The Massachusetts State House is an architectural marvel, with a golden dome sheathed in 23-carat gold leaf (the original state house's was copper). Designed by Charles Bulfinch and built on land owned by John Hancock, Paul Revere helped lay the cornerstones on July 4, 1795. Monday-Friday 10 a.m.-3:30 p.m.

USS *Constitution*
Charlestown Navy Yard, Boston National Historical Park, Constitution Rd., Boston, 617-426-1812
The oldest commissioned warship in the world got the nickname "Old Ironsides" during the War of 1812. Some 600 miles off the coast of Boston, it engaged the British HMS *Guerriere* in battle. While the *Guerriere* was badly damaged, cannonballs merely bounced off the *Constitution's* sides, as if they were made of iron (really, they're three layers of oak). In 1830, the ship was saved from the scrap heap because of public response to Oliver Wendell Holmes's poem "Old Ironsides." It was restored in 1925. May-September: daily 9 a.m.-6 p.m., October-April: daily 10 a.m.-5 p.m.

Haymarket
Blackstone Street, Boston
Rain or shine, winter or summer, Bostonians flock to Haymarket and its outdoor stalls for the freshest fruits, vegetables and seafood around.

Institute of Contemporary Art
100 Northern Ave., Boston, 617-478-3100; www.icaboston.org
In late 2006, the ICA moved into its brand new, waterfront South Boston building. The four-floor museum now has a sizable theater with walls of glass, a large outdoor deck and several galleries showing perma-

nent and temporary collections. Tuesday-Sunday.

Isabella Stewart Gardner Museum
280 The Fenway, Boston, 617-566-1401;
www.gardnermuseum.com
The museum is housed in the 19th-century home of Isabella Stewart Gardner. The collections include paintings and sculptures from around the world. On weekends in fall, winter and spring, look for free afternoon concerts. Tuesday-Sunday; concerts late September-May.

L'Arte Di Cucinare
6 Charter St., Boston, 617-523-6032;
www.cucinare.com
Michele Topor, a 30-year resident of the North End and passionate gourmet chef, leads 3 1/2-hour tours of the North End Italian markets. Reservations are required, and each tour is limited to 13 people. Wednesday, Friday-Saturday.

Louis Boston
234 Berkeley St., Boston,
617-262-6100, 800-225-5135;
www.louisboston.com
This men's and women's clothing emporium is considered among the finest in the world. Housed in the historic former museum of science building, the buyers here stock the shelves with hard-to-find labels from designers ahead of their time. Monday-Wednesday 10 a.m.-6 p.m., Thursday-Saturday 10 a.m.-7 p.m.

Louisburg Square
Louisburg Square, Beacon Hill
This lovely little residential square is one of Boston's most coveted addresses. Louisa May Alcott, William Dean Howells and other famous Bostonians—including current Senator John Kerry—have had homes here.

Make Way for Ducklings Tour
99 Bedford St., Boston, 617-426-1885;
www.historic-neighborhoods.org
This kid-friendly tour is based on Robert McCloskey's famous children's book *Make Way for Ducklings*. Other duckling-inspired events include the fancy Ducklings Day Tea held in April (reservations required) and the Mother's Day Ducklings Parade.

MDC Memorial Hatch Shell
On the Charles River, between Storrow Drive and the water;
www.mass.gov/dcr/hatch_events.htm
Packing as much as possible into the summer months, the Hatch Shell offers free entertainment nearly every night of the week. Offerings range from dance performances to rock concerts to the Boston Pops Fourth of July celebration. Early June-early September.

Minuteman Commuter Bikeway
www.minutemanbikeway.org
Begins near Alewife (T) station, goes through Lexington and Arlington and ends at Bedford. This 11-mile bike path looks like a miniature highway, complete with on- and off-ramps, a center line, and traffic signs. The trail mimics portions of Paul Revere's famous ride. Daily.

Mother Church, the First Church of Christ, Scientist Christian Science Center
Massachusetts Ave., Boston,
617-450-3793; www.tfccs.com
This is the headquarters of the Christian Science Monitor, and the home of the Mapparium, a walk-through stained-glass globe. Daily.

Museum at the John Fitzgerald Kennedy Library
617-514-1600, 866-535-1960;
www.jfklibrary.org
Designed by I. M. Pei, the library is considered one of the most beautiful contemporary works of architecture in the country. Daily 9 a.m.-5 p.m..

Museum of Afro American History
46 Joy St., Boston, 617-725-0022;
www.afroammuseum.org
The Museum of Afro American History preserves and exhibits the contributions of African-American Bostonians and New Englanders during colonial settlement and the Revolutionary War. The museum also

features workshops for kids and adults, a public lecture series, storytelling for children, and poet and author visits. Monday-Saturday 10 a.m.-4 p.m.

Museum of Fine Arts
465 Huntington Ave., Boston,
617-267-9300; www.mfa.org
The MFA, Boston's answer to New York's Met, combines classic and contemporary art with ancient artifacts. The grand white stone building is practically an exhibit in itself. Monday-Tuesday and Saturday-Sunday 10 a.m.-4:45 p.m., Wednesday-Friday to 9:45 p.m.

Museum of Science
Science Park, Charles River Dam and Storrow Dr., Boston,
617-723-2500;
www.mos.org
The MOS's entertaining exhibitions range from a T. Rex model (complete with 58 teeth) to presentations with live animals at the Wright Theater to a chick hatchery to a lighthouse that explains light, optics and color. Also onsite is the Charles Hayden Planetarium. Saturday-Thursday 9 a.m.-5 p.m., Friday to 9 p.m.

New England Aquarium
Central Wharf, Boston, 617-973-5200;
www.neaq.org
The aquarium has a colorful array of dolphins, sea lions, penguins, turtles, sharks, eels, harbor seals and fish from around the world. Every 90 minutes, sea lions perform. There's also an IMAX theater. Monday-Friday 9 a.m.-5 p.m., Saturday-Sunday, holidays to 6 p.m.

New England Aquarium Whale Watches
Central Wharf, Boston, 617-973-5206;
www.neaq.org/visit/ww.tickets.html
Stellwagen Bank, 25 miles from Boston, is a terrific area for whale-watching. From Boston, the New England Aquariums tour takes you out to the feeding grounds of a variety of whales, many of which are endangered. Purchase tickets in advance. Boston Harbor Cruises (617-227-4321; www.bostonharbor-

cruises.com) and Beantown Whale Watch (617-542-8000; www.beantownwhalewatch.com) also operate whale cruises in Boston. Mid-April-late October.

Newbury Street
1-361 Newbury St., Boston,
www.newbury-st.com
There's no better shopping street in New England than Newbury. Independent boutiques and well-known chain shops sell everything from baby gear to kitchen equipment to truffles to artwork. The street is also home to scores of spas and cafés, making it a one-stop shopping, eating and pampering destination.

Nichols House Museum
55 Mt. Vernon St., Boston, 617-227-6993;
www.nicholshousemuseum.org
(1804) Typical domestic architecture of Beacon Hill from its era; one of two homes on Beacon Hill open to the public. Attributed to Charles Bulfinch; antique furnishings and art from America, Europe and the Orient from the 17th to early 19th centuries. Collection of Rose Standish Nichols, landscape designer and writer. May-October: Tuesday-Saturday noon-4 p.m.; November-April: Thursday-Saturday noon-4 p.m.

Old South Church
645 Boylston St., Boston, 617-536-1970;
www.oldsouth.org
A church community since 1669, Old South Church has a medieval architectural style that boasts impressive mosaics, stained glass, and cherry woodwork. Worship held Sunday.

Samuel Adams Brewery
30 Germania St., Boston, 617-522-9080
Take a tour of the Boston Beer Museum and discover the critical details of the brewing process. While you're at it, sample a handful of Samuel Adams microbrews. (Tours Thursday-Saturday)

Suffolk Downs
111 Waldemar Ave., East Boston,
617-567-3900;

www.suffolkdowns.com

Seabiscuit once won at Suffolk Downs, a local track that's been operating since 1935. The track offers pari-mutuel betting, which unlike casino gambling, doesn't involve betting against the house, only against other spectators. (Daily)

The Shops at the Prudential Center

800 Boylston St., Boston, 800-746-7778; www.prudentialcenter.com

This indoor city shopping mall includes Saks Fifth Avenue, Club Monaco, Barnes and Noble and more. Daily.

Trinity Church

206 Clarendon St., Boston, 617-536-0944; www.trinitychurchboston.org

This Henry Hobson Richardson-built church was inspired by Phillips Brooks, the ninth rector of Trinity Church, and author of the Christmas carol, "O Little Town of Bethlehem." Daily.

Wang Theater/The Shubert Theater

265 and 270 Tremont St., Boston, 617-482-9393; www.wangcenter.org

Broadway shows, theater productions, dance and opera companies, and musical performers appear at the 3,600-seat Wang Theater, a world-class venue for the performing arts. The Shubert hosts an impressive array of quality local theater, dance, and opera productions, many of which appeal to children.

SPECIAL EVENTS

Boston Marathon

617-236-1652; www.bostonmarathon.org

The notoriously hilly and difficult Boston marathon is one of the most famous footraces in the world. To qualify, runners must have already posted an acceptable time in another marathon. (But that doesn't stop thousands of "scabs" from jumping into the race behind the pros.) Most of the city shuts down for the day, as fans line the route and cheer like crazy. Third Monday in April.

First Night Boston

617-542-1399; www.firstnight.org

First Night is Boston's New Year's Eve celebration. The alcohol-free event begins with a Mardi Gras–style Grand Procession and features more than 250 performances in both indoor and outdoor venues. Those who can stay awake are treated to a fireworks display at midnight.

HOTELS

★Best Western Roundhouse Suites

891 Massachusetts Ave., Boston, 617-989-1000, 888-468-3562; www.bestwestern.com

92 rooms. Pets accepted. Complimentary continental breakfast. Airport transportation available. $

★★★★★Boston Harbor Hotel

70 Rowes Wharf, Boston, 617-439-7000, 800-752-7077; www.bhh.com

Occupying an idyllic waterfront location, this quietly luxurious, subtly sophisticated hotel is located across from Boston's financial district and along a stretch of land that was once dominated by an elevated highway, but now is poised to become the new Rose Kennedy Greenway. The staff at this full-service property takes care of every possible need, and does so with aplomb. Rooms and suites are beautifully appointed in rich colors—it's worth paying extra for a room with a view. In the summer, live music, dancing and an outdoor movie night take place on the hotel's outdoor patio. The hotel's Meritage restaurant is the domain of chef Daniel Bruce, who dreams up seasonal dishes constructed of the freshest local ingredients and pairs them with imaginative wines by the glass or bottle from around the world. The Rowes Wharf water taxi whisks guests straight to the airport, avoiding Boston's notorious traffic. 230 rooms. High-speed Internet access. Three restaurants, two bars. Airport transportation available. $$$$

★★★The Colonnade Hotel

120 Huntington Ave., Boston,

617-424-7000, 800-962-3030; www.colonnadehotel.com

One of Back Bay's more family-friendly hotels, the Colonnade's big claim to fame is its roof-top pool. The only such swimming hole in the city, the 11th-floor area is typically full of bikini-clad beautiful people and the who's-who in Boston's media scene. The pool is fully catered for lunch and happy hour—the onsite bar makes great frozen cocktails—and, because of its guests-and-VIPs-only weekday policy, is generally free of crowds.

285 rooms. Wireless Internet access. Restaurant. Bar. **$$$**

★★Copley Square Hotel

47 Huntington Ave., Boston,
617-536-9000, 800-225-7062;
www.copleysquarehotel.com

143 rooms. Two restaurants, two bars. **$$**

★★★The Eliot Hotel

370 Commonwealth Ave., Boston,
617-267-1607, 800-443-5468;
www.eliothotel.com

This 95-room European-style boutique hotel is located just off the Mass Turnpike in the Back Bay, convenient to shopping, entertainment and cultural sites. A quiet elegance pervades the lobby and most of the newly renovated accommodations are spacious suites with pull-out sofas, French bedroom doors, Italian marble baths, and down comforters. The Eliot is also home to the critically acclaimed Clio and Uni restaurants that serve contemporary French-American and Japanese cuisine, respectively.

95 rooms. Wireless Internet access. Restaurant. Bar. **$$$**

★★Doubletree Guest Suites

400 Soldiers Field Rd., Boston,
617-783-0090, 800-222-8733;
www.doubletree.com

308 rooms, all suites. Restaurant. Bar. **$**

★★★The Fairmont Copley Plaza Boston

138 St., James Ave., Boston,
617-267-5300, 800-441-1414;
www.fairmont.com

Ideally situated in the heart of the Theater District, this landmark 1925 hotel is also walking distance from the Back Bay and South End. Named after the great American painter John Singleton Copley, the Fairmont is traditional and elegant—its lobby flaunts an exquisite high-domed ceiling and ornate furnishings, as well as dramatic marble pillars and elaborate rugs. Watching over all of this is Catie Copley, the hotel's resident black Lab, who's happy to be petted or taken for walks by guests.

384 rooms. High-speed Internet access. Restaurant. Bar. **$$$**

★★★★★Four Seasons Hotel Boston

200 Boylston St., Boston,
617-338-4400, 800-330-3442;
www.fourseasons.com

The Four Seasons offers its guests a prime location overlooking the Public Garden and Boston Common. The recently renovated contemporary lobby, complete with a dramatic yellow marble and black granite floor, gleams. Antiques, fine art, sumptuous fabrics, period furniture and sleek technology such as flat screen televisions and wireless Internet access bring the guest rooms and suites up to date, while impeccable and attentive service heightens the experience. Canines are pampered with everything from dog bones to a convenient dog-walking service. The Bristol Lounge is where Boston's power players come to celebrate their success.

273 rooms. High-speed Internet access. Two restaurants, two bars. Airport transportation available. **$$$$**

★Harborside Inn of Boston

185 State St., Boston,
617-723-7500, 888-723-7565;
www.harborsideinnboston.com

54 rooms. Wireless Internet access. Closed one week in late December. **$$**

★★★Hilton Boston Back Bay

40 Dalton St., Boston, 617-236-1100,
800-445-8667; www.hilton.com

Built in the age of glass-box towers, the Hilton Back Bay is a business-oriented hotel

across the street from the Hynes Convention Center. A recent renovation enhanced the hotel's amenities and upped the square footage of existing guest rooms. To further cater to its hard-working clients, the Hilton added excellent desks, a top-notch fitness club and a 24-hour business center.
385 rooms. Wireless Internet access. Restaurant, two bars. **$$**

★★★Hilton Boston Logan Airport
85 Terminal Rd., Boston,
617-568-6700, 800-445-8667;
www.hilton.com
Experiencing one of Logan's many layovers? Check into the Hilton, the airport's most convenient and comfortable hotel. A sky bridge provides pedestrians access to and from the terminals, and the hotel runs free shuttles to the airport subway stop and water taxi dock. The rooms, with their ruddy wood furniture and stocked minibars, are comfortably familiar spots to wait out a flight delay.
599 rooms. Wireless Internet access. Two restaurants, Bar. Airport transportation available. **$$**

★★Holiday Inn Select-Government Center
5 Blossom St., Boston,
617-742-7630, 800-465-4329;
www.holiday-inn.com
303 rooms. Wireless Internet access. Restaurant. Bar. **$**

★★Hotel 140
140 Clarendon St., Boston, 617-585-5600, 800-714-0140; www.hotel140.com
54 rooms. High-speed internet access. Business center. Restaurant. Fitness Room. $$

★★★Hotel Commonwealth
500 Commonwealth Ave., Boston,
617-933-5000, 866-784-4000;
www.hotelcommonwealth.com
In the heart of once-funky, now-yuppie Kenmore Square, this property is a block-long modern mammoth. The hotel now anchors the neighborhood with its gallery of upscale boutiques—don't miss the first-floor chocolatier—and two terrific restaurants. Rooms come with oversized French Empire writing desks, Frette linens, Egyptian cotton blankets, pillow-top mattresses and gleaming marble bathrooms. Fenway Park is around the corner and the Boston University campus begins a few yards up the street.
148 rooms. Wireless Internet access. Two restaurants, two bars. **$$$**

★★★Hyatt Harborside
101 Harborside Dr., Boston,
617-568-1234, 800-233-1234;
www.hyatt.com
Another Logan Airport lodging, this hotel has a friendly staff, spacious guest rooms and a meeting facility designed with the business traveler in mind. Stranded guests can enjoy the indoor lap pool or the health and fitness center—both have scenic waterfront and Boston skyline views.
270 rooms. Wireless Internet access. Restaurant. Bar. Airport transportation available. **$$**

★★★Hyatt Regency Boston Financial District
1 Ave., de Lafayette, Boston,
617-912-1234, 800-233-1234;
www.hyatt.com
When Hyatt took over this former Swisshotel, it wisely kept much of the latter's elegant décor (as well as its discounted weekend packages). Principally a business hotel, it sits a block off Boston Common at the intersection of the financial and theater districts. Public areas suggest old-world refinement with antique furniture, marble floors and Waterford crystal chandeliers. Many upper-level corner suites have city views and the trendy restaurants and nightclubs of the Ladder District are just a few steps away.
498 rooms. Wireless Internet access. Restaurant. Bar. **$$$**

★★★InterContinental Boston
510 Atlantic Ave., Boston,
617-747-1000, 800-972-3381;
www.intercontinental.com

★
★
★
★

Located in a new high-rise building in Boston's financial district, this luxury hotel is one of the city's most contemporary in design. The lobby has soaring ceilings, sleek furniture and working fireplaces. Rooms feature plush duvet-topped beds, marble bathrooms with deep soaking tubs and flat screen TVs. The hotel's Rumba bar (which spotlights rums from around the world) and 24-hour Miel restaurant are hotspots for drinking and dining.
424 rooms. Restaurant, bar. Business center. Fitness center. Indoor pool. Pets accepted, some restrictions. Valet parking only. $$$

★★★The Langham Boston
250 Franklin St., Boston,
617-451-1900, 800-791-7781;
www.langhamhotels.com
Near Faneuil Hall, the Freedom Trail and the North End, the Langham (formerly Le Meridien) is a perfect base for retracing the steps of famous patriots. The hotel's signature red awnings give way to a grand lobby done in jewel tones. The guest rooms are equally delightful—many offer wonderful views of Post Office Square. Frequented by politicos and business power players, the Julien Bar, with its "101 Martini Menu," is one of the most popular hotel bars in the city.
325 rooms. High-speed Internet access. Restaurant. Bar. Airport transportation available. $$$

★★★Lenox Hotel
61 Exeter St., Boston,
617-536-5300, 800-225-7676;
www.lenoxhotel.com
This downtown landmark is one of Boston's finest lodgings. The European-style hotel's lobby has a beautifully ornate ceiling with gilded moldings. Well-appointed guest rooms exude elegance and style. Large windows are draped in blue and gold; and some rooms have working wood-burning fireplaces. Energy-saving windows and light bulbs have won the hotel awards for environmental awareness.
212 rooms. Wireless Internet access. Restaurant. Bar. $$$

★★★Boston Marriott Copley Place
110 Huntington Ave., Boston,
617-236-5800, 877-901-2079;
www.copleymarriott.com
An enclosed walkway connects the Marriott to the shops and restaurants of the Prudential Center and Copley Place, as well as to the meeting rooms of the Hynes Convention Center. Just minutes from the Museum of Fine Arts and Newbury Street, the Marriot has one of the largest ballrooms in New England and boasts a sushi bar as one of its three restaurants.
1,147 rooms. High-speed Internet access. Three restaurants, two bars. $$

★★★Boston Marriott Long Wharf
296 State St., Boston,
617-227-0800, 800-228-9290;
www.marriott.com
Adjacent to Faneuil Hall and near the Fleet Center, this mid-20th-century hotel has rooms with stunning harbor or city skyline views. It's also a short walk to the Harbor Islands ferry, whale-watching boats, or a water taxi stand. It's not a surprise, then, that the Marriott capitalizes on the nautical theme—grand interior murals depict Long Wharf fishermen, and a railing system mimics that of a cruise ship. Summertime heaven is a bucket of steamed clams and a bottle of cold beer on the patio of Tia's on the Waterfront, the hotel's popular restaurant.
402 rooms. High-speed Internet access. Restaurant. Bar. Airport transportation available. $$

★★Courtyard Marriott Boston Tremont Hotel
275 Tremont St., Boston,
617-426-1400, 800-321-2211;
www.marriott.com
315 rooms. Wireless Internet access. $$$

★★★Millennium Bostonian Hotel
26 North St., Boston,
617-523-3600, 800-343-0922;
www.millenniumhotels.com
Those eager to be right in the mix should check into this downtown hotel. Right

★

★

★

★

★

across from tourist mecca Faneuil Hall, the Millennium is ideal for visitors who don't want to walk far to see historic attractions. Guest rooms vary from tiny to palatial; be sure to inquire carefully when booking. City Hall is nearby, so plenty of local business gets accomplished in the lobby bar and although the hotel doesn't have its own spa, guests receive a discount at the adjacent Aveda Spa.

201 rooms. High-speed Internet access. Restaurant. Bar. **$$$**

★★★Nine Zero Hotel
90 Tremont St., Boston,
617-772-5800, 866-646-3937;
www.ninezero.com

When Kimpton bought out this downtown boutique hotel last year, Nine Zero lost much of its independent character. The chain has, however, done an admirable job of sprucing up the property's rooms and introducing a menu of quirky amenities. The lobby and suites are a modern mix of nickel, chrome, stainless steel and glass, and the properly is completely wired with Internet access, stereo sound systems and flat-screen TVs. Luxe trappings include Frette linens, goose-down comforters and pillows, and local beauty guru Mario Russo's bath products.

189 rooms. Wireless Internet access. Restaurant. Bar. **$$$**

★★★Omni Parker House
60 School St., Boston,
617-227-8600, 800-843-6664;
www.omnihotels.com

The Parker House, which gave the world its eponymous dinner rolls and the Boston cream pie, is the oldest continuously operating hotel in the United States. The plush lobby and dining room, which date from just before World War I, are good examples of Edwardian excess. The guest rooms are up to modern standards, as are the sleek fitness room and private, convenient business center.

551 rooms. High-speed Internet access. Restaurant. Bar. **$$$**

★Ramada Inn
800 Morrissey Blvd., Boston,
617-287-9100; www.bostonhotel.com
177 rooms. **$**

★★★★The Ritz-Carlton, Boston Common
10 Avery St., Boston,
617-574-7100, 800-241-3333;
www.ritzcarlton.com

In a town known for its historic buildings, this contemporary hotel is a fresh and stylish alternative. Located near the city's theater district and overlooking the country's oldest public space, the Ritz-Carlton, Boston Common is convenient for business and leisure travelers alike. The guest rooms and suites have a distinctly serene feel with muted tones and polished woods. After a night of indulgence, guests often head to the massive Sports Club/LA, the city's most exclusive health club. Dogs are welcomed in style with the Pampered Pet Package, which includes bowls, biscuits and a personalized dog tag.

193 rooms. High-speed Internet access. Restaurant. Bar. **$$$$**

★★★Seaport Hotel
1 Seaport Lane, Boston,
617-385-4000, 877-732-7678;
www.seaportboston.com

It looks a bit like a beached ocean liner, but the Seaport is solidly grounded with modern rooms and impressive amenities. An above-ground, covered walkway joins the property with the World Trade Center; as such, it's home to many conferences, conventions and sales events. By 2010, developers promise the surrounding area will be packed with shops, restaurants, and galleries (right now it's a bit barren). The Seaport's health club is large and well equipped, and the restaurant is one of Boston's best for upscale seafood.

426 rooms. High-speed Internet access. Restaurant. Bar. Airport transportation available. **$$$**

★★★Sheraton Boston Hotel
39 Dalton St., Boston,

105

MASSACHUSETTS

617-236-2000, 800-325-3535;
www.sheraton.com/boston
Ideally located in the historic Back Bay and adjacent to the Hynes Convention Center, this hotel offers guests attentive service in an elegant atmosphere.
1,216 rooms. High-speed Internet access. Two restaurants, Bar. **$$$**

★★★★**Taj Boston**
15 Arlington St., Boston,
617-536-5700, 877-482-5267;
www.tajhotels.com
Boston's hotel scene changed forever last year when the Taj hotel chain bought out the old Ritz Carlton on Arlington Street. Most were cautiously optimistic the new owners would do this restored 1920s landmark justice. So far, so fabulous. In the lobby, the property looks much the same—"wedding cake" ceiling details, elaborate moldings, lavish carpets and graceful marble staircases. The guest rooms are still heavenly, with feather beds, soft robes, Molton Brown amenities and luxe marble bathrooms (suites include wood-burning fireplaces *and* a fireplace butler service). And the oldest tradition of all, the hotel's proper afternoon tea, is still going strong.
273 rooms. High-speed Internet access. Restaurant, two bars. **$$$$**

★★★**Westin Copley Place**
10 Huntington Ave., Boston,
617-262-9600, 800-937-8461;
www.westin.com/copleyplace
Rising 36-stories above the Copley Mall, this hotel is a great home base from which to explore Newbury Street, the Back Bay and the South End. Rooms are what you'd expect from a Westin—a notch above those of the other major chains.
803 rooms. High-speed Internet access. Three restaurants. Three bars. Airport transportation available. Pet. Exercise. Swim. Business Center. **$$$**

★★★★**XV Beacon**
15 Beacon St., Boston,
617-670-1500, 877-982-2226;
www.xvbeacon.com
This turn-of-the-century Beaux Arts building on Beacon Hill belies the sleek decor found within. Original artwork commissioned specifically for the hotel by well-known artists fill the walls. The eclectic guest rooms and suites are decorated in a palette of rich chocolate browns, blacks and creams. Rooms feature canopy beds with luxurious Italian linens and gas fireplaces covered in cool stainless steel. Completed in crisp white with simple fixtures, the bathrooms are a modernist's dream. The cuisine at the Federalist is delicious and fresh and the restaurant's wine list is extensive and impressive.
63 rooms. High-speed Internet access. Restaurant. Bar. Airport transportation available. Pet. Exercise. **$$$$**

SPECIALTY LODGINGS

Charles Street Inn
94 Charles St., Boston,
617-314-8900, 877-772-8900;
www.charlesstreetinn.com
Step into the past without sacrificing modern conveniences at this charming city inn. The street-level reception and staircases are rather tight, but rooms are large and regal enough to qualify as decadent. Expect to find working fireplaces, massive antique armoires and heavily draped canopy beds in most. The hotel's location is ideal for exploring Beacon Hill, downtown, or Back Bay on foot after a bounteous continental breakfast is delivered to your door.
9 rooms. Complimentary continental breakfast. Wireless Internet access. **$$$**

Gryphon House
9 Bay State Rd., Boston,
617-375-9003, 877-375-9003;
www.gryphonhouseboston.com
More of a luxury bed-and-breakfast than a hotel, this circa-1895 brownstone stands at the juncture of Back Bay and the Fenway. Each room is about the size of a studio apartment and has a working gas fireplace,

★

★

★

★

★

wet bar, and air conditioning; and is decorated in the Victorian style. The Kenmore subway stop, Boston University and Fenway Park are just moments away.

8 rooms. Complimentary continental breakfast. Wireless Internet access. **$$**

Newbury Guest House

261 Newbury St., Boston,
617-437-7666, 800-437-7668;
www.newburyguesthouse.com

A string of residences along upper Newbury Street was linked with indoor staircases and hallways to create this Back Bay bed-and-breakfast. Rooms tend to be on the small side, in part because private bathrooms were added when conversions were made. The decor is eclectic. The bed-and-breakfast offers good value for its location; just ask for a rear-facing room to escape street noise.

32 rooms. Complimentary full breakfast. Wireless Internet access. **$$**

RESTAURANTS

★★Abe & Louie's

793 Boylston St., Boston,
617-536-6300;
www.abeandlouies.com

Steak menu. Lunch, dinner, brunch. Bar. Casual attire. Reservations recommended. Valet parking. Outdoor seating. **$$$**

★★★Aquitaine

569 Tremont St., Boston,
617-424-8577;
www.aquitaineboston.com

Owned by the Aquitaine Group, this hip, modern boite is an offshoot of fellow South End restaurant Metropolis Cafe. Regulars rave about the steak frites. The wine list is intriguing, and the staff helpful. But what really makes this Tremont spot a must-visit is its creative, delicious Sunday brunch. French bistro menu. Dinner, brunch. Bar. Casual attire. Reservations recommended. Valet parking. **$$**

★★★★Aujourd'hui

200 Boylston St., Boston,
617-338-4400, 617-423-0154;
www.fourseasons.com

With floor-to-ceiling windows overlooking Boston's Public Garden, Aujourd'hui is a beautiful spot for a business lunch or an intimate dinner. Tables are set with Italian damask linens and decorated with antique plates and fresh flowers. The kitchen aims to please here, and it succeeds with an innovative selection of seasonal modern French fare prepared with regional ingredients. The predominantly American wine list complements the kitchen's talent. A lighter menu of more nutritionally responsible dishes is also available.

French menu. Dinner, Sunday brunch. Bar. Children's menu. Business casual attire. Reservations recommended. Valet parking. **$$$**

★★★Aura

1 Seaport Lane, Boston, 617-385-4300;
www.seaporthotel.com

This casually elegant waterfront restaurant is based in the Seaport Hotel. So it's no surprise its menu focuses on fish—New England clam chowder, pan-roasted Maine diver scallops, Mediterranean-style swordfish and a seared loin of yellowfin tuna all make appearances. Desserts include maple ricotta cheesecake with Concord grape sorbet and a bittersweet chocolate tart with caramel ice cream.

Seafood menu. Breakfast, lunch, dinner, late-night, brunch. Bar. Children's menu. Business casual attire. Valet parking. **$$$**

★★B & G Oysters Ltd

550 Tremont St., Boston, 617-423-0550;
www.bandgoysters.com

Seafood menu. Lunch, dinner. Casual attire. Valet parking. Outdoor seating. Closed holidays. **$$$**

★★Bob's Southern Bistro

604 Columbus Ave., Boston,
617-536-6204; www.bobthechefs.com

American menu. Dinner, brunch. Bar. Casual attire. Reservations recommended. Closed holidays. **$$**

MASSACHUSETTS

★★Bonfire
50 Park Plaza, Boston, 617-262-3473;
www.bonfiresteakhouse.com
Steak menu. Bar. Business casual attire. Reservations recommended. Valet parking. **$$$**

★★Brasserie Jo
120 Huntington Ave., Boston,
617-425-3240;
www.brasseriejoboston.com
French menu. Breakfast, lunch, dinner, late-night, brunch. Bar. Children's menu. Casual attire. Reservations recommended. Valet parking. Outdoor seating. **$$**

★★★Bravo Restaurant
465 Huntington Ave., Boston,
617-369-3487;
www.mfa.org
This bold-colored dining hall is located on the second story of the Museum of Fine Arts. The restaurant's contemporary design reflects the museum's galleries of modern art (a few works are displayed on the eatery's walls). The chef incorporates fresh, local ingredients into an eclectic American menu. Check out a wine tasting on the last Wednesday of each month.
Eclectic American menu. Lunch, dinner, brunch. Bar. Children's menu. Business casual attire. Reservations recommended. Outdoor seating. **$$$**

★★Brown Sugar Cafe- Fenway
129 Jersey St., Boston, 617-266-2928;
www.brownsugarcafe.com
Thai menu. Lunch, dinner. Casual attire. Outdoor seating. **$$**

★★The Butcher Shop
552 Tremont St., Boston, 617-423-4800;
www.thebutchershopboston.com
International menu. Lunch, dinner, brunch. Children's menu. Casual attire. Valet parking. **$$$**

★Cafe Marliave
10 Bosworth St., Boston, 617-423-6340
Italian menu. Lunch, dinner. Bar. Casual attire. Reservations recommended. Closed Sunday. **$$**

★★★The Capital Grille
359 Newbury St., Boston, 617-262-8900;
www.thecapitalgrille.com
The Capital Grille is a man's spot through and through. Dark walls and an extensive single-malt Scotch list give this high-roller-frequented steakhouse plenty of masculine character. Its generous portions of well-marbled steak, creamed spinach and buttery mashed potatoes are hearty enough for the hungriest diner. The house specialty is the gargantuan dry-aged porterhouse. Weighing in at 24 juicy, bold ounces, it should come with its own defibrillator.
Steak menu. Dinner. Bar. Business casual attire. Reservations recommended. Valet parking. **$$$**

★★Carmen
33 North Square, Boston, 617-742-6421
Mediterranean menu. Lunch, dinner. Closed Monday. Bar. Casual attire. **$$**

★★Casa Romero
30 Gloucester St., Boston, 617-536-4341;
www.casaromero.com
Mexican menu. Dinner, Sunday brunch. Bar. Outdoor seating. **$$$**

★★Chau Chow City
81 Essex St, Boston, 617-338-8158
Chinese menu. Lunch, dinner, late-night. Bar. Children's menu. Casual attire. Reservations recommended. **$$**

★Cheers
84 Beacon St., Boston, 617-227-9605;
www.cheersboston.com
American menu. Lunch, dinner. Bar. Children's menu. Casual attire. **$$**

★★Ciao Bella
240A Newbury St., Boston, 617-536-2626;
www.ciaobella.com
Italian menu. Lunch, dinner. Bar. Casual attire. Reservations recommended. Valet parking. Outdoor seating. **$$$**

★★Clarke's Turn of the Century
21 Merchants Row, Boston, 617-227-7800

American menu. Lunch, dinner, late-night. Bar. Casual attire. **$$**

★★★★Clio

370 Commonwealth Ave., Boston, 617-536-7200; www.cliorestaurant.com

Chef/owner Ken Oringer treats ingredients like notes in a melody—each one complements the next, and the result is a culinary symphony. Fresh fish plays a big role on the menu, and for those who prefer their seafood raw, Clio has a separate sashimi bar, Uni, that features a pricey selection of rare fish from around the world. The rooms are perpetually packed with Boston's media and financial elite.

French, Pan-Asian menu. Breakfast, dinner. Bar. Business casual attire. Reservations recommended. Valet parking. Closed Monday. **$$$**

★★Davide

326 Commercial St., Boston, 617-227-5745; www.davideristorante.com

Italian menu. Dinner. Bar. Valet parking. **$$**

★★★Davio's

75 Arlington St., Boston, 617-357-4810; www.davios.com

This northern Italian steakhouse has been a Boston institution for more than 20 years. Its large dining room features dramatic high ceilings, contemporary decor and imposing columns and an open kitchen lets diners watch chef Steve DiFillippo at work. Favored dishes include grilled porterhouse veal chops, hand-rolled potato gnocchi and a rich chocolate cake. Davio's To-Go Shop, serving delicious takeout such as pizza, sandwiches and dessert, is located right next door.

Italian menu. Lunch, dinner, late-night. Bar. Children's menu. Business casual attire. Reservations recommended. Valet parking. **$$$**

★Durgin Park

340 Faneuil Hall Marketplace, Boston, 617-227-2038; www.durgin-park.com

American menu. Lunch, dinner. Bar. Children's menu. Casual attire. Outdoor seating. **$$**

★★★Eastern Standard

528 Commonwealth Ave., Boston, 617-532-9100; www.easternstandardboston.com

With its prime location in the middle of newly buzzing Kenmore Square, this restaurant mixes classic French bistro décor and food with a cavernous space (that's usually packed to the rafters). The menu reads like a greatest hits of beloved comfort food dishes, from steak frites to meatloaf and mashed potatoes, viener schnitzel to beef short rib bourguignon (though there are also raw bar offerings for those in search of lighter fare). The outdoor seating is a prime warm weather people watching spot, and the bar is renowned for its expert versions of classic cocktails.

American. Breakfast, lunch, dinner. Valet parking. Outdoor dining. $$

★★Excelsior

272 Boylston St., Boston, 617-426-7878; www.excelsiorrestaurant.com/home

American menu. Dinner, late-night. Bar. Casual attire. **$$$**

★★Filippo

283 Causeway St., Boston, 617-742-4143; www.filipporistorante.com

Italian menu. Lunch, dinner. Bar. Children's menu. Valet parking. Closed Monday-Tuesday. **$$$**

★★Franklin Cafe

278 Shawmut Ave., Boston, 617-350-0010; www.franklincafe.com

American menu. Dinner, late-night. Bar. Casual attire. **$$**

★★Ginza

16 Hudson St., Boston, 617-338-2261

Japanese menu. Lunch, dinner, late-night. Casual attire. Closed Thanksgiving. **$$**

MASSACHUSETTS

★Grand Chau-Chow
45 Beach St., Boston, 617-292-5166
Chinese menu. Lunch, dinner, late-night. Casual attire. **$$**

★★★Grill 23 & Bar
161 Berkeley St., Boston, 617-542-2255; www.grill23.com
We all know the formula at steakhouses lots of beef paired with lots of testosterone, served up in a dark, wood-paneled boys club. Grill 23 serves lots of beef (seven juicy USDA Prime sirloin cuts) and ample testosterone (handsome, suited men line the bar), but this high-energy spot is anything but staid. Set in the historic Salada Tea Building, the vast space has sculptured ceilings, Corinthian columns and marble floors. It also has several non-steak options, in the form of a raw bar; lobster, shrimp, and clam entrees; caviar, sashimi and ceviche options; and plenty of lamb and poultry. Seafood, steak menu. Dinner. Bar. Business casual attire. Reservations recommended. Valet parking. **$$$**

★★★Hamersley's Bistro
553 Tremont St., Boston, 617-423-2700; www.hamersleysbistro.com
If the food were this good at home, it's doubtful you would ever bother leaving. For two decades, chef Gordon Hamersley has packed diners in nightly with his perfectly executed, seasonally influenced French bistro fare. The house specialty, chicken roasted with garlic, lemon and parsley is the perfect example of how simple food can shine. The kitchen also offers a weekly vegan special that could tantalize even the most ardent carnivore. Hamersley's eclectic wine list changes with the seasons, as does the menu, and the restaurant's staff is more than happy to help guide you to the right selection for your meal.
French bistro menu. Dinner. Bar. Casual attire. Reservations recommended. Valet parking. Outdoor seating. **$$$**

★★The Hungry I
71 1/2 Charles St., Boston, 617-227-3524

French bistro menu. Lunch, dinner, Sunday brunch. Bar. Business casual attire. Reservations recommended. Valet parking. Outdoor seating. **$$$**

★★★Icarus
3 Appleton St., Boston, 617-426-1790; www.icarusrestaurant.com
In a converted 1860s building, this South End standard shines during cold winter months, when its cozy, wood-paneled ambiance warms chilly customers. Chef Chris Douglas prepares a flavor-packed, seasonal American menu, full of dishes like slow-roasted tomato soup with Timson cheese panini, polenta with braised exotic mushrooms and duck in a cider and bourbon sauce. Come Friday nights, when a live jazz band takes the stage, and the intimate bar is the place to be. American menu. Dinner. Bar. Valet parking. **$$$$**

★Jasper White's Summer Shack
50 Dalton St., Boston, 617-867-9955
www.summershackrestaurant.com
Seafood menu. Lunch, dinner. Bar. Children's menu. Casual attire. **$$**

★★Jimmy's Harborside
242 Northern Ave., Boston, 617-423-1000; www.jimmysharborside.com
Seafood menu. Lunch, dinner. Bar. Children's menu. Casual attire. Reservations recommended. Valet parking. Outdoor seating. **$$**

★★Kashmir
279 Newbury St., Boston, 617-536-1695; www.kashmirspices.com
Indian menu. Lunch, dinner. Casual attire. Reservations recommended. Valet parking. Outdoor seating. **$$**

★★★★L'Espalier
30 Gloucester St., Boston, 617-262-3023; www.lespalier.com
Housed in a charming 19th-century townhouse, L'Espalier captures the elegance of another era, while serving French-influenced New England recipes that are

★
★
★
★
★

completely of the moment. The restaurant feels like a Merchant-Ivory film come to life. Chef Frank McClelland prepares prix fixe and tasting menus, as well as a caviar special for those feeling indulgent. A monster of a wine list offers an amazing variety of vintages, with a wide enough range to allow for great choices under $50.
French menu. Dinner, Saturday tea. Bar. Children's menu. Business casual attire. Reservations recommended. Valet parking. No Disabled Facilities. Closed Sunday-Monday in January-April and July-October. **$$$$**

★★**Lala Rokh**
97 Mt. Vernon St., Boston, 617-720-5511; www.lalarokh.com
Persian menu. Lunch, dinner. Business casual attire. **$$**

★★**Les Zygomates**
129 South St., Boston, 617-542-5108. www.winebar.com
French menu. Lunch, dinner. Bar. Casual attire. Reservations recommended. Valet parking. Closed Sunday. **$$$**

★★★**Locke-Ober**
3 Winter Place, Boston, 617-542-1340; www.lockeober.com
Established in 1875, Boston's famed Locke-Ober is a city icon. Once a stomping ground for various foodies, financiers, politicians and local glitterati, the restaurant, under the skilled leadership of chef/co-owner Lydia Shire, makes traditional American fare feel exciting. Even slightly passé dishes like beef Stroganoff made with hand-cut egg noodles and onion soup gratine taste fresh. Don't miss the signature Indian pudding for dessert.
American menu. Lunch, dinner. Bar. Business casual attire. Reservations recommended. Valet parking. Closed Sunday. **$$$**

★★**Lucia**
415 Hanover St., Boston, 617-367-2353; www.luciaboston.com

Italian menu. Lunch, dinner. Bar. Casual attire. Reservations recommended. Valet parking. **$$**

★★★**Mamma Maria**
3 North Square, Boston, 617-523-0077; www.mammamaria.com
Mamma Maria might be the North End's best restaurant—and that's saying a lot, considering every other neighborhood store front houses a trattoria. Filled nightly with celebrities and savvy locals, the romantic spot, set in an early 19th-century brick townhouse, serves a contemporary Italian menu that features seasonal ingredients and steers clear of heavy, cheesy, red-sauced pastas.
Italian menu. Dinner. Bar. Casual attire. Valet parking. **$$$**

★★★**Masa**
439 Tremont St., Boston, 617-338-8884; www.masarestaurant.com
This lively Southwestern restaurant is located on the edge of the South End, near the Chinatown and theater districts. Its lively bar area overlooks a chandelier-lit dining room, decorated with exposed brick walls, large mirrors, black-and-white checkered floors and flowing drapes. The spicy cuisine includes tapas, dinner and brunch menus. The margaritas are killer.
Southwestern menu. Dinner. Bar. Casual attire. Reservations recommended. Valet parking. Outdoor seating. **$$**

★★★★**Meritage**
70 Rowes Wharf, Boston, 617-439-3995, 800-752-7077; www.bhh.com
Chef Daniel Bruce's passion is mixing wine with food. Accordingly, his Meritage, located in the Boston Harbor Hotel, offers more than 900 bottles. He pairs his eclectic, seasonal dishes with wine flavors rather than varietals, progressing from light to heavy. Fennel-cured smoked salmon is matched with sparkling wines, while herb-and mustard-marinated filet comes with a pairing of robust reds. All menu items are available as large or small plates.

111

MASSACHUSETTS

★

★

★

★

International menu. Dinner, Sunday brunch. Bar. Business casual attire. Reservations recommended. Valet parking. Closed Monday. $$$

★★★Miel
510 Atlantic Ave., Boston,
617-747-1000, 800-327-0200;
www.intercontinentalboston.com
Miel—French for honey—is a sunny Provençal brasserie. On the ground floor of the new Intercontinental Boston, the 24-hour restaurant looks out over the revitalized waterfront. In warmer months, guests can sup on an outdoor patio. Inside, the yellow half-moon-shaped room has wrought-iron chandeliers, tile floors and a large stone hearth, plus a whole wall of olive oil jars. In addition to French classics such as Pistou soup and bouillabaisse, the chef sets up a raw bar daily.
French menu. Breakfast, lunch, dinner, late-night. Bar. Casual attire. Reservations recommended. Valet parking. Outdoor seating. $$$

★Mike's City Diner
1714 Washington St., Boston,
617-267-9393
American menu. Breakfast, lunch. Casual attire. $

★★★Mistral
223 Columbus Ave., Boston,
617-867-9300; www.mistralbistro.com
Although the vaulted ceilings and sophisticated décor may scream glam, chef/owner Jamie Mammanno's creative yet uncomplicated cuisine departs from those expectations. Menu items such as tuna tartare, grilled thin-crust pizzas and skillet-roasted Cornish game hen are complemented by a superb wine list.
French, Mediterranean menu. Dinner. Bar. Casual attire. Reservations recommended. Valet parking. $$$

★★Neptune Oyster
63 Salem St, Boston, 617-742-3424;
www.neptuneoyster.com

Seafood menu. Lunch, dinner. Bar. Casual attire. $$

★★★★No. 9 Park
9 Park St., Boston, 617-742-9991;
www.no9park.com
In the shadow of the State House on historic Beacon Hill sits Chef/owner Barbara Lynch's No. 9 Park. Her effort to support top-of-the-line local producers is evident on the seasonal menu—many ingredients are identified by farm. Perfectly prepared with a healthy dose of flavor and style, Lynch's sophisticated, tempting modern European fare runs the gamut from beef to fish to venison to pheasant. Wine director Cat Silirie selects a thoughtful and unique list, and trains the friendly wait staff to be as knowledgeable as she is.
French, Mediterranean menu. Lunch, dinner. Bar. Business casual attire. Reservations recommended. Valet parking. Closed Sunday. $$$

★★★The Oak Room
138 St., James Ave., Boston,
617-267-5300; www.theoakroom.com
This old-world steakhouse in the Fairmont Copley Plaza is steeped in Edwardian charm, as evidenced by the restored carved-plaster ceiling, baroque woodwork and garnet-red draperies. The perpetual, boisterous crowd of twenty-and thirtysomethings love the Oak Room's hearty grilled fish and beef tenderloin, oysters Rockefeller and clams casino.
American menu. Breakfast, lunch, dinner, Sunday brunch. Bar. Children's menu. Business casual attire. Reservations recommended. Valet parking. $$$

★★★The Palm
200 Dartmouth St., Boston,
617-867-9292; www.thepalm.com
"Let them eat meat!" might be an apt phrase to hang on a wall at The Palm. The local branch of the New York City favorite attracts financial moguls and out-of-town dealmakers looking to talk shop over copious amounts of perfectly seared prime beef. Tempting dessert trays include perennial

favorites such as six-layer chocolate cake and carrot cake.

Steak menu. Lunch, dinner. Bar. Children's menu. Casual attire. Reservations recommended. Valet parking. **$$$**

★★Parker's
60 School St., Boston, 617-725-1600;
www.omnihotels.com

Charles Dickens and Ralph Waldo Emerson ate here whenever in town, and John F. Kennedy's grandfather made Parker's the de facto headquarters of Massachusetts polls. The historical spot still attracts a cross-section of diners with a combination of classic and modern fare: steak au poivre with flaming tableside presentation is offered alongside pomegranate glazed chicken and salad selections include a "retro" chilled Iceberg wedge and an arugala salad with pancetta, Parmesan, and lemon-basil oil. American menu. Breakfast, lunch, dinner. Bar. Children's menu. Casual attire. Reservations recommended. Valet parking. Closed Sunday. **$$$**

★Peking Tom's
25 Kingston St., Boston, 617-482-6282;
www.pekingtom.com

Chinese menu. Lunch, dinner. Bar. Casual attire. **$$**

★★Pho Republique
1415 Washington St., Boston,
617-262-0005

Vietnamese menu. Dinner, late-night. Bar. Casual attire. **$$**

★★★Radius
8 High St., Boston, 617-426-1234;
www.radiusrestaurant.com

Chef Michael Schlow is a man who knows what diners want. First, there's the atmosphere. Radius is a chic, slick, modern space decked in silver and red décor. Second, there's the food. Schlow shows off inspired modern French cooking with spare (read: no heavy sauces) dishes prepared with infused oils, emulsions, juices, vegetable purees and reductions. Dishes are

well-textured and balanced and dessert is a heavenly experience.

French menu. Lunch, dinner. Bar. Business casual attire. Reservations recommended. Valet parking. Closed Sunday. **$$$**

★★The Red Fez
1222 Washington St., Boston,
617-338-6060; www.theredfez.com

Middle Eastern menu. Dinner, late-night, Sunday brunch. Bar. Casual attire. Outdoor seating. **$$**

★★Ristorante Toscano
47 Charles St., Boston, 617-723-4090;
www.ristorantetoscanoboston.com

Italian menu. Lunch, dinner. Bar. Business casual attire. Reservations recommended. Valet parking. Closed Sunday. **$$**

★★★Sage
1395 Washington St., Boston,
617-248-8814; www.sageboston.com

This teeny spot got a big upgrade last year when it traded its 35-seat North End space for roomy new digs in the South End. The interior is still rustic and cozy—just a bit more bustling—and chef/owner Anthony Susis is still serving modern Italian fare, including handmade pastas like gnocchi and ravioli.

Italian menu. Dinner. Casual attire. Reservations recommended. Closed Sunday. **$$$**

★★Tremont 647/Sister Sorel
647 Tremont St., Boston,
617-266-4600; www.tremont647.com

American menu. Dinner, brunch. Bar. Casual attire. Outdoor seating. **$$**

★★Sonsie
327 Newbury St., Boston,
617-351-2500; www.sonsieboston.com

International menu. Breakfast, lunch, dinner, late-night, brunch. Bar. Casual attire. Reservations recommended. Valet parking. Outdoor seating. **$$**

★★★Sorrelina
1 Huntington Ave., Boston, 617-412-4600;
www.sorrelinaboston.com

113

MASSACHUSETTS

It's hard to decide which lends more to the wow factor at this Back Bay restaurant: the sleek, contemporary design or the sophisticated Italian food. Cork floors, a white quartzite-terrazzo bar and low banquettes (all the better to see and be seen) make the room decidedly sexy. Though classics like spaghetti or veal Milanese make an appearance on the menu, chef/owner Jamie Mammano (also the talent behind Boston's Teatro, the Federalist and Mistral restaurants) dresses them up with gulf shrimp and chiles or saffron risotto. The exemplary wine list is punctuated by hard to find Italian bottles and balanced out with American and French selections.
Italian. Dinner. Valet parking. $$$

★★Tapeo
266 Newbury St., Boston,
617-267-4799; www.tapeo.com
Spanish, tapas menu. Dinner. Bar. Casual attire. Reservations recommended. Outdoor seating. $$

★★Taranta
210 Hanover St., Boston,
617-720-0052; www.tarantarist.com
Peruvian, Italian menu. Dinner. Casual attire. $$$

★★Terramia
98 Salem St., Boston, 617-523-3112;
www.terramiaristorante.com
Italian menu. Dinner. Children's menu. Reservations recommended. $$$

★★★Top of the Hub
800 Boylston St., Boston,
617-536-1775; www.topofthehub.net
If sweeping views are your thing, you'll want to add Top of the Hub to your short list of Boston must-visits. Located in Back Bay, this special-occasion spot specializes in elegant and romantic dining on the top floor of the Prudential building. The New American menu takes some chances, but for the most part stays true to the seasons, featuring a wide selection of fish, game,

pork, and beef. Main courses, such as the slow-roasted pork tenderloin (enough to feed a family of four), are ample; be prepared to share.
American menu. Lunch, dinner. Bar. Business casual attire. Reservations recommended. $$$

★★★Troquet
140 Boylston St., Boston, 617-695-9463;
www.troquetboston.com
The marriage of food and wine is the focus of this authentic Back Bay bistro. For example, owners Chris and Diane Campbell match flights of Sauvignon Blanc with a tangy fried goat cheese arugula salad, and sweet Merlots with leg of lamb. As a result, dinner becomes an education as well as a fine gastronomical experience.
American, French menu. Dinner. Bar. Business casual attire. Reservations recommended. Valet parking. Closed Sunday-Monday. $$$

★★★Union Bar and Grille
1357 Washington St., Boston,
617-423-0555; www.unionrestaurant.com
With leather banquettes and blazingly white tablecloths, Union Bar and Grille caps the gentrification of the South End's Washington Street. Stephen Sherman, the Culinary Institute of America-trained chef, produces a seasonally shifting menu that incorporates trendy dishes like tuna with grilled fennel, but also includes updated New England classics such as lobster tossed with corn and chanterelle mushrooms, and rack of lamb drizzled with fig sauce. The wine list is heavy on California and New Zealand whites. Pastry chef Joshua Steinberg's dessert menu gives diners a spot of chocolate on almost every plate.
American menu. Dinner, Sunday brunch. Bar. Casual attire. Valet parking. $$$

★★Union Oyster House
41 Union St., Boston,
617-227-2750;
www.unionoysterhouse.com

MASSACHUSETTS

★
★
★
★
★

Seafood menu. Lunch, dinner, late-night. Bar. Children's menu. Casual attire. Reservations recommended. Valet parking. **$$**

★★Via Matta
79 Park Plaza, Boston, 617-422-0008; www.viamattarestaurant.com
Michael Schlow, Christopher Myers and Esti Parsons, the savvy team behind Radius, are the folks you can thank for opening Via Matta, a trendy Italian eatery across from the Park Plaza Hotel. The place buzzes with energy, especially at lunch, as the city's power players sip Italian wine and nosh on lightly breaded Chicken Milanese. The hotspot has a shaded outdoor patio, as well as an Enoteca, a candle-lit bar area perfect for drinks and small plates. Be sure to save room for dessert—Schlow's panne cotta might be the best in Boston.
Italian menu. Lunch, dinner. Bar. Casual attire. Reservations recommended. Valet parking. Outdoor seating. Closed Sunday. **$$$**

BRAINTREE
This city, just south of Boston, is the site of second President John Adams' estate. Though Adams was away for much of their marriage, first as a European amabassador during the revolutionary war, and later in Philadelphia as president, his wife Abigail stayed behind and helped the farm and homestead flourish.
Information: South Shore Chamber of Commerce, 36 Miller Stile Rd., Quincy, 781-479-1111; www.southshorechamber.org

WHAT TO SEE AND DO
Abigail Adams House
180 Norton St., Weymouth, 781-335-4205
The birthplace of Abigail Smith Adams, daughter of a local clergyman, wife of President John Adams, mother of President John Quincy Adams. July-Labor Day: Tuesday-Sunday.

Gilbert Bean Museum
786 Washington St., Braintree, 781-848-1640
This house contains 17th- and 18th-century furnishings, military exhibits and local historical displays. Tuesday-Wednesday, Saturday-Sunday 10 a.m.-4:30 p.m.

HOTELS
★★Holiday Inn
1374 N. Main St., Randolph, 781-961-1000, 800-465-4329; www.holiday-inn.com
158 rooms. Restaurant. Bar. **$**

★Holiday Inn Express
909 Hingham St., Rockland, 781-871-5660
76 rooms. Complimentary continental breakfast. **$**

★★★Sheraton Braintree Hotel
37 Forbes Rd., Braintree, 781-848-0600, 800-325-3535; www.sheraton.com/braintree
Just 12 miles from Logan International Airport and near the JFK library and Bayside Exposition Center, the Sheraton Braintree is a good choice for those who want to visit Boston without paying the city's sky-high hotel rates. Relax in the indoor or outdoor pool, sauna and steam rooms, or enjoy an invigorating workout at the extensive on-site health club that has racquetball, aerobics and Nautilus machines.
396 rooms. Restaurant. Bar. **$**

RESTAURANTS
★★Caffe Bella
19 Warren St., Randolph, 781-961-7729
Italian menu. Dinner. Closed Sunday. Bar. **$$$**

★
★
★
★

BREWSTER

This quiet community on the inner arm of the Cape is dominated by miles of beautiful Cape Cod Bay beaches. Soft sand, gentle waves and plenty of shallow tide pools make Brewster an ideal family getaway.

Information: Cape Cod Chamber of Commerce, Highways 6 and 13, Hyannis, 508-362-3225, 888-332-2732; www.capecodchamber.org

WHAT TO SEE AND DO

Cape Cod Museum of Natural History
869 Hwy., 6A. Brewster, 508-896-3867; www.ccmnh.org
Here are exhibits on wildlife and ecology, plus a library, lectures, field walks and trips to Monomoy Island. Daily 10 a.m.-4 p.m.

Cape Cod Repertory Theater Company
3379 Hwy., 6A, Brewster, 508-896-1888; www.caperep.org
With both an indoor and outdoor theater, this troupe offers children's performances on Tuesday and Friday mornings in July and August. In addition, you'll find productions for the whole family in the outdoor theater in the woods near Nickerson State Park.

New England Fire & History Museum
1439 Main St., Brewster, 508-896-5711
This six-building complex houses an extensive collection of fire-fighting equipment. Also on hand are a diorama of Chicago's 1871 fire, antique engines, the world's only 1929 Mercedes Benz fire engine, a life-size reproduction of Ben Franklin's firehouse, a 19th-century blacksmith shop, and the largest apothecary in the country (that's 664 gold-leaf bottles of medicine). Memorial Day weekend-Labor Day: Monday-Saturday 10 a.m.-4 p.m., Sunday from noon; mid-September-Columbus Day: weekends.

Nickerson State Park
3488 Hwy., 6A, Brewster, 508-896-3491; www.state.ma.us/dem/parks/nick.htm
Nickerson State Park offers an unusual experience on Cape Cod: densely wooded areas that show no signs of the typical marshy Cape regions. The park has camping, challenging hiking trails, an 8-mile bike path, fishing, swimming, canoeing, and bird-watching. Daily.

Ocean Edge Golf Course
2660 Hwy., 6A, Brewster, 508-896-9000; www.oceanedge.com
This beautiful golf course, just a stone's throw from the ocean, offers 6,665 yards of manicured greens, plus five ponds for challenging play. Greens fees drop considerably in the off-season, and lessons from PGA pros are often available. Daily; closed for snow and inclement weather.

HOTELS

★★★Ocean Edge Resort
2907 Main St., Brewster, 508-896-9000; 800-343-6074
www.oceanedge.com
This sprawling 19th-century English country manor offers guests an oasis of comfort and privacy on Cape Cod Bay. Resort activities include golf, tennis, swimming, hiking, and biking. Kids are welcome, but romantics shouldn't shy away—the estate is big enough for everyone and every type of family.
406 rooms. Restaurant. Bar. Children's activity center. Airport transportation available. $$

SPECIALTY LODGINGS

Bramble Inn
2019 Main St., Brewster, 508-896-7644; www.brambleinn.com
8 rooms. Children over 8 years only. Complimentary full breakfast. Restaurant. Closed January-April. $

Brewster by the Sea
716 Main St., Brewster, 508-896-3910, 800-892-3910; www.brewsterfarmhouseinn.com

8 rooms. Children over 10 years only. Complimentary full breakfast. **$**

Captain Freeman Inn
15 Breakwater Rd., Brewster,
508-896-7481, 800-843-4664;
www.captainfreemaninn.com
12 rooms. Children over 10 years only. Complimentary full breakfast. Airport transportation available. **$**

Isaiah Clark House
1187 Main St., Brewster,
508-896-2223, 800-822-4001;
www.isaiahclark.com
7 rooms. Children over 10 years only. Complimentary full breakfast. **$**

Old Sea Pines Inn
2553 Main St., Brewster, 508-896-6114
www.oldseapinesinn.com
24 rooms. Children over 8 years only (except in family suites). Complimentary full breakfast. **$**

The Old Manse Inn
1861 Main St., Brewster,
508-896-3149; 866-896-3149
www.oldmanseinn.com
9 rooms. Complimentary full breakfast. **$$**

RESTAURANTS
★★★Bramble Inn
2019 Main St., Brewster, 508-896-7644;
www.brambleinn.com
Chef/owner Ruth Manchester delights guests with creative cuisine and heart-warming hospitality at this cozy eatery in Brewster's historic district. The four quaint dining rooms, including an enclosed porch, make the Bramble Inn a perfect choice for a romantic dinner.

American menu. Dinner. Bar. Business casual attire. Reservations recommended. Closed January-April. **$$$**

★★Brewster Fish House
2208 Main St., Brewster, 508-896-7867
American, seafood menu. Lunch, dinner. Closed December-April. **$$$**

★Brewster Inn and Chowder House
1993 Main St., Brewster, 508-896-7771
American menu. Lunch, dinner. Bar. Casual attire. Outdoor seating. **$$**

★★★Chillingsworth
2449 Main St., Brewster,
508-896-3640, 800-430-3640;
www.chillingsworth.com
The grand 300-year-old Chillingsworth Foster estate sprawls along the edge of the Kings Highway. For the last 30 years, its restaurant has been synonymous with epicurean eating on Cape Cod. The formal dining rooms, furnished in antiques, are spread through the central house. The seven-course dinner is a contemporary interpretation of classic French cuisine—seared veal steak with truffle risotto, for example, or lobster with sautéed spinach and fennel. Plan to dress up and spend the whole evening munching (quicker, lighter fare can be had in the more casual bistro on a glassed-in porch).
French menu. Lunch, dinner. Bar. Reservations recommended. Outdoor seating. Closed Monday; also December-mid-May. **$$$**

★★Spark Fish
2671 Main St., Brewster, 508-896-1067;
www.sparkfish.com
American menu. Dinner. Bar. Children's menu. Casual attire. Reservations recommended. Outdoor seating. **$$**

MASSACHUSETTS

BROOKLINE
What started out as a commuter community has blossomed into a booming city in its own right. Directly to the east of Boston, Brookline began in the 1600s as a summer Mecca for wealthy merchants and politicians. Centuries later, the town was still attracting notable Americans—Frederick Law Olmstead and John F. Kennedy both lived

here (the latter's boyhood home is now open to the public). Today, Brookline's much-envied, Victorian-lined shady streets are home to moneyed families and one of the best school systems in the Boston area. Washington Square, Coolidge Corner and Brookline Village, with their shops, eateries and bars, attract younger residents and out-of-towners alike.

Information: www.townofbrooklinemass.com

WHAT TO SEE AND DO

John F. Kennedy National Historic Site
83 Beals St., Brookline, 617-566-7937;
www.nps.gov/jofi
The birthplace and childhood home of the nation's 35th president has been restored to its 1917 state. Ranger-guided tours. May-October: Wednesday-Sunday 10 a.m.-4:30 p.m.

RESTAURANTS

★★★Fugakyu
1280 Beacon St., Brookline, 617-734-1268;
www.fugakyujapanese.com
For some reason, Brookline has more sushi spots than any New England city. Fugakyu stands out among all the Japanese boites. Its Coolidge Corner location is huge and heavy on the blonde wood-white screen décor. Larger parties can reserve private tatami rooms—complete with rice paper walls and sliding doors—and choose from a menu of soups, tempuras, stir-fries, noodles, pickle plates, sushi, sashimi, maki rolls and tableside braises. Diners rave about the tempura-fried green tea ice cream dessert topped with just a dab of red-bean paste.
Japanese, sushi menu. Lunch, dinner, late-night. Reservations recommended. Closed Sunday

★Rubin's Kosher Delicatessen
500 Harvard St., Brookline, 617-731-8787;
www.rubinskosher.com
Kosher deli menu. Breakfast, lunch, dinner Sunday-Thursday. Closed Saturday; Jewish holidays. **$**

★★★The Fireplace
1634 Beacon St., Brookline,
617-975-1900; www.fireplacerest.com
Thanks to its yuppified neighborhood, the Fireplace can seem like a cross between *Friends* and *Cheers,* where everyone knows everyone else, and half the diners are just stopping to chat and sip a glass of Sancerre. Hungry patrons are devoted to the hearty fare—braised brisket, grilled halibut, gingerbread pudding—much of it made from scratch in the wood-fired oven or smoke box. The eponymous hearth provides welcome warmth and added coziness in winter months. American, seafood menu. Lunch, dinner, brunch. Children's menu. Casual attire. **$$**

★★Washington Square Tavern
714 Washington St., Brookline,
617-232-8989;
www.washingtonsquaretavern.com
American menu. Dinner, Sunday brunch. Bar. Casual attire. **$$**

CAMBRIDGE

Across the Charles River from Boston, Cambridge seems a world away. Though connected to the state capital, and often lumped in with it geographically, the "People's Republic of Cambridge," as locals have christened it, has a decidedly different vibe. Famous for its universities (Harvard, M.I.T.), bustling squares and ethnically diverse residents (80 different nations are represented by the city's public school kids), the area is a melting pot of people and ideas. The gritty, nightclub-filled streets of Central Square run into the vibrant back roads of Harvard Square and the mansion-lined Brattle Street (actor John Malcovich lives here), which in turn leads into safe, family-friendly Huron Village. Farther to the east is Inman Square, a multicultural neighborhood overflowing with cafes, eateries and sweet little shops. Most of the city is easily accessible by public bus or train; those with more stamina should consider walking these historic, but very much alive, streets.

Information: Chamber of Commerce, 859 Massachusetts Ave., 617-876-4100; www.cambcc.org

WHAT TO SEE AND DO

Cambridge Antique Mall

201 Monsigenur O'Brien Hwy.,
Cambridge, 617-868-9655;
www.marketantique.com
Stroll through five floors of antique furniture, books, artwork, toys, clothing and more. Tuesday-Sunday 11 a.m.-6 p.m.

Christ Church

0 Garden St., Cambridge, 617-876-0200;
www.cccambridge.org
Dating back to 1759, this Episcopal church building is the oldest in Cambridge. The fine Georgian colonial designed by Peter Harrison was used as a barracks during the Revolution. Daily.

Formaggio Kitchen

244 Huron Ave., Cambridge, 617-354-4750;
www.formaggiokitchen.com
Whether you consider yourself a *gourmet* or a *gourmand*, you'll easily lose yourself in this culinary playground. With a selection of 200 artisan cheeses, fine pastas, international chocolates, exotic spices, mouthwatering snacks and Italian coffees, the famed Formaggio Kitchen is a food-lovers dream.

Harvard University

24 Quincy St., Cambridge,
www.harvard.edu; Information center:
1350 Massachusetts Ave., Cambridge,
617-495-1573
America's oldest university was founded in 1636. Two years later, when a minister named John Harvard died and bequested half his estate to the school, the college was named for him. The prototypical brick- and quad-filled campus spans Harvard and Radcliffe colleges, as well as 10 graduate and professional schools.

Harvard Museum of Natural History

26 Oxford St., Cambridge, 617-495-3045
The Harvard Museum of Natural History is three museums in one: a botanical museum that examines the study of plants, the museum of zoology that examines the study of animals and a geological museum that examines the study of rocks and minerals. All three explore the evolution of science and nature throughout time. Daily 9 a.m.-5 p.m.

Harvard University Art Museums

32 Quincy St., Cambridge, 617-495-9400
Visit three museums in one: the Fogg Art Museum (including wide-ranging collections of paintings and sculpture), the Busch-Reisinger Museum (which features mostly German art), and the Arthur M. Sackler Museum (ancient art, plus Asian and Islamic collections). Admission to one museum covers all three; allow a half day for all. Entry is free on Wednesdays and Saturdays until noon. Daily.

Peabody Museum of Archaeology and Ethnology

11 Divinity Ave., Cambridge, 617-496-1027
The Peabody Museum, one of the oldest anthropology museums in the world, traces human cultural history in the Western Hemisphere. Daily.

119

MASSACHUSETTS

★
★
★
★

Longfellow National Historic Site

105 Brattle St., Cambridge,
617-876-4491; www.nps.gov/long

This Georgian-style house, built in 1759, was Washington's headquarters during the 1775-1776 siege of Boston, and Henry Wadsworth Longfellow's home from 1837 until his death in 1882. Wednesday-Sunday 10 a.m.-4:30 p.m.

Massachusetts Institute of Technology

77 Massachusetts Ave., Cambridge,
617-253-1000; www.mit.edu

M.I.T. remains one of the greatest science and engineering schools in the world. On the Charles River, the campus' 135 acres house impressive neoclassic and modern buildings. Monday-Friday.

List Visual Arts Center at MIT

Wiesner Building, 20 Ames St., Cambridge,
The museum has changing exhibits of contemporary art. The MIT campus also has an outstanding permanent collection of outdoor sculpture, including works by Calder, Moore and Picasso, and significant architecture, including buildings by Aalto, Pei and Saarinen. October-June, daily.

MIT Museum

265 Massachusetts Ave., Cambridge,
617-253-4444

Collections and exhibits that interpret the Institute's social and educational history, developments in science and technology, and the interplay of technology and art. Tuesday-Friday 10 a.m.-5p.m., Saturday-Sunday from noon; closed Monday.

Radcliffe College's Schlesinger Library Culinary Collection

10 Garden St., Cambridge, 617-495-8647;
www.radcliffe.edu/schles

Through Radcliffe's culinary collection, you'll have access to more than 9,000 cookbooks. Although you can't borrow from the library, you can still tap into the books of some of the world's greatest chefs, including Samuel Narcisse Chamberlain, Julia Child and Sophie Coe. Monday-Friday.

SPECIAL EVENTS

Head of the Charles Regatta

2 Gerry's Landing Rd., Cambridge,
617-868-6200; www.hocr.org

More than 300,000 spectators from all over the world descend on Boston for this three-mile rowing race that involves 7,000 athletes and 1,470 rowing shells. Olympic and World champions race each other on the Charles River, while countless fans tailgate and cheer along the shore.

HOTELS

★★Best Western Hotel Tria

220 Alewife Brook Pkwy., Cambridge,
617-491-8000, 866-333-8742;
www.bestwestern.com

69 rooms. Complimentary continental breakfast. High-speed Internet access. Restaurant. Bar. $

★★★Charles Hotel

1 Bennett St., Cambridge,
617-864-1200, 800-882-1818;
www.charleshotel.com

Celebrities, politicians and visiting dignitaries (not to mention the wealthy parents of Harvard students) all stay at the Charles, one of Boston's most beloved hotels. The guest rooms mix Shaker-inspired design with a multitude of modern amenities such as three two-line phones, Bose Wave radios, TVs in the bathrooms and more. Dine in either of its two restaurants, and be sure to tune into the sweet sounds of jazz at the Regattabar, where swinging national bands hit the stage. In winter, the hotel's courtyard becomes an ice-skating rink, while various community events, such as a farmer's market, take place here in the summer.

294 rooms. Wireless Internet access. Restaurant. Bar. $$$

★★★Hotel @ MIT

20 Sidney St., Cambridge,
617-577-0200, 800-774-1500;
www.hotelatmit.com

This high-tech-themed hotel identifies closely with the similarly named school—it even incorporates printed circuit board designs into the bedroom furniture.

120

MASSACHUSETTS

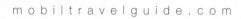

Predictably, the hotel is wired every which way, with lightning quick Internet access and Sony PlayStations in all guest rooms. The spot also functions as a conference and meeting center for cutting-edge companies in media, biotech, robotics and computing. 210 rooms. Wireless Internet access. Restaurant. Bar. **$$**

★★★Hotel Marlowe

25 Edwin H. Land Blvd., Cambridge, 617-868-8000, 800-825-7140; www.hotelmarlowe.com

The Marlowe sets itself apart from other East Cambridge lodgings with its whimsical palette of crimson, deep blue and bright gold. Surrounded by luxury condos and a shopping mall, this modern hotel is less than a block from the Museum of Science. Amenities are top of the line (Frette linens, Aveda bath products), the in-room Sony PlayStations amuse youngsters and the pet-friendly vibe (the concierge will order doggie birthday cakes from nearby Polka Dog Bakery) is a big plus for animal lovers.

236 rooms. Wireless Internet access. Restaurant. Bar. Airport transportation available. **$$$**

★★★Hyatt Regency Cambridge

575 Memorial Dr., Cambridge, 617-492-1234, 800-633-7313; www.hyatt.com

Hyatt Regency guests are afforded a level of style and comfort unexpected from the massive hotel chain. From the lavishly appointed lobby (with a large open atrium and glass elevators) to the spacious guest rooms to the darling gazebo in the well-maintained courtyard, this hotel makes patrons feel at home. Its Charles River location is 15 minutes from both Harvard Square and downtown Boston.

469 rooms. Wireless Internet access. Restaurant. Bar. **$$**

★★Boston Marriott Cambridge

2 Cambridge Center, Cambridge, 617-494-6600, 800-228-9290; www.marriott.com

431 rooms. High-speed Internet access. Two restaurants, two bars. **$$**

★★★Royal Sonesta Hotel Boston

5 Cambridge Pkwy., Cambridge, 617-806-4200, 800-766-3782; www.sonesta.com/boston

Perched on the Charles River, this hotel boasts panoramic Boston skyline views, handsomely appointed guest rooms and a state-of-the-art health spa with massage therapists, reflexology and a poolside sun deck. The property is adjacent to the Museum of Science and walking distance to the Cambridgeside Galleria, an indoor shopping mall.

400 rooms. Wireless Internet access. Two restaurants, two bars. **$$$**

★★★The Inn at Harvard

1201 Massachusetts Ave., Cambridge, 617-491-2222, 800-458-5886; www.theinnatharvard.com

Acclaimed postmodernist Cambridge architect Graham Gund showed great restraint in creating this neoclassical structure at the edge of Harvard Square. Guest rooms have a casual, homey feel, but a four-story atrium turns the reception area into a soaring library and lounge area. The university frequently books many of the rooms for visiting scholars and dignitaries; reserve months ahead of time if in town on a graduation or alumni weekend.

112 rooms. Wireless Internet access. Restaurant. Bar. **$$**

★★A Cambridge House Bed and Breakfast Inn

2218 Massachusetts Ave., Cambridge, 617-491-6300, 800-232-9989; www.acambridgehouse.com

15 rooms. Complimentary continental breakfast. Wireless Internet access. **$$**

RESTAURANTS

★★Baraka Cafe

80 1/2 Pearl St., Cambridge, 617-868-3951; www.barakacafe.com

121

MASSACHUSETTS

Tunisian. Lunch, dinner. Casual attire. Closed Monday. **$$**

★★Blue Room
1 Kendall Square, Cambridge, 617-494-9034; www.theblueroom.net
Mediterranean menu. Dinner, Sunday brunch. Bar. Casual attire. Reservations recommended. Outdoor seating. **$$$**

★★Casablanca
40 Brattle St., Cambridge, 617-876-0999; www.casablanca-restaurant.com
Mediterranean menu. Lunch, dinner. Bar. Casual attire. Reservations recommended. **$$$**

★★Chez Henri
1 Shepard St., Cambridge, 617-354-8980; www.chezhenri.com
Cuban menu, French menu. Dinner. **$$$**

★★Craigie Street Bistro
5 Craigie Circle, Cambridge, 617-497-5511; www.craigiestreetbistrot.com
French bistro, International menu. Dinner. Casual attire. Reservations recommended. Closed Monday-Tuesday; also late June-early July. **$$**

★★East Coast Grill & Raw Bar
1271 Cambridge St., Cambridge, 617-491-6568; www.eastcoastgrill.net
Seafood menu. Dinner, Sunday brunch. Bar. Casual attire. **$$**

★★★Harvest
44 Brattle St., Cambridge, 617-868-2255; www.harvestcambridge.com
Harvest's rustic ambiance—pewter tableware, dried flowers, sturdy, dark wood—is at odds with the building's modern exteriors. Inside, classic American dishes (don't miss the nightly risotto!) are served from an open kitchen in the family-friendly dining room.
American menu. Lunch, dinner, Sunday brunch. Children's menu. Outdoor seating. **$$$**

★★Helmand
143 First St., Cambridge, 617-492-4646
Afghan menu. Dinner. **$$**

★★★Oleana
134 Hampshire St., Cambridge, 617-661-0505; www.oleanarestaurant.com
Mediterranean menus are a dime a dozen in the Boston area, but few chefs coax out the cuisine's diverse influences as well as Oleana's chef/owner Ana Sortun. She gleefully matches Arabic almonds with herbs from Provence in a chicken dish, and isn't afraid to branch out with the likes of a Basque-influenced venison with caramelized turnip. Regulars would revolt if she removed the scallops with basmati-pistachio pilaf from the menu, but they'd probably come shuffling back eventually—the outdoor patio and fireplace-lit indoor rooms are too inviting to resist.
Eastern Mediterranean menu. Dinner. Bar. Casual attire. Reservations recommended. Outdoor seating. **$$$**

★★★Rialto
1 Bennett St., Cambridge, 617-661-5050; www.rialto-restaurant.com
Fresh from a complete redesign, this second floor Charles Hotel eatery is more popular than ever. Chef/owner Jody Adams's distinctive brand of boldly flavored Mediterranean-inspired fare has also been re-imagined, but her honest, straightforward approach and dedication to fresh, seasonal produce hasn't changed a bit. Her Italian-heavy menu is a masterpiece of complimentary flavors and the wine list is well-edited and approachable.
Mediterranean menu. Dinner. Bar. Business casual attire. Reservations recommended. Valet parking. **$$$**

★★★Salts
798 Main St., Cambridge, 617-876-8444; www.saltsrestaurant.com
Located between Kendall Square and Central Square, this tiny neighborhood place has a quiet and cozy atmosphere. Romantics looking for special-occasion dining can't go wrong at Salts, where the focus is on local,

122

★
★
★
★
★

organic produce. A mostly French menu pairs well with a list of some 200 French and American wines.
Contemporary American menu. Dinner. Business casual attire. Reservations recommended. Closed Sunday-Monday. **$$$**

★★Sandrine's
8 Holyoke St., Cambridge, 617-497-5300; www.sandrines.com

French bistro menu. Lunch, dinner. Bar. Business casual attire. Reservations recommended. **$$$**

★★The Elephant Walk
2067 Mass Ave., Cambridge, 617-492-6900; www.elephantwalk.com/cambridge
French, Pacific-Rim/Pan-Asian menu. Dinner. Bar. Children's menu. Casual attire. Reservations recommended. **$$$**

CAPE COD

The invention of the automobile changed Cape Cod from a group of isolated fishing villages, large estates and cranberry bogs into one of the world's prime resort areas. Today, the seaside region's population more than triples during the summertime, when 200,000 year-round residents prepare for nearly 500,000 visitors. Since World War II, hundreds of hotels and resorts have opened to accommodate the hordes of tourists (still, good luck finding a last-minute room in August), but the quaint villages themselves have remained virtually unchanged.

Seventy miles long, the Cape is a peninsula land mass in the shape of a bent arm and clenched fist. Buzzards Bay and the Cape Cod Canal mark the beginning of the Cape, Chatham and Nauset beaches are at its "elbow," and Provincetown, or P-town to those in the know, lies at its northern tip. Because the Cape extends 30 miles offshore and into the warm Gulf Stream, its climate is notably gentler than that of the mainland. As an added bonus, many Cape towns have two beaches—one bay-side, one ocean-side, both covered with fine, soft sand. All in all, the Cape's coastline stretches for a never-ending 560 miles.

123

MASSACHUSETTS

★
★
★
★

CHATHAM

Chatham is among the hubs of the Cape's social scene. Though tourists are hard to distinguish from blue-blooded locals, look closely. Year-rounders are most likely the ones sipping lemonade on the porches of their comfortable estates that look out over Pleasant Bay and Nantucket Sound. Monomoy Island, an unattached sand bar that stretches 10 miles into the sea, was once a haunt of "moon-cussers"—beach pirates who lured vessels aground with false lights.
Information: Chamber of Commerce, Chatham, 800-715-5567; www.capecodchamber.org

WHAT TO SEE AND DO
Chatham Light
Bridge and Main Streets, Chatham, 508-430-0628
This quintessential Cape lighthouse has been through many incarnations and res-

torations, but has always offered a superb view of the Atlantic and the seals on the beach below. Daily.

Monomoy National Wildlife Refuge
Monomoy Island, Chatham,

508-945-0594;
www.monomoy.fws.gov
The refuge is 2,750 acres of bird lover's paradise. The spectacle is greatest in spring, when the inhabitants exhibit bright plumage while breeding.

HOTELS

★★★The Bradford of Chatham
26 Cross St., Chatham,
508-945-1030, 888-242-8426;
www.bradfordinn.com
38 rooms. Children over 12 only. Complimentary full breakfast. **$$**

★★★Chatham Bars Inn
297 Shore Rd., Chatham,
508-945-0096, 800-527-4884;
www.chathambarsinn.com
Built in 1814, this grand Cape Cod landmark has managed to maintain most of its historic charm without falling into disrepair. The guest rooms have 180-degree views of Pleasant Bay; well-maintained gardens and a private beach (one of the few in the area) are just outside. The resort recently added a large, state-of-the-art spa that offers plenty of pampering
205 rooms. Wireless Internet access. Four restaurants, two bars. Children's activity center. Beach. Airport transportation available. **$$$$**

★Chatham Seafarer
2079 Main St., Chatham,
508-432-1739, 800-786-2772;
www.chathamseafarer.com
20 rooms. **$**

★The Chatham Motel
1487 Main St., Chatham,
508-945-2630, 800-770-5545;
www.chathammotel.com
32 rooms. Closed November-April. **$**

★★★Chatham Wayside Inn
512 Main St., Chatham,
508-945-5550, 800-242-8426;
www.waysideinn.com
This classic village inn dates to the 1860s, as evidenced by the lobby's original knotty pine flooring. The informal and cozy property has 56 large, clean and comfortable rooms—a few have private balconies and jetted tubs. The grounds are within walking distance to the water and the town center.
56 rooms. Restaurant. Bar. **$$$**

★★★Cranberry Inn
359 Main St., Chatham,
508-945-9232, 800-332-4667;
www.cranberryinn.com
Located in the historic district, this elegant inn offers guests all the comforts of home. Visitors can relax in the well-appointed guest rooms, or enjoy the picturesque view of a windmill while lazing in one of the Kennedy rocking chairs set along the expansive front porch.
18 rooms. Children over 12 years only. Complimentary full breakfast. **$**

★★★Pleasant Bay Village Resort
1191 Orleans Rd., Chatham,
508-945-1133, 800-547-1011;
www.pleasantbayvillage.com
From the exquisitely arranged rock garden, where a waterfall cascades into a stone-edged pool filled with colorful koi to the lavishly appointed gardens, this six-acre woodland retreat is timeless tranquility. Many rooms have private patios, grills and screened-in porches.
58 rooms. Closed late October-April. 11 a.m. Wireless Internet access. Restaurant. **$$**

★★★Queen Anne Inn
70 Queen Anne Rd., Chatham,
508-945-0394, 800-545-4667;
www.queenanneinn.com
34 rooms. Complimentary continental breakfast. Restaurant. Closed January. **$**

★★★Wequassett Inn
On Pleasant Bay, Chatham,
508-432-5400, 800-225-7125;
www.wequassett.com
This country inn-resort hybrid appeals to antique lovers and activity junkies alike. Located on 22 acres, the full-service spot overlooks Pleasant Bay and the Atlantic

Ocean. Suites take a cosmopolitan slant on country décor. Take advantage of the (private to everyone else) prestigious Cape Cod National Golf Club.

104 rooms. Wireless Internet access. Two restaurants, Bar. Children's activity center. Beach. Airport transportation available. Closed December-March. **$$$$**

SPECIALTY LODGINGS

Captain's House Inn

369-377 Old Harbor Rd., Chatham, 508-945-0127, 800-315-0728; www.captainshouseinn.com

Once a sea captain's estate, this pretty inn was built in 1839 and features period wallpapers, Williamsburg antiques and elegantly refined Queen Anne chairs. Many of the guestrooms are named for the ships that once sailed the nearby seas.

16 rooms. Children over 12 only. Complimentary full breakfast. **$$**

Moses Nickerson House Inn

364 Old Harbor Rd., Chatham, 508-945-5859, 800-628-6972; www.mosesnickersonhouse.com

In 1839, whaling captain Moses Nickerson built the house that's home to this quaint bed and breakfast.

7 rooms. Children over 10 years only. Complimentary full breakfast. **$**

Old Harbor Inn

22 Old Harbor Rd., Chatham, 508-945-4434, 800-942-4434; www.chathamoldharborinn.com

Built in 1933, this former residence of a prominent doctor has been renovated and is furnished with a blend of antiques and modern conveniences.

8 rooms. Children over 14 years only. Complimentary full breakfast. **$**

RESTAURANTS

★★Chatham Squire

487 Main St., Chatham, 508-945-0945; www.thesquire.com

Seafood menu. Lunch, dinner. Bar. Children's menu. Casual attire. **$$**

★★Christian's

443 Main St., Chatham, 508-945-3362; www.christiansrestaurant.com

American menu. Dinner. Closed winter. Bar. Casual attire. Reservations recommended. **$$$**

★★Impudent Oyster

15 Chatham Bars Ave., Chatham, 508-945-3545

Seafood menu. Lunch, dinner. Bar. Children's menu. Casual attire. Reservations recommended. **$$$**

★★Pate's

1260 Main St., Chatham, 508-945-9777; www.patesrestaurant.com

American menu. Dinner. Bar. Children's menu. Casual attire. Closed February-March. **$$**

★★★★Twenty-Eight Atlantic

Pleasant Bay Rd., Chatham, 508-432-5400, 800-225-7125; www.wequassett.com

Black truffle risotto, truffled salmon tartare and a petite clambake are among the enticing entrées offered at this waterfront restaurant located in the Wequassett Resort. The large, open dining room features featuring wide views of Pleasant Bay.

American menu. Breakfast, lunch, dinner. Bar. Children's menu. Business casual attire. Reservations recommended. Outdoor seating. Closed December-March. **$$$**

★★Vining's Bistro

595 Main St., Chatham, 508-945-5033; www.viningsbistro.com

International menu. Dinner. Casual attire. Closed in winter. **$$**

CONCORD

About as old-school New England as it gets, Concord (along with neighboring Lexington) boasts the title "Birthplace of the Republic." A litany of American literary greats—Ralph Waldo Emerson, Henry David Thoreau, Nathanial Hawthorne, Louisa May Alcott—once called this country town home. The area got its name from the unusual "peace and concord" between its colonial settlers and the native population in the 17th century.

Information: Concord Chamber of Commerce, 105 Everett St., Concord, 978-369-3120; www.ultranet.com/~conchamb

WHAT TO SEE AND DO

Codman House
Codman Rd., Lincoln,
781-259-8843
Originally a two-story, L-shaped Georgian mansion, this 1740 house was more than doubled in size by Federal merchant John Codman to imitate an English country residence. June-mid-October: 1st Saturday of each month, tours hourly 11 a.m.-4 p.m.

Concord Museum
200 Lexington Rd., Concord,
978-369-9763;
www.concordmuseum.org
On display are period rooms, galleries of domestic artifacts and decorative arts chronicling the history of Concord from Native American habitation to the present. Exhibits include Ralph Waldo Emerson's study, Henry David Thoreau's belongings used at Walden Pond and Paul Revere's signal lantern. Daily.

DeCordova Museum & Sculpture Park
51 Sandy Pond Rd., Lincoln,
781-259-8355; www.decordova.org
This museum has an eclectic collection of paintings, posters, photography, sculpture and media. The Sculpture Park displays large contemporary sculptures throughout 35 wooded acres. In early June, rain or shine, the museum sponsors the Annual Art in the Park Festival and Art Sale. Tuesday-Sunday 11 a.m.-5 p.m.

Drumlin Farm Education Center
208 S. Great Rd., Lincoln, 781-259-2200
A demonstration farm with domestic and native wild animals and birds, gardens and hayrides. Tuesday-Sunday and Monday holidays.

Fruitlands Museums
102 Prospect Hill Rd., Harvard,
978-456-9392
The Fruitlands Farmhouse contains the furniture, books, and memorabilia of the Alcott family and the Transcendentalists. The Shaker Museum has furniture and handicrafts, and the Picture Gallery American primitive portraits and paintings by Hudson River School artists. The American Indian Museum shows prehistoric artifacts and Native American art. Mid-May-October:Monday-Friday 11 a.m.-4 p.m., Saturday-Sunday until 5 p.m.

Great Meadows National Wildlife Refuge
Lincoln St., and Weir Hill Rd.,
Sudbury Center, 978-443-4661;
www.fws.gov/greatmeadows
Great Meadows combines terrific dirt trails with a wildlife refuge that attracts more than 200 species of birds, including the magnificent great blue heron. Daily dawn-dusk.

Gropius House
68 Baker Bridge Rd., Lincoln,
781-259-8843
This was the family home of Bauhaus architect Walter Gropius and the first building he designed after arriving in the United States in 1937. June-October: first Saturday of the month, tours every hour 11 a.m.-4 p.m.

Minute Man National Historical Park
174 Liberty St., Concord,
978-369-6993; www.nps.gov/mima
The park consists of 900 acres along the Battle Road between Lexington and Concord. Walk the 5 1/2-mile Battle Road Trail, stop at Hartwell Tavern to see reenactments of colonial life and continue to North Bridge, the site of the first battle of the Revolution-

MASSACHUSETTS

ary War (a.k.a., the shot heard round the world). Spring, summer, fall: daily; winter: Saturday-Sunday.

Old Manse
269 Monument St., Concord, 978-369-3909
This was the parsonage of Concord's early ministers, including Reverend William Emerson, Ralph Waldo Emerson's grandfather. Nathaniel Hawthorne lived here for a time and made it the setting for *Mosses from an Old Manse.* Mid-April-October: Monday-Saturday 10 a.m.-5 p.m.

Orchard House
399 Lexington Rd., Concord, 978-369-4118
Louisa May Alcott wrote *Little Women* here. Open year-round, hours vary seasonally.

Ralph Waldo Emerson House
28 Cambridge Tpke., Concord, 978-369-2236
This was Ralph Waldo Emerson's home from 1835 to 1882. Mid-April-late October: Thursday-Saturday 10 a.m.-4:30 p.m, Sunday from 1 p.m.

Sleepy Hollow Cemetery
Bedford St., Concord,
The Alcotts, Ralph Waldo Emerson, Nathaniel Hawthorne, Margaret Sidney, Daniel Chester French and Henry David Thoreau are buried here.

Walden Pond State Reservation
915 Walden St., Concord, 978-369-3254
Henry David Thoreau, the American writer and naturalist, made Walden Pond famous when he lived in a nearby rustic cabin for two years. The cabin still stands and is part of the park's collection. A 1 1/2-mile trail circles the pond, perfect for hiking, running or swimming. Get here early—before 11 a.m.—the lot closes once it's full. Daily.

Wayside
455 Lexington Rd., Concord
Well-known 19th-century authors Nathaniel Hawthorne, the Alcotts and Margaret Sidney, author of the *Five Little Peppers* books, lived here. May-October.

SPECIAL EVENTS
Patriots Day Parade
Concord, 978-369-3120, 888-733-2678
Patriots Day commemorates the Battle of Lexington and Concord, which marked the beginning of the Revolutionary War on April 18, 1775. Schools and many businesses close, and the entire city celebrates. Watch parades and reenactments of the night of Paul Revere's famous ride and at noon, the famous Boston Marathon begins in Hopkinton. Third Monday in April, one-day-only event.

HOTELS
★Best Western at Historic Concord
740 Elm St., Concord, 978-369-6100, 800-780-7234; www.bestwestern.com
106 rooms. Complimentary continental breakfast. $

★★★Colonial Inn
48 Monument Square, Concord, 978-369-9200, 800-370-9200; www.concordscolonialinn.com
Anchoring the western edge of Monument Square in historic Concord, the Colonial Inn is a short walk to the town's shops and cafes. Henry David Thoreau's family once owned the property, which has been an inn since 1889. The individually decorated guest rooms have been updated with four-poster beds. There are a variety of dining venues, including the main restaurant (for breakfast, lunch, dinner and Sunday brunch), outdoor porch (formal High Tea), and a rustic colonial tavern (beers, live jazz).
56 rooms. Wireless Internet access. Two restaurants. Two bars. $$

★★★Hawthorne Inn
462 Lexington Rd., Concord, 978-369-5610; www.concordmass.com
Built in 1870, the Hawthorne Inn is less than a mile east of the village center. The pink house is surrounded by gardens and its neighbors include Minuteman National Historic Park and the Wayside and Orchard houses. Nineteenth-century antiques, origi-

MASSACHUSETTS

nal artwork, Japanese woodcuts, pre-Columbian pottery, a kitschy collection of salt and pepper shakers and books and old maps are displayed throughout the hotel.

7 rooms. Complimentary continental breakfast. Wireless Internet access. **$$**

★★Holiday Inn
242 Adams Place, Boxborough, 978-263-8701; www.holiday-inn.com
143 rooms. Restaurant. Bar. **$**

RESTAURANTS

★★Colonial Inn
48 Monument Square, Concord, 978-369-2373, 800-370-9200; www.concordscolonialinn.com
American menu. Breakfast, lunch, dinner, Sunday brunch. Bar. Children's menu. Casual attire. Reservations recommended. Outdoor seating. **$$**

DANVERS

Settlers from Salem looking for more farmland founded this small industrial town. In 1692, Danvers was the scene of some of the most severe witchcraft hysteria—in all, 20 people were put to death here.

Information: North Shore Chamber of Commerce, 5 Cherry Hill Dr., Danvers, 978-774-8565; www.northshorechamber.org

WHAT TO SEE AND DO

Glen Magna Farms
Ingersoll St., Danvers, 978-774-9165; www.glenmagnafarms.org
A 20-room mansion with 1790-1890 furnishings and Chamberlain garden, this Derby summer house was built by Samuel McIntire. May-July: by appointment only.

Rebecca Nurse Homestead
149 Pine St., Danvers, 978-774-8799
This house, an excellent example of the New England saltbox, was the homestead of Rebecca Nurse, a saintly woman accused of and executed for witchcraft in 1692. Mid-June-mid-September: Tuesday-Sunday; mid-September-October: weekends; rest of year: by appointment.

Witchcraft Victims Memorial
176 Hobart St., Danvers,
The memorial includes the names of those who died, as well as quotes from eight victims.

HOTELS

★★Courtyard by Marriott
275 Independence Way, Danvers, 978-777-8630, 800-321-2211; www.courtyard.com

120 rooms. High-speed Internet access. Restaurant. Bar. **$**

★Days Inn
152 Endicott St., Danvers, 978-777-1030, 800-329-7466; www.daysinn.com
129 rooms. Complimentary continental breakfast. Check-in 2 p.m., check-out 11 a.m. **$**

★★★Sheraton Ferncroft Resort
50 Ferncroft Rd., Danvers, 978-777-2500, 800-325-3535; www.sheraton.com
This hotel boasts luxurious guest rooms, world class dining, and a state-of-the-art, fully-staffed business center. Guests can be pampered at the salon and day spa, enjoy a game of golf on the 18-hole Robert Trent Jones–designed course, or luxuriate in the indoor pool.
367 rooms. High-speed Internet access. Restaurant. Bar. Airport transportation available. **$$**

RESTAURANTS

★★The Hardcover
15-A Newbury St., Danvers, 978-774-1223; www.barnsiderrestaurants.com
Seafood, steak menu. Dinner. Bar. Children's menu. **$$$**

DEERFIELD

Twice destroyed by French and Native American attacks and almost forgotten by history, Deerfield was once the northwest frontier of New England. Today, it remains unspoiled by big business or big buildings, populated instead by historic homes, vast meadowlands and the nationally acclaimed prep school Deerfield Academy. The tiny village boasts one of the most beautiful lanes in America known simply as "The Street," a mile-long stretch of 80 houses dating from the 18th and early 19th centuries.

Information: Historic Deerfield, Deerfield, 413-774-5581; www.historic-deerfield.org

WHAT TO SEE AND DO

Historic Deerfield

Highways 5 and 10, Deerfield,
413-774-5581;
www.historic-deerfield.org

The town's main street maintains 14 historic houses furnished with collections of antique furniture, silver, ceramics and textiles. A 28,000-square-foot Collections Study Center features changing exhibits. Daily walking tours and antique forums and workshops are available. Daily 9:30 a.m-4:30 p.m.

Memorial Hall Museum

10 Memorial St., Deerfield,
413-774-3768;
www.deerfield-ma.org/museum.htm

Built in 1798, Deerfield Academy's first building contains colonial furnishings and Native American relics. May-October:daily 11 a.m.-5 p.m.

HOTELS

★★★Deerfield Inn

81 Old Main St., Deerfield,
413-774-5587, 800-926-3865;
www.deerfieldinn.com

Early guests once pulled up to this historic inn by stagecoach; a few years later, visitors arrived on trolleys. Today, customers pull in behind the wheels of sleek German sports cars. The 1884 inn itself, however, hasn't changed all that much—its sitting parlors still exhibit period wallpaper and antiques, and its 10 main rooms are studies in cozy New England quaintness. Modern improvements include sparkling, up-to-date bathrooms, posh four-poster beds and a 13-room barn annex. Though it's said old town ghosts wander its halls, the inn is perpetually packed; some Deerfield Academy parents book graduation rooms four years out.

23 rooms. Complimentary full breakfast. Two restaurants, Bar. **$$**

RESTAURANTS

★★★Deerfield Inn

81 Old Main St., Deerfield,
413-774-5587, 800-926-3865;
www.deerfieldinn.com

The aforementioned inn's dining room is among the finest—and only—dining options in the area. Reservations are a must, as Deerfield students typically pack the place on weeknights and weekends. The menu of classic New England cuisine changes seasonally.

American menu. Breakfast, dinner. Bar. Children's menu. Business casual attire. Reservations recommended **$$**

★★★Sienna

6B Elm St., Deerfield, 413-665-0215;
www.siennarestaurant.com

This contemporary 45-seat restaurant serves American cooking marked by French technique. Chef and owner Karl Braverman creates dishes influenced by seasonally available ingredients, such as duck with white potato, blood orange, bok choy and Spanish vinegar demi glace. American menu. Dinner. Closed Monday-Tuesday **$$**

129

MASSACHUSETTS

★

★

★

★

DENNIS

Dennis is the seat of "the Dennises," a group of Cape Cod communities that includes Dennisport, East Dennis, South Dennis and West Dennis. It was here, in 1816, that Henry Hall developed the commercial cultivation of cranberries. The town is well-known for its laid-back vibe and pristine beaches.

Information: Chamber of Commerce, 242 Swan River Rd., Dennis, 508-398-3568; www.dennischamber.com

WHAT TO SEE AND DO

Josiah Dennis Manse
77 Nobscusset Rd., Dennis, 508-385-3528
The restored home of the minister for whom the town was named has antiques, a Pilgrim chest, a children's room, a spinning and weaving exhibit and a maritime wing. July-August: Tuesday and Thursday.

SPECIAL EVENTS

Cape Playhouse
820 Main St., Dennis,
508-385-3911, 877-385-3911;
www.capeplayhouse.com
The Cape Playhouse hosts both established Broadway stars and up-and-coming actors for two-week runs of musicals, comedies and dramatic plays. It's the oldest professional summer theater in the United States. On summer Friday mornings, it has special children's performances like puppetry, storytelling and musicals. The complex also houses the Cape Museum of Fine Arts, the Playhouse Bistro and the Cape Cinema. Late June-Labor Day.

HOTELS

★Huntsman Motor Lodge
829 Main St., West Dennis,
508-394-5415, 800-628-0498;
www.thehuntsman.com
25 rooms. $

★★Lighthouse Inn
1 Lighthouse Inn Rd., West Dennis,
508-398-2244; www.lighthouseinn.com
63 rooms. Restaurant. Bar. Children's activity center. Beach. Closed mid-October-late May. $$

★Sesuit Harbor
1421 Main St., East Dennis,
508-385-3326, 800-359-0097;

www.sesuitharbormotel.com
20 rooms. Complimentary continental breakfast. $

★★Soundings Seaside Resort
79 Chase Ave., Dennisport,
508-394-6561; www.thesoundings.com
102 rooms. Restaurant. Beach. Closed mid-October-mid-May. $$

★★Three Seasons Motor Lodge
421 Old Wharf Rd., Dennisport,
508-398-6091;
www.threeseasonsmotel.com
61 rooms. Wireless Internet access. Restaurant. Beach. Closed November-April. $$

SPECIALTY LODGINGS

Isaiah Hall Bed and Breakfast Inn
152 Whig St., Dennis, 508-385-9928,
800-736-0160; www.isaiahhallinn.com
This 1857 farmhouse has rooms decorated with antiques and oriental rugs.
10 rooms. Children over 7 years only. Complimentary continental breakfast. Closed November-mid-April. $

By The Sea Guests
57 Chase Ave., Dennisport,
508-398-8685, 800-447-9202;
www.bytheseaguests.com
On a beachfront road facing Nantucket Sound, this inn has clean, bright rooms with chenille bedspreads and fine-art prints. The property's large veranda provides great scenery for morning al fresco meals.
12 rooms. Complimentary full breakfast. Beach. $$

Corsair and CrossRip Oceanfront
41 Chase Ave., Dennisport,
508-398-6600; www.corsaircrossrip.com

MASSACHUSETTS

46 rooms. Complimentary continental breakfast. Wireless Internet access. Children's activity center. Beach. Closed late October-mid-April. **$$**

RESTAURANTS

★Bob's Best Sandwiches

613 Main St., Dennisport, 508-394-8450
Deli menu. Breakfast, lunch. Children's menu. Casual attire. Outdoor seating. **$**

★★Clancy's

8 Upper County Rd., Dennisport, 508-394-6661;
www.clancysrestaurant.com
American menu. Lunch, dinner, Sunday brunch. Bar. Children's menu. Casual attire. Valet parking. Outdoor seating. **$$**

★★La Scala

106 Depot St., Dennisport, 508-398-3910
Italian menu. Dinner. Bar. Children's menu. Casual attire. Reservations recommended. **$$**

★★★Red Pheasant Inn

905 Main St., Dennis, 508-385-2133, 800-480-2133;
www.redpheasantinn.com
Housed in a 200-year-old barn, this restaurant delights romantics and gourmands alike with its quaint surroundings and fine food. The American menu consists of fish and meat specialties; lamb and game offerings change nightly. The 300-bottle wine list is enough to impress the most demanding connoisseurs.
American menu. Dinner. Bar. Reservations recommended. Valet parking. **$$$**

★★Scargo Cafe

799 Main St., Dennis, 508-385-8200, 888-355-0112; www.scargocafe.com
International menu. Lunch, dinner. Bar. Children's menu. Casual attire. Outdoor seating. **$$**

★★Swan River Seafood

5 Lower County Rd., Dennisport, 508-398-7971, 800-448-7926;
www.swanriverrestaurant.com
Seafood menu. Lunch, dinner. Bar. Children's menu. Casual attire. Reservations recommended (parties of six or more). Outdoor seating. Closed mid-October-mid-May. **$$**

EASTHAM

The *Mayflower* party met its first Native Americans in this quintessential Cape Cope town. Today, the Bay-side spot is famous for Nauset Beach, a sprawling expanse of white sand that was once a ship graveyard.
Information: Chamber of Commerce, Eastham, 508-240-7211, 508-255-3444; www.easthamchamber.com

WHAT TO SEE AND DO

Eastham Historical Society

190 Samoset Rd., Eastham, 508-255-0788;
www.easthamhistorical.org
This museum, housed in an 1869 schoolhouse, has Native American artifacts and farming and nautical implements. July-August: Monday-Friday afternoons.

Eastham Windmill

Windmill Green, Eastham, 508-240-7211

This is the oldest windmill on the Cape; built in 1680, it was restored in 1936. Late June-Labor Day: daily.

HOTELS

★Captain's Quarters

30 Captains Quarters Court, North Eastham, 508-255-5686, 800-327-7769;
www.captains-quarters.com
75 rooms. Closed mid-November-mid-April. Complimentary continental breakfast. **$**

★★Four Points by Sheraton
3800 Hwy. 6, Eastham,
508-255-5000, 800-533-3986;
www.fourpoints.com
107 rooms. Wireless Internet access. Restaurant. Bar. Airport transportation available. **$**

★★The Inn at the Oaks
3085 County Rd., Eastham,
508-255-1886, 877-255-1886;
www.inattheoaks.com
10 rooms. Complimentary full breakfast. **$$**

SPECIALTY LODGINGS
The Penny House Inn
4885 County Rd., Eastham,
508-255-6632, 800-554-1751;
www.pennyhouseinn.com
12 rooms. Children over 8 years only. Complimentary full breakfast. **$$**

The Whalewalk Inn
220 Bridge Rd., Eastham,
508-255-0617, 800-440-1281;
www.whalewalkinn.com
16 rooms. Children over 12 only. Complimentary full breakfast. **$$$**

FALL RIVER

In 1892, blue-collar Fall River was the site of one of the most famous murder trials in American history, after Lizzie Borden allegedly killed her father and stepmother with an ax (she was acquitted). Since then, the city has maintained a gritty, urban persona, thanks to its numerous industrial mills and factories.

Information: Fall River Area Chamber of Commerce, 200 Pocasset St., Fall River, 508-676-8226; www.fallriverchamber.com

WHAT TO SEE AND DO
Battleship Cove
5 Water St., Fall River, 508-678-1100
Onsite at the Cove are five World War II–era naval ships; the *Lionfish,* a World War II attack submarine; and the battleship USS *Massachusetts*. Commissioned in 1942, the latter was active in the war's European and Pacific theaters and now houses the state's official World War II and Gulf War Memorial. Also here are *PT Boat 796, PT Boat 617* and the destroyer USS *Joseph P. Kennedy Jr.,* which saw action in the Korean, Vietnam and Cuban conflicts. Daily 9 a.m.-6 p.m.

Fall River Historical Society
451 Rock St., Fall River, 508-679-1071;
www.lizzieborden.org
The 16-room Victorian mansion exhibits displays on the Fall River Steamship Line, dolls, fine art, glassware, costumes and Lizzie Borden trial artifacts. April-May, October-November: Tuesday-Friday; June-September: Tuesday-Sunday; December: Monday.

Lizzie Borden Bed and Breakfast
92 Second St., Fall River, 508-675-7333;
www.lizzie-borden.com

In 1892, Lizzie Borden's father and step-mother were found murdered in their Fall River Greek Revival house. Borden was tried for the murder, but acquitted. Enterprising souls have turned the house into a bed and breakfast, where guests can learn about the murders over a breakfast similar to the one the Bordens ate before their deaths, and even spend a chilling night in the supposedly haunted house.

HOTELS
★Hampton Inn
53 Old Bedford Rd., Westport, 508-675-8500, 800-426-7866; www.hamptoninn.com
133 rooms. Complimentary continental breakfast. Airport transportation available. **$**

★Quality Inn
1878 Wilbur Ave., Somerset, 508-678-4545, 800-228-5151; www.qualityinn.com
107 rooms. Complimentary continental breakfast. **$**

RESTAURANTS
★★The Back Eddy
1 Bridge Rd., Westport, 508-636-6500; www.thebackeddy.com
American, seafood menu. Dinner. Casual attire. Closed January-March. **$$$**

★★White's of Westport
66 State Rd., Wesport, 508-675-7185; www.lafrancehospitality.com
Seafood, steak menu. Lunch, dinner. Bar. Children's menu. **$$**

FALMOUTH
Falmouth, on the southwest corner of the Cape, boasts a whopping 68 miles of coastline and 12 public beaches. Its pride and joy is the Woods Hole Oceanographic Institution, the largest independent marine study facility in the world. Ferries run from Falmouth to Martha's Vineyard, but many vacationers make this upscale Cape town their final vacation destination. Information: Cape Cod Chamber of Commerce, Hyannis, 508-362-3225, 888-227-3263; www.capecodchamber.org

WHAT TO SEE AND DO
Ashumet Holly & Wildlife Sanctuary
Ashumet and Currier Roads, Falmouth, 508-362-1426
This is a Massachusetts Audubon Society–run 45-acre wildlife preserve with a holly trail, herb garden and observation beehive. Daily, dawn to dusk.

Bradley House Museum
573 Woods Hole Rd., Woods Hole, 508-548-7270
Featured is a model of Woods Hole circa 1895, an audiovisual show of local history, and restored ships. July-August: Tuesday-Saturday; June and September: Wednesday, Saturday; schedule may vary.

Cape Cod Kayak
1270 Hwy., 28A, Cataumet, 508-563-9377; www.capecodkayak.com

This outfitter runs guided kayak tours on area lakes, rivers and harbors. Experienced kayakers can rent boats and head out on their own for up to a week. March-November; closed December-February.

SPECIAL EVENTS
Falmouth Road Race
661 E. Main St., Falmouth, 508-540-7000; www.falmouthroadrace.com
Starting in Woods Hole and winding back into Falmouth Heights, this hilly and hot course meanders past breathtaking scenery. The 7.1-mile race has been called the Best USA Road Race by *Runners World* magazine. Entry is by lottery; those who don't get in typically join the more than 70,000 spectators who line the course. Third Sunday in August.

MASSACHUSETTS

★
★
★
★
★
★

HOTELS

★★★Coonamessett Inn
311 Gifford St., Falmouth, 508-548-2300;
www.capecodrestaurants.org
North of town, in a shady, wooded area, lies the Coonamessett Inn. The property's five buildings are spread out over six landscaped acres that also host a barn, carriage house and caretaker's cottage. Sandy beaches, harbors and myriad antique shops are all nearby. The inn's rooms are spacious, with pine furniture, sitting areas, oversized closets, fresh flowers and refrigerators. Take advantage of the complimentary continental breakfast and/or try dinner at the inn's seasonal restaurant.
28 rooms. Complimentary continental breakfast. Wireless Internet access. Restaurant. Bar. Airport transportation available. $

★Nautilus Motor Inn
539 Woods Hole Rd., Woods Hole, 508-548-1525, 800-654-2333;
www.nautilusinn.com
54 rooms. Closed late October-mid-April. $

★★★New Seabury Resort and Conference Center
Rock Landing Rd., New Seabury, 508-477-9111, 800-999-9033;
www.newseabury.com
This resort is also a residential community. It sits on 2,300 recreation-filled acres and offers rentals from early March to early January. Villa development began in 1962 and it now consists of two golf courses, 16 tennis courts, and private beaches.
160 rooms. Restaurant. Bar. Children's activity center. Airport transportation available. $

★★Ramada Inn
40 N. Main St., Falmouth, 508-457-0606, 888-744-5394;
www.innonthesquare.com
72 rooms. Restaurant. Bar. $

★Red Horse Inn
28 Falmouth Heights Rd., Falmouth,
508-548-0053, 800-628-3811;
www.redhorseinn.com
22 rooms. $

★★Sea Crest Resort
350 Quaker Rd., North Falmouth, 508-540-9400, 800-225-3110;
www.seacrest-resort.com
266 rooms. Restaurant. Bar. Children's activity center. Beach. $$

SPECIALTY LODGINGS

Capt. Tom Lawrence House
75 Locust St., Falmouth, 508-540-1445, 800-266-8139;
www.captaintomlawrence.com
Vaulted ceilings, hardwood floors, and a spiral staircase add to the romantic, old-world charm of this inn located within walking distance of the town's main street. Built in 1861, it is a former whaling captain's home.
7 rooms. Complimentary full breakfast. Closed January. $$

Elm Arch Inn
26 Elm Arch Way, Falmouth, 508-548-0133; www.elmarchinn.com
This former whaling captain's house was built in 1810. It was attacked by the British in 1814; the hole where the cannonball hit is still visible in the dining area.
24 rooms. $

Grafton Inn
261 Grand Ave. S., Falmouth, 203-531-5065; www.graftoninn.com
10 rooms. Children over 16 years only. Complimentary full breakfast. $$

Inn on the Sound
313 Grand Ave., Falmouth, 508-457-9666, 800-564-9668;
www.innonthesound.com
10 rooms. Children over 18 years only. Complimentary full breakfast. $$

Mostly Hall
27 Main St., Falmouth, 508-548-3786, 800-682-0565;
www.mostlyhall.com

134

MASSACHUSETTS

★
★
★
★
★

This 1849 plantation-style house is the only one of its kind on Cape Cod.
6 rooms. Children over 16 years only. Complimentary full breakfast. **$**

The Palmer House Inn
81 Palmer Ave., Falmouth,
508-548-1230, 800-472-2632;
www.palmerhouseinn.com
This 1901 Queen Anne–style inn and guesthouse welcomes visitors year-round. The Shining Sea Bikeway, ferries to the islands and beaches are all nearby. 16 rooms. Children over 10 only. Complimentary full breakfast. **$$**

Wildflower Inn
167 Palmer Ave., Falmouth,
508-548-9524; 800-294-5459.
www.wildflower-inn.com
Rooms at this intimate inn feature whirlpool baths, kitchenettes and period furniture. 6 rooms. Complimentary full breakfast. **$$**

RESTAURANTS
★Betsy's Diner
457 Main St., Falmouth,
508-540-0060

American menu. Breakfast, lunch, dinner. Children's menu. Casual attire. **$**

★The Flying Bridge
220 Scranton Ave., Falmouth,
508-548-2700
www.capecodrestaurants.org
Seafood menu. Lunch, dinner. Bar. Children's menu. Casual attire. Outdoor seating. Closed late November-mid-March. **$$**

★★Landfall
2 Luscombe Ave., Woods Hole,
508-548-1758;
www.woodshole.com/landfall
Seafood menu. Lunch, dinner. Bar. Children's menu. Casual attire. Reservations recommended. Outdoor seating. Closed December-March. **$$**

★★The Nimrod
100 Dillingham Ave., Falmouth,
508-540-4132;
www.thenimrod.com
American menu. Lunch, dinner, brunch. Bar. Children's menu. Casual attire. Outdoor seating. **$$**

★
★
★
★

FOXBOROUGH
This town, located between Providence and Boston, is home to Gillette Stadium, which hosts the New England Patriots football team and the New England Revolution soccer club.
Information: Neponset Valley Chamber of Commerce, 190 Vanderbilt Ave., Norwood, 781-769-1126; www.nvcc.com

WHAT TO SEE AND DO
New England Patriots
60 Washington St., Foxboro,
800-543-1776; www.patriots.com
Frequent NFL Super Bowl champions, the Patriots call Foxborough's Gillette Stadium home. Game tickets can be ultra pricey, but the arena's top-notch amenities and die-hard fans make up for its steep costs.

New England Revolution
60 Washington St., Foxboro,
877-438-7387; www.revolutionsoccer.net
One of the top teams in major league soccer, the Revolution plays its home games

at Gillette stadium. The Netside Terrace, a special seating area south of the pitch, costs $300 and includes parking, food and drinks for four. Closed October-March.

HOTELS
★★Courtyard by Marriott
35 Foxborough Blvd., Foxborough,
508-543-5222, 800-321-2211;
www.courtyard.com
161 rooms. High-speed Internet access. Restaurant. Bar. **$**

★★Holiday Inn
31 Hampshire St., Mansfield,

508-339-2200, 888-465-4329;
www.holiday-inn.com/bos-mansfield
202 rooms. Restaurant. Bar. **$**

RESTAURANTS
★★Lafayette House
109 Washington St., Foxborough,
508-543-5344; www.lafayettehouse.com
Continental, seafood menu. Lunch, dinner.
Bar. Children's menu. **$$**

GLOUCESTER
Thanks to George Clooney's tough-talking sea captian character ("Are we men, or are we Gloucestermen?") in the *Perfect Storm,* this blue-collar seaside city has experienced a recent renaissance. Tourists now crowd the streets of this growing summer resort and embark on whale-watching cruises from its harbor. Fishing is still big business here—a rumored 10,000 local men have been lost at sea in the last three centuries.
Information: Cape Ann Chamber of Commerce, 33 Commercial St., Gloucester, 978-283-1601, 800-321-0133; www.capeannvacations.com

WHAT TO SEE AND DO
Beauport, the Sleeper-McCann House
75 Eastern Point Blvd., Gloucester,
978-283-0800
(1907-1934) Henry Davis Sleeper, an early 20th-century interior designer, first built a 26-room house here in 1907. With the help of local architect Halfdan Hanson, he kept adding rooms until decades later, there were 40. Twenty-five are now on view and contain collections of antique furniture, rugs, wallpaper, ceramics and glass. Mid-May-mid-September: Monday-Friday; mid-September-mid-October: daily.

Cape Ann Historical Museum
27 Pleasant St., Gloucester, 978-283-0455
This museum has paintings by Fitz Hugh Lane, decorative arts and furnishings, and exhibitions on Cape Ann's history. Tuesday-Saturday 10 a.m-5 p.m, Sunday 1 p.m-4 p.m; closed February.

Hammond Castle Museum
80 Hesperus Ave., Gloucester, 978-283-2080;
www.hammondcastle.org
Built by inventor Dr. John Hays Hammond, Jr. to resemble a medieval castle, this museum contains a rare collection of art objects, including an 8,200-pipe organ. Memorial Day-Labor Day: daily; after Labor Day-Columbus Day: Thursday-Sunday; rest of year: Saturday-Sunday.

Sargent House Museum
49 Middle St., Gloucester,
978-281-2432
This late 18th-century Georgian residence was built for Judith Sargent, an early feminist writer and sister of Governor Winthrop Sargent. Period furniture, china, glass, silver, needlework, Early American portraits and paintings by John Singer Sargent are on display. Memorial Day-Columbus Day: Friday-Monday noon-4 p.m.

HOTELS
★Best Western Bass Rocks Ocean Inn
107 Atlantic Rd., Gloucester,
978-283-7600, 800-780-7234;
www.bestwestern.com/bassrocksoceaninn
48 rooms. Complimentary full breakfast. Closed December-March. **$$**

★The Manor Inn
141 Essex Ave., Gloucester, 978-283-0614;
www.themanorinnofgloucester.com
10 rooms. Closed November-April. Complimentary continental breakfast. **$**

★★Ocean View Inn and Resort
171 Atlantic Rd., Gloucester,
978-283-6200, 800-315-7557;
www.oceanviewinnandresort.com
62 rooms. Restaurant. **$**

MASSACHUSETTS

★
★
★
★

★

RESTAURANTS

★★Gloucester House Restaurant
7 Seas Wharf, Gloucester,
978-283-1812, 888-283-1812;
www.lobster-express.com
Seafood menu. Lunch, dinner. Bar. Children's menu. Outdoor seating. **$$**

GREAT BARRINGTON

The once tiny, locals-only town of Great Barrington has slowly become the dining, shopping and cultural center of the Southern Berkshires. Tourists mob the streets and restaurants on summer weekends, leaving residents at once miffed at the crowds and grateful for the tourism dollars. The country spot has also become popular with the New York City summerhouse set, which means things quiet down considerably in the winter. Hiking, biking, walking, skiing, snowshoeing and other outdoor activities abound here, as do music, theater and dance events.

Information: Southern Berkshire Chamber of Commerce, 362 Main St., Great Barrington, 413-528-1510; www.greatbarrington.org

WHAT TO SEE AND DO

Catamount Ski Area
Hwy. 23, Great Barrington
Night-skiing is popular at this mountain, which has four double chairlifts, a ski school, equipment rentals, a cafeteria, bar, and nursery. The longest run is two miles with a vertical drop of 1,000 feet. December-March: daily.

Colonel Ashley House
117 Cooper Hill Rd., Sheffield,
413-229-8600
The elegance of this home reflects Colonel Ashley's prominent place in society. One political meeting he held here produced the Sheffield Declaration, the forerunner to the Declaration of Independence. July-August: Wednesday-Sunday; Memorial Day-June and September-Columbus Day: weekends; open Monday.

Otis Ridge
159 Monterey Rd., Otis,
413-269-4444; www.otisridge.com
This ski resort has a double chairlift, T-bar, J-bar, three rope tows, ski patrol and school, rentals and a cafeteria. The longest run is one mile with a vertical drop of 400 feet. December-March: daily.

Ski Butternut
380 State Rd., Great Barrington,
413-528-2000, 800-438-7669;
www.butternutbasin.com
The family-friendly Butternut has a quad, triple and four double chairlifts, plus a pomalift and a rope tow. The cafeteria and wine room are better than the average ski resort's and the slalom race course frequently attracts experts. The longest run is approximately 1 1/2 miles; its vertical drop is 1,000 feet. There are also 7 miles of cross-country trails. December-March: daily.

SPECIAL EVENTS

Berkshire Craft Fair
Monument Mountain Regional High School, 600 Stockbridge Rd., Great Barrington, 413-528-3346; www.berkshirecraftsfair.org
This annual juried fair typically attracts more than 100 artisans. Mid-August.

HOTELS

★Monument Mountain Motel
249 Stockbridge Rd., Great Barrington, 413-528-3272;
www.monumentmountainmotel.com
18 rooms. **$**

SPECIALTY LODGINGS

The Egremont Inn
10 Old Sheffield Rd., South Egremont, 413-528-2111, 800-859-1780;
www.egremontinn.com
20 rooms. Complimentary continental breakfast. Restaurant. **$**

MASSACHUSETTS

Race Brook Lodge
864 S. Undermountain Rd., Sheffield,
413-229-2916, 888-725-6343;
www.rblodge.com
32 rooms. Complimentary full breakfast.
Bar. **$$**

Thornewood Inn & Restaurant
453 Stockbridge Rd., Great Barrington,
413-528-3828, 800-458-1008;
www.thornewood.com
15 rooms. Children over 12 years only. Complimentary full breakfast. Restaurant. **$$**

Windflower Inn
684 S. Egremont Rd., Great Barrington,
413-528-2720, 800-992-1993;
www.windflowerinn.com
On 10 acres of Berkshire hillside, this white clapboard country inn has a screened-in porch and antique-filled rooms. The estate dates back to the 1850s and is near the famous Tanglewood music center. 13 rooms. Complimentary full breakfast. **$$**

138 RESTAURANTS
★★★**Castle Street Cafe**
10 Castle St., Great Barrington,
413-528-5244;
www.castlestreetcafe.com
Chef/owner Michael Ballon's lively restaurant is divided into two parts: a fine-dining room and the more casual Celestial Bar. White tablecloths and candles decorate the former, while live music and multicolored pendant lamps set the tone in the (often very noisy) bar. The eatery's classic American food is consistently fresh and includes burgers and salads.
American menu. Dinner. Bar. Closed Tuesday. **$$**

★★**John Andrew's Restaurant**
Highway 23, South Egremont,
413-528-3469; www.jarestaurant.com
American menu. Dinner. Bar. Children's menu. Outdoor seating. Closed Wednesday. **$$**

★★★**Spencer's**
453 Stockbridge Rd., Great Barrington,
413-528-3828, 800-854-1008;
www.thornewood.com
Located in the turn-of-the-century Thornewood Inn, Spencer's is a mellow, cozy restaurant favored by the area's many retirees. All produce is provided by the inn's own gardens, making dishes very seasonal and flavorful.
American menu. Dinner Thursday-Saturday. Bar. Outdoor seating. **$$**

★★**The Old Mill**
53 Main St., South Egremont,
413-528-1421
American menu. Dinner. Bar. Children's menu. **$$**

HARWICH
Like many Massachusetts towns, Harwich has been immortalized in some of the country's best-known books. The pretty Cape Cod spot stars in Joseph C. Lincoln's novels, Whittier poems and James Fenimore Cooper's novel *The Spy*. Most of the area's seaside houses are owned by city dwellers who visit on weekends.
Information: Harwich Chamber of Commerce, Harwich, 508-432-1600; www.capecodchamber.org

WHAT TO SEE AND DO
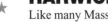
Cape Cod Baseball League
11 North Rd., Harwich, 508-432-3878;
www.capecodbaseball.org
This is baseball as it should be: local, passionate, affordable and played only with wooden bats. The 10 teams are made up of college players from around the country who live with host families for the summer. Spectators sit on wooden benches, pack picnic lunches and cheer for their favorite players during each of the season's 44 games. Mid-June-mid-August.

Harwich Historical Society

80 Parallel St., Harwich, 508-432-8089
The society has Native American artifacts, a marine exhibit, cranberry industry articles and early newspapers and photographs. It's also the site of one of the first schools of navigation in the United States. Usually mid-June-mid-October: Wednesday-Friday; schedule may vary.

SPECIAL EVENTS
Cranberry Harvest Festival
Hwy., 58 N and Rochester Rd., Harwich
A family day with an antique car show, music, arts and crafts, fireworks, carnival, and parade. One weekend in mid-September.

HOTELS
★★The Commodore Inn
30 Earle Rd., West Harwich, 508-432-1180, 800-368-1180; www.commodoreinn.com
27 rooms. Complimentary continental breakfast. Restaurant. Bar. Pool. Closed November-April. **$**

★The Sandpiper Beach Inn
16 Bank St., Harwich Port, 508-432-0485, 800-433-2234; www.sandpiperbeachinn.com
20 rooms. Beach. **$**

★Seadar Inn
1 Braddock Lane, Harwich Port, 508-432-0264, 800-888-5250; www.seadarinn.com
20 rooms. Complimentary continental breakfast. Near beach. Closed mid-October-late May. **$**

SPECIALTY LODGINGS
Cape Cod Claddagh Inn
77 Main St., West Harwich, 508-430-2440; www.capecodcladdaghinn.com
9 rooms. Complimentary full breakfast. Restaurant. Closed January-March. **$**

Country Inn
86 Sisson Rd., Harwich Port, 508-432-2769
6 rooms. Complimentary continental breakfast. Restaurant. Beach. **$**

Dunscroft By the Sea
24 Pilgrim Rd., Harwich Port, 508-432-0810, 800-432-4345; www.dunscroftbythesea.com
8 rooms. Children over 12 years only. Complimentary full breakfast. Whirlpool. **$$**

RESTAURANTS
★400 East
1421 Orleans Rd., Harwich, 508-432-1800, www.the400.com/East
American menu. Lunch, dinner, late-night. Bar. Children's menu. Casual attire. **$**

★★Ay! Caramba Cafe
703 Main St., Harwich, 508-432-9800; www.aycarambacafe.com
Mexican menu. Lunch, dinner. Bar. Children's menu. Casual attire. Outdoor seating. **$**

★★Bishop's Terrace
Route 28, West Harwich, 508-432-0253
American menu. Dinner. Bar. Children's menu. Casual attire. Closed Monday; also Thanksgiving-Memorial Day. **$$**

★★L'Alouette
787 Main St., Harwich Port, 508-430-0405; www.lalouettebistro.com
French menu. Dinner. Reservations recommended. **$$$**

MASSACHUSETTS

HYANNIS AND BARNSTABLE

The gateway to Cape Cod, Hyannis sees some six million visitors each year. Its seaside streets are well prepared, with multitudes of antique and specialty boutiques, fancy and casual eateries, libraries, museums and of course, the Kennedy Compound. In the surrounding area are tennis courts, golf courses, arts and crafts galleries and theaters. Tourist stream in and out by Amtrak rail, commuter flights, and ferries, giving this bustling city

of 14,000 a very transient feel although those in the know, stay put to decompress on the town's laid-back beaches.
Information: Chamber of Commerce, 1481 Hwy. 132, Hyannis, 508-362-5230, 877-492-6647; www.hyannis.com

WHAT TO SEE AND DO

Steamship Authority
Ocean St., Hyannis,
508-477-8600;
www.steamshipauthority.com
Catch ferries to Woods Hole, Martha's Vineyard, and Nantucket from the South Street dock.

Cape Cod Pathways
3225 Hwy. 6A, Barnstable, 508-362-3828; www.capecodcommission.org/pathways
This network of walking and hiking trails is composed of a perfect mix of dirt, sand and gravel. It links to most Cape towns, thanks to the Cape Cod Commission, which oversees the trails and produces a detailed map. In early June, hearty souls hike from one end of the cape to the other on the Cape Walk; on the October Walking Weekend, guides lead groups on short and long hikes. Daily.

Cape Cod Potato Chip Company
100 Breed's Hill Rd., Hyannis,
508-775-3358; www.capecodchips.com
Cape Cod chips, now sold all over the world, may be the area's most recognizable food product. Perhaps the best part about the onsite self-guided tour is the free samples, though seeing the chips cook in huge kettles is a close second. Monday-Friday 9 a.m.-5 p.m.

Hyannis *Whale Watcher* Cruises
Barnstable Harbor, 269 Mill Way,
Barnstable,
508-362-6088; www.whales.net
View whales aboard the *Whale Watcher,* a 297-passenger super-cruiser, custom designed and built specifically for whale-watching. An onboard naturalist narrates. April-October: daily.

John F. Kennedy Hyannis Museum
397 Main St., Hyannis, 508-790-3077

Here, photographic exhibits and a seven-minute video narrated by Walter Cronkite focus on President Kennedy's relationship with Cape Cod. Mid-April-October: Monday-Saturday 9 a.m.-5 p.m., Sunday and holidays noon-5 p.m.; rest of year: Thursday-Saturday 10 a.m.-4 p.m., Sunday and holidays noon-4 p.m.

Osterville Historical Society Museum
155 W. Bay Rd., Osterville, 508-428-5861
A sea captain's house with 18th- and 19th-century furnishings and a boat-building museum. Mid-June-September: Thursday-Sunday 1:30 p.m.-4:30 p.m.; other times by appointment.

West Parish Meetinghouse
2049 Meetinghouse Road,
West Barnstable, 508-362-4445
This building is said to be the oldest Congregational church in the country. Regular Sunday services are held here all year.

SPECIAL EVENTS

Cape Cod Oyster Festival
20 Independence Dr., Hyannis,
508-775-4746;
www.capecodoysterfestival.com
It's all you can eat at the Cape Cod Oyster fest and, thanks to local vineyards, all you can drink, too. Held at the Naked Oyster restaurant under a big tent, the event draws locals and tourists alike. Early October.

Figawi Sailboat Race and Charity Ball
70 Jobys Lane, Osterville, 508-420-5981; www.figawi.com
The largest regatta on the East Coast, Figawi features 200 sailboats racing from Hyannis to Nantucket on Saturday, then back again in a Return Race on Monday. A black tie charity ball precedes the event by one week. Held in Hyannis (and also celebrated on Nantucket) and featuring live

140

MASSACHUSETTS

bands, dancing and a big feast, it's a major social event of the year. Memorial Day weekend.

Pops by the Sea
Town Green, Hyannis, 508-362-0066;
www.artsfoundationcapecod.org
In early August, the Boston Pops makes its way to the Cape for a concert on the Hyannis Town Green. Each year brings a new celebrity guest conductor, from actors to poets to famous chefs. The performance serves as a fundraiser that supports the Arts Foundation of Cape Cod.

Willowbend Children's Charity Pro-Am
100 Willowbend Dr., Mashpee,
508-539-5030;
www.willowbendproam.com
The biggest names in professional golf pair up with celebrities for this annual charity golf event on Willowbend's course. The fee ($20) is among the lowest you can pay to watch professional golf; the proceeds benefit a variety of children's charities. Early July.

HOTELS
★Anchor-In
1 South St., Hyannis, 508-775-0357;
www.anchorin.com
43 rooms. Complimentary breakfast.

★★Cape Codder Resort & Spa
1225 Iyanough Rd., Hyannis,
508-771-3000, 888-297-2200;
www.capecodderresort.com
257 rooms. Wireless Internet access. Two restaurants. Two bars. Children's activity center. Airport transportation available. $$

★Centerville Corners Inn
1338 Craigville Beach Rd.,
Centerville,
508-775-7223, 800-242-1137;
www.centervillecorners.com
48 rooms. Complimentary continental breakfast. Wireless Internet access. Closed November-April. $

★★Courtyard by Marriott
707 Hwy., 132, Hyannis,
508-775-6600, 800-321-2211;
www.marriott.com
119 rooms. High-speed Internet access. Restaurant. Bar. Airport transportation available. $$

★★International Inn
662 Main St., Hyannis,
508-775-5600, 877-588-3353;
www.cuddles.com
141 rooms. Restaurant. Bar. $

SPECIALTY LODGINGS
Acworth Inn
4352 Old King's Hwy., Cummaquid,
508-362-3330, 800-362-6363;
www.acworthinn.com
5 rooms. Children over 12 years only. Complimentary full breakfast. $

Ashley Manor
3660 Olde King's Hwy., Barnstable,
508-362-8044, 888-535-2246;
www.ashleymanor.net
A lovely garden and gazebo adorn this beautiful inn. Unwind with a book in the library, or with afternoon tea in front of the fire.
6 rooms. Children over 14 years only. Complimentary full breakfast. $

Beechwood Inn
2839 Main St., Barnstable,
508-362-6618, 800-609-6618;
www.beechwoodinn.com
Situated near Barnstable Village, the Beechwood coordinates biking, whale-watching, and golf trips for its guests. Those looking for total relaxation can remain in their plush rooms, or hang out in the porch's rocking chairs.
6 rooms. Children over 12 only. Complimentary full breakfast. $

Captain David Kelley House
539 Main St., Centerville,
508-775-4707, 888-815-5700;
www.captaindavidkelleyhouse.com
5 rooms. Complimentary full breakfast. $

141

MASSACHUSETTS

★
★
★
☆

Honeysuckle Hill B&B
591 Old King's Hwy., West Barnstable,
508-362-8418, 866-444-5522;
www.honeysucklehill.com
5 rooms. Children over 12 years only.
Complimentary full breakfast. **$**

Sea Breeze Inn
270 Ocean Ave., Hyannis, 508-771-7213;
www.seabreezeinn.com
14 rooms. Complimentary continental breakfast. **$**

RESTAURANTS

★★**Dolphin Restaurant**
3250 Main St., Barnstable, 508-362-6610;
www.thedolphinrestaurant.com
American, seafood menu. Lunch, dinner.
Bar. Children's menu. Casual attire. Reservations recommended. **$$**

★**Egg & I**
521 Main St., Hyannis, 508-771-1596
American menu. Breakfast. Children's menu.
Casual attire. Closed November-March. **$**

★★**Five Bays Bistro**
825 Main St., Osterville, 508-420-5559;
www.fivebaysbistro.com
American menu. Dinner. Bar. Casual attire.
$$$

★★★**Naked Oyster**
20 Independence Dr., Hyannis,
508-778-6500; www.nakedoyster.com
Seafood menu. Lunch, dinner. Bar. Casual
attire. Closed Sunday. **$$**

★**Original Gourmet Brunch**
517 Main St., Hyannis, 508-771-2558;
www.theoriginalgourmetbrunch.com
American menu. Breakfast, lunch. Casual
attire. **$**

★★**Roadhouse Cafe**
488 South St., Hyannis, 508-775-2386;
www.roadhousecafe.com
Italian, seafood menu. Dinner. Bar. Casual
attire. Reservations recommended. Valet
parking. **$$**

★**Sam Diego's**
950 Iyanough Rd., Hyannis, 508-771-8816;
www.samdiegos.com
Mexican, Southwestern menu. Lunch, dinner. Bar. Children's menu. Casual attire.
Outdoor seating. **$**

★**Star City Grill**
668 Hwy., 132, Hyannis,
508-778-6767
International/Fusion menu. Lunch, dinner.
Bar. Children's menu. Casual attire. Outdoor seating. **$$**

★★★**The Paddock**
20 Scudder Ave., Hyannis, 508-775-7677;
www.paddockcapecod.com
Pressed linens and abundant flowers add
sophistication to this family- friendly restaurant. Equestrian paintings and antiques
enable a rich, classic look and the menu is
full of fresh seafood (though poultry, steak
and pasta also make appearances).
American, seafood menu. Lunch, dinner.
Bar. Children's menu. Casual attire. Reservations recommended. Valet parking.
Closed mid-November-March. **$$**

★★★**The Regatta of Cotuit**
4631 Falmouth Rd., Cotuit, 508-428-5715;
www.regattaofcotuit.com
This old 1790 stagecoach inn is run by Chef
Heather Allen, who cooks with French,
American and Asian themes. Her lacquered
duck is a neatly Americanized version of
Peking duck; her Vietnamese-style fish
and chips tempura is made from whatever
the local fishermen catch that day. Owners Wendy and Branz Bryan have accrued
a nearly legendary wine list over the last
three decades, making the Regatta a muststop for oenophiles.
American menu. Dinner. Bar. Business
casual attire. Reservations recommended.
Closed Sunday, November-April. **$$**

★**Ying's**
59 Center St., Hyannis, 508-790-2432
Asian menu. Lunch, dinner. Casual attire.
Reservations recommended. Outdoor seating.
$$

142

MASSACHUSETTS

IPSWICH

Ipswich is a summer resort town and home of Crane beach, one of the most beautiful stretches of sand in the state. The historic village has nearly 50 houses built before 1725, and many are from the 17th century.

Information: Ipswich Visitors Center-Hall Haskell House, 36 S. Main St., Ipswich, 978-356-8540

WHAT TO SEE AND DO

Clam Box of Ipswich

246 High St., Ipswich, 978-356-9707; www.ipswichma.com/clambox

This quirky roadside clam shack (the building is in the shape of an open box) is renowned for its perfectly prepared, deliciously greasy fried clams and superb lobster rolls.

Crane Beach

290 Argilla Rd., Ipswich, 978-356-4354

Among the best beaches on the Atlantic coast, Crane has five miles of sand, lifeguards, bathhouses, a refreshment stand and walking trails. Daily 8 a.m-sunset.

The John Whipple House

1 S. Village Green, Ipswich, 978-356-2811; www.ipswichmuseum.net

The 1640 house has 17th- and 18th-century furniture and a garden. May-mid-October: Wednesday-Saturday 10 a.m.-4 p.m., Sunday from 1 p.m.

John Heard House

54 S. Main St., Ipswich, 978-356-2811

Bought as memorial to Thomas F. Waters, this house has Chinese furnishings from the China sea trade. Schedule same as Whipple House.

HOTELS

★Country Garden Inn And Motel

101 Main St., Rowley, 978-948-7773, 800-287-7773; www.countrygardenmotel.com

24 rooms. $

SPECIALTY LODGINGS

Miles River Country Inn B&B

823 Bay Rd., Hamilton, 978-468-1210; www.milesriver.com

This 200-year-old rambling colonial is set on 30 acres that adjoin meadows, woodlands and marshes.

6 rooms. Complimentary full breakfast. $

RESTAURANTS

★★★1640 Hart House

51 Linebrook Rd., Ipswich, 978-356-1640; www.1640harthouse.com

Twenty years after the Pilgrims landed in the town of Ipswich, they built this now-restored property. The original room has since been sold to the Metropolitan Museum of Art.

American menu. Lunch, dinner. Bar. Children's menu. Reservations recommended. $$

LEE

Once an underappreciated Berkshire village, Lee has finally been discovered by summer and winter tourists. Its proximity to major cultural festivals and outdoor recreation makes it an ideal town in which to book an (often less-expensive) area room.

WHAT TO SEE AND DO

October Mountain State Forest

317 Woodland Rd., Lee, 413-243-1778

The forest provides fine mountain scenery overlooking 16,000 acres of hiking, hunting and snowmobiling.

Santarella

75 Main Rd., Tyringham, 413-243-2819; www.santarella.us

The former studio of sculptor Sir Henry Kitson, creator of the *Minuteman* statue in Lexington, was built in the early 1920s. The

★
★
★
★

roof was designed to look like the rolling hills of the Berkshires in autumn; the fronting rock pillars and grottoes are fashioned after similar edifices in Europe.

SPECIAL EVENTS

Jacob's Pillow Dance Festival
358 George Carter Rd., Becket,
413-243-0745
Ted Shawn Theatre and Doris Duke Theatre. America's oldest and most prestigious dance festival includes performances by international dance companies. Tuesday-Saturday, some Sundays. Late June-August.

HOTELS

★★Best Western Black Swan Inn
435 Laurel St., Lee,
413-243-2700, 800-876-7926;
www.bestwestern.com
52 rooms. Restaurant. Bar. $

SPECIALTY LODGINGS

Applegate
279 W. Park St., Lee,
413-243-4451, 800-691-9012;
www.applegateinn.com
Built in the 1920s, this Georgian Colonial is a charming bed-and-breakfast. Each room is individually decorated, and guests can stroll through six acres of rose gardens, perennial beds, and apple trees.
11 rooms. Children over 12 years only. Complimentary full breakfast. $

Chambery Inn
199 Main St., Lee, 413-243-2221,
800-537-4321; www.chamberyinn.com
This property was once the county's first parochial school. The owners saved it from destruction and kept the unique structure and original blackboards. Guests get the "menu selected" breakfasts delivered to their doors in a country basket.
9 rooms. Children over 16 years only. $$

Devonfield Inn
85 Stockbridge Rd., Lee,
413-243-3298, 800-664-0880;
www.devonfield.com

Located in the heart of the Berkshires, this Federal-era manor house offers a comfortable stay.
10 rooms. Children over 10 years only. Complimentary full breakfast. $$

Federal House Inn
1560 Pleasant St., South Lee,
413-243-1824, 800-243-1824;
www.federalhouseinn.com
This 1824 inn lies beside the Housatonic River and the Beartown State Forest. The rooms have a casual, country-style décor and include golf and tennis privileges at nearby Stockbridge Country Club.
10 rooms. Children over 12 years only. Complimentary full breakfast. Bar. $$

Historic Merrell Inn
1565 Pleasant St., South Lee,
413-243-1794, 800-243-1794;
www.merrell-inn.com
Listed on the National Register of Historic Places, this old stagecoach inn sits on two acres of picturesque Housatonic River–front property. All rooms have private baths, include a country breakfast and offer close access to the Berkshire Mountains.
10 rooms. Complimentary full breakfast. $

Morgan House
33 Main St., Lee,
413-243-3661, 877-571-0837;
www.morganhouseinn.com
11 rooms. Complimentary full breakfast. Restaurant. Bar. $

RESTAURANTS

★★Cork N' Hearth
635 Lowell St., Lee, 413-243-0535
Three dining rooms. Seafood, steak menu. Dinner. Bar. Children's menu. Closed Monday. $$

★★Sullivan Station Restaurant
109 Railroad St., Lee, 413-243-2082
American menu. Lunch, dinner. Bar. Outdoor seating. Closed two weeks in late February-early March. $$

LENOX

Lenox is the Berkshires' most talked-about town. Its name has become synonymous with rambling summer homes, fine cuisine and intellectual pursuits. The Boston Symphony orchestra calls Tanglewood its summer base, and the literati find inspiration in Edith Wharton's former grand manse, the Mount. Since not everyone can afford a second residence, many inns, bed and breakfasts, and full-service resorts have opened in the surrounding hills.
Information: Chamber of Commerce, 65 Main St., Lenox, 413-637-3646; www.lenox.org

WHAT TO SEE AND DO

Edith Wharton Estate (The Mount)

2 Plunkett St., Lenox, 413-637-1899
Edith Wharton's summer estate was planned from a book she coauthored in 1897, *The Decoration of Houses,* and built in 1902. The enormous Classical Revival house is continuously being restored. May-October: daily 9 a.m.-5 p.m.

Pleasant Valley Wildlife Sanctuary

472 Mountain Rd., Lenox, 413-637-0320
A sanctuary of the Massachusetts Audubon Society has 1,500 acres with seven miles of trails and a beaver colony. No dogs. Mid-June-Columbus Day.

Tanglewood

197 West St., Lenox, 413-637-1600
Nathaniel Hawthorne planned *Tanglewood Tales* here. Many of the 526 acres, developed into a gentleman's estate by William Aspinwall Tappan, take the form of formal gardens. Well-known today as the summer home of the Boston Symphony Orchestra, the outdoor music venue stages concerts—rock, country and classical—all season long. Daily; free except during concerts.

SPECIAL EVENTS

Shakespeare & Company

70 Kemble St., Lenox, 413-637-3353
The professional theater company performs plays by Shakespeare and Edith Wharton on four stages (one is outdoor). The main season runs from late June-early September. Tuesday-Sunday.

HOTELS

★★★★★Blantyre

16 Blantyre Rd., Lenox, 413-637-3556; www.blantyre.com

Gilded Age charm abounds at this Tudor-style mansion in the Berkshire Mountains. Blantyre's rooms maintain a decidedly British country style, with floral fabrics and overstuffed furniture. Fireplaces are available in many rooms. Activities include croquet, tennis, swimming, and the cultural festivals of Tanglewood and Jacob's Pillow. Dining at Blantyre is a special occasion, whether you're lingering over breakfast in the conservatory or enjoying a candlelit dinner. The chef even packs gourmet picnics for afternoons spent lounging within Blantyre's grounds or beyond.
25 rooms. Children over 12 years only. Complimentary continental breakfast. High-speed Internet access. Spa. Restaurant. Bar. **$$$$**

★★★Cranwell Resort Spa and Golf Club

55 Lee Rd., Lenox,
413-637-1364, 800-272-6935;
www.cranwell.com
This historic 100-year-old country hotel is set on a hill and has a 60-mile view of the southern Berkshires. Situated on 380 acres, the property has a fantastic 18-hole championship golf course that is host to Beecher's golf school. Inside the sprawling mansion are an enormous new spa and fitness center, complete with yoga studios and a pool.
108 rooms. Three restaurants, three bars. Spa. Children's activity center. **$$$**

★★★Gateways Inn

51 Walker St., Lenox,
413-637-2532, 888-492-9466;
www.gatewaysinn.com
11 rooms. Complimentary full breakfast. Restaurant. Bar. **$$**

★★★Wheatleigh

Hawthorne Rd., Lenox, 413-637-0610;
www.wheatleigh.com

Wheatleigh is a country house hotel of the finest order. The 19th-century Italianate palazzo is set on 22 acres of hills and Frederick Law Olmstead–designed gardens, and the estate shares in the grand Gilded Age heritage of the region. Guest rooms are comfortably elegant with English soaking tubs, exclusive bath amenities from Ermenegildo Zegna, raw silk coverlets and CD players. Details make the difference here, from the dazzling Tiffany windows to the ornate fireplace in the Great Hall. The restaurant, with its updated French dishes, draw gourmands.
19 rooms. Children over 9 years only. Wireless Internet access. Two restaurants, Bar. **$$$$**

★Yankee Inn

461 Pittsfield Rd., Lenox,
413-499-3700, 800-835-2364;
www.yankeeinn.com

96 rooms. Complimentary continental breakfast. Bar. **$$**

SPECIALTY LODGINGS

Apple Tree Inn

10 Richmond Mountain Rd., Lenox,
413-637-1477; www.appletree-inn.com

Just outside the center of town, the Apple Tree Inn sits on 22 hilltop acres and affords beautiful views of the Berkshires.
34 rooms. Complimentary full breakfast (off-season). Restaurant. Bar. **$$**

Birchwood Inn

7 Hubbard St., Lenox,
413-637-2600, 800-524-1646;
www.birchwood-inn.com

This bed-and-breakfast is decorated with antiques and collectables, and features meticulously kept rooms and gardens. 11 rooms. Complimentary full breakfast. Wireless Internet access. **$$**

Brook Farm Inn

15 Hawthorne St., Lenox,
413-637-3013, 800-285-7638;

www.brookfarm.com

The interior of this Victorian inn has a very literary feel, thanks to its impressive library of poetry, fiction collection and history. It is close to Tanglewood and the area's many other cultural and outdoor activities. Children over 15 years only. Complimentary full breakfast. Wireless Internet access. **$$**

Harrison House

174 Main St., Lenox, 413-637-1746;
www.harrison-house.com

The immaculate porch of this country inn overlooks Tanglewood and is directly across from Kennedy Park.
6 rooms. No children allowed. Complimentary full breakfast. **$$**

Kemble Inn

2 Kemble St., Lenox,
413-637-4113, 800-353-4113;
www.kembleinn.com

Located on three acres in the center of historic Lenox, this inn features magnificent views of the Berkshire Mountains. The guest rooms are named after American authors.
14 rooms. Children over 12 years only. Complimentary continental breakfast. **$$**

Rookwood Inn

11 Old Stockbridge Rd., Lenox,
413-637-9750, 800-223-9750;
www.rookwoodinn.com

This 1885 Victorian inn is furnished with English antiques and is located in the center of Lenox, close to the art, music, and theater of Tanglewood.
21 rooms. Complimentary full breakfast. **$$**

The Summer White House

17 Main St., Lenox,
413-637-4489, 800-382-9401;
www.thesummerwhitehouse.com

This inn is a former original Berkshire cottage built in 1885. Guest rooms feature private baths and air conditioning.
6 rooms. Children over 12 years only. Complimentary continental breakfast. **$$**

The Village Inn
16 Church St., Lenox,
413-637-0020, 800-253-0917;
www.villageinn-lenox.com
32 rooms. Complimentary full breakfast. Restaurant. Bar. **$$**

Whistler's Inn
5 Greenwood St., Lenox,
413-637-0975, 866-637-0975;
www.whistlersinnlenox.com
This inn was once the home of Ross Whistler, a railroad tycoon and nephew of the legendary American painter, James Abbott McNeil Whistler.
12 rooms. Children over 10 years only. Complimentary full breakfast. Closed November-May. **$$**

RESTAURANTS

★★★Bistro Zinc
56 Church St., Lenox, 413-637-8800;
www.bistrozinc.com
This lively hotspot is a good choice for a pre-concert meal. The contemporary décor features black-and-white herringbone tile, tin ceilings, pale yellow walls, burgundy banquettes and a large copper bar. French-American fusion standouts include ginger-encrusted salmon and entrecote aux oignons. The bar is open until 1 a.m.
French bistro menu. Lunch, dinner, late-night. Bar. Casual attire. Reservations recommended. **$$$**

★★★Blantyre
16 Blantyre Rd., Lenox, 413-637-3556;
www.blantyre.com
Dining at the 1902 mansion is a rare culinary experience. Diners enjoy pre-dinner champagne and canapes on the terrace or in the Music Room before feasting on Chef Christopher Brooks' rich, out-of-this-world fare. Antique glassware and place settings combine to create a romantic atmosphere, and the service is impeccable.
French menu. Breakfast, lunch, dinner. Jacket required. Reservations recommended. Valet parking. **$$$**

★★Café Lucia
80 Church St., Lenox, 413-637-2640
Italian, seafood menu. Dinner. Bar. Casual attire. Outdoor seating. Closed Monday in July-August, Sunday-Monday in September-June. **$$$**

★Carol's
8 Franklin St., Lenox, 413-637-8948
American menu. Breakfast, lunch, brunch. Casual attire. **$**

★★Church Street Cafe
65 Church St., Lenox, 413-637-2745;
www.churchstreetcafe.biz
American, International menu. Lunch, dinner. Bar. Children's menu. Casual attire. Reservations recommended. Outdoor seating. Closed March-April; also Sunday-Monday in May-June and September-February. **$$$**

★★★Gateways Inn
51 Walker St., Lenox,
413-637-2532, 888-492-9466;
www.gatewaysinn.com
At the Gateways, the chefs use locally grown produce and dairy products in each dish on their seasonal menu. The best seat in the house is in the main dining room: its French doors and terra cotta painted walls recall a Tuscan country inn.
American menu. Breakfast, lunch, dinner. Bar. Casual attire. Reservations recommended. Closed Monday in September-June. **$$$**

★★★Lenox 218 Restaurant
218 Main St, Lenox, 413-637-4218;
www.lenox218.com
This contemporary restaurant specializes in northern Italian dishes and can handle banquets for up to 100 people.
Italian menu. Lunch, dinner. Bar. Casual attire. Reservations recommended. **$$$**

★Panda House Chinese Restaurant
506 Pittsfield Rd., Lenox, 413-499-0660
Chinese menu. Lunch, dinner. Bar. Children's menu. Casual attire. **$$**

MASSACHUSETTS

★★★The Wyndhurst Restaurant
55 Lee Rd., Lenox, 413-637-1364;
www.cranwell.com

Cranwell Resort's main dining room is on the first floor of the 100-year-old Tudor mansion. Large windows offer vistas of the Berkshire Hills and the fireplace keeps the room warm on cold New England nights. The French and American cuisine highlights local produce, including game and cheeses.

American, French menu. Lunch, dinner. Business casual attire. Reservations recommended. Valet parking. **$$$**

★★★Wheatleigh
Hawthorne Rd., Lenox, 413-637-0610;
www.wheatleigh.com

Polished mahogany doors lead to the hotel's regal dining room, which was modeled in 1893 after a 16th-century Florentine palazzo. Dine on contemporary French cuisine in a sun-drenched room filled with oil paintings, hand-carved Chippendale chairs and a large wood-burning fireplace. Favorites on the menu include roasted Maine lobster and sweet corn soufflé with cassis ice cream.

French menu. Dinner, Sunday brunch. Bar. Business casual attire. Reservations recommended. Valet parking. **$$$$**

LEXINGTON

Lexington is often referred to as the birthplace of American liberty. On its town green, on April 19, 1775, eight Minutemen were killed in what is sometimes considered the first organized fight of the War for Independence. As the British approached, American Captain John Parker told his men: "Stand your ground. Don't fire unless fired upon. But if they mean to have a war, let it begin here!" And so it did.

Information: Chamber of Commerce Visitors Center, 1875 Massachusetts Ave., Lexington, 781-862-1450; www.lexingtonchamber.org

148

MASSACHUSETTS

WHAT TO SEE AND DO

Battle Green
Center of town

The Old Monument, the *Minuteman*-statue, and the Boulder mark the line of the Minutemen, seven of whom are buried here.

Lexington Historical Society
1332 Massachusetts Ave., Lexington, 781-862-1703; www.lexingtonhistory.org

Revolutionary period houses and guided tours.

Buckman Tavern
1 Bedford St., Lexington, 781-862-1703

The minutemen assembled here before the battle. Mid-April-May: weekends only; June-October: daily 10 a.m.-4 p.m.

Hancock-Clarke House
36 Hancock St., Lexington, 781-863-1703

Here, John Hancock and Samuel Adams were awakened by Paul Revere's alarm on April 18, 1775. Mid-April-May: weekends only; June-October: daily; tours hourly 11 a.m.-2 p.m.

Munroe Tavern
1332 Massachusetts Ave., Lexington, 781-862-1703

This was the site of the British hospital after the battle. George Washington dined here in 1789. Mid-April-October: tour at 3 p.m. daily.

National Heritage Museum
33 Marrett Rd., Lexington, 781-861-6559; www.monh.org

The museum features exhibits on American history, including that of Lexington and the Revolutionary War. Monday-Saturday 10 a.m.-5 p.m., Sunday from noon.

SPECIAL EVENTS

Reenactment of the Battle of Lexington and Concord
Lexington Green, Lexington, 781-862-1450

The yearly reenactment of the opening battle of the Revolutionary War takes place at dawn on Patriots Day and includes a parade. Monday nearest April 19.

HOTELS

★Holiday Inn Express
440 Bedford St., Lexington, 781-861-0850
204 rooms. Complimentary continental breakfast. **$**

LOWELL

In the 19th century, the powerful Merrimack River and its canals helped transform Lowell from a handicraft center to an industrial city. The Francis Floodgate, near Broadway and Clare Streets, was called "Francis's Folly" when it was built in 1848, but it saved the city from flood in 1936. A restoration of the historic canal system is currently underway, and the revitalized downtown district is sprouting urban chic stores and cafés.
Information: Greater Lowell Chamber of Commerce, 77 Merrimack St., Lowell, 978-459-8154; www. greaterlowellchamber.org

★★★Sheraton Lexington Inn
727 Marrett Rd., Lexington, 781-862-8700;
www.sheraton.com
Fifteen miles from Boston, this inn has 5,000 square feet of meeting space and an outdoor pool.
121 rooms. Restaurant. Bar. **$**

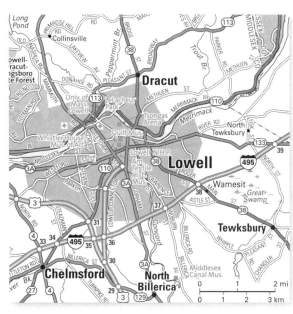

WHAT TO SEE AND DO

American Textile History Museum
491 Dutton St., Lowell, 978-441-0400;
www.athm.org
The site's permanent exhibit, "Textiles in America," features 18th- to 20th-century textiles, artifacts and machinery that show the impact of the Industrial Revolution on labor. Tuesday-Sunday.

Lowell Heritage State Park
246 Market St., Lowell, 978-453-0592
Six miles of canals and two miles of park on the bank of the Merrimack River offer boating, a boathouse, a concert pavilion and interpretive programs. Schedule varies.

Lowell National Historical Park
67 Kirk St., Lowell, 978-970-5000

www.nps.gov/lowe
The nation's first large-scale center for the mechanized production of cotton cloth, Lowell became a model for 19th-century industrial development. This park was established to commemorate Lowell's unique legacy as the most important planned industrial city in America. It includes mill buildings and a 5 1/2-mile canal system. May-Columbus Day weekend.

New England Quilt Museum
18 Shattuck St., Lowell, 978-452-4207;
www.nequiltmuseum.org
Changing exhibits feature antique, traditional, and contemporary quilts. Tuesday-Saturday 10 a.m.-4 p.m.

149

MASSACHUSETTS

Whistler House Museum of Art
243 Worthen St., Lowell, 978-452-7641;
www.whistlerhouse.org
The birthplace of the painter James Abbott
McNeill Whistler. Exhibits include several of his etchings. Wednesday-Saturday
11 a.m.-4 p.m.

HOTELS

★Best Western Chelmsford Inn
187 Chelmsford St., Chelmsford,
978-256-7511, 888-770-9992;
www.bestwestern.com/chelmsfordinn
120 rooms. High-speed Internet access. $

★Courtyard by Marriott
30 Industrial Ave. E., Lowell,
978-458-7575, 888-236-2427;
www.courtyard.com
120 rooms. High-speed Internet access.
Restaurant. $

★★Doubletree Hotel
50 Warren St., Lowell,
978-452-1200, 800-876-4586;
www.doubletree.com
252 rooms. Wireless Internet access. Restaurant. Bar. $

★★Radisson Hotel and Suites Chelmsford
10 Independence Dr., Chelmsford,
978-256-0800, 800-333-3333;
www.radisson.com
194 rooms. Restaurant. Bar. $

★★★Stonehedge Inn
160 Pawtucket Blvd.,
Tyngsboro, 978-649-4400;
www.stonehedgeinn.com
This contemporary inn is an American imitation of an English country manor. Large,
comfortable rooms have spacious bathrooms with heated towel racks. Set on the
grounds of a horse farm, the out-of-the-way

spot is perfect for a romantic rendezvous or
a corporate retreat.
30 rooms. Restaurant. Bar. $$

★★Westford Regency Inn and Conference Center
219 Littleton Rd., Westford,
978-692-8200, 800-543-7801;
www.westfordregency.com
193 rooms. Restaurant. Bar. $$

RESTAURANTS

★★Cobblestones
91 Dutton St., Lowell, 978-970-2282;
www.cobblestonesoflowell.com
American menu. Lunch, dinner, late-night.
Bar. Children's menu. Casual attire. Closed
Sunday; one week in August. $$

★★★La Boniche
143 Merrimack St., Lowell, 978-458-9473;
www.laboniche.com
Though the food is upscale, the dress is
casual at this fine restaurant. International
menu. Lunch, dinner. Closed Sunday-Monday first week of July. Bar. Casual attire.
$$

★★★Silks
160 Pawtucket Blvd., Tyngsboro,
978-649-4400; www.stonehedginn.com
Said to have one of the world's most
impressive wine caves, this out-of-the-way
restaurant is an oenophile retreat. On 36
acres of horse country farm, the Stonehedge
Inn's eatery proffers nearly 2,000 wines (its
cellar alledgedly houses more than 90,000
bottles). The food is equally impressive.
Thankfully, the service is anything but
snooty.
French menu. Breakfast, lunch, dinner,
Sunday brunch. Closed Monday. Outdoor
seating. $$$

MARBLEHEAD

Marblehead sits on a pretty peninsula 17 miles north of Boston. The town was settled in
1629 by hardy fishermen from England's West counties. It now boasts a beautiful harbor

150

MASSACHUSETTS

and a number of busy boatyards. Beaches, boating, fishing, art exhibits, and antique and curio shops abound—all combine to offer either quiet relaxation or active recreation.
Information: Chamber of Commerce, 62 Pleasant St., Marblehead, 781-631-2868; www.marbleheadchamber.org

WHAT TO SEE AND DO
Abbot Hall
188 Washington St., Marblehead, 781-631-0000
On display here are the "Spirit of '76" painting and the town's original deed. Last weekend in May-last weekend in Oct: daily; rest of year: Monday-Friday.

Jeremiah Lee Mansion
170 Washington St., Marblehead, 781-631-1069
Run by the Marblehead Historical Society, this mansion is where Generals Glover, Lafayette, and Washington were entertained. June-October: Tuesday-Saturday 10 a.m.-4 p.m.

King Hooper Mansion
8 Hooper St., Marblehead, 781-631-2608; www.marbleheadarts.org
A restored house with a garden and art exhibits. Tuesday-Saturday 10 a.m.-4 p.m., Sunday 1-5 p.m.

SPECIALTY LODGINGS
Harbor Light Inn
58 Washington St., Marblehead, 781-631-2186; www.harborlightinn.com
Each room at this inn has a fireplace, canopied bed and Jacuzzi. Continental breakfast and fresh-baked cookies are served in the colonial dining room.
21 rooms. Children over 8 only. Complimentary continental breakfast. Airport transportation available. **$**

Marblehead Inn
264 Pleasant St., Marblehead, 781-639-9999, 800-399-5843; www.marbleheadinn.com
10 rooms. Children over 10 only. Complimentary continental breakfast. **$$**

Seagull Inn
106 Harbor Ave., Marblehead, 781-631-1893; www.seagullinn.com
6 rooms. Complimentary continental breakfast. **$$**

RESTAURANTS
★★Marblehead Landing
81 Front St., Marblehead, 781-639-1266; www.thelandingrestaurant.com
Seafood menu. Lunch, dinner, Sunday brunch. Bar. Children's menu. Outdoor seating. **$$**

★★Pellino's
261 Washington St., Marblehead, 781-631-3344; www.pellinos.com
Italian menu. Dinner. Bar. Reservations recommended. **$$**

MARTHA'S VINEYARD
For an island less than 10 miles long and 20 miles wide, Martha's Vineyard has an outsized reputation. Along with neighboring Nantucket, the isle began as a whaling center and morphed into an offshore isle for the rich and fabulous. Its acres of soft, white sand beaches, grassy dunes, craggy cliffs and cultivated farmland are almost *too* postcard-perfect. Not quite as ideal are the island's lofty prices—housing, shopping and dining here all come with hefty fees. Nevertheless, tourists continually pack the streets of Edgartown, Oak Bluffs, and Vineyard Haven in the summer.
Information: Chamber of Commerce, Beach Rd., Vineyard Haven, 508-693-0085; www.mvy.com

WHAT TO SEE AND DO

Aquinnah Cliffs
State Rd., Aquinnah
These cliffs are national landmarks and the most photographed attraction on Martha's Vineyard. More than 150-feet-tall and brilliantly colored, they were formed over millions of years by glaciers. Today, the cliffs are owned by the Wampanoag Indians, who hold them sacred. At their peak sits the Aquinnah Light lighthouse, commissioned by President John Adams in 1798. At the bottom of the cliffs is beach where nude sunbathing is permitted. April-November.

Black Dog Bakery
Water St., Vineyard Haven, 508-693-4786; www.theblackdog.com
The Black Dog is more than just a bakery: it's a cultural phenomenon. Its logo—a black Labrador retriever—is omnipresent on T-shirts, hats, mugs and belts. The company's General Store has four Vineyard locations. All sell souvenirs and even dog treats. The bakery serves coffee, pastries, torts, truffles and other treats. Not to be outdone, the nearby Black Dog Tavern has tasty seafood and other island-appropriate dishes. Daily 5:30 a.m.-5 p.m., to 9 p.m. in summer.

Chicama Vineyards
Stoney Hill Rd., West Tisbury, 508-693-0309, 888-244-2262; www.chicamavineyards.com
The Vineyard was once a winemaking Mecca; today Chicama is reviving the tradition. It produces a variety of wines, including merlot, chardonnay and cabernet. The onsite store also sells vinegars and salad dressings, mustards and chutneys, and jams and jellies. Tours and wine tastings are available. Hours vary; call ahead.

Featherstone Meeting House For the Arts
Barnes Rd., Oak Bluffs, 508-693-1850; www.featherstonearts.org
This arts center offers tourists the hourly use of studios, and photography, woodworking, pottery, weaving and stained glass classes.

The Meeting House also includes a gallery of works from local artists and a camp for kids. Daily; call for studio availability.

Felix Neck Sanctuary
Edgartown-Vineyard Haven Rd., Vineyard Haven, 508-627-4850; www.massaudubon.org/nature_ connection/sancturaries/felix_neck
This 350-acre wildlife preserve is a haven for kids and bird lovers alike. Six miles of trails (guided or self-guided) meander through meadows, woods, salt marshes and beaches. The visitors center has exhibits and a gift shop. In the summer, kids enroll in the site's Fern & Feather Day Camp. Daily 8 a.m.-4 p.m.; closed Monday in September-May.

Flying Horse Carousel
33 Oak Bluffs Ave., Oak Bluffs, 508-693-9481
This carousel is the oldest in the country and a national historic landmark. Its flying horses are gorgeous, hand-carved and lifelike. Grasping the center brass ring earns you your next ride for free.

Menemsha Fishing Village
North St., Menemsha
Menemsha is a picturesque fishing village, full of cedar-sided clam shacks, fishermen in waterproof gear and lobster traps strewn about. The movie *Jaws* was filmed here, and the main street has a few cute clothing shops.

Mytoi
Dike Rd., Chappaquiddick, 508-693-7662
Although the Vineyard may not be a logical location for a Japanese garden, Mytoi has won praises for its mix of azaleas, irises, dogwood, daffodils, rhododendron and Japanese maple. The 50-year-old garden's centerpiece is a pond filled with goldfish and koi. Daily.

Oak Bluffs
In 1835, this Methodist community served as the site of annual summer camp meetings for church groups. The communal

152

MASSACHUSETTS

★
★
★
★
★

tents gave way to family tents, which in turn became wooden cottages designed to look like tents. Today, visitors to the community take in the town's resulting famous "gingerbread cottages."

The Yard
Middle Rd., Chilmark, 508-645-9662; www.dancetheyard.org
For 30 years, the Yard has hosted dance performances throughout the summer. The 100-seat theater makes its home in a renovated Chilmark barn and offers community dance classes and free performances for children and seniors. June-September.

Vincent House
Pease's Point Way, Edgartown, 508-627-4440
The oldest known house on the island, built in 1672, has been carefully restored to allow visitors to see how buildings were constructed 300 years ago. June-early October: daily 11 a.m.-3 p.m.; rest of year, by appointment.

Old Whaling Church
89 Main St., Edgartown, 508-627-4442
Built in 1843, this is a fine example of Greek Revival architecture. It's now a performing arts center with seating for 500.

Vineyard Haven and Edgartown Shopping
508-693-0085; www.mvy.com
Vineyard Haven is where most of the island's year-round residents live, so its shops are a bit less upscale than those in ritzy Edgartown, where you could spend an afternoon or even an entire day opening your wallet. In both towns, you'll find clothing boutiques (including Midnight Farm in Vineyard Haven, which is owned by Carly Simon), bookstores, jewelry shops, home accessories stores and gourmet boites.

Vineyard Museum
59 School St., Edgartown, 508-627-4441; www.marthasvineyardhistory.org
Four buildings dating back to pre-Revolutionary times join together to form the Vineyard Museum. The Thomas Cooke House, a historic colonial home, specializes in antiques and folk art; the Foster Gallery displays exhibits from the whaling industry; the Pease Galleries specialize in Native American exhibits; and the Gale Huntington Library is a useful tool for genealogy.

SPECIAL EVENTS
Striped Bass & Bluefish Derby
1A Dock St., Edgartown, 508-693-0085; www.mvderby.com
Just after midnight on the first day of the Derby, fishing enthusiasts seek out their favorite spots and cast off, hoping to land the big one. Whenever contestants haul in striped bass, bluefish, bonito or false albacore, the catch is weighed and measured at Edgartown Harbor. Prizes are awarded daily for big fish. A grand prize awaits the contestant who nets the largest catch caught during the tournament. Mid-September-mid-October.

HOTELS
★★★Beach Plum Inn
50 Beach Plum Lane, Menemsha, 508-645-9454, 877-645-7398; www.beachpluminn.com
Built in 1890 from the salvage of a shipwreck, this Vineyard inn sits on a hilltop overlooking the ocean. A stone drive and garden-like path lead to the main house. Several other cottages dot the seven-acre property.
11 rooms. Complimentary full breakfast. Restaurant. $$

★★★Harbor View Hotel
131 N. Water St., Edgartown, 508-627-7000; 800-225-6005; www.harbor-view.com
The newly renovated Harbor View combines the island's heritage with every imaginable modern amenity. Service here is top-notch, and the rooms are bright, airy and clean. Overlooking Edgartown Harbor, the hotel's lengthy veranda has many rocking chairs, the perfect perches from which to watch ship rolls in.
124 rooms. Restaurant. Bar. $

153

MASSACHUSETTS

★
★
★
★

★★★Kelley House

23 Kelley St., Edgartown,
508-627-7900, 800-225-6005;
www.kelley-house.com
53 rooms. Complimentary continental breakfast. Restaurant. **$$**

★★Mansion House Hotel & Health Club

9 Main St., Vineyard Haven,
508-693-2200, 800-332-4112;
www.mvmansionhouse.com
32 rooms. High-speed Internet access. Restaurant. Bar. **$$**

★The Nashua House Hotel

30 Kennebec Ave., Oak Bluffs,
508-693-0043; www.nashuahouse.com
16 rooms. **$**

★★★The Winnetu Inn & Resort

31 Dunes Rd., Edgartown,
508-627-4747; www.winnetu.com
This family-friendly resort has a prime location on beautiful, uncrowded South Beach just outside Edgartown. Rooms are cheerfully decorated in beachy prints and feature kitchens that can be stocked with the inn's grocery service. Activities include weekly clambakes, movie nights and rides around the property on the restored fire engine.
52 rooms. Restaurant. Bar. Children's activity center. **$$**

SPECIALTY LODGINGS

The Arbor Inn

222 Upper Main St., Edgartown,
508-627-8137, 888-748-4383;
www.mvy.com/arborinn
10 rooms. Children over 12 years only. Complimentary continental breakfast. Closed November-April. **$$**

Ashley Inn

129 Main St., Edgartown,
508-627-9655; www.ashleyinn.net
10 rooms. Children over 12 years only. Complimentary continental breakfast. **$**

Hob Knob Inn

128 Main St., Edgartown,
508-627-9510, 800-696-2723;

www.hobknob.com
The Hob Knob feels like it could be based in a mountainside forest—its cozy guest rooms, many fireplaces, and old-school dining room all recall a secluded country hideaway.
16 rooms. Complimentary full breakfast. **$$**

Colonial Inn Of Martha's Vineyard

38 N. Water St., Edgartown,
508-627-4711, 800-627-4701;
www.colonialinnmvy.com
43 rooms. Complimentary continental breakfast. Restaurant. Closed January-mid-April. **$**

Dockside Inn

Circuit Avenue Extension, Oak Bluffs,
508-693-2966, 800-245-5979;
www.vineyardinns.com/dockside.html
This gingerbread-style inn overlooks the harbor in the seaside village of Oak Bluffs and is walking distance to beaches and shopping areas.
22 rooms. Complimentary continental breakfast. Closed December-March. **$**

The Edgartown Inn

56 N. Water St., Edgartown, 508-627-4794;
www.edgartowninn.com
The inn is based in a 1798 sea captain's home. It has been a hotel of sorts since 1820.
12 rooms. Restaurant. Closed November-March. **$**

Greenwood House

40 Greenwood Ave., Vineyard Haven,
508-693-6150, 866-693-6150;
www.greenwoodhouse.com
5 rooms. Complimentary full breakfast. **$$**

The Hanover House

28 Edgartown Rd., Vineyard Haven,
508-693-1066, 800-696-8633;
www.hanoverhouseinn.com
Set on a half acre of land, this cozy bed-and-breakfast is walking distance to the ferry, shopping, restaurants, and the library. Shuttles are available for travel to Edgartown and Oak Bluffs.

154

MASSACHUSETTS

★
★
★
★
★

15 rooms. Complimentary continental breakfast. **$$**

Lambert's Cove Country Inn
Lambert's Cove Rd., Vineyard Haven, 508-693-2298; www.lambertscoveinn.com
15 rooms. Complimentary full breakfast. Restaurant (public by reservation). **$$**

The Oak House
Seaview and Pequot Avenues, Oak Bluffs, 508-693-4187; www.vineyardinns.com/oakhouse.html
10 rooms. Children over 10 years only. Complimentary continental breakfast. Closed mid-October-April. **$$**

Outermost Inn
171 Lighthouse Rd., Chilmark, 508-645-3511; www.outermostinn.com
The inn's picture windows provide excellent views of Vineyard Sound and the Elizabeth Islands.
7 rooms. Children over 12 years only. Complimentary full breakfast. Restaurant. **$$**

Pequot Hotel
19 Pequot Ave., Oak Bluffs, 508-693-5087, 800-947-8704; www.bnblist.com/ma/pequothotel
29 rooms. Complimentary continental breakfast. Closed November-April. **$**

Shiretown Inn
44 N. Water St., Edgartown, 508-627-3353; www.shiretowninn.com
35 rooms. Complimentary continental breakfast. Restaurant. Bar. Closed mid-October-April. **$**

Thorncroft Inn
460 Main St., Vineyard Haven, 508-693-3333; www.thorncroft.com
Secluded on a tree-lined, three-acre peninsula, this charming, white-shuttered house has romantic guest rooms with hot tubs and fireplaces. A full country breakfast can be eaten in the dining room or in bed.
14 rooms. Complimentary full breakfast. **$$$**

RESTAURANTS

★★★Alchemy
71 Main St., Edgartown, 508-627-9999
A smart, casual crowd, including the occasional celebrity, frequents Edgartown's popular Alchemy. The American bistro offers upscale dining—don't miss the fried risotto balls—in a relaxing, two-story atmosphere. The happening bar and lounge are packed with local revelers after hours. American menu. Lunch, dinner. Bar. Casual attire. Outdoor seating. Closed January. **$$$**

★★The Aquinnah Shop
State Rd., Aquinnah, 508-645-3142
American menu. Breakfast, lunch, dinner. Children's menu. Casual attire. Outdoor seating. Closed mid-October-Easter. **$$**

★★★Balance
57 Circuit Ave., Oak Bluffs, 508-696-3000
Balance brings a contemporary splash to Martha's Vineyard, and the flavors that come from its kitchen are as bold as its spirit. The chef is something of a local celebrity, and his touch of whimsy is evident in his creative dishes. The thriving bar scene attracts fashionable A-listers. American menu. Dinner. Bar. Casual attire. **$$**

★★★Beach Plum Inn Restaurant
50 Beach Plum Lane, Menemsha, 508-645-9454; www.beachpluminn.com
Every table at the renowned, out-of-the-way Beach Plum comes with an ocean view, making the eatery one of the most romantic places on the island. The seafood-heavy menu is nearly flawless and the four-course prix fixe menu is a delicious extravagance. American menu. Dinner. Casual attire. Outdoor seating. Closed January-early May. **$$$**

★★Cafe Moxie
48 Main St., Vineyard Haven, 508-693-1484; www.cafemoxie.com
American menu. Lunch, dinner. Casual attire. Closed Tuesday; fall-winter. **$$$**

155

MASSACHUSETTS

★★★Coach House
**131 N. Water St., Edgartown,
508-627-3761, 800-225-6005;
www.harbor-view.com**
Casual refinement is the calling card of the Coach House. The breezy Harbor View Hotel restaurant looks out over the Edgartown Harbor. An upscale crowd comes here for modern twists on old standbys at breakfast and lunch, while fresh seafood and shellfish dominate the dinner menu. The wine list is comprehensive, providing the perfect complement to an exceptional meal.
American menu. Breakfast, lunch, dinner, Sunday brunch. Bar. Children's menu. Casual attire. Reservations recommended. Valet parking. Closed Sunday-Monday evenings. **$$$**

★Coop de Ville
**Dockside Marketplace, Oak Bluffs,
508-693-3420**
Seafood menu. Lunch, dinner. Outdoor seating. **$$**

★Espresso Love Cafe
17 Church St., Edgartown, 508-627-9211
International menu. Breakfast, lunch, dinner. Children's menu. Casual attire. Reservations recommended. Outdoor seating. **$$**

★★Jimmy Sea's
**32 Kennebec Ave., Oak Bluffs,
508-696-8550**
Italian menu. Dinner. Casual attire. Outdoor seating. **$$**

★★★L'Etoile
**22 N. Water St., Edgartown,
508-627-5187; www.letoile.net**
When L'Etoile moved last year from the stuffy Charlotte Inn to a more relaxed location on North Water Street, diners breathed a sigh of relief. The food is still served in a very formal atmosphere—and still costs a pretty penny—but the overall experience is now focused on the menu, not the staff's pomp and prejudice. A new brightly col-

ored bar buts against the restaurant; either room is a worthy place to dine in style.
French menu. Dinner. Jacket required. Reservations recommended. Closed Monday-Thursday off-season. **$$$$**

★★Home Port
**512 North Rd., Menemsha,
508-645-2679; www.homeportmv.com**
Seafood menu. Dinner. Children's menu. Casual attire. Reservations recommended. Outdoor seating. Closed Labor Day-Memorial Day. **$$$**

★★Le Grenier French Restaurant
**82 Main St., Vineyard Haven,
508-693-4906;
www.legrenierrestaurant.com**
French menu. Dinner. Casual attire. Reservations recommended. **$$$**

★Lattanzi's Pizzeria
**Old Post Office Square, Edgartown,
508-627-9084; www.lattanzis.com**
Italian, pizza menu. Dinner. Children's menu. Casual attire. Reservations recommended. Outdoor seating. **$**

★Linda Jean's
34 Circuit Ave., Oak Bluffs, 508-693-4093
American menu. Breakfast, Lunch, dinner. Children's menu. Casual attire. Outdoor seating. **$**

★★Lola's Southern Seafood
**Beach Rd., Oak Bluffs, 508-693-5007;
www.lolassouthernseafood.com**
American, seafood menu. Dinner, late-night, Sunday brunch. Bar. Casual attire. **$$**

★Lookout Tavern
8 Seaview Ave., Oak Bluffs, 508-696-9844
Seafood menu. Lunch, dinner. Bar. Casual attire. Outdoor seating. Closed November-April. **$$**

★★Lure
**31 Dunes Rd., Edgartown,
508-627-3663; www.winnetu.com**
Seafood menu. Dinner. Closed Labor Day-Columbus Day Monday-Tuesday, Colum-

★
★
★
★
★

bus Day-Thanksgiving Monday-Thursday, Thanksgiving-May. **$$$**

★★★Outermost Inn
Lighthouse Rd., Aquinnah,
508-645-3511; www.outermostinn.com
As its name suggests, the Outermost Inn is far removed from the often-clogged eateries of Edgartown and Oak Bluffs. Dining here is a serene experience, thanks to the refined inn's clifftop location and relaxed elegance. Fresh herbs and vegetables grown on the property influence the creative prix fixe menu. Wine lovers, take note: the restaurant is strictly BYOB. American menu. Dinner. Reservations recommended. Closed Wednesday; also mid-October-mid-May. **$$$**

★The Newes from America
23 Kelly St., Edgartown, 508-627-4397;
www.kelley-house.com/dining
American menu. Lunch, dinner. **$**

★★Seasons Eatery
19 Circuit Ave., Oak Bluffs, 508-693-7129

American menu. Lunch, dinner. Bar. Children's menu. Casual attire. **$**

★★Square Rigger
235 State Rd., Edgartown, 508-627-9968
Seafood menu. Dinner. Bar. Casual attire. Reservations recommended. Closed January. **$$**

★★Sweet Life Cafe
63 Circuit Ave., Oak Bluffs, 508-696-0200
Seafood menu. Dinner. Reservations recommended. Outdoor seating. Closed January-March. **$$**

★★Theo's at the Inn at Blueberry Hill
74 North Rd., Chilmark,
508-645-3322, 800-356-3322;
www.blueberryinn.com
American menu. Dinner. Casual attire. **$$**

★The Wharf Pub & Restaurant
Lower Main St., Edgartown,
508-627-9966; www.wharfpub.com
Seafood menu. Lunch, dinner. Bar. Children's menu. Reservations recommended (six or more people). Closed March. **$$**

NANTUCKET
Generally regarded as even *more* exclusive than Martha's Vineyard, Nantucket is a small island full of sprawling cottages, endless soft sand beaches, first-rate restaurants and breathtaking ocean vistas. In the peak summer season, the island's population skyrockets to nearly overcrowded proportions, as day-trippers and weekenders stream from the Steamship Authority ferries. Somehow, though, the island retains its charm and its flush residents take the tourists in stride. A plethora of outdoor activity can be explored here, from biking to swimming to sailing to tennis and golf. Siasconset ('Sconset to natives) and Nantucket Town are the isle's shopping and dining hubs, though many small stores and eateries are sprinkled over the land's 49 square miles.
Information: Chamber of Commerce, 48 Main St., Nantucket, 508-228-1700
Information Bureau, 25 Federal St., Nantucket, 508-228-1700;
www.nantucketchamber.org

WHAT TO SEE AND DO
Endeavor Sailing Adventures
Straight Wharf, Nantucket,
508-228-5585; www.endeavorsailing.com
U.S. Coast Guard Captain James Genthner built his sloop, the *Endeavor*, and has been sailing it for more than 20 years. Take a 90-minute sail around Nantucket

Sound and let Genthner and his wife, Sue, introduce you to Nantucket's sights, sounds, and history. May-October; closed November-April.

Altar Rock
Off Polpis Rd., Nantucket
Altar Rock rises 90 feet above sea level

and affords stunning views of Nantucket and the surrounding Cape. Go at dawn or dusk for the best views.

Bartlett's Farm
33 Bartlett Farm Rd., Nantucket, 508-228-9403; www.bartlettsfarm.com
The Bartlett family has tilled the land of Nantucket's largest farm for nearly 200 years. Stop by for fresh vegetables, milk, eggs, cheese, freshly baked bread and cut flowers. A handful of prepared foods such as salads, pies, snacks, jams, and chutneys are also available. Daily 8 a.m.-6 p.m.

Cisco Brewers
5 Bartlett Farm Rd., Nantucket, 508-325-5929; www.ciscobrewers.com
Local beer-makers Cisco Brewers concoct dozens of micro-specialties such as Whales Tales Pale Ale, Baileys Ale, Moor Porter, Capn' Swains Extra Stout, Summer of Lager and Baggywrinkle Barleywine. Onsite are guided tours of the brewery, vineyard and distillery. Summer: Monday-Saturday 10 a.m.-6 p.m., Sunday until 5 p.m.; fall-spring: Saturday 10 a.m.-5 p.m.

First Congregational Church
62 Centre St., Nantucket, 508-228-0950
Also called the Old North Church, this spot arguably offers Nantucket's best view of the island and surrounding ocean. To enjoy it, you'll have to climb the 120-foot-tall steeple's 94 steps. Mid-June-mid-October: Monday-Saturday.

Jetties Beach
Bathing Beach Rd., Nantucket
Kid-friendly Jetties is the best bet for beach-going families. There are rest rooms, showers, changing rooms, a snack bar, lifeguards, rental chairs, a playground, volleyball and tennis courts, and a skateboarding park. You can also rent kayaks, sailboards and sailboats through Nantucket Community Sailing (508-228-5358). Daily.

Loines Observatory
59 Milk St., Nantucket,

508-228-8690; www.mmo.org
Named for the first professional female astronomer, the observatory lets guests peek through a telescope to view the star-filled Cape Cod skies. Monday, Wednesday, Friday evenings in summer, Saturday evenings year-round; closed Tuesday, Thursday, Sunday in summer, Sunday-Friday year-round.

1800 House
8 Mill St., Nantucket, 508-228-1894
This early 19th-century house has period furnishings, a large, round cellar and a kitchen garden.

Folger-Franklin Seat and Memorial Boulder
Madaket Rd., Nantucket, 508-228-1894
The birthplace of Abiah Folger, Benjamin Franklin's mother.

Hadwen House
96 Main St., Nantucket, 508-228-1894
A Greek Revival mansion with furnishings from the whaling period. Monday-Saturday 10 a.m.-5 p.m., Sunday from noon.

Jethro Coffin House (Oldest House)
16 Sunset Hill Lane, Nantucket, 508-228-1894
Built in 1686, Oldest House is, true to its name, one of the oldest houses in the United States. The building was a wedding present given to the children of two feuding families (the Gardners and the Coffins) by their in-laws, who reconciled after the happy event. Monday-Saturday 10 a.m.-5 p.m., Sunday from noon.

Old Mill
50 Prospect St., Nantucket, 508-228-1894
Believed to be the oldest windmill in the United States, this Dutch-style structure is impressive in its beauty and sheer vertical height of 50 feet. It was built in 1746 with salvaged oak that washed up on shore from shipwrecks. Inside are a research center and whaling museum. June-August: daily; call for off-season hours.

★
★
★
★
★

Miacomet Golf Course

12 W Miacomet Rd., Nantucket,
508-228-9764

Nantucket's only public golf course offers nine holes (two are par fives). Reserve a tee time at least a week in advance; the chances of playing in the summertime without a reservation are zero. Daily.

Murray's Toggery

62 Main St., Nantucket,
508-228-0437, 800-368-2134;
www.nantucketreds.com

Murray's Toggery was the first store on the island to sell Nantucket Reds, the casual pink khaki pants that have since invaded every nook of preppiness in America. Monday-Saturday 9 a.m.-7 p.m., Sunday 10 a.m.-6 p.m.; winter: Monday-Saturday 9 a.m.-5 p.m.

Nantucket Maria Mitchell Association

4 Vestal St., Nantucket,
508-228-9198; www.mmo.org

The scientific library has historical documents, science journals and Mitchell family memorabilia. There's also a natural science museum with local wildlife, and an aquarium is nearby at 28 Washington Street. Mid-June-August: Tuesday-Saturday; library also open rest of year, Wednesday-Saturday.

Nantucket Town

Nantucket, 508-228-1700;
www.nantucketchamber.org/directory/
merchants

Nantucket Town is a shopper's dream. A walk down its main street involves passing by home, clothing, culinary, boat, jewelry, art and antique shops, most of which are tasteful and well-edited.

Rafael Osona Auctions

21 Washington St., Nantucket,
508-228-3942;
www.rafaelosonaauction.com

This spot hosts estate auctions on selected weekends (call for exact dates and times) that feature treasured pieces from both the United States and Europe. Late May-early December.

Siasconset Village

East end of Nantucket Island

Siasconset lies seven miles from Nantucket Town, and can be reached by bicycle or shuttle bus (driving often takes twice as long due to traffic). This 18th-century fishing village features quaint cottages, grand mansions, restaurants, a few shops and a summer cinema.

Something Natural

50 Cliff Rd., Nantucket, 508-228-0504;
www.somethingnatural.com

Those looking for a casual breakfast or lunch should check out This off-the-beaten-path shop that makes healthy sandwiches, breads, bagels, salads, and cookies. May-October.

Strong Wings Summer Camp

9 Nobadeer Farm Rd., Nantucket,
508-228-1769; www.strongwings.org

Open for just two months every year, the Strong Wings Summer Camp enrolls kids ages 5 to 15 in three- or five-day sessions, where they explore the area, mountain bike, hike, kayak, snorkel, rock climb and boogie board. Older kids learn search-and-rescue techniques. Late June-late Aug: daily.

The Straight Wharf

Straight Wharf, Nantucket

Built in 1723, the wharf is Nantucket's launching area for sailboats, sloops and kayaks, but it's also a great shopping and eating area. Loaded with restaurants and quaint, one-room cottage shops, the wharf also features an art gallery, museum and outdoor concert pavilion.

The Sunken Ship

12 Broad St., Nantucket, 508-228-9226;
www.sunkenship.com

The Sunken Ship is a full-service dive shop that offers lessons and rentals. The general store offers an eclectic array of maritime goods. Daily; call for closures.

Theatre Workshop of Nantucket

2 Centre St., Nantucket, 508-228-4305;

159

www.theatreworkshop.com

The theater has staged comedies, dramas, plays and dance concerts since 1985. Both professionals and amateurs make up the company, which offers between six and ten performances each summer.

Windswept Cranberry Bog

Polpis Rd., Siasconset

To see how cranberries are grown and harvested, visit this 200-acre bog during the fall harvest (late September through October from dawn to dusk). At other times of the year, the bog is a peaceful place to walk and bike. Daily dawn-dusk.

Nantucket Historical Association Whaling Museum

15 Broad St., Nanutcket, 508-228-1894; www.nha.org

This museum, redesigned and reopened in 2005, is the premier institution devoted to the history of the whaling industry. Inside are a 46-foot preserved sperm whale skeleton (the whale washed ashore in 1998) and many artifacts from the island's heyday as a center for whale oil production. Mid-May through Mid-October: daily 10 a.m.-5 p.m.; Mid-October-Mid-December: Thursday-Monday 11 a.m.-4 p.m.; closed Mid-December-May.

SPECIAL EVENTS

Nantucket Arts Festival

508-325-8588; www.nantucketartscouncil.org

This week-long festival celebrates a full range of arts on the island: films, poetry and fiction, acting, dance, paintings, photography and many other forms. Look for the wet-paint sale in which you can bid on works completed just that day. Early October.

Nantucket Film Festival

508-228-6648; www.nantucketfilmfestival.org

Like other film fests, this one screens new independent movies that may not otherwise garner attention. It's attended by screenwriters, actors, film connoisseurs and occasionally, big-name celebrities. A daily event called Morning Coffee showcases a panel of the above participating in Q&As. Mid-June.

Nantucket Wine Festival

508-228-1128; www.nantucketwinefestival.com

The Great Wine in Grand Houses event allows you to visit a private mansion, sip fine vintages drawn from nearly 100 wineries and dine on food prepared by some of the area's finest chefs. Reservations are required. Mid-May.

HOTELS

★★The Beachside at Nantucket

30 N. Beach St., Nantucket, 508-228-2241, 800-322-4433; www.thebeachside.com

93 rooms. Complimentary continental breakfast. Restaurant. Bar. Closed November-April. $

★★Cliffside Beach Club

46 Jefferson Ave., Nantucket, 508-228-0618; www.cliffsidebeach.com

27 rooms, all suites. Restaurant. Bar. Beach. Closed November-April. $$

★★Harbor House Village

S. Beach St., Nantucket, 508-325-1000, 866-325-9300; www.nantucketislandresorts.com

104 rooms. Restaurant. Bar. Beach. $

★★★Jared Coffin House

29 Broad St., Nantucket, 508-228-2400; www.jaredcoffinhouse.com

60 rooms. Restaurant. Bar. $

★★Nantucket Inn

1 Miller's Way, Nantucket, 508-228-6900, 800-321-8484; www.nantucketinn.net

100 rooms. Restaurant. Bar. Airport transportation available. Closed December-March. $

★★★White Elephant Resort

50 Easton St., Nantucket, 508-228-2500, 800-445-6574;

MASSACHUSETTS

www.whiteelephantresort.com

Step back in time for a game of croquet on a sweeping, manicured lawn at this harbor-front resort. Rooms are comfortable with plush beds and luxurious bath amenities. Guests can stay in the main inn or in one of the many onsite cottages.

63 rooms. Restaurant. Bar. Closed mid December-March. **$$$**

★★★★The Wauwinet

120 Wauwinet Rd., Nantucket,
508-228-0145, 800-426-8718;
www.wauwinet.com

Staying at the Wauwinet is akin to being marooned on a remote island with impeccable service. Built in 1876 by ship captains, the Wauwinet is a grand resort, with sophisticated rooms and suites, and private beaches fronting the harbor and Atlantic Ocean. Its clay tennis courts are well-maintained, and its restaurant has a 20,000-bottle wine cellar.

36 rooms. Children over 18 only. Complimentary full breakfast. Restaurant. Tennis. Closed late October-early May. **$$$$**

SPECIALTY LODGINGS

Carlisle House Inn

26 N. Water St., Nantucket, 508-228-0720;
www.carlislehouse.com

The structure was built in 1765, and now houses an inn with rooms featuring fireplaces and four poster beds.

17 rooms. Children over 10 years only. Complimentary continental breakfast. Closed January-March. **$**

Centerboard Guest House

8 Chester St., Nantucket, 508-228-9696;
www.centerboardguesthouse.com

The updated, modern rooms at this bed and breakfast have flat screen TVs, down duvets and full baths with Caswell and Massey bath products.

8 rooms. Complimentary continental breakfast. Closed January-February. **$**

Centre Street Inn

78 Centre St., Nantucket,
508-228-0199, 800-298-0199;

www.centrestreetinn.com

Rooms in this cozy inn are named after holidays and feature antique furniture and fireplaces.

14 rooms. Complimentary continental breakfast. Closed January-April. **$**

Cobblestone Inn

5 Ash St., Nantucket, 508-228-1987;
www.nantucket.net

The petite rooms at this cozy inn have fireplaces, private baths, colorful quilts and private baths.

5 rooms. Complimentary full breakfast. Closed January-March. **$**

Martin House Inn

61 Centre St., Nantucket, 508-228-0678;
www.martinhouseinn.net

Located in a house built in 1803, this historic inn has rooms with four-poster or canopied beds and fireplaces.

13 rooms. Complimentary continental breakfast. Restaurant. **$**

Roberts House Inn

11 India St., Nantucket,
508-228-0600, 800-872-6830;
www.robertshouseinn.com

Restored in 2003, this inn has rooms furnished with antiques and reproductions and private baths.

45 rooms. Complimentary continental breakfast. **$**

Seven Sea Street Inn

7 Sea St., Nantucket, 508-228-3577;
www.sevenseastreetinn.com

Spread over three historic houses, this inn has rooms with canopied beds, high-definition TV and Jacuzzi tubs.

11 rooms. Children over 5 years only. Complimentary continental breakfast. Closed Jan-mid April. **$$**

Sherburne Inn

10 Gay St., Nantucket,
508-228-4425, 888-577-4425;
www.sherburneinn.com

Built by whaling captatin Obed Starbuck in 1831, this small inn has rooms decorated in cheerful colors. Breakfast and afternoon tea are served daily.

8 rooms. Children over 6 years only. Complimentary continental breakfast. **$**

Ships Inn

13 Fair St., Nantucket, 508-228-0040; www.shipsinnnantucket.com

12 rooms. Complimentary continental breakfast. Restaurant, bar. Closed November-April. **$$**

Vanessa Noel Hotel

5 Chestnut St., Nantucket, 508-228-5300; www.vanno.com

This petite inn, opened by a New York–based designer, is housed above her eponymous shoe boutique. Rooms are simple but luxurious with plush beds, Frette linens and Bulgari bath products.

8 rooms. Complimentary continental breakfast. High-speed Internet access. Bar. **$$$**

RESTAURANTS

★★★21 Federal

21 Federal St., Nantucket, 508-228-2121; www.21federal.net

This restaurant offers diners a rare blend of historic charm and contemporary panache. The stylishly clubby spot is a favorite haunt of the islands who's-who, both for its delectable New American cuisine and convivial bar. The well-rounded menu has a wide selection of meat, poultry, and seafood, while the award-winning wine list delights oenophiles.

American menu. Dinner. Bar. Business casual attire. Reservations recommended. Outdoor seating. Closed January-April. **$$$**

★★★American Seasons

80 Center St., Nantucket, 508-228-7111; www.americanseasons.com

American Seasons' menu is refreshingly varied if perhaps, a bit gimmicky. The menu is divided to reflect regional cuisines: New England, Down South, the Wild West and the Pacific Coast. Thanks to meticulous attention to detail and fresh, local produce, the themed meals are a success. Regulars rave about the cooking and the folk-art-

decorated, romantic dining room and patio. American menu. Dinner. Bar. Business casual attire. Reservations recommended. Outdoor seating. Closed January-March. **$$$**

★Atlantic Cafe

15 S. Water St., Nantucket, 508-228-0570

American, seafood menu. Lunch, dinner, late-night. Bar. Children's menu. Closed late December-early January. **$**

★★Black Eyed Susan's

10 India St., Nantucket, 508-325-0308

International menu. Breakfast, dinner. Casual attire. Reservations recommended. Outdoor seating. Closed Sunday; also November-March. **$$**

★★★Boarding House

12 Federal St., Nantucket, 508-228-9622; www.boardinghouse-pearl.com

Long waits are inevitable at the Boarding House, but this smart restaurant's nouveau cuisine and sexy, youthful scene make it worth the wait. Those in the know book a table outdoors to people-watch and stargaze as they eat. Others prefer the dimly lit downstairs dining room. Seafood and beef are the main inspirations behind the creative Asian-influenced menu; a comprehensive wine list ensures perfect pairings. American menu. Lunch, dinner. Bar. Reservations recommended. Outdoor seating. **$$$**

★Cambridge Street Restaurant

12 Cambridge St., Nantucket, 508-228-7109

American menu. Dinner. Bar. Casual attire. Closed January-April. **$$**

★★★Club Car

1 Main St., Nantucket, 508-228-1101; www.theclubcar.com

The Club Car lounge is housed in a renovated train club car that once ran between Steamboat Wharf and Siasconset Village. Lunches and dinners are full of sophisticated menu offerings. and A pianist performs nightly. French menu. Lunch, dinner. Bar. Business casual attire. Reservations recommended. Closed November-late May. **$$$$**

★★★Company of the Cauldron
5 India St., Nantucket, 508-228-4016; www.companyofthecauldron.com
From its ivy-covered exterior to the soft glow of its candlelit dining room to its gentle harp soundtrack, this restaurant seems crafted straight from a romance novel. The exceptional New American menu changes nightly, continuously surprising and delighting visitors with memorable dishes. International menu. Dinner. Business casual attire. Reservations recommended. Closed Monday; also Mid-December-April. **$$$**

★Downyflake
18 Sparks Ave., Nantucket, 508-228-4533
Breakfast, lunch. Casual attire. **$**

★Fog Island Cafe
7 S. Water St., Nantucket, 508-228-1818; www.fogisland.com
American menu. Breakfast, Lunch, dinner. Bar. Children's menu. Casual attire. Closed January-February. **$**

★★Le Languedoc
24 Broad St., Nantucket, 508-228-2552; www.lelanguedoc.com
French menu. Lunch, dinner. Bar. Casual attire. Reservations recommended. Outdoor seating. Closed Febuary-March. **$$$**

★★Nantucket Lobster Trap
23 Washington St., Nantucket, 508-228-4200; www.nantucketlobstertrap.com
Seafood menu. Dinner. Bar. Children's menu. Casual attire. Outdoor seating. Closed October-April. **$$$**

★★★Oran Mor
2 S. Beach St., Nantucket, 508-228-8655; www.nantucket.net/food/oranmor
Climb the stairs to Oran Mor and discover a food-lover's heaven. The fine-dining experience is capped off by a friendly, knowledgeable staff that manages to be attentive without being intrusive. The eclectic menu echoes the restaurant's accessible elegance. Organic ingredients and fresh seafood dominate the complex dishes. International menu. Dinner. Bar. Business casual attire. Reservations recommended. Closed January-March. **$$$**

★★Ropewalk
1 Straight Wharf, Nantucket, 508-228-8886; www.theropewalk.com
Seafood menu. Lunch, dinner. Bar. Children's menu. Casual attire. Outdoor seating. Closed mid-October-mid-May. **$$**

★★SeaGrille
45 Sparks Ave., Nantucket, 508-325-5700; www.theseagrille.com
Seafood menu. Lunch, dinner. Children's menu. Business casual attire. Reservations recommended. Outdoor seating. **$$**

★★★Summer House
17 Ocean Ave., Nantucket, 508-257-9976
In the tiny town of 'Sconset, distinguished by its rose-covered cottages and wind-swept bluffs, the Summer House seduces with oceanfront seating and superb cuisine. White wicker furnishings and ceiling fans set the scene for the refined New American cuisine. A more casual poolside lunch is also served. American menu. Dinner. Bar. Casual attire. Outdoor seating. Closed mid-October-mid-May. **$$$$**

★★★The Pearl
12 Federal St., Nantucket, 508-228-9701; www.boardinghouse-pearl.com
This spot was among the first to bring city chic to Nantucket. The ultra-hip eatery appeals to a young, fashionable clientele that crowds the bar area on weekend nights. Asian flavors punctuate the Pearl's seafood dishes, while the drink menu is decidedly metropolitan with various takes on martinis, cosmos and sake, in addition to a complete wine and champagne list. There are only two seatings per evening so reserve early. International menu. Dinner, late-night. Bar. Casual attire. Reservations recommended. Outdoor seating. Closed October-April. **$$$$**

163

MASSACHUSETTS

★
★
★
★
★

★★★Topper's
120 Wauwinet Rd., Nantucket,
508-228-0145, 800-426-8718;
www.wauwinet.com

Chef David Daniels lends his extensive New England-honed skills to Toppers. His signature dishes such as maple-glazed foie gras, potato-crusted Maine scallops and roasted New York duckling are all outstanding. Regulars know to order the seasonal prix fixe menu, which has locally inspired treats like lobster and chestnut soup, roasted sirloin of venison and house made ice cream. All meals can be paired with a selection from the award-winning, 900-bottle wine list.

American menu. Lunch, dinner, Sun brunch. Bar. Business casual attire. Reservations recommended. Outdoor seating. Closed late October-early May. **$$$$**

★★West Creek Cafe
11 W. Creek Rd., Nantucket, 508-228-4943
American menu. Dinner. Bar. Reservations recommended. Outdoor seating. Closed Tuesday. **$$$**

★Westender
326 Madaket Rd., Nantucket,
508-228-5100
American menu. Lunch, dinner. Bar. Closed in winter. **$$**

NEW BEDFORD

Herman Melville once said every house in New Bedford was harpooned, then reeled in from the bottom of the sea. His metaphor held some truth: in his time, the city was the greatest whaling port in the world. But in 1857, when miners struck oil in Pennsylvania, this bustling sea-dependent spot became a veritable ghost town. It was eventually rebuilt around manufacturing, but never quite recaptured the flourish of its earlier era. Today, the city is mostly urban and slight gritty. Its past can be glimpsed in its monuments and museums, and in the sea captains' homes that still line its better streets.

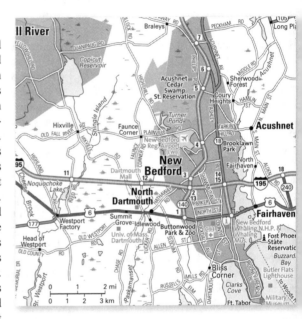

Information: Bristol County Convention & Visitors Bureau, 70 N. Second St., New Bedford, 508-997-1250, 800-288-6263; www.bristol-county.org

WHAT TO SEE AND DO

Buttonwood Park & Zoo
425 Hawthorn St., New Bedford,
508-991-6178; www.bpzoo.org
The park has a greenhouse, ball fields, tennis courts, a playground, a picnic area, and a fitness circuit. Zoo exhibits include elephants, lions, deer, bears, buffalo and a seal pool. Daily 10 a.m.-5 p.m.

New Bedford Whaling Museum
18 Johnny Cake Hill, New Bedford,
508-997-0046; www.whalingmuseum.org
The museum features an 89-foot half-scale model of the whale ship *Lagoda*. Galleries are devoted to scrimshaw, local artists, murals and a whale skeleton. Daily 9 a.m.-5 p.m.

164

MASSACHUSETTS

New Bedford-Cuttyhunk Ferry
Fisherman's Wharf at Pier 3, New Bedford,
508-992-1432
Reservations suggested. Mid-June-mid-September: daily; rest of year: varied schedule.

Rotch-Jones-Duff House and Garden Museum
396 County St., New Bedford,
508-997-1401; www.rjdmuseum.org
This Greek Revival mansion has been maintained to reflect the lives of three families that lived in the house. Daily.

Seamen's Bethel
15 Johnny Cake Hill, New Bedford,
508-992-3295
(1832) Here is the "Whaleman's Chapel" referred to by Melville in *Moby Dick*. The prow-shaped pulpit was later built to represent Melville's description. Daily.

SPECIAL EVENTS
Feast of the Blessed Sacrament
Madeira Ave., Hathaway St.,
and Tinkham St., New Bedford,
508-992-6911; www.portuguesefeast.com
This is the largest Portuguese feast in North America and features three days of entertainment, parades and amusement rides. First weekend in August.

HOTELS
★★Days Inn
500 Hathaway Rd., New Bedford,
508-997-1231, 800-329-7466;
www.daysinn.com
151 rooms. Restaurant. Bar. Airport transportation available. **$**

RESTAURANTS
★Antonio's
267 Coggeshall St., New Bedford,
508-990-3636
American, Spanish menu. Lunch, dinner. Bar. Children's menu. Casual attire. **$$**

★★Freestone's City Grill
41 William St., New Bedford,
508-993-7477; www.freestones.com
Seafood menu. Lunch, dinner. Bar. Children's menu. Casual attire. **$$**

★★★Oceanna
95 William St., New Bedford, 508-997-8465
Seafood menu. Lunch, dinner. Bar. Children's menu. Casual attire. Closed Sunday. **$$**

NEWBURYPORT
One of Massachusetts's best-kept secrets, Newburyport might be the ideal New England town. Smaller than a city but bigger than a village, this north shore spot is quaint without being saccharin, manageable without being boring. Its clean, safe streets exude history, especially those lined with stately Federalist ship captain's houses. Locals have an easy commute to Boston but rarely bother making the trip—everything they need, from sweet clothing boutiques to first-rate dining to the sandy shores of Plum Island, is right here.
Information: Greater Newburyport Chamber of Commerce & Industry, 29 State St., Newburyport, 978-462-6680; www.newburyport.chamber.org

WHAT TO SEE AND DO
Coffin House
14 High Rd., Newburyport, 978-462-2634
This old home features 17th- and 18th-century kitchens, a buttery, and parlor with early 19th-century wallpaper. June-mid-October: first Saturday of the month 11 a.m.-5 p.m.

Cushing House Museum
98 High St., Newburyport, 978-462-2681
This Federalist-style mansion was once the home of Caleb Cushing, the first U.S. envoy to China. May-November: Tuesday-Friday 10 a.m.-4 p.m., Saturday from noon.

Custom House Maritime Museum
25 Water St., Newburyport, 978-462-8681

MASSACHUSETTS

Collections of marine artifacts, ship models and navigational instruments are on display here. April-late-December: Monday-Saturday 10 a.m.-4 p.m., Sunday from 1 p.m.

Parker River National Wildlife Refuge
6 Plum Island Turnpike, Newburyport, 978-465-5753
This breath-taking natural barrier beach is 6 1/2 miles long and the home of many species of birds, mammals, reptiles, amphibians, and plants. Available are hiking, bicycling, waterfowl hunting and a nature trail. Daily.

HOTELS
★★Garrison Inn
11 Brown Square, Newburyport, 978-499-8500;
www.garrisoninn.com
24 rooms. Restaurant. Bar. Children's activity center. **$**

SPECIALTY LODGINGS
Clark Currier Inn
45 Green St., Newburyport, 978-465-8363; www.clarkcurrierinn.com
7 rooms. Complimentary full breakfast. **$**

Essex Street Inn
7 Essex St., Newburyport, 978-465-3148;
www.essexstreetinn.com
19 rooms. Complimentary continental breakfast. **$**

Morrill Place
209 High St., Newburyport, 978-462-2808
9 rooms. Complimentary continental breakfast. **$**

Windsor House
38 Federal St., Newburyport, 978-462-3778, 888-873-5296;
www.bbhost.com/windsorhouse
4 rooms. No children allowed. Complimentary full breakfast. **$$**

RESTAURANTS
★★★David's
11 Brown Square, Newburyport, 978-462-8077; www.davidstavern.com
A favorite of locals and visitors alike, this restaurant serves a wide variety of global fare.
International menu. Dinner. Bar. Children's menu. **$$$**

★★Glenn's Galley
44 Merrimac St., Newburyport, 978-465-3811; www.glennsrestaurant.com
Seafood menu. Dinner. Bar. Children's menu. Closed Monday. **$$**

★★Michael's Harborside
1 Tournament Wharf, Newburyport, 978-462-7785;
www.michaelsharborside.com
Seafood menu. Lunch, dinner. Bar. Outdoor seating. **$$**

★★Ten Center Street
10 Center St., Newburyport, 978-462-6652
American menu. Lunch, dinner, Sunday brunch. Bar. Outdoor seating. Closed Monday. **$$**

★The Grog
13 Middle St., Newburyport, 978-465-8008; www.thegrog.com
International menu. Lunch, dinner. Bar. **$$**

NEWTON
Right outside Boston, the city of Newton is made up of 13 small suburban villages best known for their well-moneyed citizens and much-envied addresses. The various main streets have become shopping and dining destinations for the family sets, while the city's five big schools—including Boston College—lend youthful energy to the area.
Information: Chamber of Commerce, 199 Wells Ave., Newton, 617-244-5300; www.nnchamber.com

WHAT TO SEE AND DO

Charles River Canoe & Kayak Center

2401 Commonwealth Ave.,
Newton, 617-965-5110;
www.ski-paddle.com/cano/canoe.htm
Tourists who aren't afraid of getting a little wet love this Charles River entry point. Kayaks and canoes are available for rent. April-October: daily.

Jackson Homestead Museum

527 Washington St., Newton,
617-552-7238
(1809) Once a station on the Underground Railroad, the home of the Newton Historical Society has changing exhibits and a children's gallery. Tuesday-Saturday and Sunday afternoon.

HOTELS

★★Holiday Inn

399 Grove St., Newton,
617-969-5300, 888-465-4329;
www.holiday-inn.com
191 rooms. Restaurant. Bar. **$**

★★★Boston Marriott Newton

2345 Commonwealth Ave., Newton,
617-969-1000, 800-228-9290;
www.marriott.com
Ideal for business travelers, the Newton Marriot has a 24-hour, self-serve business center and more than 16,000 square feet of meeting space. Its prime location along the Charles River offers a great view.
430 rooms. Restaurant. Bar. **$**

★★★Sheraton Newton Hotel

320 Washington St., Newton,
617-969-3010, 800-325-3535;
www.sheraton.com
All the rooms and suites at this recently renovated property have a creative, contemporary décor with sleek white bedding, well-designed work areas and warm, mustard-colored walls. Those not wanting to shell out for Boston rates can stay here and hop the downtown express, which departs for Faneuil Hall every 20 minutes. 272 rooms. High-speed Internet access. Restaurant. Bar. **$**

RESTAURANTS

★★★Lumiere

1293 Washington St., West Newton,
617-244-9199; www.lumiererestaurant.com
The words warm and whimsical best sum up the ambiance at this suburban French spot. The front door opens by spoon, and Scrabble tiles line the rest room doors. But the contemporary French cuisine doesn't fool around—it's fresh and straightforward, making this spot the best bistro for miles around. French, Mediterranean, Pacific menu. Dinner. **$$$**

NORTH ADAMS

No town in the Berkshires has gone through a more dramatic transformation than North Adams (well, at least not recently). Thanks to MassMoCA, the biggest modern art museum in the world, the former factory city suddenly finds itself as a booming tourist center. Boutiques and eateries have followed suit, as has a crowd of young culture vultures eager to invest in the locale's emerging spirit.
Information: Northern Berkshire Chamber of Commerce, 75 North St., Pittsfield, 413-663-3735; www.berkshirebiz.org

WHAT TO SEE AND DO

MASS MoCA

1040 Mass MoCA Way, North Adams,
413-664-4481; www.massmoca.org
The center for visual, performing and media arts features unconventional exhibits and performances by renowned artists and cultural institutions. July-early September: daily 10 a.m.-6 p.m.; rest of year: Wednesday-Monday 11 a.m.-5 p.m.

Kidspace

87 Marshall St., North Adams,
413-664-4481

The museum's children's gallery presents contemporary art in a manner that is interesting and accessible, and has hands-on activity stations where kids can create their own art. June-early September: daily noon-4 p.m.; rest of year: limited hours.

Mohawk Trail State Forest
Charlemont, 413-339-5504
The forest has spectacular scenery and swimming, fishing, hiking, winter sports, picnicking, camping and log cabins.

Mount Greylock State Reservation
Rockwell Rd., North Adams, 413-499-4262.
At 3,491 vertical feet, Mount Greylock is the highest point in the state. Fishing, hunting, cross-country skiing, picnicking and snowmobiles are allowed. Mid-May-mid-October.

Natural Bridge State Park
North Adams, 413-663-6392
This park has a water-eroded marble bridge and 550 million-year-old rock formations popularized by Nathaniel Hawthorne. Picnicking. Mid-May-mid-October.

Western Gateway Heritage State Park
115 State St., North Adams, 413-663-8059
Here are a restored freight yard with six buildings around a cobbled courtyard and detailed historic exhibits on the construction of the Hoosac Railroad Tunnel. Daily.

SPECIAL EVENTS
Fall Foliage Festival
57 Main St., North Adams, 413-664-6180; www.fallfoliageparade.com
Parade, entertainment, dancing and children's activities. Late September-early October.

La Festa
85 Main St., North Adams, 413-663-3782
A festival with ethnic food, entertainment and events. Sixteen days beginning mid-June.

HOTELS
★★Holiday Inn Berkshires
40 Main St., North Adams, 413-663-6500; www.holiday-inn.com
86 rooms. Wireless Internet access. Restaurant. Bar. **$**

★★★The Porches Inn
231 River St., North Adams, 413-664-0400; www.porches.com
Directly across from MassMoCA, this inn is housed in a row of vividly painted Victorian buildings, each of which has been restored and decorated with sleek, modern furnishings. The unlikely boutique hotel has porches and rocking chairs, but most guests ignore them in favor of the pool and luxe amenities.
52 rooms. Complimentary continental breakfast. **$$**

NORTHAMPTON
Thanks to Jonathan Edwards, a Puritan who was once regarded as the greatest preacher in New England, Northampton was the scene of a frenzied religious revival movement in the early 18th century. However, the fervor had little lasting impact on the town, which is now full of first-class theaters and restaurants, antique shops and art galleries, and up-to-date hotels and inns. The area's thriving arts scene can be partly credited to its close proximity to five colleges: Mount Holyoke, Amherst, Hampshire, Smith and the University of Massachusetts.
Information: Chamber of Commerce and Visitor Center, 99 Pleasant St., Northampton, 413-584-1900; www.northamptonuncommon.com

WHAT TO SEE AND DO
Arcadia Nature Center and Wildlife Sanctuary, Massachusetts Audubon Society
127 Combs Rd., Easthampton, 413-584-3009
On these 550 acres are an ancient oxbow of the Connecticut River, self-guided nature

trails and an observation tower. Tuesday-Sunday 9 a.m.-3 p.m.

Calvin Coolidge Memorial Room
20 West St., Northampton, 413-587-1011
On display are the local son and the late president's papers and correspondence. Monday-Thursday, Saturday; schedule may vary.

Hadley Farm Museum
208 Middle St., Hadley, 413-584-3120; www.hadleyonline.com/farmmuseum
A restored 1782 barn houses agricultural implements, tools and domestic items dating from the 1700s. May-October: Tuesday-Saturday 10 a.m.-4:30 p.m., Sunday 1:30-4:30 p.m.

Historic Northampton Museum Houses
46-66 Bridge St., Northampton, 413-584-6011
These include the 1820 Damon House and the 1730 Parsons House. Tuesday-Friday 10 a.m.-4 p.m., Saturday-Sunday from noon.

Look Park
300 N. Main St., Florence, 413-584-5457; www.lookpark.org
In the park are a miniature train, the Christenson Zoo, boating, tennis, picnicking, playgrounds, ball fields and the Pines Theater.

Smith College
33 Elm St., Northampton, 413-584-2700; www.smith.edu
With 2,700 women, this is the largest private women's liberal arts college in the United States. On campus are Paradise Pond, the Helen Hills Chapel and the William Allan Neilson Library that has more than one million volumes.

Museum of Art
Elm St., Northampton, 413-585-2760
This spot has a fine collection with emphasis on American and European art of the 19th and 20th centuries. September-May: Tuesday-Sunday; rest of year: Tuesday-Saturday.

SPECIAL EVENTS
Three-County Fair
Three-County Fairgrounds, Damon Rd., and Hwy., 9, Northampton, 413-584-2237; www.3countyfair.com
The nation's oldest agricultural fair has agricultural exhibits, horse racing and pari-mutuel betting. Labor Day week.

HOTELS
★★Clarion Hotel and Conference Center
1 Atwood Dr., Northampton, 413-586-1211, 800-582-2929; www.clarionhotel.com
122 rooms. Wireless Internet access. Restaurant. Bar. $

★★★The Hotel Northampton
36 King St., Northampton, 413-584-3100, 800-547-3529; www.hotelnorthampton.com
Built in 1927, this brick Colonial Revival building sits on a busy street opposite the restored Calvin Theater. A narrow glass greenhouse surrounds half the building, while the hotel's public areas are hung with Norman Rockwell prints and Japanese woodcuts. Colonial furnishings lend most guest rooms a stately vibe. Dining options include the light and airy Mediterranean-themed Coolidge Park Café, and the very New England Wiggins Tavern.
106 rooms. Complimentary continental breakfast. Wireless Internet access. Two restaurants. Two bars. $$

SPECIALTY LODGINGS
Autumn Inn
259 Elm St., Northampton, 413-584-7660; www.hampshirehospitality.com
Walking distance from the main gates of Smith College and a mile from downtown Northampton, this hotel sits in an old residential area. The 1960s brick property was built to resemble a colonial-era inn with a sweeping, well-manicured lawn. Its huge, wood-burning lobby is full of copper kettles and cast-iron fixtures, giving the whole room the rustic feel of a bygone era. Guests warm their feet by the fire as they nosh on the daily continental breakfast.

MASSACHUSETTS

32 rooms. Complimentary continental breakfast. **$**

ORLEANS

Orleans was supposedly named in honor of the French Duke of Orleans. Its history also includes the dubious distinction of being the only town in America to have been fired upon by the Germans during World War I. Today, tourists pass through this commercial hub along the way to Nauset Beach and the outer Cape.

Information: Cape Cod Chamber of Commerce, Highways 6 and 132, Hyannis, 508-362-3225, 888-227-3263; www.capecodchamber.org

WHAT TO SEE AND DO

Academy of Performing Arts
120 Main St., Orleans, 508-255-1963
The theater presents comedies, dramas, musicals, dance and workshops for all ages.

French Cable Station Museum
41 S. Orleans Rd., Orleans,
508-240-1735
Built in 1890 as the American end of the transatlantic cable from Brest, France, the museum has original submarine cable equipment. July-Labor Day: Tuesday-Saturday afternoons.

Nauset Beach
Beach Rd., Orleans, 508-255-1386
One of the most spectacular ocean beaches on the Atlantic coast sits within the boundaries of Cape Cod National Seashore. Swimming, surfing, fishing and lifeguards. Parking fee.

HOTELS

★Nauset Knoll Motor Lodge
237 Beach Rd., East Orleans, 508-255-2364;
www.capecodtravel.com/nausetknoll
12 rooms. Closed late October-mid-April. **$**

★Seashore Park Motor Inn
24 Canal Rd., Orleans, 508-255-2500,
800-772-6453; www.seashoreparkinn.com
62 rooms. Complimentary continental breakfast. Wireless Internet access. Airport

transportation available. Closed November-mid-April. **$**

★The Cove
13 S. Orleans Rd., Orleans,
508-255-1203, 800-343-2233;
www.thecoveorleans.com
47 rooms. Wireless Internet access. Airport transportation available. **$**

SPECIALTY LODGINGS

Ship's Knees Inn
186 Beach Rd., East Orleans,
508-255-1312; www.shipskneesinn.com
This inn—a restored sea captain's house—is walking distance to the ocean. The rooms are individually decorated in a nautical style and are furnished with antiques and four-poster beds.
16 rooms. Children over 12 years only. Complimentary continental breakfast. **$**

The Parsonage Inn
202 Main St., East Orleans,
508-255-8217, 888-422-8217;
www.parsonageinn.com
Built around 1770, this inn features cozy rooms with canopied beds and colorful quilts.
8 rooms. Children over 6 years only. Complimentary full breakfast. **$**

RESTAURANTS

★The Beacon Room
23 West Rd., Orleans, 508-255-2211;
www.beaconroom.com

170

MASSACHUSETTS

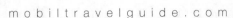

American menu. Lunch, dinner. Bar. Casual attire. Outdoor seating. **$$**

★★Barley Neck Inn
5 Beach Rd., East Orleans,
508-255-0212, 800-281-7505;
www.barleyneck.com
American menu. Dinner. Bar. Casual attire. Reservations recommended. **$$**

★★★Captain Linnell House
137 Skaket Beach Rd., Orleans,
508-255-3400; www.linnell.com
Chef/owner Bill Conway delivers a delightful dining experience at this romantic restaurant. Guests meander through the yard, complete with a Victorian gazebo, lavender bushes and ocean breezes, before settling in for candlelit dinners. Oil lamps and fresh flowers add to the main room's cozy, peaceful atmosphere. An extensive wine list is offered and the skillfully prepared menu has highlights like veal with crab, bouillabaisse, and pork tenderloin.
American menu. Dinner. Bar. Children's menu. Business casual attire. Reservations recommended. Closed Monday; also mid-February-March. **$$$**

★Double Dragon Inn
Hwys., 6A and 28, Orleans, 508-255-4100
Chinese menu. Lunch, dinner, late-night. Bar. Casual attire. **$**

★Lobster Claw
Highway 6A, Orleans, 508-255-1800;
www.lobsterclaw.com
American, seafood menu. Lunch, dinner. Bar. Children's menu. Casual attire. Closed mid-November-March. **$$**

★★Mahoney's Atlantic Bar and Grill
28 Main St., Orleans, 508-255-5505;
www.mahoneysatlantic.com
American menu. Dinner. Bar. Casual attire. **$$**

★★Nauset Beach Club Restaurant
222 E. Main St., East Orleans,
508-255-8547;
www.nausetbeachclub.com
Italian menu. Dinner. Bar. Casual attire. Reservations recommended. **$$$**

★★Old Jailhouse Tavern
28 West Rd., Orleans,
508-255-5245
American menu. Lunch, dinner, late-night, Sunday brunch. Bar. Children's menu. Casual attire. Outdoor seating. **$$**

★Sir Cricket's Fish and Chips
38 Route 6A, Orleans, 508-255-4453
Seafood menu. Lunch, dinner. Children's menu. Casual attire. **$**

★The Yardarm
48 Hwy. 28 Orleans, 508-255-4840;
www.yardarmrestaurant.com
American menu. Lunch, dinner. Bar. Children's menu. Casual attire. **$$**

PITTSFIELD

Once widely regarded as the unwelcoming, gritty epicenter of the Berkshires, Pittsfield has recently started to return to its busy, beautiful small town roots. The city's revitalized North Street once again boasts fine restaurants and shops, and its museums and theaters have also undergone facelifts. Instead of being a place visitors drive through on their way elsewhere, Pittsfield is becoming a veritable destination.
Information: Berkshire Visitors Bureau, Berkshire Common, 413-443-9186, 800-237-5747; www.berkshires.org

WHAT TO SEE AND DO
Arrowhead
780 Holmes Rd., Pittsfield,
413-442-1793

(1780) Herman Melville wrote *Moby Dick* while living here from 1850 to 1863. It's now the headquarters of the Berkshire County Historical Society. Memorial Day weekend-October: daily.

Berkshire Museum
39 South St., Pittsfield, 413-443-7171;
www.berkshiremuseum.org
This is a museum of art, natural science, and history, featuring American 19th- and 20th-century paintings; works by British and European masters; artifacts from ancient civilizations; exhibits on Berkshire County history; and children's programs. July-August: daily; rest of year: Tuesday-Sunday.

Bousquet
101 Dan Fox Dr., Pittsfield,
413-442-8316; www.bousquets.com
The ski area has two double chairlifts, three rope tows, snowmaking, ski school, rentals, a cafeteria, bar and daycare. The longest run is 1 mile with a vertical drop of 750 feet. Night skiing. December-March: daily.

Brodie Mountain
New Ashford, 413-738-5500;
www.skibrodie.com
This ski mountain has four double chairlifts, two rope tows, patrol, ski school, rentals, snowmaking, a bar, cafeteria, restaurant and a nursery. November-March: daily. It also has cross-country trails, tennis, racquetball, and winter camping.

Hancock Shaker Village
Highways 20 and 41, Pittsfield,
413-443-0188;
www.hancockshakervillage.org
A Shaker site from 1790 to 1960, this is now a living history museum of Shaker life, crafts and farming. A large collection of furniture and artifacts is housed in 20 restored buildings, including the Round Stone Barn.

Jiminy Peak
37 Corey Rd., Hancock, 413-738-5500;
www.jiminypeak.com
This ski area has a six-passenger lift, three double chairlifts, a J-bar, two quads, three triplechairs, a ski school, rentals, a restaurant, two cafeterias, a bar and a lodge. The longest run is two miles with a vertical drop 1,140 feet. Thanksgiving-early April: daily. In the summer, the mountain has trout fishing, 18-hole miniature golf course and an Alpine slide and tennis center. Memorial Day-Labor Day.

HOTELS
★★Crowne Plaza Hotel
1 West St., Pittsfield,
413-499-2000, 800-227-6963;
www.berkshirecrowne.com
179 rooms. High-speed Internet access. Restaurant. Bar. $

★★Jiminy Peak Mountain Resort
37 Corey Rd., Hancock,
413-738-5500, 800-882-8859;
www.jiminypeak.com
96 rooms. Restaurant. Children's activity center. Ski in/ski out. $

RESTAURANTS
★★Dakota
1035 South St., Pittsfield, 413-499-7900;
www.dakotarestaurant.com
American menu. Lunch, dinner, Sunday brunch. Bar. Children's menu. Casual attire. Reservations recommended. $$

172

MASSACHUSETTS

PLYMOUTH
On December 21, 1620, 102 people stepped off the *Mayflower* to found the first permanent European settlement north of Virginia: Plymouth. Plagued by exposure, cold, hunger and disease during its first American winter, the colony was nearly wiped out. But the next year, the settlers were firmly established. Their landing site is memorialized by Plymouth Rock. Today, the town doubles as a summer resort Mecca and fishing village, with tourists and locals going about their days together in ways those early citizens could hardly have imagined.
Information: Destination Plymouth, 170 Water St., Plymouth, 508-747-7525, 800-872-1620; www.visit-plymouth.com

WHAT TO SEE AND DO

Harlow Old Fort House
119 Sandwich St., Plymouth, 508-746-0012
(1677) A Pilgrim household with crafts, candle-dipping demonstrations, and an herb garden. July-August: Tuesday-Friday.

Hedge House
126 Water St., Plymouth, 508-746-0012
(1809) Here are period furnishings and special exhibits. June-October: Thursday-Saturday.

Howland House
33 Sandwich St., Plymouth, 508-746-9590
This restored 1666 Pilgrim house has 17th- and 18th-century furnishings. Memorial Day-mid-October: Monday-Saturday.

Mayflower Society House Museum
4 Winslow St., Plymouth, 508-746-2590
This is the national headquarters of the General Society of Mayflower Descendants. July-Labor Day: daily; Memorial Day weekend-June and early September-October: Friday-Sunday.

Myles Standish State Forest
194 Cranberry Rd., South Carver, 508-866-2526
The park consists of approximately 15,000 acres with swimming, fishing, boating, hiking, riding, hunting, picnicking and camping.

National Monument to the Forefathers
Allerton St., and Hwy., 44, Plymouth, 508-746-1790
This site was built between 1859 and 1889—at a cost of $155,000—to depict the virtues of the Pilgrims. At 81 feet high, it is the tallest solid granite monument in the United States. May-October: daily.

Ocean Spray Cranberry World
58 Water St., Plymouth, 508-747-2350
The center has exhibits on the history and cultivation of the cranberry. May-November.

Pilgrim Hall Museum
75 Court St., Plymouth, 508-746-1620; www.pilgrimhall.org

Decorative arts and possessions of first Pilgrims and their descendants, plus the only known portrait of a *Mayflower* passenger, are on display here. Daily; closed January.

Plymouth Colony Winery
56 Pinewood Rd., Plymouth, 508-747-3334
These working cranberry bogs are open to the public and give a good insight into cranberry harvest activities. April-late December: daily; March: Friday-Sunday; also holidays.

Plimoth Plantation/*Mayflower II*
137 Warren Ave., Plymouth, 508-746-1622; www.plimoth.org
No, it's not a typo. The Plimoth Plantation, a recreation of the 1627 Pilgrim village, uses the colony's old-fashioned spelling. Onsite actors play their roles by pretending to have zero knowledge of the 21st—or even the 18th—century; they wear and use only the clothing, equipment, tools and cookware the early settlers would have employed. The *Mayflower II* is a full-scale reproduction of the original built by J. W. & A. Upham with oak timbers, hand-forged nails, linen canvas sails and hemp rope. April-November: daily; closed December-March.

Plymouth Rock
Water St., Plymouth, 508-866-2580
The most famous rock in America, the landing site of the Pilgrims in 1620.

Provincetown Ferry
10 Town Wharf, Plymouth, 508-747-2400, 800-242-2469; www.provincetownferry.com
A round-trip passenger ferry departs State Pier in the morning and returns in the evening. Mid-June-Labor Day: daily; May-mid-June and after Labor Day-October: weekends.

Richard Sparrow House
42 Summer St., Plymouth, 508-747-1240; www.sparrowhouse.com

MASSACHUSETTS

Dating to 1640, this is Plymouth's oldest restored home. Memorial Day weekend-Thanksgiving: Monday-Tuesday, Thursday-Sunday; gallery open through late December

Spooner House
27 North St., Plymouth, 508-746-0012
This 1747 home was occupied by the Spooner family for five generations and is furnished with their heirlooms. June-October: Thursday-Saturday.

SPECIAL EVENTS
Autumnal Feasting
137 Warren Ave., Plymouth, 508-742-1622, 800-872-1620
At Plimoth Plantation's 1627 Pilgrim Village, this is a harvest celebration with Dutch colonists from Fort Amsterdam re-creating a 17th-century event. Activities, feasting, games. Columbus Day weekend.

HOTELS
★Best Western Cold Spring
188 Court St., Plymouth, 508-746-2222, 800-678-8667;
www.coldspringmotel.com
60 rooms. Complimentary continental breakfast. Closed January-March. $

★★Radisson Hotel Plymouth Harbor
180 Water St., Plymouth, 508-747-4900, 800-333-3333;
www.radisson.com

175 rooms. High-speed Internet access. Restaurant. Bar. $

SPECIALTY LODGINGS
John Carver Inn
25 Summer St., Plymouth, 508-746-7100, 800-274-1620;
www.johncarverinn.com
79 rooms. Restaurant. Bar. $$

The Colonial House Inn
207 Sandwich St., Plymouth, 508-747-4274, 866-747-4274;
www.thecolonialhouseinn.com
4 rooms. Complimentary continental breakfast. Beach. $$

The Mabbett House
7 Cushman St., Plymouth, 508-747-1044, 888-622-2388;
www.mabbetthouse.com
3 rooms. Children over 12 years only. Complimentary full breakfast. $

RESTAURANTS
★Hearth and Kettle
25 Summer St., Plymouth, 508-746-7100; www.johncarverinn.com
Seafood, steak menu. Breakfast, lunch, dinner. Children's menu. $$

174

MASSACHUSETTS

PROVINCETOWN
Though its thunder has been stolen by Plymouth and that town's famous rock, Provincetown was actually the Mayflower's first docking site. Artists of all kinds converge in P'town, as those in the know call it, for the bustling—often too crowded—summer season.
Information: Chamber of Commerce, 307 Commercial St., Provincetown, 508-487-3424; www.capecodaccess.com/provincetownchamber

WHAT TO SEE AND DO
Commercial Street
Commercial St., Provincetown
Stretching more than three miles in length, this narrow street sports art galleries, shops, clubs, restaurants and hotels. When the lane was constructed in 1835, all its houses faced the harbor. Today, most homes have

been turned 180 degrees to face the street (or had a new front door crafted on the opposite side).

Expedition Whydah's Sea Lab & Learning Center
16 MacMillan Wharf, Provincetown, 508-487-8899

This is the archaeological site of the sunken pirate ship *Whydah,* which was struck by storms in 1717. Learn about the recovery of the ship's pirate treasure, the lives and deaths of pirates and the history of the ship and its passengers. April-mid-October: daily; mid-October-December: weekends and school holidays.

Pilgrim Monument & Museum
1 High Pole Hill, Provincetown,
508-487-1310; www.pilgrim-monument.org
This is a 252-foot granite tower commemorating the Pilgrims' 1620 landing in the New World. Exhibits include whaling equipment, scrimshaw, ship models, artifacts from shipwrecks and a Pilgrim Room with a scale model diorama of the *Mayflower.* Summer: daily.

Provincetown Art Association & Museum
460 Commercial St., Provincetown,
508-487-1750; www.paam.org
Late May-Oct: daily; rest of year: weekends.

Whale Watching
306 Commercial St., Provincetown,
508-240-3636, 800-826-9300;
www.whalewatch.com
Visitors can take 3 1/2- to 4-hour trips. Research scientists from the Provincetown Center for Coastal Studies are aboard each trip to lecture on the history of whales. Mid-April-October: daily.

SPECIAL EVENTS
Provincetown Portuguese Festival
MacMillian Wharf, Provincetown,
508-487-3424
Provincetown's Portuguese community started this festival more than 50 years ago. Each year in late June, the local bishop says Mass at St. Peters Church and then leads a procession to MacMillan Wharf, where he blesses a parade of fishing boats. The festival that follows features fireworks, concerts, dancing, and Portuguese art and food. Last week in June.

HOTELS
★★★Crowne Pointe Historic Inn
82 Bradford St., Provincetown,
508-487-6767, 877-276-9631;
www.crownepointe.com
Five of the buildings at this downtown P'town inn date from the 1600s. Peaceful gardens, a fountain and a koi pond contribute to the mellow outdoor setting, while hardwood floors, antiques, crown molding and ceiling fans decorate the interiors. The guest rooms are large and offer extensive amenities; most rooms also have fireplaces and whirlpool tubs. Room rates include hearty breakfasts and evening cocktail receptions.
40 rooms. No children allowed. Complimentary full breakfast. Wireless Internet access. Restaurant. Bar. Spa. Airport transportation available. $$$

★The Masthead Resort
31-41 Commercial St., Provincetown,
508-487-0523, 800-395-5095;
www.themasthead.com
21 rooms. Wireless Internet access. Beach. $

★★Provincetown Inn
1 Commercial St., Provincetown,
508-487-9500, 800-942-5388;
www.provincetowninn.com
100 rooms. Complimentary continental breakfast. Restaurant. Bar. Beach. $

★Watermark Inn
603 Commercial St., Provincetown,
508-487-0165; www.watermark-inn.com
10 rooms, all suites. Wireless Internet access. Beach. Airport transportation available. $$

SPECIALTY LODGINGS
Fairbanks Inn
90 Bradford St., Provincetown,
508-487-0386, 800-324-7265;
www.fairbanksinn.com
14 rooms. Children over 15 years only. Complimentary continental breakfast.$

Snug Cottage
178 Bradford St., Provincetown,
508-487-1616, 800-432-2334;

175

MASSACHUSETTS

www.snugcottage.com
8 rooms. Complimentary full breakfast. **$$**

Somerset House
378 Commercial St., Provincetown,
508-487-0383, 800-575-1850;
www.somersethouseinn.com
13 rooms. Complimentary full breakfast.
Beach. **$$**

Watership Inn
7 Winthrop St., Provincetown,
508-487-0094, 800-330-9413;
www.watershipinn.com
15 rooms. Complimentary continental
breakfast. **$**

White Wind Inn
174 Commercial St., Provincetown,
508-487-1526, 888-449-9463;
www.whitewindinn.com
12 rooms. Complimentary continental
breakfast. **$**

RESTAURANTS

★★★Bistro at Crowne Pointe Inn
82 Bradford St., Provincetown,
508-487-6767; www.crownepointe.com
Paintings, fresh flowers and gleaming wood
floors set the tone at this bluff-top restaurant. The seasonal menu is skillfully served,
and guests can substitute or order options
made from scratch, without butter, cream or
fatty oils.
American menu. Dinner. Bar. Casual attire.
Reservations recommended. Valet parking.
Closed Tuesday. **$$$**

★★Cafe Edwige
333 Commercial St., Provincetown,
508-487-2008
American menu. Breakfast, dinner. Closed
weekdays Labor Day-mid-June; also October-April. **$**

★Fanizzi's by the Sea
539 Commercial St., Provincetown,
508-487-1964;
www.fanizzisrestaurant.com

American, Italian menu. Lunch, dinner.
Bar. Children's menu. Casual attire. Reservations recommended. **$$$**

★★Front Street
230 Commercial St., Provincetown,
508-487-9715;
www.frontstreetrestaurant.com
Italian menu. Dinner. Bar. Casual attire.
Reservations recommended. Closed January-April. **$$**

★★Lobster Pot
321 Commercial St., Provincetown,
508-487-0842; www.ptownlobsterpot.com
Seafood menu. Lunch, dinner. Bar. Children's menu. Casual attire. Closed December-March. **$$$**

★★Lorraine's Restaurant
133 Commercial St., Provincetown,
508-487-6074;
www.lorrainesrestaurant.com
Mexican menu. Dinner. Bar. Children's
menu. Casual attire. Reservations recommended. Closed December-March. **$$**

★★Martin House
157 Commercial St., Provincetown,
508-487-1327; www.themartinhouse.com
American menu. Dinner, brunch. Bar. Reservations recommended. Outdoor seating.
Closed Monday-Wednesday; also January.
$$$

★★The Mews Restaurant & Cafe
429 Commercial St., Provincetown,
508-487-1500; www.mews.com
International menu. Dinner, Sunday brunch.
Bar. Casual attire. **$$**

★★Napi's
7 Freeman St., Provincetown,
508-487-1145, 800-571-6274;
www.napis-restaurant.com
International menu. Dinner. Bar. Children's
menu. Casual attire. Reservations recommended. **$$**

★★★Red Inn Restaurant
15 Commercial St., Provincetown,

MASSACHUSETTS

★

★

★

★

★

508-487-7334, 866-473-3466;
www.theredinn.com
One of the best parts about this restaurant is its view. The harbor, the bay, Long Point lighthouse and the shores of the Outer Cape are all on panoramic display. Diners get an eyeful as they chomp on the house specialty—a tasty porterhouse steak. New American menu. Dinner, brunch. Bar. Business casual attire. Reservations recommended. $$$

★★Sal's Place
99 Commercial St., Provincetown, 508-487-1279;
www.salsplaceofprovincetown.com
Italian menu. Dinner. Children's menu. Casual attire. Reservations recommended. Outdoor seating. Closed November-April. $$

ROCKPORT

Rockport is a year-round artists' colony. A weather-beaten shanty on one of its many wharves has been the subject of so many paintings that it's now referred to as "Motif No. 1." Studios, galleries and summer cottages dot the shore of this quiet Cape Ann town, while tourists cruise its streets.

Information: Chamber of Commerce, Rockport, 978-546-6575, 888-726-3922; www.rockportusa.com

WHAT TO SEE AND DO
Old Castle
Granite and Curtis Streets, Rockport, 978-546-9533
This 1715 structure is a fine example of early 18th-century architecture and exhibits. July-August: daily; rest of year: by appointment.

Sandy Bay Historical Society & Museums
40 King St., Rockport, 978-546-9533
The museum has early American and 19th-century rooms and objects and exhibits on fishing, the granite industry, and the Atlantic cable. Mid-June-mid-September: daily; rest of year: by appointment.

The Paper House
52 Pigeon Hill St., Rockport, 978-546-2629
Newspapers were used in the construction of this house and its furniture. April-October.

SPECIAL EVENTS
Rockport Chamber Music Festival
3 Main St., Rockport, 978-546-7391; www.rcmf.org
Soloists and chamber ensembles of international acclaim have performed at this art colony since 1982. A lecture series and family concert are also featured. Four weekends in June or July.

HOTELS
★★★Emerson Inn by the Sea
1 Cathedral Ave., Rockport, 978-546-6321, 800-964-5550;
www.emersoninnbythesea.com
This traditional country inn has hosted guests at its Pigeon Cove location since 1846. From March through the end of December, visitors can take in ocean views from the pool, porch, restaurant and half the guest rooms.
36 rooms. Restaurant. Spa. $

★★★Seacrest Manor
99 Marmion Way, Rockport, 978-546-2211; www.seacrestmanor.com
The staff at this country inn is amazingly attentive (without being annoying). Guests can have traditional afternoon tea at the manor or rent one of the onsite bicycles and take a ride.
7 rooms. Complimentary full breakfast. Restaurant for inn guests only. Closed December-March. $$

★★★Seaward Inn & Cottages
44 Marmion Way, Rockport,

978-546-3471, 877-473-2927;
www.seawardinn.com
39 rooms. Complimentary full breakfast. Restaurant. Airport transportation
available. **$**

★★Turk's Head Motor Inn
151 South St., Rockport,
978-546-3436; www.turksheadinn.com
28 rooms. Restaurant. **$**

★★★Yankee Clipper Inn
127 Granite St., Rockport,
978-546-3407, 800-545-3699;
www.yankeeclipperinn.com
One of a few coastal inns open year-round,
this seaside resort has rolling country
gardens, a heated pool and a comfortable
atmosphere. Its Veranda Restaurant features elegant American-Continental cuisine.
16 rooms. Complimentary full breakfast.
Outdoor saltwater pool. Airport transportation available. Closed January-February.
$$

SPECIALTY LODGINGS
Addison Choate Inn
49 Broadway, Rockport,
978-546-7543, 800-245-7543;
www.addisonchoateinn.com
This Cape Ann bed-and-breakfast is less than
an hour's drive north of Boston.
8 rooms. Children over 11 years only. Com-
plimentary continental breakfast. **$**

The Inn On Cove Hill
37 Mount Pleasant St., Rockport,
978-546-2701, 888-546-2701;

www.innoncovehill.com
This inn was built in 1791 from proceeds of
pirates' gold found nearby.
8 rooms. Complimentary continental break-
fast. Closed mid-October-mid-April. **$**

Linden Tree Inn
26 King St., Rockport,
978-546-2494, 800-865-2122;
www.lindentreeinn.com
18 rooms. Complimentary full breakfast. **$**

Pegleg Restaurant and Inn
1 King St., Rockport,
978-546-2352, 800-346-2352;
www.cape-ann.com/pegleg
33 rooms. Complimentary continental break-
fast. Restaurant. Closed November-March.
$

Rocky Shores Inn & Cottages
65 Eden Rd., Rockport,
978-546-2823, 800-348-4003
11 rooms. Complimentary full breakfast.
Closed mid-October-mid-April. **$**

The Tuck Inn B&B
17 High St., Rockport,
978-546-7260, 800-789-7260;
www.thetuckinn.com
13 rooms. Complimentary continental
breakfast. **$**

RESTAURANTS
★Brackett's Oceanview
25 Main St., Rockport, 978-546-2797;
www.bracketts.com
Seafood menu. Lunch, dinner. Closed mid-
October-March. **$$**

SALEM

Despite its picturesque, idyllic streets, famous native son Nathaniel Hawthorne, and its
legacy as a major shipbuilding center, Salem will always be known for the brutal blip in its
history. In 1692, at the peak of the town's infamous witch trials, 19 people were hanged on
Gallows Hill, another was "pressed" to death and at least two others died in jail. A museum
now memorializes the terrible events and much of the town's tourist trade revolves around
the old trials.
Information: Chamber of Commerce, 63 Wharf St., Salem, 978-744-0004; www.salem-
chamber.org

WHAT TO SEE AND DO

House of Seven Gables
54 Turner St., Salem, 978-744-0991;
www.7gables.org
Nathaniel Hawthorne's 1851 novel of the same name is said to have been inspired by this home. Daily; closed the first three weeks in January.

Peabody Museum & Essex Institute
East India Square, Salem,
978-745-9500, 866-745-1876
The Peabody Museum, founded by sea captains in 1799, features five world-famous collections in 30 galleries. Daily.

Crowninshield-Bentley House
126 Essex St., Salem, 978-745-9500
Reverend William Bentley, minister and diarist, lived here from 1791 to 1819. June-October: daily; rest of year: Saturday-Sunday, holidays.

Gardner-Pingree House
128 Essex St., Salem, 978-745-9500
1804) Designed by McIntire, this house has been restored and handsomely furnished. June-October: daily; rest of year: Saturday-Sunday, holidays.

John Ward House
161 Essex St., Salem, 978-745-9500
Seventeenth-century furnishings. June-October: daily; rest of year: Saturday-Sunday, holidays.

Peirce-Nichols House
80 Federal St., Salem, 978-745-9500
1782) One of the finest examples of McIntire's architectural genius, this home is authentically furnished. By appointment only.

Pioneer Village: Salem in 1630
Forest River Park off West St.,
Salem, 978-744-0991
A reproduction of an early Puritan settlement, the village has dugouts, wigwams and thatched cottages peopled by costumed interpreters. Late April-late November, daily.

Ropes Mansion and Garden
318 Essex St., Salem, 978-745-9500
This is a restored gambrel-roofed, Georgian and colonial mansion furnished with period pieces. The garden, laid out in 1912, is known for its beauty and variety. June-October: daily; limited hours Sunday.

Salem Maritime National Historic Site
174 Derby St., Salem, 978-740-1660;
www.nps.gov/sama
Here are nine acres of historic waterfront. Self-guided and guided tours. Daily.

Derby House
174 Derby St., Salem, 978-740-1660
This was the home of maritime merchant Elias Hasket Derby, one of the country's first millionaires. The Garden features roses, herbs and 19th-century flowers.

Salem Witch Museum
19 1/2 Washington Square, Salem,
978-744-1692;
www.salemwitchmuseum.com
The Salem witch trials of 1692 are recreated here with a 30-minute narrated presentation that uses special lighting and life-size figures. (The exhibit may be too frightening for young children.) Slightly less gruesome is the town's October Salem's Haunted Happenings, a Halloween festival that features street merchants, plays, witchy games and haunted houses. Daily.

Witch Dungeon Museum
16 Lynde St., Salem, 978-741-3570;
www.witchdungeon.com
Onsite is a reenactment of the witch trial of Sarah Good and a tour through a re-created dungeon where accused witches awaited trial. April-November: daily.

Witch House
310 Essex St., Salem, 978-744-8815
This was the home of witchcraft trial judge Jonathan Corwin; some of the accused witches may have been examined here. May-early November: daily 10 a.m.-5 p.m.

179

MASSACHUSETTS

HOTELS

★★Hawthorne Hotel
18 Washington Square W., Salem,
978-744-4080, 800-729-7829;
www.hawthornehotel.com
89 rooms. Restaurant. **$**

SPECIALTY LODGINGS

Salem Inn
7 Summer St., Salem,
978-741-0680, 800-446-2995;
www.saleminnma.com
With individually appointed rooms and
suites, many of which feature Jacuzzis,
kitchenettes and fireplaces, this inn provides
comfort and luxury without assaulting
your wallet. Season packages available.
33 rooms. Complimentary continental
breakfast. **$**

RESTAURANTS

★★Grape Vine
26 Congress St., Salem, 978-745-9335;

www.grapevinesalem.com
American, Italian menu. Dinner. Bar. Out-
door seating. **$$$**

★★★Lyceum
43 Church St., Salem,
978-745-7665;
www.lyceumsalem.com
One of the area's best restaurants, this com-
fortable dining room is located in the build-
ing where Alexander Graham Bell made his
first call in 1877.
American menu. Lunch, dinner, Sunday
brunch. Bar. **$$**

★Victoria Station
86 Wharf St., Salem, 978-745-3400;
www.victoriastationinc.com
Seafood, steak menu. Lunch, dinner. Bar.
Children's menu. Outdoor seating. **$**

180 SANDWICH

Sandwich was the first established town on Cape Cod. Today, it's famous for its eponymous
glass.
Information: Cape Cod Canal Region Chamber of Commerce, 70 Main St., Buzzards Bay,
508-759-6000; www.capecodcanalchamber.org

WHAT TO SEE AND DO

Heritage Plantation
67 Grove St., Sandwich, 508-888-3300;
www.heritageplantation.org
The Heritage Plantation has an eclectic
mix of beautiful gardens, folk art, antique
cars and military paraphernalia. Highlights
include the 1800-era Old East Windmill
and a restored 1912 carousel. Call ahead to
find out about unique exhibits, displays, and
concerts. (May-October: daily; November-
April: Wednesday-Sunday)

Hoxie House & Dexter Gristmill
Water St., Sandwich, 508-888-1173
These are restored mid-17th-century build-
ings with an operating mill. Mid-June-mid-
October: daily.

Sandwich Glass Museum
129 Main St., Sandwich, 508-888-0251
Here is an internationally renowned collection of Sandwich Glass. April-October:
daily.

HOTELS

★★★Dan'l Webster Inn
149 Main St., Sandwich,
508-888-3622, 800-444-3566;
www.danlwebsterinn.com
54 rooms. Restaurant. Bar. **$$**

★Earl Of Sandwich Motel
378 Hwy., 6A, East Sandwich,
508-888-1415, 800-442-3275;
www.earlofsandwich.com
24 rooms. Complimentary continental
breakfast. **$**

MASSACHUSETTS

★
★
★
★
★

★Shady Nook Inn & Motel

14 Old Kings Hwy., Sandwich,
508-888-0409, 800-338-5208;
www.shadynookinn.com
30 rooms. $

★Spring Hill Motor Lodge

351 Hwy., 6A, East Sandwich,
508-888-1456, 800-647-2514;
www.springhillmotorlodge.com
24 rooms. $

SPECIALTY LODGINGS

The Belfry Inn & Bistro

8 Jarves St., Sandwich,
800-844-4542, 800-844-4542;
www.belfryinn.com
14 rooms. Children over 10 years only.
Complimentary full breakfast. Restaurant.
$$

Isaiah Jones Homestead

165 Main St., Sandwich,
508-888-9115, 800-526-1625;
www.isaiahjones.com
An American flag and flower-lined porch
adorn the exterior of this 1849 Victorian
home. The guest rooms, decorated with
antiques and country-patterned fabrics, are
an ideal place from which to explore the
Cape's many historic sites.
7 rooms. Children over 16 years only. Com-
plimentary full breakfast. $

Village Inn

4 Jarves St., Sandwich,
508-833-0363, 800-922-9989;

www.capecodinn.com
This federal style building was constructed
in 1830.
8 rooms. Children over 8 years only. Com-
plimentary full breakfast. $

RESTAURANTS

★★Aqua Grille

14 Gallo Rd., Sandwich,
508-888-8889;
www.aquagrille.com
American, seafood menu. Lunch, dinner.
Bar. Children's menu. Casual attire. Outdoor
seating. Closed November-mid-April. $$

★★Beehive Tavern

406 Hwy., 6A, Sandwich, 508-833-1184
American, seafood menu. Lunch, dinner.
Bar. Children's menu. Casual attire. $$

★★★The Dan'l Webster Inn

149 Main St., Sandwich,
508-888-3623, 800-444-3566;
www.danlwebsterinn.com
A former 1800s stagecoach inn once
frequented by its namesake, this hotel offers
both a tavern and a white-tablecloth dining
room. Chef and co-owner Robert Cata-
nia buys some of his fish and hydroponic
vegetables from a local aquafarm, and he
has built his wine list around his culinary
aspirations.
American menu. Breakfast, lunch, dinner,
Sunday brunch. Bar. Children's menu.
Business casual attire. Reservations recom-
mended. Valet parking. $$

SPRINGFIELD

Springfield has a fine library, museums and a symphony orchestra, but it's best known for
being a serious industrial city on the Connecticut River.
Information: Greater Springfield Convention & Visitors Bureau, 1441 Main St., Springfield,
413-787-1548, 800-723-1548; www.myonlinechamber.com

WHAT TO SEE AND DO

Basketball Hall of Fame

1150 W. Columbus Ave., Springfield,
413-781-6500; www.hoophall.com
This sports spot includes exhibits on the game
and its teams and players. Inside the ball-

shaped building are free movies, video highlights and life-size action blow-ups of Hall
of Famers. Major features include "Hoopla,"
a 22-minute film, and "The Spalding Shoot-
Out," which allows visitors to try scoring
baskets from a moving sidewalk. Daily.

Indian Motorcycle Museum

33 Hendee St., Springfield,
413-737-2624

This was part of the vast complex where Indian motorcycles were made until 1953. On display are historical cycles, an early snowmobile, and a 1928 roadster. Daily.

Springfield Armory National Historic Site

1 Armory Square, Springfield,
413-734-8551; www.nps.gov/spar

The old U.S. armory contains one of the largest collections of military small arms in the world. Exhibits include the "Organ of Guns," made famous by Longfellow's poem "The Arsenal at Springfield." Tuesday-Saturday.

Springfield Museums at the Quadrangle

220 State St., Springfield, 413-263-6800; www.springfieldmuseums.org

The site includes four museums and a library. The **George Walter Vincent Smith Art Museum** houses a collection of Asian armor, arms, jade, bronzes and rugs. The **Connecticut River Valley Historical Museum** includes genealogy and a local history library. The **Museum of Fine Arts** has 20 galleries and an outstanding collection of American and European works. The **Science Museum** has an exploration center, early aviation exhibit, aquarium, planetarium, African hall and dinosaur hall. All buildings Wednesday-Sunday.

Storrowton Village

Eastern States Exposition,
1305 Memorial Ave., West Springfield,
413-205-5051

This group of restored Early American buildings includes a meeting house, schoolhouse, and blacksmith shop. June-August: Tuesday-Saturday; rest of year: by appointment.

SPECIAL EVENTS

Eastern States Exposition (The Big E)

1305 Memorial Ave., West Springfield,
413-737-2443; www.thebige.com

The largest fair in the Northeast has entertainment, exhibits, an historic Avenue of States, Storrowton Village, a horse show, agricultural events and a "Better Living Center" exhibit. September.

HOTELS

★Hampton Inn

1011 Riverdale St., West Springfield,
413-732-1300, 800-426-7866;
www.hamptoninn.com

126 rooms. Complimentary continental breakfast. **$**

★★Holiday Inn Downtown

711 Dwight St., Springfield,
413-781-0900, 888-465-4329;
www.holiday-inn.com

242 rooms. Wireless Internet access. Restaurant. Bar. **$**

★★★Marriott Springfield

1500 Main St., Springfield, 413-781-7111,
800-228-9290; www.marriott.com

At the Marriot Springfield, it's all about the beds. With extra-thick mattresses, duvets

bed skirts and plush pillows, the sweet sleep spots are reason enough to book a room here. Those needing extra incentive should take note of the in-room 32″ flat-screen TVs and polished granite bathrooms. The hotel is also connected via enclosed walkway to a mall and complex that includes restaurants, art galleries, an African-American history museum and a billiards parlor.
265 rooms. Wireless Internet access. Two restaurants, Bar. **$$**

★★★**Sheraton Springfield Monarch Place Hotel**
1 Monarch Place, Springfield,
413-781-1010;
www.sheraton-springfield.com
The Sheraton's Athletic Club is the largest hotel health club west of Boston. It's open to all guests and has two dozen cardio machines, free weights, a 50-foot swimming pool,

a racquetball court, an indoor golf range and a myriad of fitness classes. Hotel spa services include everything from tanning to massages to manicures. Guest rooms in this contemporary, urban spot surround a 12-story atrium, and the public areas feature local touches such as a folk art mural of Springfield's historical highlights. Business travelers should ask for a smart room, which comes with a photocopier and fax machine.
325 rooms. Wireless Internet access. Two restaurants, Bar. **$$**

RESTAURANTS
★★**Student Prince & Fort**
8 Fort St., Springfield, 413-788-6628;
www.studentprince.com
German menu. Lunch, dinner. Bar. Casual attire. Reservations recommended. Valet parking. **$$**

STOCKBRIDGE
Stockbridge's main drag was made forever famous by small-town life chronicler Norman Rockwell. The fact that the town still looks much as it appeared in his drawings continuously delights tourists, who crowd the area's shops and eateries in the summertime. West Stockbridge, by contrast, is a completely restored market village. Its own Main Street is lined with renovated, well-kept storefronts.
Information: Stockbridge Chamber of Commerce, 6 Elm St., Stockbridge, 413-298-5200; www.stockbridgechamber.org

WHAT TO SEE AND DO
Berkshire Botanical Garden
Highways 102 and 183, Stockbridge, 413-298-3926; www.berkshirebotanical.org
This 15-acre botanical garden has perennials, shrubs, trees, antique roses, ponds, a wildflower exhibit, vegetable gardens and demonstration greenhouses. Garden shop; special events, lectures; picnicking. May-October: daily.

Chesterwood
284 Main St., Stockbridge, 413-298-3579; www.chesterwood.org
This was the grand early 20th-century summer residence and studio of Daniel Chester French, sculptor of the *Minute Man* statue in Concord and the Lincoln Memorial in Washington, DC. May-October: daily.

Mission House
1 Sergeant St., Stockbridge, 413-298-3239
The house built in 1739 for the missionary Reverend John Sergeant and his wife, Abigail Williams, is now a museum of colonial life. Memorial Day weekend-Columbus Day weekend: daily.

Naumkeag
1 Seargeant St., Stockbridge, 413-298-3239
Stanford White designed this Norman-style "Berkshire cottage" in 1886. The interior has antiques, Oriental rugs and a collection of Chinese export porcelain. The gardens include terraces of tree peonies, fountains, and a birch walk. Memorial Day weekend-Columbus weekend: daily.

Norman Rockwell Museum
9 Glendale Rd., Stockbridge,
413-298-4100; www.nrm.org
His eponymous museum maintains and
exhibits the nation's largest collection of
original art by Norman Rockwell. Daily.

HOTELS

★★★The Red Lion Inn
30 Main St., Stockbridge, 413-298-5545;
www.redlioninn.com
Along with the street it sits on, the Red
Lion Inn was immortalized by Norman
Rockwell in his hearty, happy Stockbridge
street scenes. Its guest rooms are well-
appointed, though a bit snug. For roomier
digs, book one of the inn's off-site suites,
which are sprinkled among a handful of
buildings throughout town, such as the former studio of artist Daniel Chester French
and the former home of the Stockbridge
Volunteer Fire Department.
108 rooms. Two restaurants, Bar. **$$**

★★★Williamsville Inn
Hwy., 41, West Stockbridge,
413-274-6118; www.williamsvilleinn.com
Run by a German husband and wife team,
the Williamsville Inn is a cross between
Shaker austerity and three-star comfort.
Its blond wood floors are spotless, as are
its white bed linens and bath towels. Fresh
flowers lightly scent each room, and guests
can walk through the property's extensive
gardens.
16 rooms. Complimentary full breakfast.
Restaurant. Bar. **$**

SPECIALTY LODGINGS

Inn at Stockbridge
Hwy., 7 N., Stockbridge,
413-298-3337; www.stockbridgeinn.com
An in-room decanter of port. Breakfast in
a formal dining room. A large parlor with
fireside chairs. A stroll through 12 secluded
acres. Sound appealing? This 1906 Geor-
gian-style inn has just eight guest rooms,
allowing each visitor to savor the above
amenities. The Cottage House, added in
1997, has four junior suites. The Barn, built

in 2001, provides four deluxe suites. 16
rooms. Children over 12 years only. Com-
plimentary full breakfast. **$$$**

The Taggart House
18 W. Main St., Stockbridge,
413-298-4303, 800-918-2680;
www.taggarthouse.com
This lovingly restored 1800s country house
fronts the Housatonic River. It is luxurious
and intimate, and replete with fine antiques.
4 rooms. Children over 18 years only. Com-
plimentary full breakfast. **$$$**

RESTAURANTS

★Michael's Restaurant & Pub
5 Elm St., Stockbridge, 413-298-3530;
www.michaelsofstockbridge.com
American, Italian menu. Lunch, dinner,
late-night. Bar. Children's menu. Casual
attire. Reservations recommended. **$$**

★★★The Red Lion
30 Main St., Stockbridge, 413-298-5545;
www.redlioninn.com
This inn's candlelit dining room is filled
with antiques, colonial pewter and crystal.
The contemporary New England menu
emphasizes local, seasonal produce and
offers several vegetarian options.
American menu. Lunch, dinner. Bar. Children's menu. Business casual attire. Reservations recommended. Outdoor seating.
$$$

★★★Williamsville Inn
Hwy. 41, West Stockbridge, 413-274-6118;
www.williamsvilleinn.com
This cozy dining room has an open fire-
place and plenty of candlelight. But what's
really special about the German eatery is its
open kitchen—guests can watch chef/owner
Erhard Wendt at work in his yellow-walled
space (he often invites diners back for a
closer look). The food is rich and savory—
don't pass up any of the desserts.
French, German menu. Dinner, brunch. Bar.
Casual attire. Reservations recommended.
Outdoor seating. **$$$**

SUDBURY

This leafy northwestern Boston suburb was founded in 1638.

Information: Board of Selectmen, Loring Parsonage, 288 Old Sudbury Rd., Sudbury, 978-443-8891

WHAT TO SEE AND DO

Martha Mary Chapel

72 Wayside Inn Rd., Sudbury Center

Built and dedicated by Henry Ford in 1940, this was a nondenominational, nonsectarian chapel. It's now used primarily for weddings. By appointment.

HOTELS

★★Best Western Royal Plaza Hotel & Trade Center

181 W. Boston Post Rd., Marlborough, 508-460-0700, 888-543-9500;
www.bestwestern.com
431 rooms. Restaurant. Bar. $$

★Clarion Hotel

738 Boston Post Rd., Sudbury, 978-443-2223, 800-637-0113;
www.clarionhotel.com
39 rooms. Complimentary full breakfast. $$

★★Radisson Hotel Marlborough

75 Felton St., Marlborough, 508-480-0015, 800-333-3333;
www.radisson.com
206 rooms. Restaurant. Bar. $

SPECIALTY LODGINGS

The Arabian Horse Inn

277 Old Sudbury Rd., Sudbury, 978-443-7400, 800-272-2426;
www.arabianhorseinn.com
5 rooms. Complimentary full breakfast. $$

Longfellows Wayside Inn

72 Wayside Inn Rd., Sudbury, 978-443-1776, 800-339-1776;
www.wayside.org
A literary shrine, this is America's oldest operating inn. Originally restored by Henry Ford, it was badly damaged by fire in December 1955, and restored again by the Ford Foundation. It's now a national historic site. On its grounds are the Wayside Gristmill and Redstone School.
10 rooms. Complimentary full breakfast. Restaurant. Bar. $

RESTAURANTS

★★Longfellow's Wayside Inn

72 Wayside Inn Rd., Sudbury Center, 978-443-1776;
www.wayside.org
Seafood, steak menu. Lunch, dinner. Bar. Children's menu. $$

TRURO & NORTH TRURO

Truro is perhaps the most sparsely settled part of Cape Cod, with great stretches of rolling moorland dotted only occasionally by small cottages. On the hill above the Pamet River marsh are two early 19th-century churches—one is the town hall. The surrounding countryside is popular with artists and writers.

Information: Cape Cod Chamber of Commerce, Highways 6 and 132, Hyannis, 508-362-3225, 888-227-3263; www.capecodchamber.org

WHAT TO SEE AND DO

Highland Light/Cape Cod Light

Highland Light Rd., North Truro, 508-487-1121;
www.lighthouse.cc/highland
This was the first lighthouse on Cape Cod. Built in 1798 and fueled with whale oil, it was rebuilt in 1853 and switched to an automated facility in 1986. It now shines for 30 miles, the longest visible range of any lighthouse on the Cape. Thoreau once stayed here. The museum next door, housed in a historic building, is open from June through September and highlights the area's fishing and whaling heritage. May-late October: daily.

Truro Historical Society Museum
6 Highland Rd., North Truro, 508-487-3397
The collection of artifacts from the town's past include shipwreck mementos, whaling gear, ship models, 17th-century firearms, a pirate chest and period rooms. June-September, Monday-Saturday 10 a.m.-4:30 p.m, Sunday from 1 p.m..

HOTELS
★Crow's Nest Resort
496 Shore Rd., North Truro,
508-487-9031, 800-499-9799;
www.caperesort.com
33 rooms. Closed December-March. Beach. $

RESTAURANTS
★Adrian's
535 Hwy. 6, North Truro, 508-487-4360;
www.adriansrestaurant.com
Italian menu. Breakfast, dinner. Bar. Children's menu. Outdoor seating. Closed mid-October-mid-May. $$

★★Blacksmith Shop Restaurant
17 Truro Center Rd., Truro, 508-349-6554
Seafood, steak menu. Dinner. Bar. Children's menu. Casual attire. Reservations recommended. Closed Monday-Wednesday in the off-season. $$

★★Montano's
481 Hwy. 6, North Truro, 508-487-2026;
www.montanos.com
Italian, seafood menu. Dinner. Bar. Children's menu. Casual attire. $$

WALTHAM
The name Waltham, taken from the English town of Waltham Abbey, means "a home in the forest." And, indeed, this Boston suburb is based in a wooded area, but it's not completely countrified. The town is a mix of McMansions, industry and academia—Bentley, Brandeis and Regis colleges are based here.
Information: Waltham West Suburban Chamber of Commerce, 84 South St., Waltham, 781-894-4700; www.walthamchamber.com

WHAT TO SEE AND DO
Brandeis University
415 South St., Waltham, 781-736-2000;
www.brandeis.edu
(1948) This was the first Jewish-founded nonsectarian university in the United States. Its 250-acre campus includes Three Chapels, the Rose Art Museum (September-May: Tuesday-Sunday), the Spingold Theater Arts Center (plays presented October-May) and the Slosberg Music Center (September-May).

Gore Place
52 Gore St., Waltham, 781-894-2798;
www.goreplace.org
A living history farm, Gore Place has changing exhibits and 40 acres of cultivated fields. The mansion, designed in Paris and built in 1805, has 22 rooms filled with examples of Early American, European and Asian antiques. Mid-April-mid-November: Thursday-Monday hourly tours 1 p.m.-4 p.m.

Lyman Estate
185 Lyman St., Waltham, 781-893-7232
Designed in1793 by Samuel McIntire for Boston merchant Theodore Lyman, this home was enlarged and remodeled in the 1880s. Its five operating greenhouses contain grape vines, camellias, orchids and herbs. The house is open by appointment for groups only. Monday-Saturday, also Sunday afternoons.

HOTELS
★★Doubletree Hotel
550 Winter St., Waltham,
781-890-6767, 800-222-8733;
www.doubletree.com
275 rooms, all suites. Restaurant. Bar. $

★★Home Suites Inn
455 Totten Pond Rd., Waltham,
781-890-3000, 866-335-6175;
www.homesuitesinn.com
116 rooms, all suites. Complimentary continental breakfast. Restaurant. Bar. **$**

★★★The Westin Waltham-Boston
70 Third Ave., Waltham,
781-290-5600, 800-228-3000;
www.westin.com
Just 15 minutes from downtown Boston, this modern hotel has rooms geared toward the business traveler.
376 rooms. Restaurant. Bar. Airport transportation available. **$$**

RESTAURANTS
★★★Grille at Hobbs Brook
550 Winter St., Waltham,

781-487-4263
Many of the Grille's menu ingredients come from its onsite garden. The plush setting is a quiet, relaxing place to dine.
American menu. Breakfast, lunch, dinner. Bar. Children's menu. **$$$**

★★★Il Capriccio
888 Main St., Waltham, 781-894-2234
Gauzy drapes and glass partitions give this innovative restaurant a chic, urban look.
Italian menu. Dinner. Bar. Closed Sunday. **$$$**

★★Tuscan Grill
361 Moody St., Waltham, 781-891-5486;
www.tuscangrillwaltham.com
Italian menu. Dinner. Bar. **$$**

WELLFLEET
Once a fishing town, Wellfleet dominated the New England oyster business in the latter part of the 19th century. It is now a summer resort and an art gallery town, and there's still plenty of oysters.
Information: Chamber of Commerce, Wellfleet, 508-349-2510;
www.wellfleetchamber.com

WHAT TO SEE AND DO
Historical Society Museum
266 Main St., Wellfleet, 508-349-9157;
www.wellfleethistoricalsociety.com
Marine items, whaling tools, Marconi memorabilia, needlecraft, photograph collection, marine and primitive paintings are on display here. Late June-early September: Tuesday-Saturday; schedule may vary.

Wellfleet Bay Wildlife Sanctuary
291 Hwy. 6, South Wellfleet, 508-349-2615;
www.wellfleetbay.org
Operated by the Massachusetts Audubon Society, the sanctuary has self-guiding nature trails and a natural history summer day camp for children. Memorial Day-Columbus Day: daily; rest of year: Tuesday-Sunday.

Wellfleet Drive-In Theater
Hwy. 6, Wellfleet, 508-349-7176;
www.wellfleetdrivein.com

This is the only outdoor theater on the Cape. It projects a family-oriented double feature every evening under the stars. Mid-Oct-ober-mid-April.

HOTELS
★★Wellfleet Motel & Lodge
146 Hwy. 6, South Wellfleet,
508-349-3535, 800-852-2900;
www.wellfleetmotel.com
65 rooms. Restaurant. Bar. **$**

SPECIALTY LODGINGS
Inn At Duck Creek
70 Main St., Wellfleet, 508-349-9333;
www.innatduckcreeke.com
25 rooms. Complimentary continental breakfast. Closed November-April. **$**

RESTAURANTS
★Moby Dick's
Hwy. 6, Wellfleet, 508-349-9795;

www.mobydicksrestaurant.com
Seafood menu. Lunch, dinner. Children's menu. Casual attire. Outdoor seating. Closed mid-October-April. **$$**

★★Van Rensselaer's Restaurant & Raw Bar
1019 Hwy. 6, South Wellfleet,
508-349-2127; www.vanrensselaers.com
American, seafood menu. Breakfast, dinner. Bar. Children's menu. Casual attire. Outdoor seating. Closed late October-early April. **$$**

WILLIAMSTOWN

Most things in this northern Berkshires town are centered around Williams College, one of the best liberal arts school in the country. The very quiet, very remote hamlet is a perfect setting for a school campus, and a drive through the area reveals myriad playing fields and students shuffling to class.

WHAT TO SEE AND DO

Sterling and Francine Clark Art Institute
225 South St., Williamstown,
413-458-2303; www.clarkart.edu
This museum houses more than 30 paintings by Renoir and other French Impressionists, as well as English and American silver and works by American artists like Homer, Sargent, Cassatt and Remington. July-Labor Day: daily; rest of year: Tuesday-Sunday.

Williams College
54 Sawyer Library Dr., Williamstown,
413-597-3131; www.williams.edu
This private liberal arts college has a student body of 1,950 and an idyllic campus. Its Chapin Library of rare books is one of the nation's finest and houses the four founding documents of the United States. The Hopkins Observatory has planetarium shows and the Adams Memorial Theater presents plays.

Williams College Museum of Art
15 Lawrence Hall Dr., Williamstown,
413-597-2429
This spot is considered one of the finest college art museums in the country; it houses approximately 11,000 pieces. Tuesday-Saturday 10 a.m.-5 p.m., Sunday from 1 p.m. and Monday, holidays.

HOTELS

★★★1896 House
910 Cold Spring Rd., Williamstown,
413-458-1896, 888-999-1896;
www.1896house.com
Among other options, guests can choose to stay in a brook- or pond-side room at this old inn. The Brookside suite, hidden from the road by trees, features Cushman rock maple furniture, luxurious amenities and a beautiful gazebo. The Pondside room has slightly fewer frills.
29 rooms. Complimentary continental breakfast. Restaurant. **$**

★Berkshire Hills Motel
1146 Cold Spring Rd., Williamstown,
413-458-3950, 800-388-9677;
www.berkshirehillsmotel.com
21 rooms. Complimentary buffet breakfast **$**

★Four Acres Motel
213 Main St., Williamstown, 413-458-8158;
www.fouracresmotel.com
31 rooms. Complimentary continental breakfast. **$**

★★★The Orchards
222 Adams Rd., Williamstown,
413-458-9611, 800-225-1517;
www.orchardshotel.com
Grand gates of Vermont granite lead into this European chateau-style property just east of the village center. The rooms are reminiscent of those in an English country side, with bay windows and marble-floored baths, and the public spaces are plush with Oriental rugs and Austrian crystal chandeliers. The onsite restaurant serves a mix

of continental and American cuisine; visitors can dine outdoors in the garden during summer months.

49 rooms. Wireless Internet access. Restaurant. Bar. **$$**

★★★Williams Inn

Highways 7 and 2, Williamstown, 413-458-9371, 800-828-0133; www.williamsinn.com

Since it's located on the college campus, the Williams Inn often hosts parents and families of students, as well as visiting professors and lecturers. The staff is friendly and creates an at-home feel, and the spot's live entertainment—from jazz to acoustic guitar to cabaret—is a community favorite.

125 rooms. High-speed Internet access. Restaurant, bar. **$$**

RESTAURANTS

★★★Gala Restaurant & Bar

222 Adams Rd., Williamstown, 413-458-9611, 800-225-1517; www.galarestaurant.com

At Gala, in the Orchards hotel, gold and red brocade chairs and white tablecloths dress the room's interior. The bar area has fireside couches and walls adorned with large nature photographs. High-quality local ingredients go into the chef's classic American dishes, which include apple- and cheddar-stuffed pork chop, merlot-braised New Zealand lamb shank, and seared Atlantic salmon. A wine cellar with a tasting room is used for chef's tables and private functions.

American menu. Breakfast, lunch, dinner, Sunday brunch. Bar. Casual attire. Reservations recommended. Outdoor seating. **$$**

★★Jae's Inn

777 Cold Spring Rd., Williamstown, 413-458-8032; www.jaesinn.com

Korean menu. Lunch, dinner. Bar. Children's menu. Casual attire. Reservations recommended. Outdoor seating. **$$**

★★Water Street Grill

123 Water St., Williamstown, 413-458-2175

American menu. Lunch, dinner. Bar. Children's menu. Casual attire. **$$**

WORCESTER

One of the largest cities in New England, Worcester is an important industrial center. It's also another academic powerhouse—within city limits are 12 colleges.

Information: Worcester County Convention & Visitors Bureau, 30 Worcester Center Blvd., Worcester, 508-753-2920; www.worcester.org

WHAT TO SEE AND DO

American Antiquarian Society

185 Salisbury St., Worcester, 508-755-5221

This research library has the largest collection of source materials pertaining to the first 250 years of American history. Monday-Friday; Guided tours Wednesday afternoons.

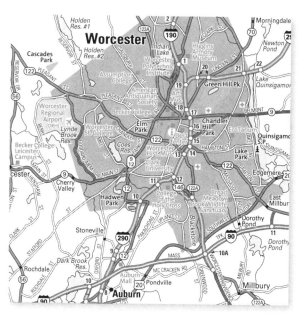

EcoTarium
222 Harrington Way, Worcester,
508-929-2700; www.ecotarium.org
This museum has environmental science exhibits, a solar/lunar observatory, a multimedia planetarium theater, and an African Hall. Tuesday-Saturday 10 a.m.-5 p.m., Sunday from noon.

John H. Chaffy Blackstone River Valley National Heritage Corridor
414 Massasoit Rd., Worcester, 508-755-8899
This 250,000-acre region extends southward to Providence, Rhode Island and includes many points of historical and cultural interest.

Salisbury Mansion
40 Highland St., Worcester, 508-753-8278
This was the house of leading businessman and philanthropist Stephen Salisbury.

Worcester Art Museum
55 Salisbury St., Worcester,
508-799-4406; www.worcesterart.org
Fifty centuries of paintings, sculpture, decorative arts, prints, drawings and photography from America to ancient Egypt are on display here. Wednesday-Sunday.

HOTELS

★★★Beechwood Hotel
363 Plantation St., Worcester,
508-754-5789, 800-344-2589;
www.beechwoodhotel.com
The hotel has a 24-hour fitness room and business center which makes it ideal for business travelers. A polished foyer with marble floors, a small fireside seating area, and antique, stained-glass windows spice up the lobby.
73 rooms, Wireless Internet access. Restaurant. Bar. **$$**

★★★Crowne Plaza Hotel
10 Lincoln Square, Worcester,
508-791-1600, 877-227-6963;
www.cpworcester.com
The Crowne Plaza is modern and close to shopping malls and the booksellers' marketplace and within 10 minutes of most area businesses. It also has a large indoor/outdoor pool and a courtyard landscaped with holly and flowering fruit trees. Ask for a room with a balcony, where you can enjoy morning coffee and a view of Lincoln Square.
243 rooms. Wireless Internet access. Restaurant. Bar. **$**

RESTAURANTS

★★★Castle
1230 Main St., Leicester,
508-892-9090;
www.castlerestaurant.com
Owned and operated by the Nicas family since 1950, this "castle," complete with turrets, towers and a moat, always provides a unique dining experience. Choose from one of the two distinctly different dining rooms, the Crusader or the Camelot; each has its own creative menu. French menu. Lunch, dinner. Closed Monday. Bar. Children's menu. Outdoor seating. **$$$**

YARMOUTH

Much of the Yarmouth area was developed on the strength of its 19th-century seafaring and fishing industries. Well-preserved houses line Main Street, where well-preserved locals shop and stroll.
Information: Yarmouth Area Chamber of Commerce, Yarmouth, 800-732-1008; www.capecodchamber.org

WHAT TO SEE AND DO

Cape Symphony Orchestra
712A Main St., Yarmouth Port,
508-362-1111;
www.capesymphony.org
This 90-member professional orchestra performs 15 indoor concerts throughout the year at Barnstable High School's 1,400-seat auditorium. Selections range from classical to pops to special children's events. September-May; also two concerts in summer.

Winslow Crocker House
250 Hwy. 6A, South Yarmouth,
617-227-3957
This is a Georgian house adorned with 17th-, 18th-, and 19th-century furnishings collected in the early 20th century. June-October: first Saturday of the month.

HOTELS

★All Season Motor Inn
1199 Main St., South Yarmouth,
508-394-7600, 800-527-0359;
www.allseasons.com
114 rooms. Restaurant. $

★★Best Western Blue Water on the Ocean
291 S. Shore Dr., South Yarmouth,
508-398-2288, 800-367-9393;
www.bestwestern.com
106 rooms. Restaurant. Bar. Children's activity center. Beach. $$

★★Blue Rock Resort
39 Todd Rd., South Yarmouth,
508-398-6962, 800-780-7234;
www.redjacketresorts.com
44 rooms. Restaurant. Bar. Closed late-October-March. $

★Gull Wing Suites
822 Main St., South Yarmouth,
508-394-9300, 877-984-9300;
www.gullwinghotel.com
136 rooms. $

★★★Liberty Hill Inn
77 Main St., Yarmouth Port,
508-362-3976, 800-821-3977;
www.libertyhillinn.com
The stately, whitewashed building that houses this charming inn was built in 1825. Rooms have antique furniture and oriental rugs and some bathrooms have original clawfoot tubs.
9 rooms. Complimentary full breakfast. Check-in 3-9 p.m., check-out 11 a.m. Airport transportation available. $

★★Red Jacket Beach
1 S. Shore Dr., South Yarmouth,
508-398-6941, 800-672-0500;
www.redjacketbeach.com
150 rooms. Restaurant. Bar. Children's activity center. Closed late October-March. $$

★★Riviera Beach Resort
327 S. Shore Dr., South Yarmouth,
508-398-2273, 800-227-3263;
www.rivieraresort.com
125 rooms. Restaurant. Bar. Children's activity center. Beach. Closed November-March. $$

SPECIALTY LODGINGS

Captain Farris House Bed & Breakfast
308 Old Main St., South Yarmouth,
508-760-2818, 800-350-9477;
www.captainfarris.com
This bed-and-breakfast has beautifully landscaped lawns and breathtaking views. Guests can take advantage of nearby sailing, canoeing, kayaking, and windsurfing. Antique shopping, bird-watching and the John F. Kennedy Museum are also nearby.
10 rooms. Children over 10 years only. Complimentary full breakfast. Check-in 3-7 p.m., check-out 11 a.m. Restaurant. Whirlpool. $

Colonial House Inn & Restaurant
277 Main St., Yarmouth Port,
508-362-4348, 800-999-3416;
www.colonialhousecapecod.com
21 rooms. Complimentary full breakfast. Restaurant. Bar. $

Inn at Lewis Bay
57 Maine Ave., West Yarmouth,

508-771-3433, 800-962-6679;
www.innatlewisbay.com
Located in a quiet seaside neighborhood just one block from Lewis Bay, this Dutch colonial bed-and-breakfast serves a bountiful meal each morning and refreshments each afternoon. 6 rooms. Children over 12 years only. Complimentary full breakfast. Check-in 3-8 p.m. Check-out 11 a.m. **$**

RESTAURANTS

★★Abbicci
43 Main St., Yarmouth Port,
508-362-3501;
www.abbicci.com
Mediterranean menu. Lunch, dinner. Bar. Business casual attire. Reservations recommended. **$$**

★★Ardeo
23V Whites Path, South Yarmouth,
508-760-1500;
www.ardeocapecod.com
Mediterranean menu. Lunch, dinner. Bar. Children's menu. Casual attire. **$$**

★★Inaho
157 Main St., Yarmouth Port,
508-362-5522.

Japanese, sushi menu. Dinner. Casual attire. **$$**

★★Riverway Lobster House
1338 Route 28, South Yarmouth,
508-398-2172;
www.riverwaylobsterhouse.com
American menu. Dinner. Bar. Children's menu. Casual attire. Reservations recommended. Closed Monday in January-April. **$$**

★★Skipper Restaurant
152 S. Shore Dr., South Yarmouth,
508-394-7406;
www.skipper-restaurant.com
Seafood menu. Lunch, dinner. Bar. Children's menu. Casual attire. Outdoor seating. Closed mid-October-mid-April. **$$**

★★Yarmouth House
335 Main St., West Yarmouth,
508-771-5154;
www.yarmouthhouse.com
Seafood, steak menu. Lunch, dinner. Bar. Children's menu. Casual attire. Reservations recommended. **$$**

MASSACHUSETTS

NEW HAMPSHIRE

NEW HAMPSHIRE'S MOTTO, AS PROUDLY PROCLAIMED ON ITS LICENSE PLATES, IS "LIVE FREE or Die", a reference to the state's revolutionary spirit. Some from the surrounding states like to tease that the motto should be "Live Free *and* Die" because the granite state has markedly fewer laws restricting personal freedoms than any other state, from no helmet laws for motorcyclists to no seatbelts laws in cars. But this atmosphere of free living is what is attracting more and more newcomers to New Hampshire, who come here for the low taxes and beautiful mountain scenery.

New Hampshire is famous for the important role it plays in national politics. It traditionally holds the first presidential primary in the country, placing the laser focus of the media on its many small towns, their inhabitants and their voting habits.

The mountains in New Hampshire are known for their rugged "notches" (called "gaps" and "passes" elsewhere) and the old valley towns offer a serene beauty. Some of the best skiing in the East is available at several major resorts here. The state's many parks, antiques shops, art and theater festivals and county fairs are also popular attractions, and more than half of New England's covered bridges are in New Hampshire.

In 1623, David Thomson and a small group of colonists settled on the New Hampshire coast near Portsmouth. These early settlements were part of Massachusetts. In 1679, they became a separate royal province under Charles the Second. In 1776, the Provincial Congress adopted a constitution making New Hampshire the first independent colony, seven months before the Declaration of Independence was signed. Although New Hampshire was the only one of the 13 original states not invaded by the British during the Revolution, its men fought long and hard on land and sea to bring about the victory. This strong, involved attitude continues in New Hampshire to this day.

★ SPOTLIGHT

★ Tupperware was invented in Berlin, New Hampshire in 1938.

★ The oldest ski club in America was formed by a group of Scandinavians in Berlin in 1882.

★ The first U.S. public library was opened in Peterborough in 1837.

★ Open since 1789, the John Hancock Inn in Hancock is the oldest operating tavern in New England.

BARTLETT

Bartlett is home to Attitash ski resort, popular in the area for its focus on snowboarding.
Information: Mount Washington Valley Chamber of Commerce, N. Main St., North Conway, 603-356-5701; www.mtwashingtonvalley.org

WHAT TO SEE AND DO
Attitash Bear Peak Ski Resort
Highway 302, Bartlett,
New Hampshire,
603-374-2368; www.attitash.com
Two high-speed quad, three quad, three triple, three double chairlifts; three surface lifts; patrol, school, rentals; snowmaking; nursery; cafeteria; bar. Longest run 1 3/4 mile; vertical drop 1,750 feet. Mid-November-late April: daily. **Summer recreation**: Alpine slide, waterslides, scenic chairlift, horseback riding, mountain biking, hiking, driving range

Mid-June-Labor Day: daily; Memorial Day-mid-June and early September-mid-October: weekends; fees.

HOTELS
★★Attitash Grand Summit Resort And Conference Center
Highway 302, Bartlett,
603-374-1900, 800-862-1600;
www.attitashmtvillage.com
253 rooms. Restaurant. Bar. Indoor pool, two outdoor pools, whirlpool. Tennis. Ski in/ski out. **$**

BRETTON WOODS

Bretton Woods is located in the White Mountains on a long glacial plain next to Mount Washington and the Presidential Range. Mount Washington was first sighted in 1497; however, settlement around it did not begin until 1771 when the Crawford Notch, which opened the way through the mountains, was discovered. In the 1770s, Governor Wentworth named the area Bretton Woods for his ancestral home in England. This historic name was set aside in 1832 when all the tiny settlements in the area were incorporated under the name of Carroll. For a time, a railroad through the notch brought as many as 57 trains a day and the area grew as a resort spot. A string of hotels sprang up, each more elegant and fashionable than the last. In 1903, the post office, railroad station and express office reverted to the traditional name—Bretton Woods. Today, Bretton Woods is a resort area at the base of the mountain.

★
★
★
★
★

WHAT TO SEE AND DO
Bretton Woods Ski Area
Hwy. 302, Bretton Woods, 603-278-3320;
www.brettonwoods.com
Two high-speed quad, triple, two double chairlifts, three surface lifts; patrol, school, rentals, snowmaking; restaurant, cafeteria, bar; child care; lodge. Longest run two miles; vertical drop 1,500 feet. Thanksgiving-April: daily. Night skiing early December-March: Friday-Saturday. 48 miles of cross-country trails.
Crawford Notch State Park
Hwy. 302, Bretton Woods, 603-374-2272
One of the state's most spectacular passes. Mounts Nancy and Willey rise to the west; Mounts Crawford, Webster and Jackson to the east. Park headquarters is at the former site of the Samuel Willey house. The family of six and two hired men died in a landslide in 1826 when they rushed out of their house, which was left untouched. Fishing, trout-feeding pond. Hiking, walking trails on the Appalachian system. Picnicking, conces-

sion. Camping. Interpretive center. Late-May-mid-October.

HOTELS
★★★Mount Washington Hotel
Hwy. 302, Bretton Woods,
603-278-1000, 800-258-0330;
www.mtwashington.com
This landmark hotel is a true retreat in every way. Enjoy golfing, horseback riding and bicycle riding during the day and live music, fine dining and dancing at night to live jazz or big band music.
200 rooms. Two restaurants. Five bars. Children's activity center. Fitness room. Indoor pool, outdoor pool. Golf, 27 holes. Tennis. Business center. **$$$**

RESTAURANTS
★Fabyan's Station
Highway 302, Bretton Woods,
603-278-2222; www.mtwashington.com
American menu. Lunch, dinner. Bar. Children's menu. Casual attire. **$$**

CONCORD

New Hampshire, one of the original 13 colonies, entered the Union in 1788, but its capital was in dispute for another 20 years. Concord finally won the honor in 1808. Building began for the state house immediately and finally finished in 1819. The legislature is the largest (more than 400 seats) of any state. Concord is the financial center of the state and offers a diverse range of industry as well.

Information: Chamber of Commerce, 40 Commercial St., 603-224-2508; www.concordnhchamber.com

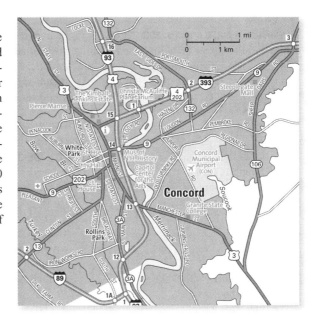

SPOT★LIGHT

★PRESIDENT FRANKLIN PIERCE WAS BORN IN CONCORD IN 1804.

★CONCORD'S FRANKLIN PIERCE LAW SCHOOL IS THE ONLY LAW SCHOOL IN THE STATE.

WHAT TO SEE AND DO

Canterbury Shaker Village
288 Shaker Rd., Canterbury, 603-783-9511;
www.shakers.org
Pay homage to New Hampshire's Shaker heritage with a visit to this National Historic Landmark museum, which offers guided and self-guided tours and a variety of exhibits. Mid-May–late-October: daily 10 a.m.-5 p.m.; November-December: Saturday-Sunday 10 a.m.-4 p.m.;

Christa McAuliffe Planetarium
2 Institute Dr., Concord, 603-271-7831;
www.starhop.com
This living memorial to New Hampshire teacher Christa McAuliffe, who died aboard the U.S. space shuttle *Challenger* on January 28, 1986, offers a variety of shows designed for all ages in a 92-seat theater. Some shows are aimed at the very young while others boast 3-D computer graphic effects likely to impress all ages. Daily; call or visit website for show schedule.

Granite State Candy Shoppe
13 Warren St., Concord,
603-225-2591, 888-225-2531;
www.nhchocolates.com
Founded in 1927 by a Greek immigrant, Granite State Candy Shoppe is an old-fashioned candy store with a motto, "We're in the happiness business." The candy shoppe is now owned by the founder's grandchildren, who still use many of his original copper kettles and dip each chocolate one by one.

Museum of New Hampshire History
6 Eagle Square, Concord, 603-228-6688;
www.nhhistory.org
Historical museum (founded 1823) with permanent and changing exhibits, including examples of the famed Concord Coach; museum store. Tuesday-Saturday, also Sunday afternoons.

NEW HAMPSHIRE

★
★
★
★

Pierce Manse

14 Penacook St., Concord, 603-225-4555
Home of President Franklin Pierce from
1842 to 1848. Reconstructed and moved
to the present site; contains many original
furnishings and period pieces. Mid-June-
mid-October: Tuesday-Saturday; also by
appointment.

State House

107 N. Main St., Concord, 603-271-2154
Hall of Flags; statues, portraits of state
notables. Monday-Friday.

HOTELS

★Comfort Inn

71 Hall St., Concord,
603-226-4100, 877-424-6423;
www.comfortinn.com
100 rooms. Pets accepted, some restrictions;
fee. Complimentary continental breakfast.
Indoor pool, whirlpool. **$**

★Hampton Inn

515 South St., Bow,
603-224-5322, 800-426-7866;
www.hamptoninn.com
145 rooms. Complimentary continental
breakfast. Indoor pool, whirlpool. **$**

★★★Colby Hill Inn

The Oaks, Henniker, 603-428-3281,
800-531-0330; www.colbyhillinn.com
This classic New England country inn offers
individually decorated rooms and fine-
dining in a beautiful, wooded setting.
14 rooms. Children over 7 years only. Complimentary full breakfast. Wireless Internet
access. Restaurant. Bar. Outdoor pool. **$$**

RESTAURANTS

★★Angelina's Ristorante Italiano

11 Depot St., Concord, 603-228-3313;
www.angelinasrestaurant.com
American, Italian menu. Lunch, dinner.
Casual attire. Reservations recommended.
Closed Sunday. **$$**

★Arnie's Place

164 Loudon Rd., Concord, 603-228-3225;
www.arniesplace.com
American menu. Lunch, dinner. Children's
menu. Casual attire. Outdoor seating. No
credit cards accepted. **$**

★Boar's Tavern

Routes 106 and 129, Loudon,
603-798-3737; www.boarstavern.com
American menu. Lunch, dinner. Bar. Casual
attire. **$$**

★★Colby Hill Inn

The Oaks, Henniker, 603-428-3281;
www.colbyhillinn.com
Regional menu. Dinner. Business casual
attire. Reservations recommended. **$$$**

★★Longhorn Steakhouse

217 Loudon Rd., Concord, 603-228-0655;
www.longhornsteakhouse.com
Steak menu. Lunch, dinner. Bar. Children's
menu. Casual attire. **$$**

★Makris Lobster and Steak House

354 Sheep Davis Rd., Concord,
603-225-7665; www.eatalobster.com
Seafood, steak menu. Lunch, dinner, late-
night. Bar. Children's menu. Casual attire.
Outdoor seating. **$$**

★Red Blazer Restaurant

72 Manchester St., Concord,
603-224-4101; www.redblazer.cc
American menu. Lunch, dinner. Bar. Chil-
dren's menu. Casual attire. **$$**

★Sal's Just Pizza

80 Storrs St., Concord, 603-226-0297;
www.sals-pizza.com
Pizza. Lunch, dinner. Children's menu.
Casual attire. Outdoor seating. No credit
cards accepted. **$**

NEW HAMPSHIRE

DIXVILLE NOTCH

The small village of Dixville Notch shares its name with the most northern White Mountain passes. The Notch cuts through the mountain range between Kidderville and Errol. At its narrowest point, east of Lake Gloriette, is one of the most impressive views in the state. Every four years, Dixville Notch is invaded by the national news media, who report the nation's first presidential vote tally shortly after midnight on election day.

WHAT TO SEE AND DO

Balsams/Wilderness Ski Area

Highway 26, Dixville Notch,
603-255-3400, 800-255-0600;
www.thebalsams.com

Chairlift, two T-bars; patrol, school, rentals, snowmaking; restaurant, cafeteria, bar, nursery, resort. Longest run one mile; vertical drop 1,000 feet. December-March:daily. Cross-country trails.

HOTELS

★★★The Balsams

Highway 26, Dixville Notch,
603-255-3400, 800-255-0600;
www.thebalsams.com

The Balsams has impressive architecture and a bucolic setting. Built just after the Civil War, this 15,000-acre resort offers downhill skiing, cross-country skiing, snowboarding and ice skating, while warmer months are spent playing golf or tennis and enjoying the great outdoors on nature walks. Operating on the all-inclusive American plan, the Balsams makes gourmet dining an integral part of the experience here.

212 rooms. Two restaurants. Two bars. Fitness room. Outdoor pool. Golf, 27 holes. Tennis. Ski in/ski out. Airport transportation available. $$

DOVER

With its historic trails and homes, Dover is the oldest permanent settlement in New Hampshire. The town contains the only known existing colonial garrison.
Information: Chamber of Commerce, 299 Central Ave., 603-742-2218, www.dovernh.org

WHAT TO SEE AND DO

Woodman Institute

182-190 Central Ave., Dover, 603-742-1038
Garrison House (1675), the only garrison in New Hampshire now visible in nearly its original form. Woodman House (1818), residence of the donor, is now a natural history museum with collections of minerals, Native American artifacts and displays of mammals, fish, amphibians, reptiles, birds, insects; war memorial rooms. Senator John P. Hale House (1813) contains articles of Dover history and antique furniture. May-November: Wednesday-Sunday afternoons; December: Saturday-Sunday afternoons.

HOTELS

★Days Inn

481 Central Ave., Dover,
603-742-0400, 800-329-7466;
www.dover-durham-daysinn.com

50 rooms. Pets accepted. Complimentary continental breakfast. Outdoor pool, whirlpool. $

RESTAURANTS

★★★Maples

17 Newmarket Rd., Durham,
603-868-7800, 888-399-9777;
www.threechimneysinn.com

This restaurant provides service in an old New England setting that includes dark wood tables and large, comfortable chairs. In the summertime, the patio is open for dining and in the winter, the fireplace provides a cozy atmosphere.
American menu. Lunch, dinner. Outdoor seating. $$$

★Newick's Seafood

431 Dover Point Rd., Dover,
603-742-3205; www.newicks.com
Seafood menu. Lunch, dinner. $$

★

★

★

★

★

EXETER

A respected preparatory school and colonial houses are a large part of Exeter's radical history. The town had its beginnings in religious non-conformity, led by Reverend John Wheelwright and Anne Hutchinson, both of whom were banished from Massachusetts for heresy. There was an anti-British scuffle in 1734, and by 1774 Exeter was burning Lord North in effigy and talking of liberty. It was made the capital of the state during the Revolution. Exeter is the birthplace of Daniel Chester French and John Irving.

Information: Exeter Area Chamber of Commerce, 120 Water St., 603-772-2411; www. exeterarea.org

WHAT TO SEE AND DO

American Independence Museum
1 Governors Lane, Exeter, 603-772-2622
www.independencemuseum.org
Site of Revolutionary War–era state treasury building; grounds house Folsom Tavern (1775). May-October: Wednesday-Saturday.

Phillips Exeter Academy
20 Main St., Exeter, 603-772-4311;
www.exeter.edu
(1781) (990 students) A prestigious college preparatory school on 400 acres with more than 100 buildings. Co-ed school for grades 9-12. Founded by John Phillips, who sought a school for "students from every quarter." Exeter is known for its student diversity. On campus there is a contemporary library (1971), designed by Louis I. Kahn; the Frederick R. Mayer Art Center; and the Lamont Art Gallery.

FRANCONIA

Franconia is the gateway to the White Mountains. From here, explore the area's best hiking and skiing and in the fall, leaf peeping, as the annual pilgramage to view the changing colors of the leaves is affectionately called.

Information: Franconia Notch Chamber of Commerce, 603-823-5661, 800-237-9007; www.franconianotch.org

WHAT TO SEE AND DO

Frost Place
Ridge Rd., Franconia, 603-823-5510;
www.frostplace.org
Two furnished rooms of Robert Frost's home open to public; memorabilia; poetry trail; 25-minute video. July-Columbus Day: Wednesday-Monday afternoons; Memorial Day-June: Saturday-Sunday afternoons.

New England Ski Museum
Franconia Notch Pkwy., Franconia,
603-823-7177, 800-639-4181;
www.nesm.org
Details history of skiing in the East; exhibits feature skis and bindings, clothing, art and photographs; vintage films. Gift shop.

Memorial Day-Columbus Day and December-March:daily.

HOTELS

★★Franconia Village Hotel
87 Wallace Hill Rd., Franconia,
603-823-7422, 888-669-6777;
www.franconiahotel.com
61 rooms. Pets accepted, some restrictions; fee. Complimentary continental breakfast. Restaurant. Bar. Fitness room. Indoor pool.
$

★Stonybrook Motel & Lodge
1098 Profile Rd., Franconia,
603-823-5800, 800-722-3552;
www.stonybrookmotel.com

23 rooms. Complimentary continental breakfast. Children's activity center. Indoor pool, outdoor pool. **$**

★★Sugar Hill Inn
Highway 117, Franconia,
603-823-5621, 800-548-4748;
www.sugarhillinn.com
15 rooms. Complimentary full breakfast. Wireless Internet access. Restaurant (public by reservation). Bar. Spa. Closed one week in April. **$$**

★★★Franconia Inn
1300 Easton Rd., Franconia,
603-823-5542, 800-473-5299;
www.franconiainn.com
Located in the White Mountains, but still close to the town center, this charming inn welcomes guests into an informal country home atmosphere. The comfortable guest rooms are spacious and onsite activities include horseback riding, mountain biking, fishing and croquet.
34 rooms. Complimentary full breakfast. Restaurant. Bar. Outdoor pool, whirlpool. Tennis. Closed April-mid-May. **$**

★★★Lovetts Inn
1474 Profile Rd., Franconia,
603-823-7761, 800-356-3802;
www.lovettsinn.com
Breathe in the fresh country air at this historic, romantic inn surrounded by the White Mountains. Well appointed and charming, the inn has a rustic feel. The town center is a short drive away.
18 rooms. Pets accepted; fee. Complimentary full breakfast. Wireless Internet access. Restaurant. Bar. Outdoor pool. Closed April. **$$**

SPECIALTY LODGINGS

Hilltop Inn
1348 Main St., Sugar Hill,
603-823-5695; 800-770-5695.
www.hilltopinn.com
Built in 1895; rooms feature antiques, quilts.

6 rooms. Pets accepted, some restrictions; fee. Complimentary full breakfast. **$**

Sunset Hill House–A Grand Inn
231 Sunset Hill Rd., Sugar Hill,
603-823-5522, 800-786-4455;
www.sunsethillhouse.com
Built in 1882; beautiful view of mountains. 28 rooms. Complimentary full breakfast. Restaurant. Outdoor pool. Golf. **$$$**

RESTAURANTS

★★★The Franconia Inn
1300 Easton Rd., Franconia,
603-823-5542, 800-473-5299;
www.franconiainn.com
Surrounded by hills and mountains, this restaurant offers New American cuisine, drawing on regional specialties and influenced by the rich heritage of the area. Main courses include filet mignon with crab cakes and pepper-seared Atlantic salmon. American menu. Breakfast, dinner. Closed April-mid-May. Bar. Children's menu. Casual attire. Reservations recommended. **$$**

★★Horse & Hound
205 Wells Rd., Franconia,
603-823-5501, 800-450-5501;
www.horseandhoundnh.com
American menu. Dinner. Closed Sunday-Wednesday. Bar. Casual attire. Reservations recommended. Outdoor seating. **$$**

★★Lovetts Inn by Lafayette Brook
1474 Profile Rd., Franconia,
603-823-7761;
www.lovettsinn.com
American menu. Breakfast, dinner. Bar. Casual attire. Reservations recommended. Outdoor seating. **$$**

★★Polly's Pancake Parlor
672 Highway 117, Sugar Hill,
603-823-5575;
www.pollyspancakeparlor.com
American menu. Breakfast, lunch. Closed November-April. Children's menu. **$$**

FRANCONIA NOTCH STATE PARK

This seven-mile pass and state park, a deep valley of 6,440 acres between the Franconia and Kinsman ranges of the White Mountains has been a top tourist attraction since the mid-19th century. Mounts Liberty (4,460 feet), Lincoln (5,108 feet) and Lafayette (5,249 feet) loom in the east, and Cannon Mountain (4,200 feet) presents a sheer granite face. The Pemigewasset River follows the length of the Notch. The park offers various recreational activities, including swimming at Sandy Beach; fishing and boating on Echo Lake (junction Highway 18 and I-93 exit 3); hiking; eight-mile paved bike path through the Notch; skiing; picnicking; camping. Fees for some activities.
Information: Franconia Notch State Park, Franconia, 603-823-5563

WHAT TO SEE AND DO

Cannon Mountain Ski Area
Franconia Notch State Pkwy., Franconia, 603-823-8800; www.cannonmt.com
Tramway, two quad, three triple, two double chairlifts, pony lift; patrol, school, rentals; snowmaking; cafeterias, bar (beer and wine); nursery. New England Ski Museum. Longest run two miles and vertical drop 2,146 feet. Late November-mid-April: daily. Tramway rising 2,022 feet vertically over a distance of one mile in six minutes. Also operates Memorial Day-mid-October: daily; rest of year: weekends (weather permitting).

Flume Gorge & Park Information Center
Franconia Notch State Pkwy., Franconia, 603-745-8391; www.flumegorge.com
Narrow, natural gorge and waterfall along the flank of Mount Liberty, accessible by stairs and walks. Information center offers a 15-minute movie every half-hour introducing the park. Interpretive exhibits. Gift shop, cafeteria. Mid-May-late-October, daily.

Old Man of the Mountain Historic Site
1, 200 ft., above Profile Lake, Franconia, Notch State Pkwy.
Discovered in 1805, the craggy likeness of a man's face was formed naturally of five layers of granite and was 40 feet high. It tumbled down on May 3, 2003. It was also known as the "Great Stone Face."

GORHAM

Located near the Presidential Range of the White Mountains, at the north end of Pinkham Notch, Gorham is the center for summer and winter sports. The Peabody River merges with the Androscoggin in a series of falls and there is a Ranger District office of the White Mountain National Forest here.
Information: Northern White Mountains Chamber of Commerce, 164 Main St., Berlin, 603-752-6060, 800-992-7480; www.northernwhitemountains.com

WHAT TO SEE AND DO

Moose Brook State Park
30 Jimtown Rd., Gorham, 603-466-3860
Views of the Presidential Range of the White Mountains; good stream fishing area. Swimming, bathhouse; picnicking; camping. Hiking to Randolph Range. Late May-early-September. Standard fees.

HOTELS

★Mt. Madison Motel
365 Main St., Gorham, 603-466-3622, 800-851-1136; www.mtmadisonmotel.com
33 rooms. Pets accepted, some restrictions. Outdoor pool. $

★★Royalty Inn
130 Main St., Gorham, 603-466-3312, 800-437-3529; www.royaltyinn.com
90 rooms. Pets accepted, some restrictions. Restaurant. Bar. Fitness room. Indoor pool, outdoor pool. $

NEW HAMPSHIRE

RESTAURANTS

★★Yokohama
288 Main St., Gorham, 603-466-2501

Japanese menu. Lunch, dinner. Children's menu. Closed Monday; also two weeks in spring and two weeks in fall. **$$**

HAMPTON BEACH

This beachfront town has an old-fashioned boardwalk and plenty of sandy beaches. An annual seafood festival, held the week after Labor Day, is the town's biggest event.
Information: Chamber of Commerce, 1 Park Ave., 603-926-8717, 800-438-2826; www. hamptonbeaches.com

WHAT TO SEE AND DO

Fuller Gardens
10 Willow Ave., North Hampton, 603-964-5414; www.fullergardens.org
Former estate of the late Governor Alvan T. Fuller featuring extensive rose gardens, annuals, perennials, Japanese garden and conservatory. Mid-May-mid-October: daily.

Hampton Beach State Park
Hwy. 1A, Hampton Beach, 603-926-3784
Sandy beach on Atlantic Ocean. Swimming, bathhouse. Also here is the Sea Shell, a band shell and amphitheater. Camping (hook-ups). Standard fees. Late-May-Labor Day: daily.

Tuck Memorial Museum
40 Park Ave., Hampton, 603-929-0781
Home of Hampton Historical Society. Antiques, documents, photographs, early postcards, tools and toys; trolley exhibit; memorabilia of Hampton history. Restored one-room schoolhouse; fire station. Mid-June-mid-September.

HOTELS

★★Ashworth By The Sea
295 Ocean Blvd., Hampton Beach, 603-926-6762, 800-345-6736; www.ashworthhotel.com
105 rooms. Three restaurants, bar. Indoor pool. **$$**

★Hampshire Inn
20 Spur Rd., Seabrook, 603-474-5700, 800-932-8520; www.hampshireinn.com
35 rooms. Complimentary continental breakfast. Fitness room. Indoor pool, whirlpool. Airport transportation available. **$**

★★Hampton Falls Inn
11 Lafayette Rd., Hampton Falls, 603-926-9545, 800-356-1729; www.hamptonfallsinn.com
47 rooms. Pets accepted, some restrictions. Wireless Internet access. Restaurant. Indoor pool, whirlpool. **$**

★★Inn Of Hampton
815 Lafayette Rd., Hampton, 603-926-6771, 800-423-4561; www.theinnofhampton.com
71 rooms. Restaurant. Bar. Children's activity center. Fitness room. Indoor pool. Business center. **$**

★★Lamie's Inn & Old Salt Restaurant
490 Lafayette Rd., Hampton, 603-926-0330, 800-805-5050; www.lamiesinn.com
32 rooms. Pets accepted, some restrictions; fee. Complimentary continental breakfast. Restaurant. Bar. **$**

SPECIALTY LODGINGS

D. W.'s Oceanside Inn
365 Ocean Blvd., Hampton Beach, 603-926-3542, 866-623-2674; www.oceansideinn.com
This early 1900s beach house overlooking the Atlantic Ocean is an ideal getaway. The décor is colonial and some rooms have canopied beds.
9 rooms. No children allowed. Complimentary full breakfast. Beach. Closed mid-October-mid-May. **$$**

HANOVER

Established four years after the first settlers came here, Dartmouth College is an integral part of Hanover. Named for the Earl of Dartmouth, the school was founded by the Reverend Eleazar Wheelock "for the instruction of the youth of Indian tribes . . . and others." An ivy league college famous for its party scene, Dartmouth was the inspiration for the film *Animal House*.
Information: Chamber of Commerce, 216 Nugget Bldg., Main St., 603-643-3115; www.hanoverchamber.org

WHAT TO SEE AND DO

Dartmouth College
Main and Wheelock Streets, Hanover, 603-646-1110; www.dartmouth.edu
(1769) (5,400 students) This Ivy League school is renowned for its business school and top-notch academics.

Enfield Shaker Museum
24 Caleb Dyer Lane, Enfield, 603-632-4346; www.shakermuseum.org
Museum devoted to Shaker culture on the site where the Shakers established their Chosen Vale in 1793. Includes exhibits, craft demonstrations, workshops, special programs and extensive gardens.

Saint-Gaudens National Historic Site
Route 12A, Cornish, 603-675-2175; www.nps.gov/saga
Former residence and studio of sculptor Augustus Saint-Gaudens (1848-1907). Saint-Gaudens' famous works *The Puritan*, *Adams Memorial* and *Shaw Memorial* are among the 100 works on display. Also includes formal gardens and works by other artists; sculptor-in-residence; interpretive programs. Memorial Day-October: daily.

Webster Cottage
32 N. Main St., Hanover, 603-643-6529
(1780) Residence of Daniel Webster during his last year as a Dartmouth College student; colonial and Shaker furniture and Webster memorabilia. Memorial Day-mid-October: Wednesday, Saturday-Sunday afternoons.

HOTELS

★★Fireside Inn & Suites
25 Airport Rd., West Lebanon, 603-298-5900, 877-258-5900; www.afiresideinn.com

126 rooms. High-speed Internet access. Fitness room. **$$**

★★★Hanover Inn
Main and Wheelock Streets., Hanover, 603-643-4300, 800-443-7024; www.hanoverinn.com
This inn is located just minutes from Dartmouth College. The guest rooms are decorated with a colonial motif and guests have access to athletic facilities at the university.
92 rooms. Pets accepted; fee. High-speed Internet access, wireless Internet access. Restaurant. Bar. Fitness room. Airport transportation available. **$$$**

SPECIALTY LODGINGS

Alden Country Inn
1 Market St., Lyme, 603-795-2222, 800-794-2296; www.aldencountryinn.com
Original inn and tavern built in 1809; antique furnishings.
15 rooms. Complimentary full breakfast. Restaurant. Bar. **$**

Dowd's Country Inn
On the Common, Lyme, 603-795-4712, 800-482-4712; www.dowdscountryinn.com
This charming New England inn is located 10 miles north of Dartmouth College. Close to the Lyme commons, this property is surrounded by trees.
23 rooms. Complimentary full breakfast. **$$**

RESTAURANTS

★★Jesse's
Lebanon Rd., Hanover, 603-643-4111; www.blueskyrestaurants.com

NEW HAMPSHIRE

Steak menu. Lunch, dinner. Bar. Children's menu. Outdoor seating. **$$**

★**Molly's**
43 S. Main St., Hanover, 603-643-2570; www.mollysrestaurant.com
American menu. Lunch, dinner. Bar. **$$**

HOLDERNESS

Holderness is the shopping center and post office for Squam Lake the second-largest lake in the state, and neighboring Little Squam. Fishing, boating, swimming, water sports and winter sports are popular in this area. The movie *On Golden Pond* was filmed here.

WHAT TO SEE AND DO

Squam Lakes Natural Science Center

23 Science Center Rd., Holderness, 603-968-7194; www.nhnature.org

If this attraction looks familiar, perhaps you'll recognize it as the site where the 1981 movie, *On Golden Pond,* with Henry Fonda and Katharine Hepburn, was filmed. Walking through the woods of this 200-acre wildlife sanctuary, you'll see black bears, deer, bobcats, otters, mountain lions, foxes and birds of prey in enclosed trailside exhibits. You can also take the Explore Squam boat tour. Picnicking. May-early November: daily 9:30 a.m.-4:30 p.m.

HOTELS

★★★Manor On Golden Pond

Manor Dr., Holderness, 603-968-3348, 800-545-2141; www.manorongoldenpond.com

Modeled after an English country estate, this inn is located on the shore of Squam Lake. Activities include tennis, badminton, croquet and access to a private beach. 25 rooms. Children over 12 years only. Complimentary full breakfast. Wireless Internet access. Restaurant. Bar. Indoor pool. Tennis. **$$$**

SPECIALTY LODGINGS

Glynn House Inn

59 Highland St., Ashland, 603-968-3775, 800-637-9599; www.glynnhouse.com

This restored 1896 Queen Anne/Victorian is conveniently located near Squam Lake in the White Mountains. The interior is tastefully decorated and guest rooms are nicely appointed. Lakes Region dining, attractions and activities are all nearby. 13 rooms. Children over 12 years only. Complimentary full breakfast. **$$**

Inn On Golden Pond

Route 25, Holderness, 603-968-7269; www.innongoldenpond.com

Built in 1879; fireplace; individually-decorated rooms. 8 rooms. Children over 10 years only. Complimentary continental breakfast. **$**

RESTAURANTS

★Common Man

60 Main St., Ashland, 603-968-7030; www.thecman.com

American menu. Lunch, dinner. Bar. Children's menu. Casual attire. Outdoor seating. **$$**

★★Corner House Inn

22 Main St., Center Sandwich, 603-284-6219; www.cornerhouseinn.com

American menu. Lunch, dinner, brunch. Bar. Children's menu. Casual attire. Reservations recommended. **$$**

★★★Manor on Golden Pond

Manor Dr., Holderness, 603-968-3348; www.manorongoldenpond.com

Dinner at this cozy inn on Squam Lake is a romantic experience. The location, high on a hill, provides spectacular views. The frequently changing a la carte menu includes New American dishes like duck hash Napolean and sauted mahi mahi.
American menu. Dinner. Bar. Business casual attire. Reservations recommended. Valet parking. **$$$**

NEW HAMPSHIRE

JACKSON

At the south end of Pinkham Notch, Jackson is a center for skiing and a year-round resort. The Wildcat River rushes over rock formations in the village; Wildcat Mountain is to the north. A covered bridge (circa 1870) spans the Ellis River.

Information: Chamber of Commerce, 603-383-9356; www.jacksonnh.com

WHAT TO SEE AND DO

Black Mountain

Hwy. 16B, Jackson, 603-383-4490; www.blackmt.com

Triple and double chairlifts, J-bar, patrol, school, rentals, cafeteria, nursery. Longest run is one mile; vertical drop 1,100 feet.

Jackson Ski Touring Foundation

Main St., and Highway 16A, Jackson, 603-383-9355; www.jacksonxc.org

Maintains 95 miles of cross-country trails, connecting inns and ski areas. Instruction, rentals, rescue service. December-mid-April, daily.

HOTELS

★Lodge at Jackson Village

153 Highway 16, Jackson, 603-383-0999, 800-233-5634; www.lodgeatjacksonvillage.com

32 rooms. Complimentary full breakfast. High-speed Internet access, wireless Internet access. Outdoor pool, whirlpool. Tennis. **$$**

★★Storybook Resort Inn

Highways 302 and 16, Glen, 603-383-6800; www.storybookresort.com

78 rooms. Restaurant. Bar. Fitness room. Indoor pool, two outdoor pools, children's pool. Tennis. **$**

★★Eagle Mountain House

Carter Notch Rd., Jackson, 603-383-9111, 800-966-5779; www.eaglemt.com

97 rooms. Wireless Internet access. Restaurant. Bar. Fitness room. Outdoor pool, whirlpool. Golf, 9 holes. Tennis. Ski in/ski out. **$$**

★★★Wentworth Resort Hotel

1 Carter Notch Rd., Jackson, 603-383-9700, 800-637-0013;

www.thewentworth.com

This elegant country inn, built in 1869, has been in continuous operation for more than a century. Located in the White Mountains, the year-round resort offers a fine-dining restaurant and recreational facilities.

51 rooms. Restaurant. Bar. Outdoor pool. Golf, 18 holes. Tennis. Ski in/ski out. Airport transportation available. **$$**

★★★Inn At Thorn Hill

Thorn Hill Rd., Jackson, 603-383-4242, 800-289-8990; www.innatthornhill.com

This historic inn puts a premium on luxury. Rooms have plush, down duvet-topped beds, Jacuzzi tubs and TV/DVD players. A full, gourmet breakfast is served each morning in the inn's restaurant.

25 rooms. Children over 8 years only. Complimentary full breakfast. High-speed Internet access, wireless Internet access. Restaurant. Bar. Fitness room, spa. Outdoor pool, whirlpool. Ski in/ski out. **$$$**

★★★Inn at Ellis River

17 Harriman Rd., Jackson, 603-383-9339, 800-233-8309; www.innatellisriver.com

This luxurious inn offers rooms with period furnishings and a wide variety of amenities. Some rooms have whirlpool tubs or balconies and most have fireplaces. The area surrounding the inn offers year-round activities such as cross-country skiing, golf, fishing, swimming and kayaking.

21 rooms. Children over 12 years only. Complimentary full breakfast. Restaurant. Bar. Outdoor pool. **$**

SPECIALTY LODGINGS

Dana Place Inn

Highway 16, Jackson, 603-383-6822, 800-537-9276;

www.danaplace.com
30 rooms. Pets accepted, some restrictions. Complimentary full breakfast. Restaurant. Bar. Indoor pool, children's pool, whirlpool. Golf. Tennis. Business center. **$$**

Nestlenook Farm Resort
Dinsmore Rd., Jackson,
603-383-9443, 800-659-9443;
www.luxurymountaingetaways.com
Located on the river, this restored Victorian building is one of the oldest in Jackson (1770). Furnishings include antiques, Tiffany lamps and 18th-century parlor stoves. 7 rooms, all suites. No children allowed. Complimentary full breakfast. Outdoor pool. Closed two weeks in April. **$$**

RESTAURANTS
★★Christmas Farm Inn
Highway 16B, Jackson,
603-383-4313, 800-443-5837;
www.christmasfarminn.com
American menu. Breakfast, dinner. Bar. Children's menu. Casual attire. Reservations recommended. **$$$**

★★★Inn at Thorn Hill
Thorn Hill Rd., Jackson,
603-383-4242, 800-289-8990;
www.innatthornhill.com
The dining room at this restaurant has views of the countryside and a wood-burning fireplace. The menu changes seasonally and offers options such as pan-seared tuna, grilled beef tenderloin and petite rack of veal. An extensive wine list is offered. American menu. Breakfast, dinner. Bar. Business casual attire. Reservations recommended. Outdoor seating. **$$$**

★Red Parka Pub
Highway 302, Glen, 603-383-4344;
www.redparkapub.com
Steak menu. Dinner. Bar. Children's menu. Outdoor seating. **$**

★★Wildcat Inn & Tavern
Highway 16A, Jackson,
603-383-4245, 800-228-4245;
www.wildcattavern.com
American menu. Lunch, dinner. Bar. Children's menu. Casual attire. Reservations recommended. Outdoor seating. **$$$**

205

★
★
★
★

KEENE
A modern commercial city, Keene is the chief community of the Monadnock region. Its industries manufacture many products including furniture, machinery, textiles and toys.
Information: Chamber of Commerce, 48 Central Square., 603-352-1303; www.keenechamber.com

WHAT TO SEE AND DO
Colony Mill Marketplace
222 West St., Keene, 603-357-1240;
www.colonymill.com
Restored 1838 textile mill now transformed into regional marketplace with dozens of specialty shops, an antique center, numerous dining options and varied entertainment. Daily.

Horatio Colony House Museum
199 Main St., Keene, 603-352-0460;
www.horatiocolonymuseum.org
Stately Federalist home (1806) of the son of prominent Keene mill owners. Features treasures collected from Colony's world travels; books, art, antique furniture. May-mid-October: Wednesday-Sunday; rest of year: by appointment.

Wyman Tavern
339 Main St., Keene, 603-352-1895
The 1762 scene of the first meeting of Dartmouth College trustees in 1770; now furnished in 1820s-style. June-September, Thursday-Saturday.

HOTELS
★★Best Western Sovereign Hotel
401 Winchester St., Keene,
603-357-3038, 800-780-7234;
www.bestwestern.com

131 rooms. Pets accepted; fee. Complimentary full breakfast. Restaurant. Bar. Indoor pool. **$**

RESTAURANTS

★★176 Main
176 Main St., Keene,
603-357-3100; www.176main.com

American menu. Lunch, dinner. Bar. Children's menu. Outdoor seating. Closed holidays. **$$**

★The Pub
131 Winchester St., Keene, 603-352-3135;
www.thepubrestaurant.com
American menu. Breakfast, lunch, dinner. Bar. Children's menu. **$**

LACONIA

On four lakes (Winnisquam, Opechee, Pauqus Bay and Winnipesaukee), Laconia is the commercial center of this area, known as the "Lakes Region." Besides the resort trade, it has numerous factories whose products include knitting machinery, hosiery, knitted fabrics, ball bearings and electronic components. The headquarters of the White Mountain National Forest is also located here.
Information: Chamber of Commerce, 11 Veterans Sq., 603-524-5531; www.laconia-weirs.org

WHAT TO SEE AND DO

M/S Mount Washington
Weirs Beach, 603-366-5531, 888-843-6686;
www.cruisenh.com
Cruise the waters of Lake Winnipesaukee, the largest lake in New Hampshire, and enjoy scenic mountain views aboard the M/S *Mount Washington*, which offers daily scenic and dinner dance cruises. Ports of call include Weirs Beach, Wolfeboro, Meredith, Alton Bay and Center Harbor. Mid-May-October; check website or call for schedule.

HOTELS

★★B. Mae's Resort Inn & Suites
Routes 11 and 11B, Gilford,
603-293-7526, 800-458-3877;

www.bmaesresort.com
82 rooms. Complimentary continental breakfast. Restaurant. Bar. Fitness room. Indoor pool, outdoor pool, whirlpool. **$**

★Barton's Motel
1330 Union Ave., Laconia, 603-524-5674;
www.bartonsmotel.com
41 rooms. Beach. Outdoor pool. **$**

RESTAURANTS

★Naswa Beach Bar and Grill
1086 Weirs Blvd., Laconia, 603-366-4341;
www.naswa.com
American menu. Lunch, dinner. Bar. Children's menu. Casual attire. Outdoor seating. **$$**

LINCOLN/NORTH WOODSTOCK

In a spectacular mountain setting, the villages of Lincoln and Woodstock lie at the junction of the road through Franconia Notch State Park and the Kancamagus Scenic Byway.
Information: Chamber of Commerce, Lincoln, 603-745-6621, 800-227-4191; www.linwoodcc.org

WHAT TO SEE AND DO

Loon Mountain Recreation Area
Hwy. 112, Lincoln, 603-745-8111;
www.loonmtn.com

A 7,100-foot gondola, two triple and four double chairlifts, one high-speed quad chairlift, pony lift, patrol, school, rentals, shops, snowmaking, restaurant, bar, nursery, lodge. Longest run 2 1/2

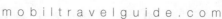

miles; vertical drop 2,100 feet. (Late November-mid-April, daily). Cross-country trails (December-March). Summer activities include mountain biking (rentals), bike tours, in-line skating, horseback riding, skate park, climbing wall. Gondola also operates Memorial Day-mid-October: daily.

Lost River Gorge
Lost River Rd., North Woodstock, 603-745-8031
Natural boulder caves, largest known granite pothole in the eastern United States; Paradise Falls; boardwalks with 1,900-foot glacial gorge; nature garden with 300 varieties of native shrubs and flowers; geology exhibits. Cafeteria, picnicking. Mid-May-mid-October: daily. Appropriate outdoor clothing recommended.

SPECIAL EVENTS
New Hampshire Highland Games
Loon Mountain, 603-229-1975, 800-358-7268; www.nhscot.org
Largest Scottish gathering in the eastern United States. Bands, competitions, concerts, workshops. Three days in September.

HOTELS
★★Indian Head Resort
664 U.S. Route 3, Lincoln, 603-745-8000, 800-343-8000; www.indianheadresort.com
98 rooms. Restaurant. Bar. Fitness room. Indoor pool, outdoor pool, whirlpool. Tennis. $

★★InnSeason Resorts South Mountain
Main St., Route 112, Lincoln, 603-745-2244, 800-654-6183; www.innseasonresorts.com
84 rooms. Fitness room. Indoor pool. $

★★Woodwards Resort
527 U.S. Route 3, Lincoln,
603-745-8141, 800-635-8968; www.woodwardsresort.com
80 rooms. Restaurant. Bar. Indoor pool. $$

★★Mountain Club on Loon
90 Loon Mountain Rd., Lincoln, 603-745-2244, 800-229-7829; www.mtnclub.com
This ski area is located at the base of Loon Mountain on the scenic Kancamagus Highway. This property offers lifts, ski shops and shuttle services, along with many on-site activities.
234 rooms. Two restaurants. Bar. Children's activity center. Fitness room, spa. Indoor pool, outdoor pool, children's pool, whirlpool. Ski in/ski out. $$

SPECIALTY LODGINGS
Woodstock Inn
135 Main St., North Woodstock, 603-745-3951, 800-321-3985; www.woodstockinnnh.com
Victorian house (1890).
24 rooms. Complimentary full breakfast. Restaurant. Bar. $

RESTAURANTS
★★Common Man
Pollard Rd., Lincoln, 603-745-3463; www.thecman.com
American menu. Dinner. Bar. Children's menu. $$

★★Gordi's Fish & Steak House
Kancamagus Hwy., Lincoln, 603-745-6635
Seafood, steak menu. Lunch, dinner. Bar. Children's menu. $$$

★Truants Taverne
96 Main St., North Woodstock, 603-745-2239
American menu. Lunch, dinner. Bar. Children's menu. $$

207

NEW HAMPSHIRE

★
★
★
★

LITTLETON

Littleton is a resort area a few miles northwest of the White Mountain National Forest, which maintains a Ranger District office in nearby Bethlehem. It is a regional commercial center, with industries that produce abrasives and electrical component parts. The Ammonoosuc River falls 235 feet on its way through the community.

Information: Chamber of Commerce, 120 Main St., 603-444-6561; www.littletonareachamber.com

WHAT TO SEE AND DO

Littleton Historical Museum

1 Cottage St., Littleton, 603-444-6435
Photographs, arts and crafts, stereographs, local memorabilia. April-November, Wednesday, or by appointment.

HOTELS

★★Eastgate Motor Inn

335 Cottage St., Littleton,
603-444-3971, 866-640-3561;
www.eastgatemotorinn.com
55 rooms. Pets accepted, some restrictions; fee. Complimentary continental breakfast. Restaurant. Bar. Outdoor pool, children's pool. $

★★★Adair Country Inn

80 Guider Lane, Bethlehem,
603-444-2600, 888-444-2600;
www.adairinn.com
Built in 1927, this inn is situated on 200 landscaped acres designed by the Olmsted Brothers. Guest rooms are furnished with antiques and original artwork and include afternoon tea and homemade desserts.

10 rooms. Children over 12 years only. Complimentary full breakfast. Wireless Internet access. Restaurant. Tennis. Closed three weeks in April and November. $$

SPECIALTY LODGINGS

Thayer's Inn

111 Main St., Littleton,
603-444-6469, 800-634-8179;
www.thayersinn.com

Historic inn (1843); antiques, library, sitting room. Cupola open to the public.
39 rooms. Pets accepted, some restrictions. $

★★Wayside

3738 Main St., Bethlehem,
603-869-3364, 800-448-9557;
www.thewaysideinn.com
26 rooms. Complimentary full breakfast. Restaurant. Bar. Tennis. Closed April and November. $

RESTAURANTS

★★Clam Shell

274 Dells Rd., Littleton, 603-444-6445
American, seafood menu. Lunch, dinner. Bar. Children's menu. $$

★Eastgate

335 Cottage St., Littleton, 603-444-3971;
www.eastgatemotorinn.com
American menu. Dinner. Bar. $

★★Italian Oasis

106 Main St., Littleton, 603-444-6995
Italian menu. Lunch, dinner. Bar. Converted Victorian home (circa 1890). Outdoor seating. $$

★★Rosa Flamingos

Main St., Bethlehem, 603-869-3111
Italian menu. Lunch, dinner, brunch. Bar. Children's menu. Casual attire. Reservations recommended. Outdoor seating. $$

★
★
★
★
★

MANCHESTER

Manchester is a city that has refused to bow to economic adversity. When the Amoskeag Manufacturing Company (cotton textiles), which had dominated Manchester's economy, failed in 1935, it left the city poverty-stricken. However, a group of citizens bought the plant for $5 million and revived the city. Now Manchester is northern New England's premier financial center.

Information: Chamber of Commerce, 889 Elm St., 603-666-6600; www.manchester-chamber.org

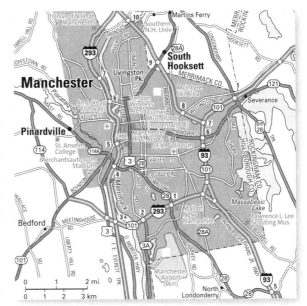

WHAT TO SEE AND DO

Currier Museum of Art

201 Myrtle Way, Manchester, 603-669-6144; www.currier.org

One of New England's leading small museums; 13th-to 20th-century European and American paintings and sculpture; New England decorative art; furniture, glass, silver and pewter; changing exhibitions, concerts, films, other programs. Tours of Zimmerman House, designed by Frank Lloyd Wright (call for reservations and times, fee). Wednesday-Monday.

Manchester Historic Association Millyard Museum

129 Amherst St., Manchester, 603-622-7531; www.manchesterhistoric.org

Museum and library with collections illustrating life in Manchester from pre-colonial times to present; permanent and changing exhibits; firefighting equipment; decorative arts, costumes, paintings. Tuesday-Saturday.

Science Enrichment Encounters Museum

200 Bedford St., Manchester, 603-669-0400; www.see-sciencecenter.org

More than 60 interactive, hands-on exhibits demonstrate basic science principles. Daily.

HOTELS

★★Quality Inn Bedford

121 S. River Rd., Bedford, 603-622-3766, 800-424-6423; www.wayfarerinn.com

190 rooms. Pets accepted; fee. Complimentary continental breakfast. Restaurant. Bar. Fitness room. Indoor pool, outdoor pool. Airport transportation available. $

★★Four Points by Sheraton

55 John Devine Dr., Manchester, 603-668-6110, 800-368-7764; www.fourpoints.com/manchester

120 rooms. Pets accepted; fee. High-speed Internet access, wireless Internet access. Restaurant. Bar. Fitness room. Indoor pool, whirlpool. Airport transportation available. $

★★Radisson Hotel Manchester

700 Elm St., Manchester, 603-625-1000, 800-333-3333; www.radisson.com/manchesternh

251 rooms. Pets accepted. High-speed Internet access, wireless Internet access. Restaurant. Bar. Fitness room. Indoor pool,

★
★
★
★

whirlpool. Airport transportation available. $

★★★Bedford Village Inn
2 Olde Bedford Way, Bedford,
603-472-2001, 800-852-1166;
www.bedfordvillageinn.com
This stately New England inn, a converted 1800s barn, offers all-suite accommodations and four-poster beds, Italian marble and whirlpool bathtubs.
14 rooms, all suites. Wireless Internet access. Restaurant. Bar. Airport transportation available. **$$$**

RESTAURANTS
★★★Bedford Village Inn
2 Village Inn Way, Bedford,
603-472-2001, 800-852-1166;
www.bedfordvillageinn.com

Originally part of a working farm (1810), this inn is surrounded by pristine gardens. Choose from eight separate dining rooms, each with its own distinct character (hand-painted murals, swag drapes, area rugs, or a roaring fireplace). The kitchen offers updated regional New England cuisine using only the freshest local ingredients.

American menu. Breakfast, lunch, dinner. Business casual attire. Reservations recommended. **$$$**

★Puritan Backroom
245 Hooksett Rd., Manchester,
603-623-3182; www.puritanbackroom.com
American menu. Lunch, dinner. Bar. Children's menu. Casual attire. Outdoor seating. **$$**

MEREDITH

Between Lakes Winnipesaukee and Waukewan in the Lakes Region, Meredith is a year-round recreation area.

Information: Chamber of Commerce, 272 Daniel Webster Hwy., 603-279-6121, 877-279-6121; www.meredithcc.org

WHAT TO SEE AND DO
League of New Hampshire Craftsmen—Meredith/Laconia Arts & Crafts
279 Daniel Webster Hwy., Meredith,
603-279-7920; www.nhcrafts.org
Work by some of New Hampshire's finest craftspeople. Daily.

Winnipesaukee Scenic Railroad
Meredith, 603-279-5253; www.hoborr.com
Scenic train rides along the shore of Lake Winnipesaukee. Board in Meredith or Weirs Beach. Memorial Day-October. Fall foliage trains to Plymouth.

HOTELS
★★★The Inn At Bay Point
312 Daniel Webster Hwy., Meredith,
603-279-7006, 800-622-6455;
www.millfalls.com
Right on the edge of Lake Winnipesaukee, this inn offers guests views of the lake from the large, comfortable rooms and also from

the dining area. Canoeing and other water sports are among the outdoor activities offered here, and there are plenty of shops and dining options in the surrounding area.

24 rooms. Complimentary continental breakfast. Restaurant. Bar. Spa. Closed midweek in winter. **$$**

SPECIALTY LODGINGS
Olde Orchard Inn
108 Lee Rd., Moultonborough,
603-476-5004, 800-598-5845;
www.oldeorchardinn.com
This quaint inn was built in 1790 and was converted to a bed-and-breakfast 150 years later. The cozy lounge has a fireplace.
9 rooms. Complimentary full breakfast. **$**

The Inn at Mill Falls
312 Daniel Webster Hwy., Meredith,
603-279-7006, 800-622-6455;
www.millfalls.com

210

NEW HAMPSHIRE

★
★
★
★
★

54 rooms. Two restaurants, bar. Fitness room, spa. Indoor pool. **$$**

RESTAURANTS

★Hart's Turkey Farm
Highways 3 and 104, Meredith, 603-279-6212; www.hartsturkeyfarm.com

American menu. Breakfast, lunch, dinner, brunch. Children's menu. Casual attire. **$$**

★★Mame's
8 Plymouth St., Meredith, 603-279-4631; www.mamesrestaurant.com
American, Italian menu. Lunch, dinner, brunch. Bar. Children's menu. Casual attire. Reservations recommended. **$$**

MOUNT WASHINGTON

Mount Washington is the central peak of the White Mountains and the highest point in the northeastern United States (6,288 feet). At the summit, there is a 54-acre state park with an information center, first-aid station, restaurant and gift shop. The mountain has the world's first cog railway, completed in 1869; a road to the top dates to 1861. P. T. Barnum called the view from the summit "the second-greatest show on earth."

The weather on Mount Washington is so violent that the timberline is at about 4,000 feet; in the Rockies it is nearly 10,000 feet. In the treeless zone are alpine plants and insects, some unique to the region. The weather station here recorded a wind speed of 231 miles per hour in April, 1934—a world record. The lowest temperature recorded was -49°F; the year-round average is below freezing. The peak gets nearly 15 feet of snow each year.

WHAT TO SEE AND DO

Cog Railway
Highway 302, Bretton Woods, 603-846-5404, 800-922-8825; www.thecog.com
Allow at least three hours for round trip. May-Memorial Day weekend: weekends; after Memorial Day weekend-November: daily.

Great Glen Trails
Highway 16, Gorham, 603-466-2333; www.greatglentrails.com
Located at the base of Mount Washington, this all-season, non-motorized, recreational trails park features biking programs (rentals), hiking programs (guided or self-guided), kayak and canoe tours and workshops in summer; cross-country skiing, snowshoeing and snow tubing in winter. Daily; closed April. For a detailed brochure with schedule and fees, visit Highway 16, Pinkham Notch, Gorham.

Mount Washington Auto Road
Highway 16, Gorham, 603-466-3988; www.mt-washington.com
The trip to the summit of Mount Washington takes approximately 30 minutes each way. Make sure your car is in good condition; check brakes before starting. Mid-May-mid-October: daily, weather permitting. Guided tour service available: daily.

Mount Washington Summit Museum
Highway 302, Sargent's Purchase. Top of Mount Washington; 603-466-3388
Displays on life in the extreme climate of the summit; rare flora and fauna; geology, history. Memorial Day-Columbus Day: daily.

211

NEW HAMPSHIRE

NASHUA

Originally a fur trading post, Nashua's manufacturing began with the development of Merrimack River water power early in the 19th century. The city is the second largest in New Hampshire.

Information: Greater Nashua Chamber of Commerce, 146 Main St., 603-881-8333; www.nashuachamber.com

WHAT TO SEE AND DO

Silver Lake State Park
Silver Lake Rd., Hollis, 603-465-2342
One-thousand-foot beach on a 34-acre lake; swimming, bathhouse; picnicking. Late June-Labor Day.

HOTELS

★Fairfield Inn
4 Amherst Rd., Merrimack, 603-424-7500, 800-228-2800; www.fairfieldinn.com
116 rooms. Complimentary continental breakfast. Outdoor pool. **$**

★★★Crowne Plaza
2 Somerset Pkwy., Nashua, 603-886-1200, 800-962-7482; www.crowneplazanashua.com
Just 15 miles from Manchester Airport and 40 miles from Boston's Logan Airport, this full-service hotel is in the heart of New Hampshire's high-tech area.
230 rooms. High-speed Internet access. Restaurant. Bar. Fitness room. Indoor pool. Airport transportation available. **$$**

★★Holiday Inn Nashua
9 Northeastern Blvd., Nashua, 603-888-1551, 888-801-5661.
208 rooms. Pets accepted; fee. High-speed Internet access, wireless Internet access. Restaurant. Bar. Fitness room. Outdoor pool.

★★★Sheraton Nashua Hotel
11 Tara Blvd., Nashua, 603-888-9970, 800-325-3535; www.sheraton.com
This contemporary hotel with Tudor-style architecture offers a comfortable stay for both business and leisure travelers. It is located near the highway in a corporate park with 16 acres of landscaped grounds. 336 rooms. Pets accepted, some restrictions. Wireless Internet access. Restaurant. Bar. Indoor pool, outdoor pool, whirlpool. Airport transportation available. **$$**

NEW LONDON

Located in the Lake Sunapee recreational area, this town has a charming main street and is close to many cross-country skiing and hiking trails.

Information: Chamber of Commerce, Main St., 603-526-6575, 877-526-6575; www.newlondonareanh.com

NEW HAMPSHIRE

HOTELS

★★★Inn at Pleasant Lake

853 Pleasant St., New London,
603-526-6271, 800-626-4907;
www.innatpleasantlake.com

Situated between the lake and Mount Kearsarge, this gabled country inn is decorated like a comfortable house and has access to a private beach.
10 rooms. Complimentary full breakfast. High-speed Internet access, wireless Internet access. Restaurant. Beach. Closed one week in April and two weeks in November. **$$**

New London Inn

353 Main St., New London,
603-526-2791, 800-526-2791;
www.newlondoninn.us

This historic inn is located on the main street of a quaint town. Each room is uniquely decorated, and some feature Jacuzzi tubs or TV/DVD players.
24 rooms. Pets accepted. Complimentary full breakfast. Wireless Internet access. Restaurant. Bar. Closed one week in November.**$**

SPECIALTY LODGINGS

Follansbee Inn

Highway 114, North Sutton,
603-927-4221, 800-626-4221;
www.follansbeeinn.com

This homey 1840 country inn, located on the south shore of Keyzar Lake, has a wraparound porch and individually decorated rooms.
18 rooms. Children over 10 years only. Complimentary full breakfast. **$**

RESTAURANTS

★★Millstone

74 Newport Rd., New London,
603-526-4201;
www.millstonerestaurant.com

American menu. Lunch, dinner, Sunday brunch. Bar. Children's menu. Casual attire. **$$**

★★New London Inn

353 Main St., New London,
603-526-2791, 800-526-2791;
www.newlondoninn.net

American menu. Dinner, Sunday brunch. Bar. Children's menu. Casual attire. Reservations recommended. Outdoor seating. Closed Monday. **$$**

NORTH CONWAY

The heart of the famous Mount Washington Valley region of the White Mountains, this area also includes Bartlett, Glen, Jackson, Conway, Redstone, Kearsarge and Intervale. Mount Washington, seen from the middle of Main Street, is one of the great views in the East.
Information: Mount Washington Valley Chamber of Commerce, 1267 Main St.,
603-356-5701, 800-367-3364; www.mtwashingtonvalley.org

WHAT TO SEE AND DO

Conway Scenic Railroad

38 Norcross Circle, North Conway,
603-356-5251; www.conwayscenic.com

Steam and diesel trains depart from restored Victorian station (1874) for an 11-mile (55-minute) round trip. The Valley Train explores the Saco River valley. Mid-May-October: daily; mid-April-mid-May, November-December: weekends. The Notch Train travels through Crawford Notch Mid-September-mid-October: daily; late June-mid-September: Tuesday-Thursday, Saturday. Railroad museum.

Echo Lake State Park

Highway 302, 603-356-2672

Mountain lake in the shadow of White Horse Ledge. Scenic road to 700-foot Cathedral Ledge, a dramatic rock formation; panoramic views of the White Mountains and the Saco River Valley. Swimming, picnicking. Late June-Labor Day.

Mount Cranmore

Highway 302, 800-786-6754;
www.cranmore.com

Express quad, triple, double chairlift to summit, three double chairlifts to north, south and east slopes, four surface lifts, patrol, school, rentals, snowmaking, restaurant, bar, day care. Longest run 1 3/4 miles; vertical drop 1,200 feet. November-April: daily.

HOTELS

★★Best Western Red Jacket Mountain View Resort & Conference Center
Highway 16, North Conway,
603-356-5411, 800-752-2538;
www.bestwestern.com
148 rooms. Wireless Internet access. Two restaurants, bar. Children's activity center. Fitness room, spa. Indoor pool, outdoor pool, whirlpool. Tennis. **$$**

★Comfort Inn
2001 White Mountain Highway,
North Conway, 603-356-8811,
866-647-8483; www.comfortinnnh.com
59 rooms. Complimentary continental breakfast. Wireless Internet access. Children's activity center. Fitness room. Indoor pool. **$**

★★The Fox Ridge
White Mountain Highway; Highway 16,
North Conway, 603-356-3151,
800-343-1804; www.redjacketresorts.com
136 rooms. Wireless Internet access. Restaurant. Bar. Children's activity center. Fitness room. Indoor pool, outdoor pool, whirlpool. Tennis. **$$**

★★Green Granite Inn
Highways 16 and 302, North Conway,
603-356-6901, 800-468-3666;
www.greengranite.com
91 rooms. Complimentary full breakfast. Children's activity center. Fitness room. Indoor pool, outdoor pool. **$$**

★★North Conway Grand Hotel
72 Common Court, North Conway,
603-356-9300, 800-648-4397;
www.northconwaygrand.com
200 rooms. Restaurant. Bar. Children's activity center. Fitness room. Indoor pool, whirlpool. Tennis. **$$**

★North Conway Mountain Inn
Main St., North Conway,
603-356-2803, 800-319-4405;
www.northconwaymountaininn.com
32 rooms. **$**

★Swiss Chalets Village Inn
Highway 16A, Intervale,
603-356-2232, 800-831-2727;
www.swisschaletsvillage.com
42 rooms. Pets accepted; fee. Complimentary continental breakfast. Outdoor pool. **$**

★★★White Mountain Hotel & Resort
W. Side Rd., North Conway,
603-356-7100, 800-533-6301;
www.whitemountainhotel.com
Beneath the Whitehorse and Cathedral ledges and Echo State Park, this elegant English country inn offers outdoor activities including cross-country skiing, hiking and rock climbing.
80 rooms. High-speed Internet access, wireless Internet access. Restaurant. Bar. Children's activity center. Fitness room. Outdoor pool, whirlpool. Golf, 9 holes. Tennis. Ski in/ski out. **$$**

SPECIALTY LODGINGS

1785 Inn
3582 N. White Mountain Hwy.,
North Conway, 603-356-9025,
800-421-1785; www.the1785inn.com
This colonial-style building (1785) is located on six acres and features original fireplaces and Victorian antiques. The inn has views of Mount Washington.
17 rooms. Complimentary full breakfast. Restaurant. Bar. **$**

Buttonwood Inn on Mt. Surprise
Mt. Surprise Rd., North Conway,
603-356-2625, 800-258-2625;
www.buttonwoodinn.com
Located on 17 wooded acres on the mountainside, this Cape Cod–style building (1820s) features antiques and a library.
10 rooms. Children over 12 years only. Complimentary full breakfast. Outdoor pool. **$$**

★
★
★
★
★

Cranmore Mountain Lodge

859 Kearsarge St., North Conway,
603-356-2044, 800-356-3596;
www.cml1.com

Located on 12 acres, this historic guest house (1860) was once owned by Babe Ruth's daughter and son-in-law. There are farm animals and a duck pond on the grounds.
21 rooms. Outdoor pool. **$**

Darby Field Country Inn

185 Chase Hill Rd., Albany,
603-447-2181, 800-426-4147;
www.darbyfield.com

This inn has views of the Presidential Mountains.
13 rooms. Children over 8 years only. Complimentary full breakfast. Outdoor pool. **$$**

Eastman Inn

2331 White Mountain Highway,
North Conway, 603-356-6707,
800-626-5855; www.eastmaninn.com

This classic three-story Victorian inn (1777) features a wraparound veranda and rich and tasteful decor. The central location is close to shopping and attractions in town.
14 rooms. Children over 15 years only. Complimentary full breakfast. **$$**

Merrill Farm Resort

428 White Mountain Hwy., North Conway,
603-447-3866, 800-445-1017;
www.merrillfarm.com

Just south of the town's center, this converted farmhouse (1885) is located on the Saco River and has cottages for overnight stays.

Nearby activities and attractions include skiing, golfing, covered bridges and shopping.
62 rooms. Complimentary continental breakfast. Indoor pool, whirlpool. **$**

Snowvillage Inn

Stewart Rd., Snowville,
603-447-2818, 800-447-4345;
www.snowvillageinn.com

18 rooms. Pets accepted, some restrictions. Complimentary full breakfast. Restaurant, bar. **$$**

RESTAURANTS

★★★1785 Inn

3582 White Mountain Hwy., North Conway,
603-356-9025, 800-421-1785;
www.the1785inn.com

This restaurant offers an extensive continental menu that includes creative veal chops with mushroom and cabernet sauvignon reduction and seared sea scallops with leeks and artichokes.
American, continental menu. Dinner. Bar. Casual attire. **$$**

★Bellini's

1857 White Mountain Hwy., North Conway,
603-356-7000; www.bellinis.com

American, Italian menu. Lunch, dinner. Bar. Children's menu. Casual attire. Outdoor seating. **$$**

★Horsefeathers

Main St., North Conway, 603-356-2687;
www.horsefeathers.com

American menu. Lunch, dinner, brunch. Bar. Children's menu. Casual attire. **$$**

PETERBOROUGH

This was the home of composer Edward MacDowell (1861-1908). Edward Arlington Robinson, Stephen Vincent Bent, Willa Cather and Thornton Wilder, among others, worked at the MacDowell Colony, a thriving artists' retreat, which made Peterborough famous.
Information: Greater Peterborough Chamber of Commerce, 603-924-7234;
www.peterboroughchamber.com

WHAT TO SEE AND DO

Miller State Park

Route 101 E., Peterborough, 603-924-3672

Atop the 2,288-foot Pack Monadnock Mountain; walking trails on summit; scenic drive; picnicking. June-Labor Day: daily; May and

Labor Day-November: Saturday-Sunday and holidays.

Peterborough Historical Society
19 Grove St., Peterborough, 603-924-3235
Exhibits on the history of the area; historical and genealogical library. Monday-Saturday.

HOTELS
★★★Hancock Inn
33 Main St., Hancock,
603-525-3318, 800-525-1789;
www.hancockinn.com
In operation since 1789, the interior of this country inn is reminiscent of 18th-century New England. Sit by the fire in the red-walled dining room and order the famous Shaker cranberry pot roast.
15 rooms. Pets accepted. Complimentary full breakfast. Wireless Internet access. Restaurant. Bar. **$$**

PLYMOUTH
Since 1795, Plymouth's varied industries have included lumber, pig iron, mattresses, gloves and sporting goods. It has been a resort center since the mid-19th century.
Information: Chamber of Commerce, 603-536-1001, 800-386-3678; www.plymouthnh.org

WHAT TO SEE AND DO
Mary Baker Eddy Historic House
58 Stinson Lake Rd., Rumney, 603-786-9943
Residence of Mary Baker Eddy from 1860 to 1862, prior to the founding of the Christian Science Church. May-October: Tuesday-Sunday.

HOTELS
★Cobblestone Inn
304 Main St., Plymouth, 603-536-2330; www.cobblestoneinnh.com
38 rooms. Pets accepted. Complimentary continental breakfast. Outdoor pool. **$**

216

★
★
★
★
★

PORTSMOUTH
A tour of Portsmouth's historic houses reveals architecture from the Colonial and Federal periods into the 19th century. The one-time capital of New Hampshire, Portsmouth was also the home port of a dynasty of merchant seamen who grew rich and built accordingly. The U.S. Navy Yard, located in Kittery, Maine, on the Piscataqua River, has long been Portsmouth's major industry. The peace treaty ending the Russo-Japanese War was signed at the Portsmouth Navy Yard in 1905.
Information: Greater Portsmouth Chamber of Commerce, 500 Market St., 603-436-3988; www.portsmouthchamber.org

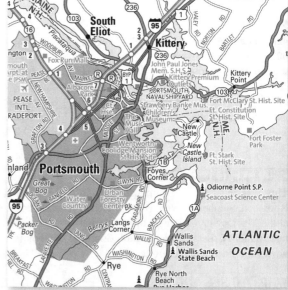

WHAT TO SEE AND DO

Children's Museum of Portsmouth

280 Marcy St., Portsmouth, 603-436-3853;
www.childrens-museum.org

Arts and science museum featuring mock submarine, space shuttle, lobster boat, exhibits and gallery. Summer and school vacations: daily; rest of year: Tuesday-Sunday.

Fort Constitution

New Castle, 603-436-1552

(1808) The first cannon was placed on this site in 1632; in 1694, it was known as Fort William and Mary. Information about a British order to stop gunpowder from coming into the colonies, brought by Paul Revere on December 13, 1774, caused the Sons of Liberty from Portsmouth, New Castle, and Rye to attack and capture a fort that held five tons of gunpowder the next day. Much of this powder was used at Bunker Hill by the Patriots. This uprising against the King's authority was one of the first overt acts of the Revolution. Little remains of the original fort except the base of its walls. Fort Constitution had been built on the same site by 1808; granite walls were added during the Civil War. Mid-June-early September: daily; late May-mid-June, late September-mid-October: weekends, holidays only.

Fort Stark State Historic Site

Wild Rose Lane, New Castle,
603-436-1552

A former portion of the coastal defense system dating to 1746, exhibiting many of the changes in military technology from the Revolutionary War through World War I. The fort is situated on Jerry's Point, overlooking the Piscataqua River, Little Harbor and Atlantic Ocean. Late May-mid-October: daily.

Isles of Shoals

315 Market St., Portsmouth, 603-431-5500

The M/V *Thomas Laighton* makes cruises to historic Isles of Shoals. Lobster clambake river cruises, fall foliage excursions and others. Party ship. Mid-June-Labor Day: daily.

Governor John Langdon House

143 Pleasant St., Portsmouth,
603-436-3205

(1784) John Langdon served three terms as governor of New Hampshire and was the first president *pro tempore* of the U.S. Senate. The house's exterior proportions are monumental and the interior is embellished with excellent woodcarving and fine Portsmouth-area furniture. George Washington was entertained here in 1789. Surrounded by landscaped grounds with gazebo, rose and grape arbor and restored perennial garden beds. Tours June-mid-October: Friday-Sunday.

John Paul Jones House

43 Middle St., Portsmouth, 603-436-8420

(1758) Where the famous naval commander twice boarded; now a museum containing period furniture, collections of costumes, china, glass, documents, weapons. Guided tours June-mid-October: daily.

Moffatt-Ladd House

154 Market St., Portsmouth, 603-436-8221

Built in 1763 by Captain John Moffatt; later the home of General William Whipple, his son-in-law, a signer of the Declaration of Independence. Many original 18th and 19th-century furnishings. Formal gardens. Mid-June-mid-October, daily.

Rundlet-May House

364 Middle St., Portsmouth, 603-436-3205

Federalist, three-story 1807 mansion. House sits on terraces and retains its original 1812 courtyard and garden layout; landscaped grounds. House contains family furnishings and accessories, including many fine examples of Federalist craftsmanship and the latest technologies of its time. Guided tours. Grounds available for rental. June-October: first Saturday of the month.

Warner House

150 Daniel St., Portsmouth, 603-436-5909

(1716) One of New England's finest Georgian houses, with scagliola in the dining room, restored mural paintings on the staircase walls, a lightning rod on the west wall

217

said to have been installed by Benjamin Franklin in 1762, five portraits by Joseph Blackburn, appropriate furnishings. Guided tours. June-mid-October: Monday-Saturday; Sunday afternoons.

Wentworth-Gardner House
50 Mechanic St., Portsmouth,
603-436-4406
(1760) Excellent example of Georgian architecture. Elaborate woodwork and main staircase. Mid-June-mid-October: Tuesday-Saturday afternoons.

Strawbery Banke Museum
454 Court St., Portsmouth, 603-433-1100;
www.strawberybanke.org
Restoration of a 10-acre historic waterfront neighborhood; site of the original Portsmouth settlement. 42 buildings dating from 1695 to 1950. Includes nine houses: Captain Keyran Walsh House (1796), Governor Goodwin Mansion (1811), Chase House (1762), Captain John Wheelwright House (1780), Thomas Bailey Aldrich House (1790), Drisco House (1790s), Rider-Wood House (1840s), Abbott Grocery Store (1943) and the William Pitt Tavern (1766). Shops, architectural exhibits, pottery shop and demonstrations, family programs and activities, special events, tours. May-October: Monday-Saturday, Sunday afternoons; November-April: Thursday-Sunday; closed January.

HOTELS

★Fairfield Inn
650 Borthwick Ave., Portsmouth,
603-436-6363, 800-228-2800;
www.marriott.com/psmfi
105 rooms. Complimentary continental breakfast. High-speed Internet access, wireless Internet access. Outdoor pool. $

★★Holiday Inn
300 Woodbury Ave., Portsmouth,
603-431-8000, 888-465-4329;
www.holiday-inn.com
130 rooms. Restaurant. Bar. Fitness room. Indoor pool. $$

★The Port Inn
505 Highway 1 Bypass S., Portsmouth,
603-436-4378, 800-282-7678;
www.theportinn.com
57 rooms. Complimentary continental breakfast. High-speed Internet access, wireless Internet access. Outdoor pool. $

★★★Sheraton Harborside Hotel Portsmouth
250 Market St., Portsmouth,
603-431-2300, 800-325-3535;
www.sheratonportsmouth.com
This large New England–style hotel features a brick and granite exterior with large-paneled windows. The interior is inviting and stylish, and the location is in the downtown historic district on the Piscataqua River.
220 rooms. Pets accepted, some restrictions. Restaurant. Bar. Fitness room. Indoor pool. Business center. $$

SPECIALTY LODGINGS
Sise Inn
40 Court St., Portsmouth,
603-433-1200, 877-747-3466;
www.siseinn.com
This Queen Anne–style home was built in 1881 for the prosperous businessman and merchant John E. Sise.
34 rooms. Complimentary full breakfast. Wireless Internet access. $$

SALEM
This southern New Hampshire town was once part of Massachusetts. Many of its residence commute to Boston.
Information: Greater Salem Chamber of Commerce, 224 N. Broadway, 603-893-3177;
www.salemnhchamber.org

WHAT TO SEE AND DO

America's Stonehenge
105 Haverhill Rd., North Salem, 603-893-8300; www.stonehengeusa.com
A megalithic calendar site dated to 2000 BC, with 22 stone buildings on more than 30 acres. The main site features a number of stone-constructed chambers and is surrounded by miles of stone walls containing large, shaped monoliths that indicate the rising and setting of the sun at solstice and equinox, as well as other astronomical alignments, including lunar. Daily.

Robert Frost Farm
Highway 28, Derry, 603-432-3091
Home of poet Robert Frost from 1900 to 1911; period furnishings; audiovisual display; poetry-nature trail. Mid-June-Labor Day: Wednesday-Sunday; mid-May-mid-June: weekends.

HOTELS

★Fairfield Inn
8 Keewaydin Dr., Salem, 603-893-4722, 800-228-2800; www.fairfieldinn.com
105 rooms. Pets accepted; fee. Complimentary continental breakfast. Outdoor pool. $

★★Holiday Inn
1 Keewaydin Dr., Salem, 603-893-5511, 888-465-4329; www.holiday-inn.com
85 rooms. Pets accepted; fee. Complimentary continental breakfast. Restaurant. Fitness room. Outdoor pool. $

SUNAPEE

This is a year-round resort community on Lake Sunapee and a popular weekend and summer escape for Bostonians.

Information: New LondonLake Sunapee Region Chamber of Commerce,603-526-6575, 877-526-6575; www.lakesunapeenh.org

WHAT TO SEE AND DO

Snowhill at Eastman Ski Area
6 Club House Lane, Grantham, 603-863-4500; www.eastman-lake.com
Ski Touring Center has 30 kilometers of cross-country trails; patrol, school, rentals; bar, restaurant. Summer facilities include Eastman Lake (swimming, boating, fishing); 18-hole golf, tennis, indoor pool, hiking. December-March: daily.

HOTELS

★Burkehaven at Sunapee
79 Burkehaven Hill Rd., Sunapee, 603-763-2788, 800-567-2788; www.burkehavenatsunapee.com
10 rooms. Outdoor pool. Tennis. $

SPECIALTY LODGINGS

Candlelite Inn
5 Greenhouse Lane, Bradford, 603-938-5571, 888-812-5571; www.candleliteinn.com
Built in 1897; gazebo porch.
6 rooms. Complimentary full breakfast. $

Dexters Inn & Tennis Club
258 Stagecoach Rd., Sunapee, 603-763-5571, 800-232-5571; www.dextersnh.com
On 20-acre estate.
2 story. Pets accepted, some restrictions; fee. Complimentary full breakfast. Outdoor pool. Tennis. $$

TWIN MOUNTAIN

Information: Chamber of Commerce, 800-245-8946; www.twinmountain.org

HOTELS

★Four Seasons Motor Inn
Birch Rd., and Route 3, Twin Mountain,
603-846-5708, 800-228-5708;
www.4seasonsmotorinn.com
24 rooms. Outdoor pool. **$**

★Shakespeare's Inn
675 Highway 3, Twin Mountain,
603-846-5562, 888-846-5562;
www.shakespearesinn.com
33 rooms. Restaurant. Outdoor pool. Tennis. **$**

SPECIALTY LODGINGS

Northern Zermatt Inn & Motel
529 Highway 3 N., Twin Mountain,
603-846-5533, 800-535-3214;
www.zermattinn.com
Former boarding house (circa 1900) for
loggers and railroad workers.
17 rooms. Pets accepted, some restrictions.
Complimentary continental breakfast. Outdoor pool. **$**

WATERVILLE VALLEY

Although the resort village of Waterville Valley was developed in the late 1960s, the surrounding area has attracted tourists since the mid-19th century, when summer vacationers stayed at the Waterville Inn. Completely surrounded by the White Mountain National Forest, the resort, approximately 11 miles northeast of Campton, offers a variety of winter and summer activities and spectacular views of the mountains.
Information: Waterville Valley Region Chamber of Commerce, Campton, 603-726-3804, 800-237-2307; www.watervillevalleyregion.com

WHAT TO SEE AND DO

Waterville Valley Ski Area
1 Ski Area Rd., Waterville Valley,
800-468-2553; www.waterville.com
Three double, two triple chairlifts, two quad chairlifts, T-bar, J-bar, four platter pulls, patrol, school, retail, rental and repair shops, snowmaking, restaurants, lounge and nursery. 52 ski trails; longest run three miles; vertical drop 2,020 feet. Half-day rates. Mid-November-mid-April, daily. Ski Touring Center with 46 miles of cross-country trails, rentals, school, restaurants. Summer facilities include nine-hole golf, 18 clay tennis courts, small boating, hiking, fishing, bicycling; entertainment. Indoor sports center (daily). Contact Waterville Valley Resort, Town Square.

HOTELS

★★Snowy Owl Inn
4 Village Rd., Waterville Valley,
603-236-8383, 800-766-9969;
www.snowyowlinn.com
83 rooms. Pets accepted, some restrictions.
Complimentary continental breakfast.
Fitness room. Indoor pool, outdoor pool, whirlpool. **$**

★★Valley Inn & Tavern
1 Tecumseh Rd., Waterville Valley,
603-236-8336, 800-343-0969;
www.valleyinn.com
52 rooms. Complimentary continental breakfast. Restaurant. Bar. Fitness room. Indoor/outdoor pool, whirlpool. **$**

RESTAURANTS

★★William Tell
Route 49, Thornton, 603-726-3618;
www.nhwilliamtell.com
American, Continental menu. Dinner. Bar. Children's menu. Outdoor seating. Closed Wednesday. **$$**

White Mountain National Forest

This national forest includes the Presidential Range and a large part of the White Mountains. With more than 100 miles of roads and 1,128 miles of foot trails, there is much to see. The Appalachian Trail, with eight hostels, winds over some spectacular peaks—eight tower more than a mile above sea level (the highest is Mount Washington at 6,288 feet). Twenty-two mountains rise more than 4,000 feet and there are several well-defined ranges, divided by deep "notches" and broader valleys. Clear streams, mountain lakes and ponds dot the landscape and deer, bears, moose and bobcats roam throughout the area.

There is lodging within the forest; for information and reservations, contact the Appalachian Mountain Club, Pinkham Notch, Gorham, New Hampshire 03581. 603-466-2727. There are also many resorts, campsites, picnicking and recreational spots in private and state-owned areas. A visitor center (daily) is at the Saco Ranger Station, 33 Kancamagus Highway, Conway, New Hampshire 03818. 603-447-5448. Information stations are also located at exits 28 and 32, off Interstate 93 and at Franconia Notch State Park Visitor Center. For further information, contact the Supervisor, White Mountain National Forest, 719 N. Main St., Laconia, New Hampshire 03246. 603-528-8721.

The following cities and villages in and near the forest are included in this book: Bartlett, Bretton Woods, Franconia, Franconia Notch State Park, Gorham, Jackson, Lincoln/North Woodstock Area, Mount Washington, North Conway, Pinkham Notch, Twin Mountain and Waterville Valley.

WOLFEBORO

Wolfeboro has been a resort area for more than two centuries. It's the oldest summer resort in America, but come winter, it's a ski touring center with 40 miles of groomed trails. Information: Chamber of Commerce, 312 Central Ave., 603-569-2200, 800-516-5324; www.wolfeborochamber.com

WHAT TO SEE AND DO

Clark House
37 S. Main St., Wolfeboro, 603-569-4997
Wolfeboro Historical Society is housed in the Clark family homestead (1778), a one-room schoolhouse (circa 1820) and a firehouse museum. Clark House has period furnishings and memorabilia; the firehouse museum contains restored firefighting equipment dating to 1842. July-August, Wednesday-Saturday.

Wright Museum
77 Center St., Wolfeboro, 603-569-1212; www.wrightmuseum.org
Showcases American enterprise during World War II. Collection of tanks, Jeeps and other military vehicles, period memorabilia. May-October, daily; weekends only April and November; closed December-March.

HOTELS

★★★The Wolfeboro Inn
90 N. Main St., Wolfeboro, 603-569-3016, 800-451-2389; www.wolfeboroinn.com
Built in 1812, this inn is located on Lake Winnipesaukee in one of America's oldest summer resort towns. Many rooms offer Wolfeboro Bay views and all include a boat ride and private beach access during summer months.
40 rooms. Complimentary continental breakfast. Restaurant. Bar. **$$**

RHODE ISLAND

★

★

★

★

★

RHODE ISLAND

RHODE ISLAND'S MOTTO IS "HOPE," BUT A MORE APPROPRIATE MAXIM MIGHT BE "SIZE DOESN'T matter." Yes, the wee state is the smallest in the nation, more petite even than most neighboring state counties. But its pint size belies its influence as a historical, cultural, and natural Mecca—one that road trippers would be remiss to miss. For starters, the Ocean State has more than 400 miles of coastline, replete with sunning, swimming, sailing and fishing enclaves. Then there are the inland 1,000 or so square miles, studded with postcard-perfect working farms, quaint Colonial inns and protected nature reserves. Cities such as Providence and Newport supply the state with first-rate lodging and modern cuisine, while isles like Block Island give the harried a place to unwind.

All of this would no doubt have blown the feather cap off explorer Giovanni da Verrazano, who landed in Narragansett Bay in 1524, but it might not have surprised Roger Williams. Like thousands after him, Williams moved to Rhode Island to get away from it all. True, the "all" in his case was the puritanical tyranny of Massachusetts but still, his tolerant 1636 settlement set the tone for times to come. The area quickly became known for its policy of religious and political freedom and, in 1663, King Charles II granted it a royal charter, creating the state of Rhode Island.

Since then, the region has become a seat of firsts: Rhode Islanders were among the first colonists to attack the British; on May 4, 1776, the state was the first to proclaim independence (a full two months before the Declaration was signed); resident Samuel Slater built America's first water-powered cotton mill in 1790; and, in 1876, Newport held the country's first-ever polo match. And it may not have been the first watering hole ever built, but Newport's 1673 White Horse Tavern is the oldest operating pub in the United States. It's small, but sturdy and still going strong. Information: www.visitrhodeisland.com

★ SPOTLIGHT

★ Rhode Island is the smallest state in the country.

★ In 1895, the state was home to the first open golf tounament.

BLOCK ISLAND

Twelve miles off the state mainland and a short ferry ride from Montauk, Block Island seems a world away. Blessedly absent from the 21-square-mile retreat are Long Island's social-climbing weekenders and Newport's summer hordes. The scene here just feels milder and, technically, it is—once named Rhode Island's "air conditioned" resort, the atoll is up to 15 degrees cooler than the rest of the state. Named for Dutch explorer

RHODE ISLAND'S EASTERN COASTLINE

Summer in Rhode Island's South County means beaches, boating and basking in the sun. It also means tourists galore. Navigating Newport traffic in August can bring out road rage in the mildest mannered of drivers; waiting in epic lines for ice cream can be a chore. Escape the crowds by taking a daytrip along the state's quiet eastern coastline, through the (almost) untouched towns of Bristol, Tiverton and Little Compton. From downtown Providence, take Highway 195 east to exit 7, Highway 114 South. Drive through Barrington, Warren and Bristol. (Dozens of antique and second-hand shops line Warren's Main and Water streets.) Highway 114 becomes Hope Street in Bristol, where stately Federal-era houses (many of them now B&Bs) hint at the town's pre-Civil War wealth. Continue over the Mount Hope Bridge into Portsmouth, and turn left onto Highway 24. Cross the Sakonnet River Bridge into Tiverton, and turn right onto Highway 77 South. At the lone traffic light on 77, an intersection with Highway 179, is Tiverton Four Corners. Pause here for shopping and lunch at the town's boutiques and eateries, and don't miss a cone from1920s sweet shop Gray's Ice Cream. Continue south on 77 toward Little Compton, past open fields with panoramic views of Narragansett Bay. Once a productive agricultural area, Little Compton is now a wealthy summer community; the restored-farmhouses-cum-stately-estates are a sight to be seen. You can double back on the same route or turn right onto Highway 24 North in Tiverton and drive into Fall River, Massachusetts, then head west to Providence on Highway 195. **Approximately 40 miles.**

224

RHODE ISLAND

Adriaen Block, who landed here in 1614, the island was once a low-key fishing and farming community. Today, it's still low-key, and draws burnt-out city slickers and nature enthusiasts to its white-sanded shores. More than 40 rare and endangered species of plants and animals live here; most are protected by public land trusts like The Nature Conservancy, which designated Block Island "one of the twelve last great places in the Western Hemisphere."

Information: Chamber of Commerce, Water Street, Block Island, 401-466-2982, 800-383-2474; www.blockislandchamber.com

WHAT TO SEE AND DO

Mohegan Bluffs
West of the Southeast Light lighthouse off Mohegan Trail, these grand 185-foot clay cliffs provide sightseers with an unparalleled ocean view.

New Harbor
One mile west of the Mohegan Bluffs on Ocean Avenue, the mammoth New Harbor was formed when town planners cut through a sand bar to merge the sea with Great Salt Pond.

North Light
Built in 1867 at the tip of the island near Settler's Rock, this former lighthouse now houses a maritime museum. Its surrounding dunes host a seagull rookery and wildlife sanctuary.

HOTELS

★★Spring House
52 Spring St., Block Island,
401-466-5844, 800-234-9263;
www.springhousehotel.com
50 rooms. Closed in winter. Complimentary continental breakfast. Restaurant. Bar. Airport transportation available. **$$**

SPECIALTY LODGINGS

The 1661 Inn & Guest House
1 Spring St., Block Island,
401-466-2421, 800-626-4773;
www.blockislandresorts.com
21 rooms. Complimentary full breakfast.
Airport transportation available. **$$$**

RESTAURANTS

★Finn's Seafood
212 Water St., Block Island, 401-466-2473
Seafood menu. Lunch, dinner. Bar. Children's menu. Casual attire. **$$**

★★★Hotel Manisses Dining Room
1 Spring St., Block Island, 401-466-2836;
www.blockislandresorts.com
A discreet, knowledgeable staff welcomes diners to this stately restaurant praised for its seafood-heavy contemporary American menu. Romantics favor dining in the glass-enclosed garden room; sweet tooths adore rich homemade desserts like layered banana cream cake and Italian-Style hot chocolate. American menu. Dinner. Closed November-April. Bar. Reservations recommended. Outdoor seating. **$$$**

★Mohegan Cafe
Water St., Block Island, 401-466-5911
American menu. Lunch, dinner. Bar. Casual attire. **$$**

BRISTOL

Quaint little Bristol's history is surprisingly rife with strife. In the late 1600s, the Native American rebel leader King Philip headquartered his Wampanoag troops in the area, preparing them for the country's first major Colonist vs. Indian battle. The resulting year-long King Philip's War began and ended on the Bristol peninsula, between Mount Hope and Narragansett bays. Civil War officer—and later, state governor and senator—General Ambrose Burnside also earned his military stripes in Bristol, which by the turn of the 18th century had become the fourth-busiest port in the United States. Today, the town is well-known for its postcard-perfect, sea-side feel and the storied Herreshoff Boatyard where many an America's Cup champion was built.
Information: East Bay County Chamber of Commerce, 654 Metacom Ave., Warren, 401-245-0750; www.eastbaychamber.org

WHAT TO SEE AND DO

Blithewold Mansion and Gardens
101 Ferry Rd., Bristol, 401-253-2707;
www.blithewold.org
The 45-room mansion, with its manicured trees, flowers and gardens combine with a sweeping sea view to put visitors' aesthetic senses on overload. Concerts are held on the grounds in the summer. Mansion, mid-April-Columbus Day: Wednesday-Sunday 10 a.m.-4 p.m.; grounds, daily 10 a.m.-5 p.m.

Coggeshall Farm Museum, Colt State Park
Poppasquash Rd., Bristol, 401-253-9062
Set in the middle of Colt State Park, this working 18th-century farm has fresh vegetables and herbs, as well as colonial craft demonstrations. Visitors with extra time can cruise the park's three-mile scenic drive around the former Colt family estate on Narragansett Bay, or take advantage of area fishing, boating, hiking, picnicking and seasonal concerts in Stone Barn. Farm museum, March-September: daily 10 a.m.-6 p.m.; October-February: daily 10 a.m.-dusk.

Herreshoff Marine Museum
1 Burnside St., Bristol, 401-253-5000;
www.herreshoff.org
The Herreshoff Manufacturing Company produced some of the world's greatest yachts, including eight winners of the America's Cup. Permanent exhibits include big boats, steam engines, and photographs and memorabilia from the "golden age of yachting." May-October: daily 10 a.m.-5 p.m.

225

RHODE ISLAND

★
★
★
★

SPECIALTY LODGINGS

Rockwell House Inn
610 Hope St., Bristol,
401-253-0040, 800-815-0040;
www.rockwellhouseinn.com
One block from Bristol Harbor, this 1809 inn is set on a half-acre of land that boasts the state's largest tulip tree. Guest rooms are filled with antique furniture and cooled by new ceiling fans. The restored property features a mix of architectural styles— Federal, Georgian, Victorian—and is walking distance to Narragansett Bay and Bristol's many antiques shops and restaurants.
4 rooms. Children over 12 years only. Complimentary full breakfast. **$$**

Williams Grant Inn
154 High St., Bristol,
401-253-4222, 800-596-4222;
www.wmgrantinn.com
5 rooms. Children over 12 years only. Complimentary full breakfast. **$**

RESTAURANTS

★★Lobster Pot
119-121 Hope St., Bristol, 401-253-9100;
www.lobsterpotri.com
American, seafood menu. Lunch, dinner. Closed Monday; also two weeks in March. Bar. Business casual attire. Reservations recommended. Outdoor seating. **$$**

★★The Nat Porter
125 Water St., Warren, 401-289-0373;
www.natporter.com
American, seafood menu. Dinner. Bar. Casual attire. Reservations recommended. Closed Monday. **$$**

KINGSTON

Home to the University of Rhode Island, Kingston is a melting pot of enterprising coeds and laid-back old-timers. The city's early settlers were farmers, and their legacy lives on in the Biscuit City neighborhood's water-powered mill. Legal eagles love Kingston for its legislative lore—the state constitution and an early anti-slavery law were ratified here. A fertile flood plain lies on the outskirts of town; geologists believe it was once an ancient river.
Information: Chamber of Commerce, 328 Main St., Wakefield; 401-783-2801;
www.southcountyri.com

WHAT TO SEE AND DO

Kingston Library
2605 Kingston Rd., Kingston,
401-783-8254;
web.provlib.org/SkiLib/skk.html
Once visited by George Washington and Benjamin Franklin, the library housed the Rhode Island General Assembly when the British occupied Newport. Monday-Saturday.

SPECIAL EVENTS

Wakefield Rotary Balloon Festival
University of Rhode Island, 404 Wordens Pond Rd., Kingston, 401-783-1770
The two-day event features hot air balloon rides, parachute demonstrations, arts and crafts, and music. Late July or early August.

SPECIALTY LODGINGS

Larchwood Inn
521 Main St., Wakefield,
401-783-5454, 800-275-5450;
www.larchwoodinn.com
20 rooms. Restaurant. Bar. **$**

RESTAURANTS

★★Larchwood Inn
521 Main St., Wakefield,
401-783-5454, 800-275-5450;
www.larchwoodinn.com
American menu. Breakfast, lunch, dinner. Closed Monday. Bar. Children's menu. Casual attire. Reservations recommended. Outdoor seating. **$$**

NARRAGANSETT

Before there was Monte Carlo, there was Narragansett. The southern Rhode Island city was once home to a lavish McKim, Mead and White designed casino. Several summer "cottages" and hotels were built to house the well-heeled who flocked here to hobnob and gamble in the late 19th and early 20th centuries. The casino was devastated by fire in 1900, but its Tower still stands on Ocean Road. Today, Narragansett—named for its indigenous people—counts fishing and tourism as its leading industries. The city is also home to the University of Rhode Island's renowned Graduate School of Oceanography.

Information: Narragansett Chamber of Commerce, The Towers Narragansett Visitors Center, Ocean Rd., Narragansett; 401-783-7121; www.narragansettri.com/chamber

WHAT TO SEE AND DO

Block Island Ferry
Galilee State Pier, 304 Great Island Rd., Point Judith, 401-783-4613
Automobile ferries to Block Island from Point Judith and Newport. Daily.

Point Judith
1460 Ocean Rd., Narragansett, 401-789-0444
The lighthouse and station are closed to the public, but strolling Point Judith's historical grounds is free.

South County Museum
Strathmore St., Narragansett, 401-783-5400; www.southcountymuseum.org
The museum exhibits 19th-century Rhode Island antique costumes, vehicles, toys, and nautical equipment, as well as farm and blacksmithing displays. Also: a historic country kitchen, general store, cobbler's shop, and a complete turn-of-the-century letterpress print shop. May-June, September-October: Friday-Saturday 10 a.m.-4 p.m., Sunday noon-4 p.m.; July-Aug: Wednesday-Saturday 10 a.m.-4 p.m., Sunday noon-4 p.m.

The Towers
35 Ocean Rd., Narragansett, 401-782-2597; www.thetowersri.com
In 1900, McKim, Mead, and White's grandiose casino—the landmark that solidified Narragansett as a summer Mecca to the rich and fashionable—was destroyed by fire. This Romanesque arch entryway, flanked by conical towers, is the only structural element that remains. Various public events throughout summer.

SPECIAL EVENTS

Mid-Winter New England Surfing Championship
Narragansett Town Beach, 170 Clarke Rd., Narragansett, 401-723-8795; www.sne.surfesa.org
For information, contact the Northeastern Surfing Association, 126 Sayles Ave., Pawtucket, 02860. Third Saturday in February.

RESTAURANTS

★★Coast Guard House
40 Ocean Rd., Narragansett, 401-789-0700; www.thecoastguard.house.com
American, seafood menu. Lunch, dinner, Sunday brunch. Bar. Children's menu. Casual attire. Outdoor seating. Closed early January-mid-February. $$

RHODE ISLAND

NEWPORT

Had Jay Gatsby had a second summer home, it might have been in Newport. The laid-back resort town was once the epicenter of East Coast summer society, where the rich and fabulous—August Belmont, Ward McAllister, William Astor, Stuyvesant Fish—built mega-mansions along the city's now-public Cliff Walk. Their lavish and often outrageous soirees, some costing upwards of $300,000, were the talk of early 20th century Rhode Island. World War I dampened the revelry considerably, though many modern-day blue bloods still flock here for various seasonal affairs.

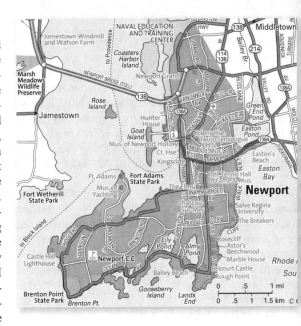

Social registries aside, Newport is home to Rhode Island's first school and newspaper, as well as the country's earliest Quaker and Jewish communities. During the Revolution, it was occupied by the British for two years, before being recaptured by French allies. Throughout its history, the city has been famous for its boating and yachting culture—shipbuilders and sailors still abound in town.

Information: Newport County Convention & Visitors Bureau, 23 America's Cup Ave., Newport, 401-849-8048, 800-976-5122; www.gonewport.com

SPOT★ LIGHT

★NEWPORT HOSTED THE FIRST AMERICAN CIRCUS IN 1774.

★JOHN F. AND JACQUELINE KENNEDY WERE MARRIED IN NEWPORT IN 1953.

★THE FIRST JAIL SENTENCE FOR SPEEDING WAS ISSUED IN NEWPORT IN 1904.

WHAT TO SEE AND DO

Brick Market

127 Thames St., Newport, 401-846-0813; www.brickmarketnewport.com

Home of the Newport Historical Society, the Brick Market was built by Touro Synagogue architect Peter Harrison in 1762. The restored building, which once served as a market and granary, is now full of boutiques and restaurants. Daily.

Cliff Walk

Memorial Blvd., Newport, 401-847-1355; www.cliffwalk.com

This scenic walk overlooking the Atlantic Ocean adjoins many of Newport's famous cottages. It was designated a National Recreational Trail in 1975.

Friends Meeting House

Farewell and Marlborough Streets, Newport, 401-846-0813; www.newporthistorical.org

The site of the New England Yearly Meeting of the Society of Friends from 1699 to 1905. The expanded meeting house spans three centuries of architecture and construction. Guided tours through Newport Historical Society. Mid-June-August: Thursday-Saturday, tours hourly 10 a.m.-3 p.m.; otherwise by appointment.

Historic Mansions and Houses

Combination tickets to the Elms, the Breakers, Rosecliff, Marble House, Hunter House, Chateau-sur-Mer, Kingscote and Green Animals topiary gardens are available at any of these houses.

Astor's Beechwood

580 Bellevue Ave., Newport, 401-846-3772
Italianate summer residence of Mrs. Caroline Astor—that's *the* Mrs. Astor. A theatrical tour of house includes actors portraying Mrs. Astor's servants and society guests. Mid-May-mid-December: daily; rest of year: weekends only.

Belcourt Castle

657 Bellevue Ave., Newport, 401-846-0669
Designed by Richard Morris Hunt in French château style, this 1891-era 62-room house was the residence of Oliver Hazard Perry Belmont and his wife, Alva Vanderbilt Belmont. Belmont loved horses and his stables sit inside the main structure. The castle contains the largest collection of antiques and objets d'art in Newport. Tea served. Special events scheduled throughout year. Daily; closed January.

Breakers

44 Ochre Point Ave., Newport,
401-847-1000
The 70-room, northern Italian palazzo designed by Richard Morris Hunt is the largest of all Newport cottages. The children's playhouse cottage has a scale-size kitchen, fireplace and playroom. The mansion was built for Mr. and Mrs. Cornelius Vanderbilt in 1895. Daily.

Chateau-sur-Mer

474 Bellevue Ave., Newport, 401-847-1000
This 1852 Victorian mansion was remodeled in 1872 by Richard Morris Hunt and has landscaped grounds with a Chinese moon gate. Built for William S. Wetmore, who made his fortune in the China trade. Late June-early October, daily.

Edward King House

Aquidneck Park, 35 King St., Newport,
401-846-7426, 866-878-6954
Richard Upjohn's 1895 mansion is considered one of the finest Italianate houses in the country. It's now used as senior citizens' center. Monday-Friday.

Elms

367 Bellevue Ave., Newport, 401-847-1000
Modeled after the 18th-century Chateau d'Asnieres near Paris, this restored cottage from Newport's gilded age boasts elaborate interiors and formal, sunken gardens. The 1901 home was built for Edward J. Berwind, a Philadelphia coal magnate. May-October: daily; November-March: Saturday-Sunday.

Hunter House

54 Washington St., Newport, 401-847-1000
An outstanding example of Colonial architecture, the 1748 Hunter House features a gambrel roof, 12-on-12 panel windows and a broken pediment doorway. It's furnished with pieces by famous 18th-century cabinetmakers Townsend and Goddard. Late June-late September: daily.

Kingscote

253 Bellevue Ave., Newport, 401-847-1000
A Gothic Revival cottage designed by Richard Upjohn. In 1881, McKim, Mead, and White added the "aesthetic" dining room, which features a Tiffany-glass wall and Chinese paintings and porcelains. Built for George Noble Jones of Savannah, Georgia, Kingscote is considered the nation's first true summer "cottage." June-October: daily.

Marble House

596 Bellevue Ave., Newport, 401-847-1000
The front gates, entrance and central hall of this 1892 house are modeled after Versailles. It's named for the many kinds of marble used on its interior, which also features lavish use of gold. Original furnishings include dining room chairs made of gilded bronze. It was built for Mrs. William K. Vanderbilt. On display are yachting memorabilia and a restored

★
★
★
★

Chinese teahouse where Mrs. Vanderbilt held suffragette meetings. April-October: daily; rest of year: weekends.

Rosecliff

548 Bellevue Ave., Newport, 401-847-6543
Modeled by Stanford White after the Grand Trianon at Versailles, Rosecliff has the largest private ballroom in Newport and a famous heart-shaped staircase. It was built for socialite Mrs. Hermann Oelrichs in 1902. April-early November: daily.

Samuel Whitehorne House

416 Thames St., Newport, 401-849-7300
The 1811 house has exquisite furniture, silver and pewter made by 18th-century artisans, plus Chinese porcelain, Irish crystal, Pilgrim-era furniture and a garden. May-October: Monday, Thursday-Friday 11 a.m.-4 p.m.; Saturday-Sunday 10 a.m.-4 p.m.; winter by appointment.

Wanton-Lyman-Hazard House

17 Broadway, Newport, 401-846-0813
This 1675 house is the oldest in Newport, and one of the finest Jacobean homes in New England. It was the site of the 1765 Stamp Act riot. Its 18th-century garden has been restored. Guided tours. Mid-June-late August: Thursday-Saturday; 5 tours daily; closed holidays.

Whitehall Museum House

311 Berkeley Ave., Middletown, 401-846-3116.
A restored, 1729 hip-roofed country house built by Bishop George Berkeley, the British philosopher and educator. July-Labor day: Tuesday-Sunday 10 a.m.-5 p.m.; otherwise by appointment.

International Tennis Hall of Fame & Museum

194 Bellevue Ave., Newport, 401-849-3990, 800-457-1144;
www.tennisfame.org/museum
The world's largest tennis museum features interactive and dynamic exhibits detailing the history of the sport. Tennis equipment, fashions, trophies and memorabilia are on display in the famous Newport Casino, built in 1880 and designed by McKim, Mead and White. Daily. Grass courts available May-October.

Newport Art Museum and Art Association

76 Bellevue Ave., Newport, 401-848-8200; www.newportartmuseum.com
Changing exhibitions of contemporary and historical art are housed in the 1864 mansion designed by Richard Morris Hunt in the "Stick-Style" and in the 1920 Beaux Arts building. Available are lectures, performing arts events, evening musical picnics and tours. Columbus Day-Memorial Day: Tuesday-Saturday 10 a.m.-4 p.m. Sunday noon-4 p.m.; rest of the year Monday-Saturday 10 a.m.-5 p.m., Sunday noon-5 p.m.

Old Stone Mill

Touro Park, Mill St., and Bellevue Ave., Newport, 401-846-1398
The origin of this circular stone tower supported by arches is unknown. Although excavations (1948-1949) have disproved it, some people still believe it was built by Norsemen.

Redwood Library and Athenaeum

50 Bellevue Ave., Newport, 401-847-0292; www.redwoodlibrary.org
Designed by master Colonial architect Peter Harrison, this is thought to be oldest library building (1750) in continuous use in United States. It was used by English officer as a club during Revolution. Collection include original books and early portraits Monday, Friday-Saturday 9:30 a.m. 5:30 p.m.; Tuesday-Thursday to 8 p.m. Sunday 1-5 p.m.

Touro Synagogue National Historic Site

85 Touro St., Newport, 401-847-4794; www.tourosynagogue.org
The first synagogue (1763) in America, a Georgian masterpiece by the country's first architect, Peter Harrison, the Touro contains the oldest Torah in North America examples of 18th-century crafts and a letter from George Washington.

RHODE ISLAND

★
★
★
★
★

Trinity Church

Queen Anne Square, Newport,
401-846-0660
The first Anglican parish in the state (1698), the Trinity has been in continuous use since it was built. George Washington and philosopher George Berkeley were communicants. Interior features Tiffany windows and an organ tested by Handel before being shipped from London. Tours.

SPECIAL EVENTS

Newport Music Festival

Newport, 401-849-0700;
www.newportmusic.org
Chamber music held in Newport's fabled mansions. Three concerts daily. Mid-July.

Newport Winter Festival

23 America's Cup Ave., Newport,
401-847-7666, 800-326-6030;
www.newportevents.com/winterfest
Ten days of food, festivities and music with more than 200 cultural and recreational events and activities. Mid-February.

HOTELS

★★ Beech Tree Inn

34 Rhode Island Ave., Newport,
401-847-9794, 800-748-6565;
www.beechtreeinn.com
8 rooms. Wireless Internet access. $$

★★★Castle Hill Inn & Resort

590 Ocean Dr., Newport,
401-849-3800, 888-466-1355;
www.castlehillinn.com
Right off the famous Ocean Drive is the colossal city landmark. Converted in 1974, the mansion has uninterrupted water views. Romantic and quiet (no kids allowed in the lobby!), the resort spans the main house, the adjacent Harbor House, a guest chalet and newly renovated private cottages. Most rooms are filled with original antiques, gas fireplaces, marble baths and canopy beds. If you can tear yourself away from your suite, don't miss the lobby's evening fireside s'mores.

35 rooms. Complimentary full breakfast. Wireless Internet access. Restaurant. Two bars. Beach. Airport transportation available. $$$$

★★Courtyard Marriott

9 Commerce Dr., Middletown,
401-849-8000, 888-686-5067;
www.courtyard.com
148 rooms. High-speed Internet access. Restaurant. Airport transportation available. $$

★★★Hotel Viking

1 Bellevue Ave., Newport,
401-847-3300, 800-556-7126;
www.hotelviking.com
First built in 1926, the Hotel Viking, in Newport's Historic Hill neighborhood, is listed on the National Register of Historic Places. But don't mistake it for a stodgy old inn—sure, it has four-poster beds and antique-looking furniture, but the spot is also home to a modern, full-service spa. The Viking's vistas are sweeping, thanks to its off-the-beaten-path hilltop location far away from tourists, yet close enough to attractions like the Tennis Hall of Fame. 222 rooms. High-speed Internet access. Restaurant. Bar. Airport transportation available. $$$

★★★Hyatt Regency Newport

1 Goat Island, Newport,
401-851-1234, 888-591-1234;
www.newport.hyatt.com
On the tip of Goat Island, the Hyatt Regency overlooks Newport's harbor, Narragansett Bay and Jamestown Bridge. Pillow-top mattresses, plush duvets and Portico toiletries lend each room a home-away-from-home feel, while a kid-friendly outdoor pool reminds guests they're on vacation (though business travelers can still sit in on conferences in the hotel's wired work center). No seaside trip is complete without a clambake and the Hyatt delivers this, too with two do-it-yourself waterfront fire pits. 264 rooms. Wireless Internet access. Two restaurants, bar. Airport transportation available. $$$

231

RHODE ISLAND

★★Hydrangea House Inn
16 Bellevue Ave., Newport,
401-846-4435, 800-945-4667;
www.hydrangeahouse.com
6 rooms. Complimentary full breakfast. Free long distance phone calls and Internet access. **$$$**

★★Ivy Lodge
12 Clay St., Newport,
401-849-6865, 800-834-6865;
www.ivylodge.com
8 rooms. Complimentary full breakfast. Wireless Internet access. Airport transportation available. Business center. **$$$**

★★Melville House
39 Clarke St., Newport,
401-847-0640, 800-711-7184;
www.melvillehouse.com
6 rooms. Children over 12 years only. Complimentary full breakfast. Wireless Internet access. Airport transportation available. No Disabled Facilities. **$$**

★★Mill Street Inn
75 Mill St., Newport,
401-849-9500, 800-392-1316;
www.millStreetinn.com
23 rooms, all suites. Complimentary full breakfast. Wireless Internet access. **$$$**

★★★Marriott Newport
25 America's Cup Ave., Newport,
401-849-1000, 800-458-3066;
www.newportmarriott.com
The nautical-themed Marriott Newport somehow seamlessly blends big-city service with small-town charm. Massive, suspended sails hover over a lounge in the waterfront-facing, multi-level lobby; upstairs, sailboat-patterned quilts lay across white guestroom duvets.
319 rooms. Internet access. Restaurant. Bar. Airport transportation available. **$$$**

★★★Newport Harbor Hotel and Marina
49 America's Cup Ave., Newport,
401-847-9000, 800-955-2558;
www.newporthotel.com
Want to live like the Astors but lacking a seaside manse? Check in to the Newport Harbor Hotel. The Queen Ann Square spot overlooks its own 60-slip marina off Narragansett Bay. The surrounding acres include first-rate restaurants and shops, 19th-century mansions, a golf course, tennis courts and local wineries. Low-key blue and grey furniture decorates the hotel's lobby and guest rooms are stocked with televisions, DVDs, and video games.
133 rooms. High-speed Internet access. Restaurant. Bar. Airport transportation available. **$$$**

★★Pilgrim House
123 Spring St., Newport,
401-846-0040, 800-525-8373;
www.pilgrimhouseinn.com
11 rooms. Children over 12 years only. Complimentary continental breakfast. Wireless Internet access. Airport transportation available. **$$**

★★★The Francis Malbone House
392 Thames St., Newport,
401-846-0392, 800-846-0392;
www.malbone.com
Few historic inns still take pride in serving a *real* afternoon tea (most have gone the way of instant Lipton and tired store-bought pastries). At the Malbone House, however, decorum still reigns with complimentary daily tea service and better yet, a full gourmet breakfast. The rooms are spacious, immaculate and tasteful, with Jacuzzis and fireplaces and fluffy comforters. The house itself dates back to 1760 and is convenient walking distance from Newport's shops and eateries. 20 rooms. Complimentary full breakfast. Wireless Internet access. Airport transportation available. **$$$**

RESTAURANTS

★★★Canfield House
5 Memorial Blvd., Newport, 401-847-0416;
www.canfieldhousenewport.com
This elegant restaurant once housed Newport's only gambling casino. Today, it is a place where both locals and tourists come for traditional American fare such as steaks,

★
★
★
★
★

lamb and local seafood. High ceilings, dark wood paneling, crystal chandeliers, a prominent stained-glass window and other refined touches make any meal here a celebration. Al fresco dining is available on the covered porch during the warmer months, and more casual meals are available in the cellar pub.

American menu. Dinner. Bar. Children's menu. Business casual attire. Reservations recommended. Valet parking. Outdoor seating. Closed Monday. **$$**

★★La Forge Casino Restaurant
186 Bellevue Ave., Newport, 401-847-0418;
www.laforgerestaurant.net

American menu. Lunch, dinner, Sunday brunch. Bar. Children's menu. Casual attire. Outdoor seating. No Disabled Facilities. **$$**

★★Rhode Island Quahog Company
250 Thames St., Newport, 401-848-2330;
www.quahog.com

Seafood menu. Lunch, dinner. Bar. Children's menu. Casual attire. Reservations recommended. Outdoor seating. Closed January-February. **$$**

★★★White Horse Tavern
26 Marlborough St., Newport,
401-849-3600;
www.whitehorsetavern.com

If walls could talk, the White Horse Tavern's dark wooden planks would have much to say—built in 1673, the downtown tavern is America's oldest watering hole. Its litany of owners have thankfully left well-enough alone and the pub's brown clapboard exterior and dimmed interior with stone fireplaces and exposed ceiling beams smack of centuries-old character. The only thing updated is the food, a menu of well-executed regional New England entrees.

American menu. Lunch, dinner, Sunday brunch. Bar. Business casual attire. Reservations recommended. Outdoor seating. **$$$**

PROVIDENCE

Grateful that God's providence had led him to this spot, Roger Williams founded a town and named it accordingly. The early 1636 settlement, more farm town than urban center, soon morphed into an important port and industrial hub. Clipper ships left the harbor to explore China and the West Indies. Silver and jewelry artisans set up shop along the city's Colonial-lined streets.

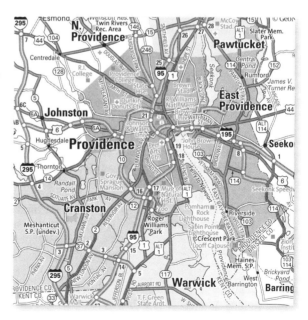

Today, Rhode Island's capital is the biggest metropolis in the state—which, with 160,000 residents isn't saying too much—and best-known for its outstanding universities: the liberal, Ivy league Brown, and the funky, alternative Rhode Island School of Design. Students are fixtures in the myriad coffee shops and bars of bustling Thayer Street, while local Goodfellas frequent the trattorias of Federal Hill, Providence's Little Italy. The up-and-coming downtown now has an upscale mall, modern convention center and a booming

RHODE ISLAND

★
★
★
★

nightlife scene. Still, perhaps in deference to the deferential Roger Williams himself, the city has maintained much of its old charm—contemporary hotels and office buildings share streets with historic houses, and the views of Narragansett Bay are as striking as ever.
Information: Providence Warwick Convention & Visitors Bureau,
1 W. Exchange St., Providence, 401-274-1636, 800-233-1636; www.pwcvb.com

WHAT TO SEE AND DO

Arcade
65 Weybosset St., Providence,
401-861-9150;
www.pwcvb.com
America's first indoor shopping mall, built in 1828, has national landmark status and more than 35 specialty shops and restaurants.

Brown University
45 Prospect St., Providence,
401-863-2378; www.brown.edu
Founded as Rhode Island College in 1764, the school was renamed for major benefactor Nicholas Brown in 1804. The 7,500-student Ivy is the seventh-oldest university in the country; its many libraries are free and open to the public.

First Unitarian Church
1 Benevolent St., Providence,
401-421-7970;
www.firstunitarianprov.org
At the top of this 1816 building is the largest bell ever cast by Paul Revere.

Governor Stephen Hopkins House
15 Hopkins St., Providence, 401-421-0694
Visit the home of the 10-time governor of Rhode Island (he signed the Declaration of Independence) lived here. April-December: Wednesday, Saturday 1-4 p.m., also by appointment.

John Brown House
52 Power St., Providence, 401-273-7507;
www.rihs.org

George Washington was once a guest at this Georgian manse that now houses a museum of 18th-century china, glass and paintings, as well as John Brown's chariot, the oldest surviving American-made vehicle. January-April: Friday-Saturday 10:30 a.m.-4:30 p.m.; May-December Tuesday-Saturday 10:30 a.m.-4:30 p.m.

Culinary Archives & Museum
315 Harborside Blvd., Providence,
491-598-2805
Dubbed the "Smithsonian of the food service industry," this museum contains more than 200,000 items related to the culinary arts. Tuesday-Sunday 10 a.m.-5 p.m.

Old State House
150 Benefit St., Providence, 401-222-2678
The state General Assembly met here between 1762 and 1900. Independence was proclaimed in the State House two months before the Declaration was signed in Philadelphia. Monday-Friday.

Providence Athenaeum Library
251 Benefit St., Providence, 401-421-6970
www.providenceathenaeum.org
Housed in a Greek Revival building designed by William Strickland, this is one of the oldest subscription libraries in the United States. The rare book room includes original Audubon elephant folios and a small art collection. September-May: Monday-Thursday 9 a.m.-7 p.m., Friday-Saturday to 5 p.m., Sunday 1-5 p.m.; June-Labor Day: Monday-Thursday 9 a.m.-7 p.m., Friday to 5 p.m., Saturday to 1 p.m.; closed first two weeks in August.

234

RHODE ISLAND

Providence Children's Museum

100 South St., 401-273-5437;
www.childrenmuseum.org
Many hands-on exhibits, including a time-travel adventure through Rhode Island's multicultural history, a wet-and-wild exploration of water and a hands-on geometry lab, entertain kids at the museum. September-March: Tuesday-Sunday 9 a.m.-6 p.m.; April-Labor Day: daily 9 a.m.-6 p.m.

Rhode Island School of Design

2 College St., Providence, 401-454-6100;
www.risd.edu
Nearly two thousand students are enrolled in one of the country's leading art and design schools.

Rhode Island State House

82 Smith St., Providence, 401-222-2357;
www.state.ri.us
Inside the 1901 capitol, designed by McKim, Mead, and White, is an original Gilbert Stuart portrait of George Washington. Monday-Friday 9-11 a.m.; closed second Monday in August.

Roger Williams National Memorial

282 N. Main St., Providence, 401-521-7266
At the site of the old town spring, this 4 1/2-acre park, commemorates Roger Williams and the founding of Providence. Daily.

Roger Williams Park

1000 Elmwood Ave., Providence,
401-785-9450;
www.providenceri.com/government/parks
The park has 430 acres of woodlands, waterways, and winding drives, plus greenhouses and a Japanese garden. Daily.

Museum of Natural History and Cormack Planetarium

1000 Elmwood Ave., Providence,
401-785-9450
Anthropology, geology, astronomy and biology displays; educational and performing arts programs. Daily 10 a.m.-5 p.m.; planetarium: September-June Saturday-Sunday, July-August Tuesday.

Roger Williams Park Zoo

1000 Elmwood Ave., Providence,
401-785-3510
Ideal for kids, the zoo has a nature center, tropical building, African plains and Marco Polo exhibits, and more than 600 animals. Daily.

SPECIAL EVENTS

Spring Festival of Historic Houses

21 Meeting St., Providence, 401-831-7440;
www.ppsri.og
Sponsored by the Providence Preservation Society, the festival runs tours of grand old private houses and gardens. Third weekend in June.

WaterFire

Waterplace Park, 101 Regent Ave.,
Providence, 401-272-3111;
www.waterfire.org
Floating bonfires in the Providence River are accompanied by music. Weekends, late May-late October.

HOTELS

★★Christopher Dodge House

11 W. Park St., Providence, 401-351-6111;
www.providence-hotel.com
14 rooms. Complimentary full breakfast. High-speed Internet access. Airport transportation available. $

★★Courtyard by Marriott Providence Downtown

32 Exchange Terrace, Providence,
401-272-1191, 800-321-2211;
www.courtyard.com
216 rooms. High-speed Internet access. Two restaurants. Bar. Airport transportation available. $$

★★★Marriott Providence

1 Orms St., Providence,
401-272-2400, 800-937-7768;
www.marriottprovidence.com
Just off I-95, the Marriott can't be beat for convenience. Thanks to well-appointed rooms—think cushy arm chairs, stately desks and a pillow menu—it's hard to beat for hospitality as well. Even kids get

RHODE ISLAND

★
★
★
★
★

special treatment here in the form of poolside sand competitions and hotel-run scavenger hunts. Outside are rows of classic Rhode Island Colonial homes, as well as plenty of shopping and eating options. 351 rooms. High-speed Internet access. Restaurant. Bar. Airport transportation available. **$$**

★★Radisson Hotel Providence Harbor
220 India St., Providence,
401-272-5577, 800-333-3333;
www.radisson.com/providenceri
136 rooms. High-speed Internet access. Restaurant. Bar. Whirlpool. Airport transportation available. **$**

★★★The Westin Providence
1 W. Exchange St., Providence,
401-598-8000, 800-301-1111;
www.westin.com/providence
The downtown Westin is attached—via sky bridge—to Providence Place, the city's major mall. If browsing hundreds of boutiques isn't your thing, though, the modern two-tower hotel provides plenty of other distractions in the form of a pool, fitness classes and extensive in-suite entertainment. Each room comes with Starwood's signature "Heavenly Bed" and a flat-screen TV, cordless phone, dual-head shower and better-than-average minibar. Even canine guests are welcome—they get their own bowls, treats and "Heavenly" dog beds. 364 rooms. High-speed Internet access. Two restaurants. Two bars. Airport transportation available. **$$$**

RESTAURANTS

★★Adesso
161 Cushing St., Providence,
401-521-0770;
www.zerotosixfigures.com/adesso
California, Italian menu. Lunch, dinner, late-night. Bar. Casual attire. Reservations recommended. Valet parking. **$$$**

★★★Al Forno
577 S. Main St., Providence, 401-273-9760;
www.alforno.com

Local favorite Al Forno has turned out primo pasta dishes for nearly three decades. Chef-owners (and cookbook authors) Johanne Killeen and George Germon preside over their rustic, two-story waterfront spot, infusing the Italian menu with Tuscan and Provencal flair. Must-eat dishes include the house-made gnocchi with spicy sausage and the artery-clogging baked pasta with cream and four cheeses.
Italian menu. Dinner. Bar. Casual attire. Valet parking. Outdoor seating. Closed Sunday-Monday. **$$$**

★The Cactus Grille
800 Allens Ave., Providence, 401-941-0004
Mexican menu. Lunch, dinner. Bar. Children's menu. Casual attire. **$$**

★★Hemenway's Seafood Grill
1 Providence-Washington Plaza,
Providence, 401-351-8570
Seafood menu. Lunch, dinner. Bar. Outdoor seating. **$$**

★★★★Mill's Tavern
101 N. Main St., Providence, 401-272-3331
Mills Tavern has a knack for improving on the classics. From its smart design and young, energetic vibe to its appealing menu, this winning restaurant housed in a former mill turns tradition on its head. The menu echoes the classic-contemporary sentiment with a wide variety of creatively prepared American seasonal dishes, many utilizing the kitchen's wood-burning oven, wood grill and rotisserie. The warm, knowledgeable staff provides professional and thorough service without being stuffy or intrusive.
Contemporary American menu. Dinner. Bar. Business casual attire. Reservations recommended. Valet parking. **$$$**

★★★New Rivers
7 Steeple St., Providence, 401-751-0350;
www.newriversrestaurant.com
Fake fruit and wall-mounted plates can often turn a good kitchen into kitsch. But while both Lucite pears and Majolica pottery are incorporated into New Rivers

décor, the overall ambiance is comfortable, not cheesy. The colorful downtown American bistro's seasonal menu is full of fresh, local ingredients; standout dishes include poached rabbit loin in sweet pea broth and roasted trout with cracked wheat and beets.

American menu. Dinner. Bar. Business casual attire. Reservations recommended. Closed Sunday. **$$$**

★★Pane E Vino

365 Atwells Ave., Providence,
401-223-2230; www.panevino.net

Italian menu. Dinner. Bar. Business casual attire. Reservations recommended. Valet parking. **$$$**

★★★Pot Au Feu

44 Custom House St., Providence,
401-273-8953; www.potaufeuri.com

A formal, upstairs salon and a relaxed downstairs bistro make up Pot Au Feu, a traditional French bistro in the heart of Providence. The classic and regional French dishes—onion soup, salade nicoise, sweet and savory crepes—are authentic and delicious. The exposed brick walls and candlelit tables create a warm and cozy atmosphere.

French bistro menu. Lunch, dinner. Bar. Business casual attire. Reservations recommended. Closed Sunday. **$$**

WARWICK

Sometimes pretty, sometimes gritty, Warwick often gets an (unfair) bad rap. The state's second-largest city is home to T.F. Green International airport and countless industrial warehouses, *but* it also has 39 miles of Narragansett Bay coastline and more than 15 picturesque marinas. Less populated than Providence, Warwick still has plenty of shopping and eating destinations, and its decentralized geography has given rise to a number of postcard-perfect villages such as Pawtuxet, Cowesett and Conanicut.

Information: City Hall, 3275 Post Rd., 401-738-2000, 800-492-7942; www.warwickri.com

WHAT TO SEE AND DO

Historic Pontiac Mills

334 Knight St., Warwick, 401-737-2700;
www.visitwarwickri.com

A restored 1863 mill complex houses nearly 80 small businesses, artisans and shops, with an open-air market on weekends. Daily.

Walking Tour of Historic Apponaug Village

3275 Post Rd., Warwick, 800-492-7942;
www.visitwarwickri.com

More than 30 historic and architecturally interesting buildings comprise this walking tour; brochure available through Warwick City.

SPECIAL EVENTS

Gaspee Days

Warwick, 401-781-1772, 800-492-7942;
www.gaspee.com

A celebration of the capture and burning of the British schooner Gaspee by Rhode Island patriots includes arts and crafts, concerts, footraces, battle reenactments, parades and contests. May-June.

Warwick Heritage Festival

Warwick City Park, Warwick,
401-738-2000, 800-492-7942;
www.visitwarwickri.com

A weekend reenactment of the city's history. November, Veterans Day weekend.

HOTELS

★★★Crowne Plaza

801 Greenwich Ave., Warwick,
401-732-6000, 800-227-6963;
www.crowneplaza.com

Stranded travelers breathe a sigh of relief when checking into the Crowne Plaza. Three miles from the airport is this tastefully decorated hotel which offers a sleep

amenity package. It includes an eye mask, drape clip, ear plugs, lavender spray and a night light. Rooms come standard with marble baths, dark wooden desks, CD players, bathrobes and upscale toiletries, making overnights a genuine pleasure.
266 rooms. High-speed Internet access. Restaurant. Bar. Airport transportation available. $$

★★Radisson Airport Hotel
2081 Post Rd., Warwick, 401-739-3000, 800-333-3333; www.radisson.com/warwickri
111 rooms. Complimentary continental breakfast. High-speed Internet access. Restaurant. Bar. Airport transportation available. $$

WESTERLY

Tourists looking for Newport's panache without its crowds would do well to look toward Westerly. The quiet seaside city and surrounding hamlets, including the very WASPy Watch Hill, are full of grand old-money cottages and quaint small-town streets. Founded in 1669, Westerly is among the state's oldest settlements and the seat of once-booming granite quarries. Today, the southwestern Rhode Island locale counts tourism and fishing gear among its top industries.

Information: Westerly-Pawcatuck Area Chamber of Commerce, 1 Chamber Way, Westerly, 401-596-7761, 800-732-7636; www.westerlychamber.org

WHAT TO SEE AND DO

Babcock-Smith House
124 Granite St., Westerly, 401-596-5704; www.babcock-smithhouse.com
This 1732 two-story, gambrel-roofed Georgian mansion was once home to Dr. Joshua Babcock, Westerly's first physician. Today, its furniture collection spans 200 years. Late May-October: Saturday 2-5 p.m.; also Friday 2-5 p.m. July-August; otherwise by appointment.

Misquamicut State Beach
257 Atlantic Ave., Westerly, 401-596-9097; www.riparks.com/misq.uamicut.htm
Soft sands and gentle waves make Misquamicut the perfect place to lay a towel. Swimming, bathhouse, fishing, picnicking, concession. Memorial Day-Labor Day: daily 9 a.m.-6 p.m.

Watch Hill
Watch Hill, Westerly, 401-596-7761; www.westerlychamber.org
A Newport-like historic community of handsome summer houses, many of which date from the 1870s.

Watch Hill Lighthouse
Watch Hill, 14 Lighthouse Rd., Westerly, 401-596-7761
The granite lighthouse was built in 1856 to replace the wooden 1807 structure. Museum exhibits. July-August: Tuesday, Thursday 1-3 p.m.

HOTELS

★Breezeway Resort
70 Winnapaug Rd., Misquamicut Beach, 401-348-8953, 800-462-8872; www.breezewayresort.com
50 rooms. Complimentary continental breakfast. Bar. Pool $

★★Shelter Harbor Inn
10 Wagner Rd., Westerly, 401-322-8883, 800-468-8883; www.shelterharborinn.com
24 rooms. Complimentary full breakfast. Restaurant. Bar. Tennis Courts. $

★Winnapaug Inn
169 Shore Rd., Westerly, 401-348-8350, 800-288-9906; www.winnapauginn.com
49 rooms. Complimentary continental breakfast. High-speed Internet access. Restaurant. Bar. Pool. $$

SPECIALTY LODGINGS

Villa Bed & Breakfast

190 Shore Rd., Westerly,
401-596-1054, 800-722-9240;
www.thevillaatwesterly.com

This B&B doubles as a romantic hideaway—it comes complete with flower gardens, Italian porticos and verandas. Al fresco diners are fans of the Villa's complimentary poolside breakfast; beachgoers love its proximity to Misquamicut Beach. Block Island, Foxwoods Casino and the Mystic Aquarium are all short rides away. 5 rooms. Complimentary continental breakfast. $

RHODE ISLAND

240

★

★

★

★

★

VERMONT

GREEN ROLLING HILLS, PICTURE PERFECT VILLAGES, FIELDS DOTTED WITH BLACK AND WHITE cows. Vermont is every bit as bucolic as most imagine. But under that peaceful surface is an independent spirit that makes Vermont one of the most progressive, liberal states in the country. Vermonters are proudly individualist and even retain a bit of the 60s hippie spirit—recently, one town threatened to secede from the U.S. over the Iraq war, and several towns have fought fiercely (but unsuccessfully) to stop Wal-Mart from opening in the state. And while modern Vermont is progressively leftist (it was one of the first states to sanction civil unions), that independent spirit is nothing new.

In 1724, Vermont became the last New England state to be settled. Ethan Allen and his Green Mountain Boys made Vermont famous when they took Fort Ticonderoga from the British in 1775. Claimed by both New York and New Hampshire, Vermont framed a constitution in 1777. It was the first state to prohibit slavery and the first to provide universal male suffrage, regardless of property or income. For 14 years, Vermont was an independent republic, running its own postal service, coining its own money, naturalizing citizens of other states and countries and negotiating with other states and nations. In 1701, Vermont became the 14th state.

Tourism is a driving force in Vermont, with every town sprinkled with quaint bed and breakfasts, inns and restaurants. The state's many ski resorts often get top marks by national publications. A strong, organic and environmentalist movement exists here, and chains are rare. It's not unusual to buy your gas from an independent gas station, or turn to a local bookshop for the latest bestseller.

That kind of grass roots populism is refreshing in an ever-homogenous America. Here you'll find tiny villages, outstanding fresh, organic food, top-notch skiing and the best maple syrup in the country. Burlington is a funky, artsy college town, while Montpelier is one of the country's prettiest state capitals. In between is a delightful landscape of adorable villages, each with a unique and proud character of its own.
Information: www.travel-vermont.com

241

VERMONT

★ SPOTLIGHT

★ Vermonter Calvin Coolidge was the only U.S. president to be born on the Fourth of July.

★ More people in Vermont live in a rural setting than an urban setting.

★ Vermont produces more than 500,000 gallons of maple syrup each year.

ARLINGTON
Arlington, located in Southwestern Vermont, lies between the Green Mountains and the Taconic range. There are five mountain peaks located in the town.

WHAT TO SEE AND DO
Norman Rockwell Exhibition
3772 Hwy. 7A, Arlington, 802-375-6423;
www.vmga.org/bennington/
normrockwell.html

Hundreds of magazine covers, illustrations, advertisements, calendars and other printed works are displayed in a historic 1875 church in the illustrator's hometown. Hosts are Rockwell's former models. Daily.

HOTELS

★Candlelight Motel
4893 Hwy. 7A, Arlington,
802-375-6647; 800-348-5294;
www.candlelightmotel.com
17 rooms. Complimentary continental breakfast. Outdoor pool. **$**

★★★Arlington Inn
3904 Highway 7A and 313W, Arlington,
802-375-6532, 800-443-9442;
www.arlingtoninn.com
Built in 1848, this Greek Revival–style mansion has been an inn since 1888 and is listed on the National Register of Historic Places. Spread throughout the main house and several converted outbuildings, the guest rooms feature antiques, double-sided fireplaces and Jacuzzi tubs. If you'd like a more historic room, opt for the main house; the carriage house and parsonage have been renovated with modern architectural details, such as cathedral ceilings and skylights. The three-acre grounds include a walking path, gazebo and small stone fountain with waterfall.
18 rooms. Complimentary full breakfast. Restaurant. Bar. **$$**

★★★Arlington's West Mountain Inn
River Rd., and Highway 313, Arlington,
802-375-6516; www.westmountaininn.com
This historic white, seven-gabled inn was built in 1849 and opened as an inn in 1978. Located on a mountainside overlooking the Battenkill River, the interior of the inn is furnished with a mix of antiques and country classics (pine paneling, fireplace, books, chess and checkers). Nearby activities include hiking, snowshoeing, canoeing, tubing, tennis and golf.
20 rooms. Complimentary full breakfast. Restaurant. Bar. **$$**

SPECIALTY LODGINGS

Hill Farm Inn
458 Hill Farm Rd., Arlington,
802-375-2269; 800-882-2545.
www.hillfarminn.com
North of Arlington's town center on 50 acres fronting the Battenkill River, this inn has a historic guest house (1790), a classic white farmhouse (1830) and several outlying cottages housing family suites and efficiencies. Sheep, goats and chickens wander about outside to amuse kids and adults alike. Inside, the guest rooms have simple country charm—there are no phones, but some rooms have televisions.
15 rooms. Complimentary full breakfast. **$**

RESTAURANTS

★★★Arlington Inn
3904 Highway 7A, Arlington,
802-375-6532, 800-443-9442;
www.arlingtoninn.com
This historic landmark inn was built in 1848 as a private home and has been in operation since 1888. The Victorian dining room serves classic dishes such as beef stroganoff and filet mignon.
American menu. Dinner. Bar. Children's menu. Business casual attire. Reservations recommended. Closed Monday; last week in April-first week in May; also Sunday in off-season. **$$$**

BENNINGTON

Bennington was headquarters for Ethan Allen's Green Mountain Boys—known to New Yorkers as the "Bennington Mob"—in Vermont's long struggle with New York. On August 16, 1777, this same "mob" won a decisive battle of the Revolutionary War. Bennington has three separate areas of historic significance: the Victorian and turn-of-the-century buildings downtown; the colonial houses, church and commons in Old Bennington (1 mile W.); and the three covered bridges in North Bennington.

Information: Information Booth, 100 Veterans Memorial Dr., 802-447-3311, 800-229-0252; www.bennington.com

WHAT TO SEE AND DO

Bennington Battle Monument

15 Monument Circle, Old Bennington, 802-447-0550; www.dhca.state.vt.us

A 306-foot monolith commemorates a Revolutionary War victory. Elevator to observation platform Mid-April-October, daily 9 a.m.-5 p.m.

Bennington College

Highway 67A and College Dr., Bennington, 802-442-5401; www.bennington.edu

(1932) Introduced progressive methods of education; became co-educational in 1969. The Visual and Performing Arts Center has special exhibits. Summer programs and performances.

Bennington Museum

75 Main St., Bennington, 802-447-1571; www.benningtonmuseum.org

Early Vermont and New England historical artifacts, including American glass, paintings, sculpture, silver, furniture; Bennington pottery, Grandma Moses paintings, 1925 "Wasp" luxury touring car. Schoolhouse Museum contains Moses family memorabilia, Bennington flag, other Revolutionary War collections. Thursday-Tuesday 10 a.m.-5 p.m. Genealogical library (by appointment.)

Old First Church

One Monument Circle, Old Bennington, 802-447-1223; www.oldfirstchurchbenn.org

(1805) Example of early colonial architecture; original box pews; Asher Benjamin steeple. Guided tours. Memorial Day-June: weekends; July-mid-October: Monday-Saturday 10 a.m.-noon, 1-4 p.m.; Sunday 1-4 p.m.

Old Burying Ground

Monument Ave., Bennington, 802-447-3311

Poet Robert Frost and those who died in the Battle of Bennington are all buried here.

Park-McCullough House Museum

Park and West St., North Bennington, 802-442-5441; www.parkmccullough.org

A 35-room 1865 Victorian mansion with period furnishings, stable with carriages. costume collection, Victorian gardens, child's playhouse. Special events are held throughout the year. Mid-May-mid-October: daily, tours 10 a.m.-3 p.m.

Woodford State Park

142 State Park Rd., Woodford, 802-447-7169

At 2,400 feet, this 400-acre park has the highest elevation of any park in the state. Swimming, fishing, boating (no motors; rentals), nature and hiking trails, picnicking, tent and trailer sites (dump station). Memorial Day-Columbus Day.

HOTELS

★Best Western

220 Northside Dr., Bennington, 802-442-6311, 800-780-7234; www.bestwestern.com

58 rooms. Complimentary continental breakfast. Outdoor pool. Near Bennington College. **$**

★★★Four Chimneys Inn

21 West Rd., Bennington, 802-447-3500; www.fourchimneys.com

This elegant 1783 inn is set on 11 acres of trees and rolling grass fields. Guest rooms blend modern amenities with an old-world feel.

11 rooms. Complimentary full breakfast. Restaurant. Bar. **$$**

★Hampton Inn

51 Hannaford Square, Bennington, 802-440-9862, 800-426-7866; www.hamptoninn.com

243

VERMONT

Complimentary breakfast. Pool. Fitness center. Pets not accepted. **$**

SPECIALTY LODGINGS
South Shire Inn
124 Elm St., Bennington, 802-447-3839; www.southshire.com

This inn is reminiscent of the Victorian era from its shingled facade to the mahogany paneling, leaded glass doors and ornate moldings of its common rooms. All rooms have period furnishings.
9 rooms. Children over 12 years only. Complimentary full breakfast. High-speed Internet access. **$$**

BRANDON
Brandon is a resort and residential town located at the western edge of the Green Mountains. The first U.S. electric motor was made in nearby Forestdale by Thomas Davenport.
Information: Brandon Area Chamber of Commerce, 802-247-6401; www.brandon.org

WHAT TO SEE AND DO
Mount Independence
Highways 22A and 73 W., Orwell, 802-759-2412; www.historicvermont.org/sites
Wooded bluff on shore of Lake Champlain, part of the Revolutionary War defense complex. Fort built in 1776 across from Fort Ticonderoga to house 12,000 troops and to protect colonies from northern invasion; evacuated in 1777. Least disturbed major Revolutionary War site in the country; four marked trails show ruins of fort complex. Late May-mid-October: daily 9:30 a.m.-5 p.m.

Stephen A. Douglas Birthplace
2 Grove St. (Highway 7), Brandon, 802-247-6401
Cottage where the "Little Giant", once the Democratic nominee for president who lost to Abraham Lincoln, was born in 1813. Douglas attended Brandon Academy before moving to Illinois in 1833. By appointment.

HOTELS
★★★Lilac Inn
53 Park St., Brandon, 802-247-5463, 800-221-0720; www.lilacinn.com
This colonial home, built in 1909, is on the National Register of Historic Places. Enjoy a book in the library, practice on the putting green or take a drive to nearby historic Fort Ticonderoga. The inn is decorated in Victorian style and rooms feature antiques, historical prints and artwork. Extensive gardens are found in back, along with a patio and gazebo.
9 rooms. Pets accepted; fee. Children over 12 permitted. Complimentary full breakfast. Restaurant. Bar. **$$**

SPECIALTY LODGINGS
The Brandon Inn
20 Park St., Brandon, 802-247-5766, 800-639-8685; www.historicbrandoninn.com
Built in 1786.
37 rooms. Restaurant. Bar. Outdoor pool. **$$**

BRATTLEBORO
The first settlement in Vermont was at Fort Dummer (two miles south) in 1724.
Information: Brattleboro Area Chamber of Commerce, 180 Main St., 802-254-4565; www.brattleboro.com

WHAT TO SEE AND DO
Brattleboro Museum & Art Center
10 Vernon St., Brattleboro, 802-257-0124;

www.brattleboromuseum.org
Exhibits change periodically and feature works by New England artists; frequent

performances and lecture programs. May-February: Wednesday-Monday 11 a.m.-5 p.m.; closed July 4, November 25; also August 2-5, November 1-4.

Creamery Bridge
Guilford St., & Route 9 W., Brattleboro, 802-254-4565
(1879) One of Vermont's best-preserved covered bridges.

Harlow's Sugar House
563 Bellows Falls Rd., Putney, 802-387-5852; www.vermontsugar.com
Observe working sugarhouse (March-mid-April). Maple exhibit and products. Pick your own fruit in season: strawberries, blueberries, raspberries, apples; cider in fall. Daily; closed January-February.

HOTELS
★Latchis Hotel
50 Main St., Brattleboro, 802-254-6300, 800-254-6304; www.latchis.com
30 rooms. Complimentary continental breakfast. Wireless Internet access. **$**

★★Quality Inn
1380 Putney Rd., Brattleboro, 802-254-8701, 800-228-5151; www.qualityinnbrattleboro.com
98 rooms. Complimentary continental breakfast. High-speed Internet access, wireless Internet access. Restaurant. Bar. Fitness room. Indoor pool, outdoor pool. **$**

BURLINGTON
Located on Lake Champlain, Burlington is the largest city in Vermont. It's the site of the oldest university and the oldest daily newspaper (1848) in the state, the burial place of Ethan Allen and the birthplace of philosopher John Dewey. It has a diverse range of industries and the lakefront area offers a park, dock and restaurants.
Information: Lake Champlain Regional Chamber of Commerce, 60 Main St., 802-863-3489, 877-686-5253; www.vermont.org

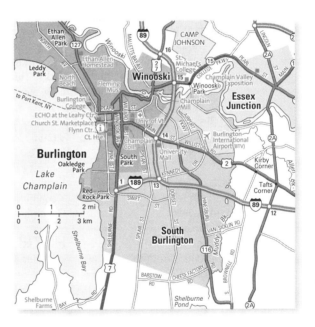

VERMONT

★
★
★
★
★

WHAT TO SEE AND DO
Bolton Valley Ski/Summer Resort
4302 Bolton Access Rd., Bolton Valley, 877-926-5866; www.boltonvalleyvt.com

Resort has quad, four double chairlifts, one surface lift, school, patrol, rentals, snowmaking, cafeteria, restaurants, bar, nursery. Forty-three runs, longest run over three miles, vertical drop 1,600 feet. November-April:

daily. Sixty-two miles of cross-country trails. Also summer activities.

Church Street Marketplace
135 Church St., Burlington,
802-863-1648;
www.churchstmarketplace.com
Four traffic-free blocks, from the Unitarian Church, designed in 1815 by Peter Banner, to City Hall at the corner of Main Street. Buildings are a mix of Art Deco and 19th-century architectural styles and house more than 100 shops, restaurants, galleries and cafes. The brick promenade offers vendors and street entertainers.

Ethan Allen Homestead and Museum
1 Ethan Allen Homestead,
Burlington, 802-865-4556;
www.ethanallenhomestead.org
Ethan Allen had a colorful history as a frontiersman, military leader, land specu- lator, suspected traitor and prisoner of war. This preserved pioneer homestead was Allen's last home. Here you'll find a re-created hayfield and kitchen gardens, plus the 1787 farmhouse. One-hour guided tours are available. Monday-Saturday 10 a.m.-4 p.m., Sunday 1-4 p.m.; tours available June-October.

Ethan Allen Park
North Ave. and Ethan Allen Pkwy.,
Burlington, 802-863-3489;
www.enjoyburlington.com/Parks/
EthanAllen Park.cfm
Part of Ethan Allen's farm. Ethan Allen Tower, Memorial Day-Labor Day: Wednes- day-Sunday afternoons and evenings with view of Adirondacks and Lake Champlain to the west, Green Mountains to the east. Picnicking.

Lake Champlain Chocolates
750 Pine St., Burlington,
802-864-1808, 800-465-5909;
www.lakechamplainchocolates.com
Large glass windows give visitors a view of the chocolate-making process at this small-scale factory. The gift shop onsite usually features in-store chocolate-

making demonstrations on Saturdays, when the factory itself is closed. Tours: Monday-Friday 9 a.m.-2 p.m. on the hour; factory store: Monday-Saturday 9 a.m.- 6 p.m., Sunday noon-5 p.m.

University of Vermont
Waterman Bldg., 85 S. Prospect St.,
Burlington, 802-656-3480; www.uvm.edu
(1791) (10,000 students) Fifth-oldest university in New England. Graduate and undergraduate programs. On campus is the Billings Center, the Bailey-Howe Library, the largest in the state, the Georgian-designed Ira Allen Chapel, named for the founder, and the Old Mill, a classroom building with cor- nerstone laid by General Lafayette in 1825.

SPECIAL EVENTS

Discover Jazz Festival
230 College St., Burlington, 802-863-7992;
www.discoverjazz.com
A jazz extravaganza with more than 150 live performances taking place in city parks, clubs and restaurants. Ten days in early June.

Vermont Mozart Festival
802-862-7352; www.vtmozart.com
Features 26 chamber concerts in pictur- esque Vermont settings including the Trapp Family Meadow, Basin Harbor Club in Vergennes and Shelburne Farms on Lake Champlain. Mid-July-early August.

HOTELS

★★Best Western Windjammer Inn & Conference Center
1076 Williston Rd., South Burlington,
802-863-1125, 800-371-1125;
www.bestwestern.com/windjammerinn
159 rooms. Pets accepted, some restrictions; fee. Complimentary continental breakfast. Restaurant. Fitness room. Indoor pool, out- door pool, whirlpool. Airport transportation available. $

★Comfort Inn
1285 Williston Rd., South Burlington,
802-865-3400, 877-424-6423;
www.choicehotels.com

★
★
★
★
★

105 rooms. Pets accepted, some restrictions; fee. Complimentary continental breakfast. Fitness room. Outdoor pool. **$**

★★Doubletree Hotel
1117 Williston Rd., South Burlington,
802-658-0250, 800-222-8733;
www.doubletree.com
130 rooms. Pets accepted, some restrictions; fee. Restaurant. Bar. Fitness room. Indoor pool, children's pool. Airport transportation available. **$**

★Holiday Inn Express
1712 Shelburne Rd., South Burlington,
802-860-1112, 866-762-7870;
www.innvermont.com
84 rooms, all suites. Complimentary continental breakfast. Airport transportation available. **$**

★★★The Inn at Essex—A Summit Hotel
70 Essex Way, Essex,
802-878-1100, 800-727-4295;
www.innatessex.com
Each room at this inn is individually decorated with 18th-century period-style furniture. The meals are prepared by the New England Culinary Institute.
97 rooms. Pets accepted, some restrictions; fee. Restaurant. Airport transportation available. **$$**

★★★Sheraton Burlington Hotel and Conference Center
870 Williston Rd., South Burlington,
802-865-6600, 800-677-6576;
www.sheratonburlington.com

This full-service hotel is the only Sheraton located in Vermont. Rooms are comfortable with plush beds and wireless internet.
309 rooms. Pets accepted. Restaurant. Bar. Fitness room. Indoor pool, whirlpool. Airport transportation available. Business center. **$**

RESTAURANTS

★Daily Planet
15 Center St., Burlington, 802-862-9647
International menu. Dinner, late-night. Bar. Children's menu. Casual attire. Reservations recommended. Outdoor seating. **$$**

★★Ice House
171 Battery St., Burlington, 802-864-1800
American menu. Lunch, dinner. Bar. Children's menu. Casual attire. Reservations recommended. Outdoor seating. **$$**

★★★Pauline's
1834 Shelburne Rd., South Burlington,
802-862-1081; www.paulinescafe.com
This two-story restaurant serves fresh seasonal ingredients and a seafood-heavy menu. A $30 two-course dinner-for-two menu is offered at opening Sunday through Thursday.
American menu. Lunch, dinner, Sunday brunch. Bar. Children's menu. Outdoor seating. **$$**

★★Perry's Fish House
1080 Shelburne Rd., South Burlington,
802-862-1300; www.perrysfishhouse.com
Seafood menu. Dinner, Sunday brunch. Bar. Children's menu. **$$**

VERMONT

DORSET
This charming village is surrounded by hills that are 3,000 feet high. In 1776, the Green Mountain Boys voted for Vermont's independence here and in 1785, the first marble quarry in the country was opened on nearby Mount Aeolus.
Information: Dorset Chamber of Commerce, 802-867-2450; www.dorsetvt.com

SPECIAL EVENTS
Dorset Theatre Festival
Dorset Playhouse, Cheney Rd.,
Dorset, 802-867-2223;
www.dorsettheatrefestival.com
Professional theater company presents six productions each season. Mid-June-Labor Day.

HOTELS

★★★Dorset Inn
8 Church St. & Route 30, Dorset,
802-867-5500, 877-367-7389;
www.dorsetinn.com
Located where the Green Mountain Boys plotted their fight against the British, the Dorset Inn combines colonial elements with modern amenities. Guest rooms feature private baths, antique furnishings and wall-to-wall carpet. Telephones are not included in rooms, but some offer televisions. Established in 1796, this is the oldest continuously operating inn in Vermont. The onsite restaurant serves high-end comfort food, made from locally farmed products—dishes include smoked salmon and Asian spiked shrimp skewers. 29 rooms. Pets accepted, some restrictions; fee. Complimentary full breakfast. Wireless Internet access. Restaurant. Bar. Spa. **$$**

★★★Inn at West View Farm
2928 Highway 30, Dorset,
802-867-5715, 800-769-4903;
www.innatwestviewfarm.com
This restored farmhouse overlooks the Vermont countryside. Rooms have CD players, Caswell Masey bath products and beds topped with down duvets.
10 rooms. Complimentary full breakfast. Restaurant. Bar. **$**

SPECIALTY LODGINGS

Barrows House Inn
3156 Highway 30, Dorset,
802-867-4455, 800-639-1620;
www.barrowshouse.com
28 rooms. Pets accepted, some restrictions; fee. Check-in 2 p.m., check-out 11 a.m. Restaurant. Bar. Outdoor pool. Tennis. **$$**

RESTAURANTS

★★★Barrows House Inn
3156 Highway 30, Dorset,
802-867-4455, 800-639-1620;
www.barrowshouse.com
Choose to sit in the clubby tavern, the bright greenhouse, on the small outdoor patio or in the more formal dining room while enjoying the regional cuisine served at this inn. American menu. Breakfast, dinner. Bar. Children's menu. Casual attire. Reservations recommended. Outdoor seating. **$$**

★★Inn at West View Farm
2928 Route 30, Dorset,
802-867-5715, 800-769-4903;
www.innatwestviewfarm.com
American menu. Dinner. Bar. Business casual attire. Reservations recommended. Closed Tuesday-Wednesday. **$$$**

FAIRLEE
This town is located near the New Hampshire border and on Lake Morley.
Information: Town Offices, Main St., 802-333-4363

HOTELS

★★Lake Morey Resort
185 Clubhouse Rd., Fairlee,
802-333-4311, 800-423-1211;
www.lakemoreyresort.com
144 rooms. Restaurant. Bar. Children's activity center. Fitness room. Indoor pool, outdoor pool, whirlpool. Golf. Tennis. **$**

GRAFTON
This New England village is a blend of houses, churches, galleries, antiques shops —all circa 1800. Founded in pre-Revolutionary times under the patronage of George III, Grafton became a thriving mill town and modest industrial center after the damming of the nearby Saxton River. When water power gave way to steam, the town declined. Rescued, revived and restored by the Windham Foundation, its beauty remains in tact. A creek runs through the picturesque town, a favorite among photographers.

WHAT TO SEE AND DO

Grafton Ponds Cross-Country Ski Center
Townshend Rd., Grafton,
800-843-1801
Featuring more than 16 miles of groomed trails, a skiing school, rentals, concessions and a warming hut. December-March: daily. In summer, walking and fitness trails (no fee)

The Old Tavern at Grafton
92 Main St., Grafton, 800-843-1801
www.old-tavern.com
(1801) Visited by many famous guests over the years, including several presidents and authors; names inscribed over the desk. Furnished with antiques and colonial decor. Former barn converted to lounge; annex is restored from two houses; dining by reservations. May-March: daily.

HOTELS

★★★Old Tavern At Grafton
92 Main St., Grafton,
802-843-2231, 800-843-1801;
www.old-tavern.com
This New England inn features guest rooms with antique Chippendale and Windsor furnishings. The inn serves afternoon tea, and has tennis courts and bicycles. 46 rooms. Closed Apr. Children over 7 years only. Complimentary full breakfast. Restaurant. Bar. Tennis. **$**

SPECIALTY LODGINGS

Inn At Woodchuck Hill Farm
Middletown Rd., Grafton, 802-843-2398;
www.woodchuckhill.com
First farmhouse in town (1790). On 200 acres with a pond. 10 rooms. Complimentary full breakfast. **$**

JEFFERSONVILLE

249

This village, located in the mountains of Vermont's Northern Kingdom, has a population of less than 600. Smugglers' Notch ski resort is located here.
Information: Smugglers' Notch Area Chamber of Commerce, www.smugnotch.com

WHAT TO SEE AND DO

Smugglers' Notch
4323 Highway 108 S., Jeffersonville,
802-644-8851, 800-451-8752;
www.smuggs.com
Resort has five double chairlifts, three surface lifts, school, rentals, snowmaking, concession area, cafeteria, restaurants, a nursery and a lodge. Sixty runs, longest run over three miles; vertical drop 2,610 feet. Thanksgiving-mid-April, daily). More than 25 miles of cross-country trails (December-April: daily; rentals), ice skating. Summer activities include 10 swimming pools, three water slides, tennis, miniature golf, driving range.

HOTELS

★★Smugglers' Notch Resort
4323 Highway 108 S., Jeffersonville,
802-644-8851, 800-451-8752;
www.smuggs.com
525 rooms. Restaurant. Bar. Children's activity center. Fitness room. Eight outdoor pools, whirlpool. Tennis. Ski in/ski out. Airport transportation available. **$**

SPECIALTY LODGINGS

Sinclair Inn Bed & Breakfast
389 Highway 15, Jericho,
802-899-2234, 800-433-4658;
www.sinclairinnbb.com
This restored Queen Anne Victorian inn was built in 1890. 6 rooms. Children over 12 years only. Complimentary full breakfast. **$**

VERMONT

KILLINGTON

One of New England's most popular ski towns, Killington attracts scores every year thanks to its reliable and early-season snowmaking. The bars and lounges around Killington become a lively singles scene for skiing Bostonians come winter.

Information: Killington Chamber of Commerce, 802-773-4181, 800-337-1928; www.killingtonchamber.com

WHAT TO SEE AND DO

Gifford Woods State Park
34 Gifford Woods, Killington, 802-775-5354
This 114-acre park has fishing and boat access to Kent Pond. Foot trails (Appalachian Trail passes through park). Virgin forest with picnic facilities. Tent and trailer sites (dump station). Standard fees. Memorial Day-Columbus Day.

Killington Resort
4763 Killington Rd., Killington,
802-422-3261, 800-621-6867;
www.killington.com
Comprises 1,200 acres with seven mountains (highest elevation 4,241 feet). Two gondolas, six high-speed quad, six quad, six triple, four double chairlifts, eight surface lifts, patrol, school, rentals, snowmaking, mountaintop restaurant (with observation decks), six cafeterias, bars, children's center, nursery and lodging. More than 200 runs, with the longest run 10 miles, with a vertical drop 3,150 feet. Snowboarding; snow tubing. October-June: daily.

Pico Alpine Slide and Scenic Chairlift
4763 Killington Rd., Killington,
866-667-7426
Chairlift to top of mountain slope; control speed of own sled on the way down. Sports center and restaurant below. Late-May-mid-October.

HOTELS

★★Cascades Lodge
58 Old Mill Rd., Killington Village,
802-422-3731, 800-345-0113;
www.cascadeslodge.com
46 rooms. Pets accepted, some restrictions; fee. Complimentary full breakfast. Restaurant. Bar. Fitness room. Indoor pool, whirlpool. Ski in/ski out. $

★Econo Lodge Killington Area
51 Route 4, Mendon,
800-992-9067, 800-553-2666
30 rooms. Pets accepted. Complimentary continental breakfast. Children's activity center. Outdoor pool, whirlpool. $

★★Grey Bonnet Inn
831 Hwy. 100, Killington,
802-775-2537, 800-342-2086;
www.greybonnetinn.com
40 rooms. Restaurant. Bar. Fitness room. Indoor pool, outdoor pool, whirlpool. Tennis. Closed April-May, late October-late November. $

★★Killington Pico Motor Inn
64 Hwy. 4, Killington
802-773-4088, 800-548-4713;
www.killingtonpico.com
28 rooms. Complimentary full breakfast. Restaurant. Bar. Outdoor pool, whirlpool. $

★Sherburne-Killington Motel
1946 Hwy. 4, Killington,
802-773-9535, 800-366-0493;
www.lodgingkillington.com
20 rooms. Complimentary continental breakfast. Outdoor pool. $

★★Summit Lodge
Killington Mountain Rd., Killington,
802-422-3535, 800-635-6343;
www.summitlodgevermont.com
45 rooms. Complimentary full breakfast. Wireless Internet access. Restaurant. Bar. Two outdoor pools, whirlpool. Tennis. $

★★★Cortina Inn and Resort
103 Hwy. 4, Killington,
802-773-3333, 800-451-6108;
www.cortinainn.com

250

VERMONT

Open year-round, this inn offers a perfect weekend retreat. Rooms are cozy and feature wireless internet and Direct TV. 97 rooms. Pets accepted; fee. Complimentary full breakfast. Restaurant. Bar. Fitness room. Indoor pool, whirlpool. Tennis. Airport transportation available. **$**

★★★Inn Of The Six Mountains
2617 Killington Rd., Killington,
802-422-4302, 800-228-4676;
www.sixmountains.com
Located close to Killington ski resort, this inn offers an easy location from which to hit the slopes early in the morning. Cedars restaurant serves breakfast and the lounge is a great place for an après-ski drink.
100 rooms. Complimentary full breakfast. Restaurant. Bar. Fitness room. Indoor pool, outdoor pool, whirlpool. Tennis. **$**

★★★Red Clover Inn
7 Woodward Rd., Mendon,
802-775-2290, 800-752-0571;
www.redcloverinn.com
This 1840s country inn features views of the Green Mountains. Some rooms have fireplaces and four-poster beds.
14 rooms. Children over 12 years only. Complimentary full breakfast. Wireless Internet access. Restaurant. Bar. **$$**

SPECIALTY LODGINGS
Vermont Inn
Hwy. 4, Killington,
802-775-0708, 800-541-7795;
www.vermontinn.com
18 rooms. Children over 6 years only. Restaurant. Bar. Fitness room. Outdoor pool, whirlpool. Tennis. Closed mid-April-late-May. **$$**

RESTAURANTS
★★★Hemingway's
4988 Hwy. 4, Killington, 802-422-3886;
www.hemingwaysrestaurant.com
Housed in a charming 19th-century house, Hemingway's offers a six-course menu, a four-course vegetable menu and a three-course prix fixe menu. Everything is prepared with seasonal ingredients, regional seafood and farm-raised poultry and game. Known for its robust, American fare, the menu features dishes such as pecan-crusted Vermont lamb with crispy potatoes and green beans, and wood-grilled quail with cheddar corn cakes and black-eyed pea vinaigrette. International menu. Dinner. October-mid-November. Bar. Casual attire. Closed Monday-Tuesday; also mid-April-mid-May. **$$$$**

★★★Red Clover
7 Woodward Rd., Mendon,
802-775-2290, 800-752-0571;
www.redcloverinn.com
This 19th-century farmhouse inn offers sophisticated dining in four candlelit rooms. The menu changes frequently and entrees include oven-roasted quail on a Tuscan bean salad and cider-marinated-salmon. American menu. Breakfast, dinner. Bar. Business casual attire. Reservations recommended. Closed Monday-Wednesday. **$$$**

★★Vermont Inn
Hwy. 4, Killington, 802-775-0708,
800-541-7795; www.vermontinn.com
Located in the Vermont Inn, this restaurant features a large wood-burning fireplace, exposed beams and views of the front lawn and mountains.
American menu. Dinner. Bar. Children's menu. Casual attire. Reservations recommended. Closed three weeks in April and May. **$$**

251

VERMONT

LONDONDERRY
A tiny town of less than 2,000 residents, this village is located close to Magic Mountain ski resort.
Information: Londonderry Area Chamber of Commerce Mountain Marketplace, 802-824-8178; www.londonderryvt.com

HOTELS

★★Dostal's Resort Lodge
441 Magic Mountain Access Rd.,
Londonderry, 802-824-6700,
800-255-5373; www.dostals.com
50 rooms. Pets accepted; fee. Restaurant.
Bar. Indoor pool, outdoor pool, whirlpool.
Tennis. Closed November-mid-December.
$

SPECIALTY LODGINGS

Frog's Leap Inn
7455 Highway 100, Londonderry,
802-824-3019, 877-376-4753;
www.frogsleapinn.com
This historic building (1842) is situated on 32
wooded acres.

17 rooms. Pets accepted; fee. Restaurant. Outdoor pool. Tennis. Closed three weeks in April and one week in November. $

Londonderry Inn
8 Melendy Hill Rd., Londonderry,
802-824-5226, 800-644-5226;
www.londonderryinn.com
Built in 1826, this inn used to be a farmhouse. 25 rooms. Complimentary continental breakfast. Restaurant. Outdoor pool. $

Swiss Inn
249 Highway 11, Londonderry,
802-824-3442, 800-847-9477;
www.swissinn.com
19 rooms. Complimentary full breakfast. Restaurant. Bar. Outdoor pool. Tennis. $

LUDLOW

This southwestern Vermont town is close to Okemo Mountain and Ascutney Mountain ski resorts.
Information: Ludlow Area Chamber of Commerce, Okemo Market Place, 802-228-5830

WHAT TO SEE AND DO

Crowley Cheese Factory
103 Healdville Rd., Healdville,
802-259-2340;
www.crowleycheese-vermont.com
(1882) Oldest cheese factory in the United
States that still makes cheese by hand.
Display of tools used in early cheese factories and in home cheesemaking. Watch
the process and sample the product.
Monday-Friday.

Green Mountain Sugar House
820 Highway 100 N., Ludlow,
800-643-9338; www.gmsh.com
Working maple sugar producer on shore of
Lake Pauline.

HOTELS

★★★The Governor's Inn
86 Main St., Ludlow,
802-228-8830, 800-468-3766;
www.thegovernorsinn.com
The challenging slopes of Okemo Mountain
are just a short distance from the Governor's
Inn. A shuttle takes guests to the base of the

mountain from the inn. The building dates
to 1890 and is a Victorian masterpiece.
Many rooms have period antiques and gas-lit stoves or fireplaces. Diners taken with
the cuisine at the restaurant can participate in one of the Culinary Magic Cooking
Seminars.
9 rooms. Children over 12 years only.
Complimentary full breakfast. Restaurant.
Closed late December; also two weeks in
April and two weeks in November. $$

SPECIALTY LODGINGS

Andrie Rose Inn
13 Pleasant St., Ludlow,
802-228-4846, 800-223-4846;
www.andrieroseinn.com
Built in 1829, this inn is at the base of
Okemo Mountain.
23 rooms. Complimentary full breakfast. $

Combes Family Inn
953 E. Lake Rd., Ludlow,
802-228-8799, 800-822-8799;
www.combesfamilyinn.com

This restored farmhouse (1891) is situated on 50 acres of land near Lake Rescue. 11 rooms. Pets accepted. Restaurant. Closed mid-April-mid-May. $

Golden Stage Inn
399 Depot St., Proctorsville,
802-226-7744, 800-253-8226;
www.goldenstageinn.com

9 rooms. Restaurant (public by reservation), bar. Outdoor pool. $$

Inn at Water's Edge
45 Kingdom Rd., Ludlow,
802-228-8143, 888-706-9736;
www.innatwatersedge.com
11 rooms. Complimentary full breakfast. $$

LYNDONVILLE

Lyndonville, located in the valley of the Passumpsic River, is home to several small industries and a trading center for the surrounding dairy and stock raising farms. Five covered bridges, the earliest dating to 1795, are found within the town limits.
Information: Lyndon Area Chamber of Commerce, 802-626-9696; www.lyndonvermont.com

WHAT TO SEE AND DO
Burke Mountain Ski Area
Rte. 114 E. & E. Burke, Lyndonville,
802-626-3322, 888-287-5388;
www.skiburke.com
Area has two chairlifts, one Pomalift, J-bar, school, rentals and snowmaking; two cafeterias, two bars, nursery. Forty-three runs, longest run approximately 2 1/2 miles, with a vertical drop of 2,000 feet. More than 57 miles of cross-country trails. Thanksgiving-early April: daily.

HOTELS
★Colonnade Inn
28 Back Center Rd., Lyndonville,
802-626-9316, 877-435-5688

40 rooms. Complimentary continental breakfast. $

SPECIALTY LODGINGS
The Wildflower Inn
2059 Darling Hill Rd., Lyndonville,
802-626-8310, 800-627-8310;
www.wildflowerinn.com
Family-oriented inn on 500 acres; barns, farm animals, sledding slopes. Art gallery. 25 rooms. Complimentary full breakfast. Restaurant. Children's activity center. Outdoor pool, children's pool, whirlpool. Tennis. Closed two weeks in April and November. $

MANCHESTER
Manchester and Manchester Center have been among Vermont's best-loved year-round resorts for 100 years. The surrounding mountains and the ski business add to their popularity. Bromley Mountain, Stratton Mountain and other areas lure thousands each year and a Ranger District office of the Green Mountain National Forest is located here.
Information: Manchester and the Mountains Regional Chamber of Commerce, 5046 Main St., 802-362-2100, 800-362-4144; www.manchestervermont.net

253

VERMONT

★
★
★
★
★

WHAT TO SEE AND DO

American Museum of Fly Fishing

410 Main St., Manchester,
802-362-3300; www.amff.com

Founded in 1968 by fishermen who wanted to ensure that the history of their sport would not be lost, this museum is a mecca for anglers of all ages. Collection of fly-fishing memorabilia and tackle of many famous persons, including Dwight D. Eisenhower, Ernest Hemingway, Andrew Carnegie, Winslow Homer, Bing Crosby and others. Monday-Friday 10 a.m.-4 p.m.

Emerald Lake State Park

65 Emerald Lake Lane, North Dorset,
802-362-1655

This 430-acre park has rich flora in a limestone-based bedrock. Swimming beach, bathhouse, fishing (also in nearby streams), boating (rentals), nature and hiking trails, picnicking, concession. Tent and trailer sites (dump station). Standard fees. Memorial Day-Columbus Day.

Equinox Sky Line Drive

1A St. and Bruno Dr., Manchester and Manchester Center, 802-362-1114; www.equinoxmountain.com/skylinedrive

A spectacular five-mile paved road that rises from 600 to 3,835 feet. Parking and picnic areas are along the road and a view from top of Mount Equinox. Fog or rain may make mountain road dangerous and travel inadvisable. May-October: daily. No large camper vehicles.

Historic Hildene

1005 Hildene Rd., Manchester, 802-362-1788;
www.hildene.org

(1904) The 412-acre estate of Robert Todd Lincoln (Abraham Lincoln's son) includes a 24-room Georgian manor house, held in the family until 1975. Original furnishings, carriage barn, formal gardens, nature trails. Tours. Mid-May-October: daily 9:30 a.m.-3 p.m.; November-May: Thursday-Monday 11 a.m.-3 p.m.

Manchester Designer Outlets

Highways 11 and 30, Manchester Center,
802-362-3736;
www.manchesterdesigneroutlets.com

Many outlet stores can be found in this area, mainly along Highway 11/30 and at the intersection of Highway 11/30 and Highway 7A. Contact the Chamber of Commerce (802-362-2100) for a complete listing of stores.

HOTELS

★Aspen Motel

5669 Main St., Manchester Center,
802-362-2450;
www.thisisvermont.com/aspen

24 rooms. Outdoor pool. **$**

★Manchester View

Hwy. 7A and High Meadow Way,
Manchester Center,
802-362-2739, 800-548-4141;
www.manchesterview.com

35 rooms. Complimentary continental breakfast. Outdoor pool. **$**

Palmer House

5383 Main St., Manchester Center,
802-362-3600, 800-917-6245;
www.palmerhouse.com

50 rooms. Children over 12 years only. Complimentary continental breakfast. Fitness room. Indoor pool, outdoor pool, whirlpool. Golf, 9 holes. Tennis. **$**

★★★Village Country Inn

3835 Main St., Manchester,
802-362-1792, 800-370-0300;
www.villagecountryinn.com

A perfect romantic getaway. This historic mansion has rooms adorned with lace, chintz, mirrored armoires, antique collectibles, canopied beds and fireplaces. The on-site restaurant, Angel, is decorated in a cheerful garden style and features American cuisine.

32 rooms. Pets accepted, some restrictions; fee. Children over 12 years only. Complimentary full breakfast. Restaurant. Bar. Outdoor pool. **$$**

★★★The Equinox
3567 Main St., Manchester Village,
802-362-4700, 866-346-7625;
www.equinox.rockresorts.com
Open since 1769, the Equinox, listed on
the National Register of Historic Places, is
located in the shadow of Mount Equinox.
This premier resort has long been a favorite of notables, including the Lincolns,
Tafts and Roosevelts. From world-class
golf at the Gleneagles golf course, skiing
at nearby Stratton and Bromley mountains,
Orvis fly fishing and shooting schools, and
its very own falconry center, this place is
a paradise for sports enthusiasts. A luxe
new spa is located on site, as are three
restaurants.
180 rooms. Pets accepted, some restrictions;
fee. Wireless Internet access. Three restaurants, two bars. Fitness room, fitness
classes available, spa. Indoor pool, whirlpool. Golf, 18 holes. Tennis. Ski in/ski out.
Airport transportation available. Business
center. $$$

★★★Reluctant Panther Inn and Restaurant
39 West Rd., Manchester,
802-362-2568, 800-822-2331;
www.reluctantpanther.com
This inn was built in 1850 by a wealthy
blacksmith. The owners have refurbished
the property, retaining two of the original
fireplaces.
21 rooms. Children over 14 years only. Com-
plimentary full breakfast. Restaurant. Bar.
$$

SPECIALTY LODGINGS
1811 House
Main St., Manchester,
802-362-1811, 800-432-1811;
www.1811house.com
Each guest room at this inn is named for
individuals who were prominent in the
history of Manchester. Gardens surround
around the inn.
13 rooms. Children over 16 years only Com-
plimentary full breakfast. Bar. Tennis. $$

Inn at Manchester
3967 Main St., Manchester,
802-362-1793, 800-273-1793,
www.innatmanchester.com
This 19th-century Victorian structure has
been beautifully restored to its original
grandeur.
18 rooms. Children over 8 years only. Com-
plimentary full breakfast. Wireless Internet
access. Outdoor pool. $$

The Inn at Ormsby Hill
1842 Main St., Manchester, 802-362-1163
Hospitality and relaxation await at this
tranquil location surrounded by views of
the Green Mountains. The common areas
feature a collection of china and unique
fireplaces.
10 rooms. Complimentary full breakfast.
$$

Manchester Highlands Inn
216 Highland Ave., Manchester Center,
802-362-4565, 800-743-4565;
www.highlandsinn.com
Views of Mount Equinox can be seen from
this Victorian inn. Plenty of outlet shopping
is nearby.
15 rooms. Complimentary full breakfast.
Wireless Internet access. Outdoor pool. $$

Wilburton Inn
River Rd., Manchester Village,
802-362-2500, 800-648-4944;
www.wilburton.com
Set on a hill that overlooks the Battenkill
Valley, this 20-acre Victorian estate offers
guests numerous on-site activities as well as
nearby shopping.
36 rooms. Complimentary full breakfast.
Outdoor pool. $$

SPAS
★★★Avanyu Spa at the Equinox Resort
3567 Main St., Manchester Village,
802-362-4700
This recently constructed 13,000-square-
foot spa has a 75-foot heated indoor pool,
state-of-the-art fitness center, 10 treatment
rooms, saunas and steam baths. Treatments
include the Gentle Rain body treatment,

VERMONT

where a sea salt, maple or citrus scrub is followed with a warm waterfall shower and an application of a rich body cream. Massage therapies like Flowing Water, Rolling Thunder and Dancing Wind simulate nature's energies through effleurage, deep tissue and gentle massage techniques.

MIDDLEBURY

Benjamin Smalley built the first log house here just before the Revolution. In 1800, the town had a full-fledged college and, by 1803, there was a flourishing marble quarry and a women's academy run by Emma Hart Willard, a pioneer in education for women. Today, Middlebury is known for Middlebury College. A Ranger District office of the Green Mountain National Forest is also located here, and a map and guides for day hikes on Long Trail are available.

Information: Addison County Chamber of Commerce Information Center, 2 Court St., 802-388-7951, 800-733-8376; www.midvermont.com

WHAT TO SEE AND DO

Congregational Church
27 N. Pleasant St., Middlebury, 802-388-7634
(1806-1809) Built after a plan in the *Country Builder's Assistant* and designed by architect Lavius Fillmore. Architecturally, one of the finest in Vermont.

Middlebury College
Middlebury College, Route 30, Middlebury, 802-443-5000;
www.middlebury.edu
(1800) (1,950 students) Famous for the teaching of arts and sciences, summer language schools; Bread Loaf School of English and Writers' Conference.

Bread Loaf
Middlebury College, Freeman International Center, Middlebury, 802-443-5418
Site of nationally known Bread Loaf School of English in June and annual Writers' Conference in August. Also site of Robert Frost's cabin. In winter, it is the Carroll and Jane Rikert Ski Touring Center.

Middlebury College Snow Bowl
Route 125, Middlebury, 802-388-7951
Area has triple, two double chairlifts, patrol, school, rentals, snowmaking, cafe-teria. Fourteen runs. Early December-early April, daily.

Vermont State Craft Center at Frog Hollow
1 Mill St., Middlebury, 802-388-3177, 888-388-3177;
www.froghollow.org
Restored mill overlooking Otter Creek Falls houses an exhibition and sales gallery with works of more than 300 Vermont artists. Special exhibitions, classes and workshops. (Spring-fall: daily; rest of year: Monday-Saturday.

SPECIAL EVENTS

Festival on the Green
Middlebury Green, Main St. and Highway 7, Middlebury, 802-388-0216;
www.festivalonthegreen.org
Village green. Classical, modern and traditional dance; chamber and folk music; theater and comedy presentations. Early July.

Winter Carnival
Middlebury College, Highway 30, Middlebury, 802-443-3100
The oldest and largest student-run carnival in the country includes fireworks, an ice show and ski competitions; held on the campus of Middlebury College. Late February.

HOTELS

★★Middlebury Inn
24 Court House Square, Middlebury, 802-388-4961, 800-842-4666;
www.middleburyinn.com

VERMONT

★

★

★

★

★

45 rooms. Pets accepted, some restrictions. Complimentary continental breakfast Restaurant. Bar. **$$**

★★★Swift House Inn
25 Stewart Lane, Middlebury,
802-388-9925, 866-388-9925;
www.swifthouseinn.com
This inn has three separate buildings, each with its own character and charm. Rooms are individually decorated and feature four-poster beds and handmade quilts.

Pets accepted, some restrictions; fee. Complimentary continental breakfast. Restaurant. **$$**

SPECIALTY LODGINGS
Waybury Inn
457 E. Main, East Middlebury,
802-388-4015, 800-348-1810;
www.wayburyinn.com
Constructed as a stagecoach stop; an inn since 1810. Near Middlebury College. 14 rooms. Pets accepted. Complimentary full breakfast. Restaurant. Bar. **$**

MONTPELIER
Vermont's capital is one of the nation's most picturesque, located on the banks of the Winooski River and made up of quaint brick buildings. A popular summer vacation area, Montpelier absorbs the overflow from the nearby ski areas in winter.
Information: Central Vermont Chamber of Commerce, Barre, 802-229-5711; www.central-vt.com

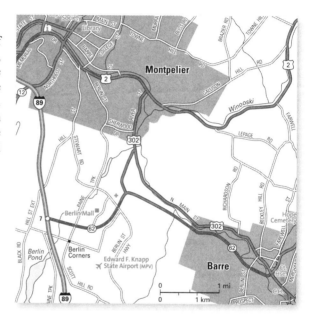

VERMONT

★MONTPELIER IS THE SMALLEST STATE CAPITAL IN THE COUNTRY.
★THE NEW ENGLAND CULINARY INSTITUTE IS LOCATED IN MONTPELIER.
★THE CITY IS THE ONLY U.S. CAPITAL WITHOUT A MCDONALD'S.

WHAT TO SEE AND DO
Morse Farm
1168 County Rd., Montpelier,
802-223-2740, 800-242-2740;
www.morsefarm.com
Maple sugar and vegetable farm in rustic, wooded setting. Tour of sugar house; view sugar-making process in season March-April. Slide show explains process off-season. Gift shop. Daily.

State House
115 State St., Montpelier, 802-828-2228,
www.leg.state.vt.us/sthouse/sthouse.htm
(1859) Made of Vermont granite; dome covered with gold leaf. Monday-Friday 8 a.m.-4 p.m.; guided tours, July-mid-October: Monday-Friday 10 a.m.-3:30 p.m., Saturday 11 a.m.-2:30 p.m.

Thomas Waterman Wood Art Gallery

36 College St., Montpelier, 802-828-8743;
www.twwoodgallery.org
Oils, watercolors and etchings by Wood and other 19th-century American artists. Also, American artists of the 1920s and 30s, changing monthly exhibits of works of contemporary local and regional artists. Tuesday-Wednesday, Friday-Sunday noon-4 p.m.; Thursday to 8 p.m.

Vermont Historical Society Museum

109 State St., Montpelier, 802-828-2291;
www.vermonthistory.org
Historical exhibits. Tuesday-Sunday; closed holidays.

HOTELS

★Comfort Inn

213 Paine Turnpike N., Montpelier,
802-229-2222, 800-424-6423;
www.choicehotels.com
89 rooms. Complimentary continental breakfast. Bar. Airport transportation available. $

★★★Capitol Plaza Hotel and Conference Center

100 State St., Montpelier,
802-223-5252, 800-274-5252;
www.capitolplaza.com
Across the street from the historic State House, this hotel has served Vermont's lawmakers and tourists since the 1930s.
56 rooms. Restaurant. Bar. $

★★★Inn At Montpelier

147 Main St., Montpelier,
802-223-2727;
www.innatmontpelier.com
Re-visit the early 1800s at this historic inn. Comprised of two stately buildings, this inn showcases Greek and Colonial Revival woodwork, numerous fireplaces and a spectacular front staircase.
19 rooms. Complimentary continental breakfast. $

★★★The Inn On The Common

1162 N. Craftsbury Rd., Craftsbury Common, 802-586-9619, 800-521-2233;
www.innonthecommon.com
This inn is made up of three restored Federal-style houses that feature colorful gardens and wooded hillsides.
16 rooms. Pets accepted, some restrictions; fee. Restaurant. Bar. Outdoor pool. Tennis. $$

SPECIALTY LODGINGS

Northfield Inn

228 Highland Ave., Northfield,
802-485-8558; www.thenorthfieldinn.com
This inn was built in 1901and is furnished with period pieces.
28 rooms. Children over 15 years only. Complimentary full breakfast. $

RESTAURANTS

★★Chef's Table

118 Main St., Montpelier, 802-229-9202;
www.neci.edu/restaurants.html
International menu. Dinner. Bar. Closed Sunday-Monday. $$$

NEWFANE

Originally settled high on Newfane Hill, this postcard-perfect Vermont town was a favorite vacation spot for American poet Eugene Field.
Information: Town Clerk, 802-365-7772; www.newfanevt.com

WHAT TO SEE AND DO

Scott Covered Bridge

Route 30, Townshend, 802-257-0292
(1870) Longest single span in the state (166 feet), built with lattice-type trusses. Together the three spans total 276 feet.

Other two spans are of king post-type trusses.

Townshend State Forest

2755 State Forest Rd., Townshend,
802-365-7500

A 1,690-acre area with foot trail to Bald Mountain (1,580 feet). Swimming at nearby Townshend Reservoir Recreation Area, hiking trails, picnic sites, tent and trailer sites. Standard fees. May-Columbus Day.

HOTELS

★★★Windham Hill Inn
311 Lawrence Dr., West Townshend, 802-874-4080, 800-944-4080; www.windhamhill.com
This charming and elegant 1825 country estate features rooms with fireplaces, spa or soaking tubs and plush beds. The onsite restaurant serves full country breakfasts and simple, well-prepared dinners.
21 rooms. Children over 12 years only. Restaurant. Outdoor pool. Tennis. **$$**

SPECIALTY LODGINGS

Four Columns Inn
21 West St., Newfane, 802-365-7713, 800-787-6633; www.fourcolumnsinn.com
Located in the center of Newfane and at the foot of a private mountain, this 16-room inn combines historic charm with modern flair. While some rooms are without TVs, all have wireless Internet access. The decor is old-fashioned, with sleigh and iron four-poster beds. Many suites have two-sided fireplaces and most rooms have whirlpools or soaking tubs.

16 rooms. Pets accepted, some restrictions; fee. Complimentary continental breakfast. Restaurant. Bar. Outdoor pool. **$$$**

RESTAURANTS

★★★Four Columns
21 West St., Newfane, 802-365-7713, 800-787-6633; www.fourcolumnsinn.com
Chef Greg Parks offers innovative and contemporary cuisine and an award-winning wine list at this welcoming inn. Dinner often features dishes such as grilled angus tenderloin with green peppercorn vinaigrette. American menu. Breakfast for inn guests only, dinner. Bar. Casual attire. Reservations recommended. Outdoor seating. Closed Tuesday. **$$$**

★★★Old Newfane Inn
Highway 30, Newfane, 802-365-4427, 800-784-4427; www.oldnewfaneinn.com
Timbered ceilings and brick fireplaces add to the colonial charm of this historic 1787 landmark. The restaurant specializes in European classics such as chateaubriand and veal goulash.
Continental, French menu. Dinner. Bar. Casual attire. Reservations recommended. Closed Monday; April-mid-May, November-mid-December. **$$**

★
★
★
★
★
★

NORTH HERO

This far northern Vermont town borders Lake Champlain and is close to both New York State and Quebec, Canada.
Information: Champlain Islands Chamber of Commerce, 802-372-8400; www.champlainislands.com

WHAT TO SEE AND DO
North Hero State Park
3803 Lakeview Dr., North Hero, 802-372-8727
A 399-acre park located in the north part of the Champlain Islands; extensive shoreline on Lake Champlain. Swimming, fishing, boating (ramps), hiking trails, playground,

tent and trailer sites (dump station). Standard fees. Memorial Day-Labor Day.

SPECIAL EVENTS
Royal Lippizan Stallions of Austria
Knight Point State Park, 44 Knight Point Rd., North Hero, 802-372-8400, 800-262-5226; www.herrmannslipizzans.com

Summer residence of the stallions. Performances Thursday and Friday evenings, Saturday and Sunday afternoons. For ticket prices, contact Chamber of Commerce. July-August.

HOTELS
★★Shore Acres Inn
237 Shore Acres Dr., North Hero, 802-372-8722; www.shoreacres.com
23 rooms. Pets accepted; fee. Restaurant. Bar. Tennis. **$**

★★★North Hero House Inn
Highway 2, North Hero, 802-372-4732, 888-525-3644; www.northherohouse.com
This inn, built in 1800, is surrounded by spectacular views of the Green Mountains and Mount Mansfield. Activities are available year-round.

26 rooms. Complimentary continental breakfast. Restaurant. Bar. Tennis. **$$**

SPECIALTY LODGINGS
Thomas Mott Alburg Homestead B&B
63 Blue Rock Rd., Alburg, 802-796-4402, 800-348-0843; www.thomas-mott-bb.com
This restored farmhouse (1838) overlooks the lake.
4 rooms. Children over 6 years only. Complimentary full breakfast. **$**

RESTAURANTS
★★North Hero House
Highway 2, North Hero, 802-372-4732, 888-525-3644; www.northherohouse.com
American menu. Breakfast for inn guests only, dinner, Sunday brunch. Bar. Outdoor seating. **$$**

PLYMOUTH

This town hasn't changed much since July 4, 1872, when Calvin Coolidge was born in the back of the village store (which is still in business today). A country road leads to the cemetery where the former president and six generations of his family are buried. Nearby is the Coolidge Visitors Center and Museum, which displays historical and presidential memorabilia.
Information: Town of Plymouth, 802-672-3655

WHAT TO SEE AND DO
President Calvin Coolidge Homestead
Coolidge Memorial Dr., Plymouth Notch, 802-672-3773; www.dhca.state.vt.us
In 1923, Calvin Coolidge was sworn in by his father in his house's sitting room, which has been restored to its early-20th-century appearance. The Plymouth Historic District also includes the General Store that was operated by the president's father, the house where the president was born, the village dance hall that served as the 1924 summer White House office, the Union Church with its Carpenter Gothic interior, the Wilder House (birthplace of Coolidge's mother), the Wilder Barn with 19th-century farming equipment, a restaurant and a visitor center with museum. Late-May-mid-October: daily 9:30 a.m.-5 p.m.

HOTELS
★Farmbrook Motel
706 Highway 100A, Plymouth, 802-672-3621; www.farmbrookmotel.net
12 rooms. **$**

★★★Hawk Inn and Mountain Resort
Route 100 S., Plymouth, 802-672-3811, 800-685-4295; www.hawkresort.com
From rooms at the inn to luxurious mountainside villas on the resort's nearly 1,200 acres, guests will enjoy privacy and a variety of onsite activities including a spa and stables.
200 rooms. Restaurant. Bar. Children's activity center. Fitness room. Indoor pool, outdoor pool, whirlpool. Tennis. Airport transportation available. **$$$**

RUTLAND

This is Vermont's second-largest city. Its oldest newspaper, the *Rutland Herald*, has been published continuously since 1794. The world's deepest marble quarry is in West Rutland and the office of the supervisor of the Green Mountain National Forest is located here. Information: Chamber of Commerce, 256 N. Main St., 802-773-2747; www.rutlandvermont.com

WHAT TO SEE AND DO

Hubbardton Battlefield and Museum
5696 Monument Hill Rd., East Hubbardton, 802-759-2412; www.dhca.state.vt.us
On July 7, 1777, the Green Mountain Boys and colonial troops from Massachusetts and New Hampshire stopped British forces pursuing the American Army from Fort Ticonderoga. This was the only battle of the Revolution fought on Vermont soil and the first in a series of engagements that led to the capitulation of Burgoyne at Saratoga. Visitor Center with exhibits. Battle monument, trails, picnicking. Memorial Day-Columbus Day: Wednesday-Sunday 9:30 a.m.-5 p.m.

New England Maple Museum
Highway 7, Pittsford, 802-483-9414; www.maplemuseum.com
One of the largest collections of antique maple sugaring artifacts in the world; two large dioramas featuring more than 100 hand-carved figures; narrated slide show; demonstrations, samples of Vermont foodstuffs; craft and maple product gift shop. Late-May-October: daily 8:30 a.m.-5:30 p.m.; November-December, mid-March-late-May: daily 10 a.m.-4 p.m.; closed January-February.

Norman Rockwell Museum
654 Highway 4 E., Rutland, 802-773-6095; www.normanrockwellvt.com
More than 2,000 pictures and Rockwell memorabilia spanning 60 years of the artist's career. Includes the Four *Freedoms*, Boy Scout series, many magazine covers, including all 323 from the *Saturday Evening Post* and nearly every illustration and advertisement. Daily.

Wilson Castle
W. Proctor Rd., Center Rutland,
802-773-3284; www.wilsoncastle.com
This 32-room 19th-century mansion features 19 open proscenium arches, 84 stained-glass windows, 13 imported tile fireplaces, a towering turret and parapet; European and Asian furnishings; art gallery; sculpture; 15 other buildings. Picnic area. Guided tours. Late-May-late-October: daily 9 a.m.-6 p.m.; Christmas tours.

HOTELS

★Best Western Inn & Suites Rutland/Killington
1 Route 4 E., Rutland,
802-773-3200, 800-720-7234;
www.bestwestern-rutland.com
56 rooms. Complimentary continental breakfast. Wireless Internet access. Fitness room. Outdoor pool. Tennis. $$

★★Comfort Inn
19 Allen St., Rutland,
802-775-2200, 800-432-6788;
www.choicehotels.com
104 rooms. Pets accepted, some restrictions; fee. Complimentary continental breakfast. Wireless Internet access. Restaurant. Bar. Indoor pool, whirlpool. Business center. $

★★Holiday Inn Rutland/Killington
2111 Highway 7 S., Rutland,
802-775-1911, 800-462-4810;
www.ichotelsgroup.com/h/d/6c/1/en/hd/rutvt
151 rooms. Pets accepted; fee. Wireless Internet access. Restaurant. Bar. Fitness room. Indoor pool, whirlpool. Airport transportation available. Business center. $$

★★★Mountain Top Inn
195 Mountain Top Rd., Chittenden,
800-445-2100, 800-445-2100;
www.mountaintopinn.com
Located in the Green Mountains of Vermont close to Killington ski resort,

VERMONT

the guest rooms at this inn are rustic and cozy, with down duvets and rich toiles and chintzes.

60 rooms. Closed April and first three weeks in November. Pets accepted; fee. Restaurant. Bar. Outdoor pool. Golf. Tennis. $$

SPECIALTY LODGINGS
Inn at Rutland
70 N. Main St., Rutland,
802-773-0575, 800-808-0575;
www.innatrutland.com

This Victorian mansion was built in 1893 and has been completed restored to its former elegance.

11 rooms. Complimentary full breakfast. $

Maplewood Inn
1108 S. Main St., Fair Haven,
802-265-8039, 800-253-7729;
www.maplewoodinn.net
Listed on the National Register of Historic Places, this Greek Revival inn has rooms with period decor and is perfect for a romantic getaway.

5 rooms. Pets accepted, some restrictions. Complimentary full breakfast. $

SHELBURNE
With the Adirondack Mountains on the west and the Green Mountains on the east, Shelburne is a small, friendly town that borders Lake Champlain. The Shelburne Museum has one of the most comprehensive exhibits of early American life.
Information: Town Hall, 5420 Shelburne Rd., 802-985-5110; www.shelburnevt.org

WHAT TO SEE AND DO
Shelburne Farms
1611 Harbor Rd., Shelburne,
802-985-8686; www.shelburnefarms.org
Built at the turn of the 20th century, this is the former estate of Dr. Seward Webb and his wife, Lila Vanderbilt. Located on the shores of Lake Champlain, the grounds, landscaped by Frederick Law Olmstead and forested by Gifford Pinchot, once totaled 3,800 acres. Structures include the Webbs' mansion, Shelburne House, a 110-room summer "cottage" built in the late 1800s on a bluff overlooking the lake, a five-story farm barn, and the coach barn, once the home of prize horses. Tours Memorial Day-mid-October: daily 9 a.m.-5:30 p.m.; off-season, daily 10 a.m.-5 p.m. Also, hayrides, walking trail. Visitor center, 802-985-8442. Cheese shop (all year, daily). Overnight stays available.

Shelburne Museum
5555 Shelburne Rd., Shelburne,
802-985-3346; www.shelburnemuseum.org
Founded by Electra Webb, daughter of Sugar King H. O. Havemeyer, this collection of Americana is located on 45 acres with 37 historic buildings containing items such as historic circus posters, toys, weather vanes, trade signs and an extensive collection of wildfowl decoys and dolls. American and European paintings and prints (including works by Monet and Grandma Moses) are on display as well. Also here is the 220-foot side-wheel steamboat *Ticonderoga*, which carried passengers across Lake Champlain in the early part of the century and is now the last vertical beam passenger and freight side-wheel steamer intact in the United States. There is a working carousel and a 5,000-piece hand-carved miniature traveling circus, a fully intact lighthouse, a one-room schoolhouse, an authentic country store, the only two-lane covered bridge with footpath in Vermont, blacksmith shop, printing and weaving demonstrations, farm equipment and more than 200 horse-drawn vehicles on display. May-October:daily 10 a.m.-5 p.m.

Vermont Teddy Bear Company
6655 Shelburne Rd., Shelburne,
802-985-1319; www.vermontteddybear.com

262

VERMONT

★
★
★
★
★

The guided tour at this factory shows the process of handcrafting these famous stuffed animals. The onsite gift shop ensures that you won't go home empty handed—the Bear Shop opens at 9 a.m. daily. Call for a tour schedule.

Vermont Wildflower Farm
4750 Shelburne Ave., Shelburne,
802-425-3641;
www.vermontwildflowerfarm.com

Acres of wildflower gardens, flower fields and woodlands, pond and brook. April-October, daily 10 a.m.-5 p.m.

HOTELS
★**Days Inn**
3229 Shelburne Rd., Shelburne,
802-985-3334, 800-329-7466;
www.daysinnshelburne.com
58 rooms. Complimentary continental breakfast. Outdoor pool. **$**

SPRINGFIELD

The cascades of the Black River once provided power for the machine tool plants that stretch along Springfield's banks. Lord Jeffrey Amherst started the Crown Point Military Road to Lake Champlain from here in 1759. Springfield has been the home of many New England inventors and is also the headquarters of the Amateur Telescope Makers who meet at Stellafane, an observatory site west of Highway 11.
Information: Chamber of Commerce, 14 Clinton St., 802-885-2779; www.springfieldvt.com

WHAT TO SEE AND DO
Eureka Schoolhouse
Charlestown Rd., Springfield,
802-885-2779
Oldest schoolhouse in the state, built in 1790. Nearby is a 100-year-old lattice-truss covered bridge. Memorial Day-Columbus Day, Wednesday-Monday 10 a.m.-4 p.m.

Reverend Dan Foster House & Old Forge
2656 Weathersfield Center Rd.,
Weathersfield, 802-263-5230.;
www.weathersfield.org
Historic parsonage (1785) contains antique furniture, textiles, utensils, farm tools; old forge has working machinery and bellows. Guided tours. For further information contact the Chamber of Commerce. Mid-June-October: Thursday-Monday 2-5 p.m. or by appointment.

Springfield Art and Historical Society
Miller Art Center, 9 Elm Hill, Springfield,
802-885-2415; www.millerartcenter.org
American art and artifacts. Collections include Richard Lee pewter, Bennington pottery, 19th-century American paintings, costumes, dolls and toys. Springfield historical items. Changing exhibits. Mid-

April-October: Tuesday-Friday 10 a.m.-4 p.m., Saturday 10 a.m.-1 p.m.

HOTELS
★**Holiday Inn Express**
818 Charlestown Rd., Springfield,
802-885-4516; 800-465-4329;
www.vermonthi.com
88 rooms. Pets accepted; fee. Complimentary continental breakfast. Wireless Internet access. Fitness room. Indoor pool. Business center. **$$**

★★★**The Inn at Weathersfield**
1342 Highway 106, Weathersfield,
802-263-9217; www.weathersfieldinn.com
This colonial countryside inn is full of charm and tranquility. Shopping, state parks, hiking, skiing and sleigh and carriage rides are just minutes away. Gourmet, candlelit dinners are served in a dining room that includes an eclectic mix of original wood beams and rustic tables. A natural amphitheater on the grounds is used in summer for performances by local musicians, and also for weddings.
12 rooms. Children over 14 years only. Complimentary full breakfast. Wireless

Internet access. Restaurant. Bar. Airport transportation available. $$

SPECIALTY LODGINGS
Hartness House
30 Orchard St., Springfield,
802-885-2115, 800-732-4789;
www.hartnesshouse.com

This lodging is part historic inn, part aviation museum and working observatory. A former Vermont governor, James Hartness was an inventor who built a series of underground tunnels where he could work without being disturbed. He was also an aviation pioneer who was fascinated with astronomy and telescope making. Today three of the workrooms in Hartness' underground tunnels have been turned into a museum. The underground tunnels also lead to the original 1903 Hartness House, containing 14 guest rooms above. Two wings wrap around the pool, one with eight rooms, the other with 24. The Hartness House is surrounded by woods and winding nature trails—the innkeepers will be happy to make you a sack lunch to take along on a hike.

43 rooms. Pets accepted, some restrictions; fee. Complimentary full breakfast. Wireless Internet access. Restaurant. Bar. Outdoor pool. $

Stone Hearth Inn
698 Highway 11 W., Chester,
802-875-2525, 888-617-3656;
www.thestonehearthinn.com

Restored farm house (1810); antiques. 10 rooms. Complimentary full breakfast. Bar. $$

ST. JOHNSBURY

This town was named for Ethan Allen's French friend, John Hector St. John de Crevecoeur, author of *Letters from an American Farmer*. The town gained fame when Thaddeus Fairbanks invented the platform scale in 1830. Fairbanks scales, maple syrup and manufacturing are among this town's major industries.

Information: Northeast Kingdom Chamber of Commerce, 357 Western Ave., 802-748-3678, 800-639-6379; www.vermontnekchamber.org

WHAT TO SEE AND DO
Fairbanks Museum and Planetarium
1302 Main St., St. Johnsbury,
802-748-2372; www.fairbanksmuseum.org

Exhibits and programs on natural science, regional history, archaeology, anthropology, astronomy and the arts. More than 4,500 mounted birds and mammals, antique toys, farm, village and craft tools; Northern New England Weather Broadcasting Center; planetarium; Hall of Science; special exhibitions in Gallery Wing. Monday-Saturday, also Sunday afternoons. Planetarium (July-August: daily; rest of year: Saturday-Sunday only).

Maple Grove Farms of Vermont Factory Tours & Maple Museum
1052 Portland St., St. Johnsbury,
802-748-5141; www.maplegrove.com

Learn about Vermont's maple syrup industry on this factory tour, which offers glimpses into the process of making pure syrup and maple candy. Also, taste the various grades of syrup available in the Cabin Shop. May-December, Monday-Friday 8 a. m.-2 p.m.

SPECIAL EVENTS
St. Johnsbury Town Band
Courthouse Park, St. Johnsbury,
802-748-8891

One of the oldest continuously performing bands (since 1830) in the country plays weekly outdoor evening concerts. Contact the Chamber of Commerce for further information. Monday, mid-June-late August.

HOTELS
★The Fairbanks Inn
401 Western Ave., St. Johnsbury,

802-748-5666; www.stjay.com
46 rooms. Pets accepted; fee. Complimentary continental breakfast. Outdoor pool. **$**

★Holiday Motel
222 Hastings St., St. Johnsbury,
802-748-8192
34 rooms. Pets accepted, some restrictions; fee. Outdoor pool. **$**

★★★Rabbit Hill Inn
48 Lower Waterford Rd., Lower Waterford,
802-748-5168, 800-762-8669;
www.rabbithillinn.com
This old-fashioned inn dates to 1795. Rooms are decorated in a crisp, colonial style. Befitting a bed-and-breakfast, there is a lavish morning buffet, afternoon tea and five-course dinners.

19 rooms. Children over 13 years only. Complimentary full breakfast. Restaurant. Bar. Closed first two weeks of April and first two weeks of November. **$$**

RESTAURANTS
★★★Rabbit Hill
48 Lower Waterford Rd., Lower Waterford,
802-748-5168, 800-762-8669;
www.rabbithillinn.com
This charming country inn has an acclaimed restaurant where fresh seasonal ingredients are the focus. Roasted rack of lamb comes with thyme-whipped potatoes, while seared duck breast is served with currant and pear-laced bulghar wheat, Brussels sprouts and peach chutney.
American menu. Breakfast, dinner. Bar. Reservations recommended. **$$$**

STOWE
Stowe is a year-round resort area, with more than half of its visitors coming during the summer. Mount Mansfield, Vermont's highest peak (4,393 feet), offers skiing, snowboarding, snowshoeing and skating in the winter. Summer visitors can experience outdoor concerts, hiking, biking, golf, tennis and many events and attractions, including a Ben & Jerry's ice cream factory tour. Information: Stowe Area Association, Main St., 802-253-7321, 877-467-8693; www.gostowe.com

265

WHAT TO SEE AND DO
Alpine Slide
Stowe Mountain Resort, Spruce Peak,
Stowe, 802-253-3000, 800-253-4754;
www.stowe.com
Chairlift takes riders to a 2,300-foot slide that runs through the woods and open field. Speed controlled by rider. Late June-Labor Day: daily 10 a.m.-5 p.m.; September-mid-October: weekends.

Mount Mansfield State Forest
This 38,000-acre forest can be reached from Underhill Flats, off Highway 15, or from Stowe through Smugglers' Notch, north on Highway 108. The Long Trail leads to the summit of Mount Mansfield from the north and south. There are three state recreation areas in the forest. **Smugglers' Notch** (802-253-4014 or 802-479-4280) and **Underhill** (802-899-3022 or 802-879-5674) areas offer hiking, skiing, snowmo-

biling, picnicking, camping (dump station). **Little River Camping Area** (802-244-7103 or 802-479-4280), northwest of Waterbury, offers swimming, fishing, boating (rentals for campers only), hiking, camping. Memorial Day-Columbus Day.

Stowe Mountain Resort
5781 Mountain Rd., Stowe,
802-253-3000, 800-253-4754;
www.stowe.com
Resort has quad, triple and six double chairlifts, Mighty-mite handle tow, patrol, school, rentals, snowmaking, cafeterias, restaurants, bar, entertainment, nursery. Forty-seven runs, longest run more than 3 1/2 miles; vertical drop 2,360 feet. Night skiing. Mid-November-mid-April: daily. Summer activities include three outdoor swimming pools, alpine slide (mid-June-early September, daily), mountain biking (rentals), gondola

rides, in-line skate park, fitness center, spa, recreation trail, tennis, golf.

Mount Mansfield Gondola
Stowe Mountain Resort,
5781 Mountain Rd., Stowe,
802-253-3000, 800-253-4754;
An eight-passenger enclosed gondola ride to the summit of Vermont's highest peak. Spectacular view of the area. Restaurant and gift shop. Mid-June-mid-October, daily 10 a.m.-5 p.m.

SPECIAL EVENTS
Stoweflake Balloon Festival
Stoweflake Mountain Resort & Spa,
1746 Mountain Rd., Stowe,
800-253-2232;
www.stoweflake.com
Stoweflake Resort Field, Highway 108. More than 20 balloons launched continuously. Second weekend in July.

HOTELS
★★Edson Hill Manor
1500 Edson Hill Rd., Stowe,
802-253-7371, 800-621-0284;
www.edsonhillmanor.com
25 rooms. Pets accepted, some restrictions. Complimentary full breakfast. Restaurant. Bar. Indoor pool. Ski in/ski out. **$$**

★★Grey Fox Inn and Resort
990 Mountain Rd., Stowe,
802-253-8921, 800-544-8454;
www.stowegreyfoxinn.com
38 rooms. Complimentary full breakfast. Restaurant. Bar. Children's activity center. Fitness room. Indoor pool, outdoor pool, whirlpool. **$**

★★Golden Eagle Resort
511 Mountain Rd., Stowe,
802-253-4811, 800-626-1010;
www.goldeneagleresort.com
94 rooms. Restaurant. Children's activity center. Fitness room. Indoor pool, two outdoor pools, whirlpool. Tennis. **$$**

★★★Stoweflake Mountain Resort & Spa
1746 Mountain Rd., Stowe,

802-253-7355, 800-253-2232;
www.stoweflake.com
This resort, the oldest in Stowe, recently underwent a major room renovation, and added a 50,000-square-foot spa. Rooms are decorated in country quilts and feature pillowtop beds and down duvets. The restaurant serves innovative takes on American cuisine.
117 rooms. High-speed Internet access. Restaurant. Bar. Fitness room, fitness classes available, spa. Indoor pool, outdoor pool, whirlpool. Golf, 9 holes. **$$$**

★★Trapp Family Lodge
700 Trapp Hill Rd., Stowe,
802-253-8511, 800-826-7000;
www.trappfamily.com
Channel your inner Julie Andrews at this Tyrolean resort run by the Von Trapp family, the inspiration for the movie *The Sound of Music*. The rustic lodge overlooks a beautiful mountain range and is accented with handcarved balustrades, pitched gables and a cedar shake roof. Activities include croquet, hiking, horse-drawn sleigh rides, pastry classes and cross-country skiing.
96 rooms. Wireless Internet access. Restaurant. Bar. Fitness room. Indoor pool, outdoor pool. Tennis. **$$**

★★★Green Mountain Inn
18 S. Main St., Stowe,
802-253-7301, 800-253-7302;
www.greenmountaininn.com
This historic (yet modernized) colonial inn is surrounded by charming stores, galleries and restaurants.
104 rooms. Wireless Internet access. Restaurant. Bar. Fitness room. Outdoor pool. **$$**

★★★Ye Olde England Inne
433 Mountain Rd., Stowe,
802-253-7558, 800-477-3771;
www.englandinn.com
This elegant 1893 English inn offers rooms decorated in English chintzes and antiques. Mr. Pickwick's Polo Pub is a great spot to grab a meal.

VERMONT

30 rooms. Complimentary full breakfast. Wireless Internet access. Restaurant. Bar. Outdoor pool, whirlpool. **$$**

Topnotch Resort and Spa
4000 Mountain Rd., Stowe,
888-460-5567; www.topnotchresort.com
This classic New England ski resort is slated to close for complete renovations in spring 2008. While the rooms, lobby and lounge areas are under construction, the resort's sprawling new spa, Norma's restaurant and resort townhouses will be open for visitors.

SPECIALTY LODGINGS
Fitch Hill Inn
258 Fitch Hill Rd., Hyde Park,
802-888-3834, 800-639-2903;
www.fitchhillinn.com

This tranquil setting is 15 minutes north of Stowe and is located on three acres of woods and gardens. Guest rooms are decorated in a country style featuring quilts and lace curtains.
6 rooms. Complimentary full breakfast. Whirlpool. **$$**

Stone Hill Inn
89 Houston Farm Rd., Stowe,
802-253-6282; www.stonehillinn.com
This inn is close to all the antique shops, restaurants and activities the town has to offer. Trails, snowshoes, tobogganing and sledding are offered on-site.
9 rooms. Closed April; also mid-November-mid-December. No children allowed. Complimentary full breakfast. Wireless Internet access. Whirlpool. **$$$**

STRATTON
Stratton Mountain is the main attraction in this central Vermont town. The ski resort has a reputation as a superb mountain for families.
Information: www.stratton.com

WHAT TO SEE AND DO
Stratton Mountain
Stratton Mountain Rd., Londonderry,
802-297-4211; www.stratton.com
A high-speed gondola, two high-speed six-passenger chairlifts, three quads, one triple and two double chairlifts, two surface lifts, patrol, school, rentals, snowmaking, cafeterias, restaurants, bars, nursery, sports center. Ninety runs, longest run three miles; vertical drop 2,003 feet. Mid-November-mid-April: daily. More than 17 miles of cross-country trails (December-March: daily), rentals, snowboarding. Summer activities include gondola ride, horseback riding, tennis, golf (school), festivals, concert series.

SPECIAL EVENTS
Vermont Arts & Fine Crafts Festival
Stratton Mountain Ski Resort, Stratton Mountain Rd., Stratton Mountain,
www.vtartsfestival.com
Paintings, photography, sculpture and crafts; special performing arts events, craft demonstrations. Labor Day Weekend.

HOTELS
★★The Inn at Stratton Mountain
61 Middle Ridge Rd., Stratton,
802-297-2500, 800-787-2886;
www.stratton.com
119 rooms. Children's activity center. Fitness room. Indoor pool, three outdoor pools, whirlpool. Golf. Tennis. Ski in/ski out. **$**

VERMONT

SWANTON
The location of this town, just two miles east of Lake Champlain, makes it a popular resort spot.
Information: Chamber of Commerce, 802-868-7200

WHAT TO SEE AND DO

Missisquoi National Wildlife Refuge
29 Tabor Rd., Swanton, 802-868-4781;
www.fws.gov/refuges
More than 6,400 acres, including much of
the Missisquoi River delta on Lake Champlain. Primarily a waterfowl refuge (best in
April, September and October), but other
wildlife and birds may be seen. Fishing,
hunting, hiking and canoe trails. Daily.

HOTELS

★★Tyler Place Family Resort
1 Old Dock Rd., Highgate Springs,
802-868-4000; www.tylerplace.com
39 rooms. Restaurant. Bar. Children's activity center. Fitness room. Indoor pool, outdoor pool, children's pool. Tennis. Closed
Labor Day-late May. $

VERGENNES

The oldest city in Vermont and the third oldest in New England, Vergennes is one of the
smallest incorporated cities in the nation (one square mile).
Information: Vergennes Chamber of Commerce; 802-877-0080

WHAT TO SEE AND DO

Button Bay State Park
5 Button Bay State Park Rd.,
Vergennes, 802-475-2377
This 236-acre park on a bluff overlooking
Lake Champlain was named for the button-
like formations in the clay banks. Spectacular views of Adirondack Mountains.
Swimming pool, fishing, boating (rentals),
nature and hiking trails, picnicking, tent
and trailer sites (dump station). Museum,
naturalist. Memorial Day-Columbus Day.

John Strong Mansion
6656 Highway 17 W., West Addison,
802-759-2309
(1795) Federalist house, restored and furnished in the period. Memorial Day-Labor
Day: Saturday-Sunday 10 a.m.-5 p.m.

Rokeby Museum
4334 Highway 7, Ferrisburgh,
802-877-3406; www.rokeby.org
(Circa 1785) The ancestral home of
abolitionist Rowland T. Robinson was a
station for the Underground Railroad. Artifacts and archives of four generations of the
Robinson family. Set on 85 acres, the farm-
stead includes an ice house, a creamery
and a stone smokehouse. Special events are
offered year-round. Tours. Mid-May-mid-
October, house tours: Thursday-Sunday
11 a.m., 12:30 p.m., 2 p.m.; grounds:
Tuesday-Sunday 10 a.m.-4 p.m.

HOTELS

★★★Basin Harbor Club
4800 Basin Harbor Rd., Vergennes,
802-475-2311
Located on Lake Champlain, this hotel
offers accommodations in the lodge or in
the cottages spread out over the property.
Fresh local ingredients are used to prepare
the breakfast and dinner served in the main
dining room.
117 rooms. Pets accepted, some restrictions; fee. Restaurant. Bar. Children's
activity center. Fitness room. Beach. Outdoor pool. Golf. Tennis. Airport transportation available. Closed November-mid-
May. $$

SPECIALTY LODGINGS

Strong House Inn
94 W. Main St., Vergennes, 802-877-3337;
www.stronghouseinn.com
This historic Federal-style inn is furnished
in period furniture and antiques and is set
on six acres of walking trails, gardens
and ponds. Nearby are many activities,
including hiking, golfing, cycling and
fishing.
14 rooms. Children over 8 years only. Com-
plimentary full breakfast. $$

★
★
★
★
★

WAITSFIELD

This region, known as "the Valley," is a popular area in summer as well as in the winter ski season. Rolling hills and bucolic farms dot the countryside.
Information: Sugarbush Chamber of Commerce, General Wait House, Highway 100, 802-496-3409, 800-828-4748; www.sugarbushchamber.org

WHAT TO SEE AND DO
Mad River Glen Ski Area
Highway 17, Waitsfield, 802-496-3551; www.madriverglen.com
This ski resort has the country's oldest single chairlift, which was fully restored in 2006. Mad River Glen does not make snow, so conditions here depend on the weather. Area has three double and two single chairlifts, patrol, school, rentals, cafeterias, restaurant, bar, nursery. Forty-four runs, longest run three miles; vertical drop 2,000 feet. December-April, daily.

HOTELS
★★Tucker Hill Inn
65 Marble Hill Rd., Waitsfield, 802-496-3983, 800-543-7841; www.tuckerhill.com
22 rooms. Restaurant. Bar. Outdoor pool. Tennis. $$

SPECIALTY LODGINGS
1824 House Inn Bed and Breakfast
2150 Main St., Waitsfield, 802-496-7555, 800-426-3986; www.1824house.com
This restored 1824 farmhouse features feather beds, Oriental rugs and down quilts.
8 rooms. Complimentary full breakfast. Whirlpool. $

The Inn at the Round Barn
1661 E. Warren Rd., Waitsfield, 802-496-2276; www.theroundbarn.com

Located on more than 200 acres of mountains, ponds and meadows, this inn has a round barn that is fully restored and is the setting for weddings, meetings and other functions.
12 rooms. Complimentary full breakfast. Indoor pool. $$

Lareau Farm Country Inn
48 Lareau Rd., Waitsfield, 802-496-4949, 800-833-0766; www.lareaufarminn.com
Farmhouse and barn built by the area's first physician. 13 rooms. Complimentary full breakfast. $

The Waitsfield Inn
5267 Main St., Waitsfield, 802-496-3979, 800-758-3801; www.waitsfieldinn.com
14 rooms. Closed April, November. $

RESTAURANTS
★Restaurant Den
5153 Main St., Waitsfield, 802-496-8880
American menu. Lunch, dinner. Bar. Outdoor seating. Closed holidays. $$

★★The Steak Place at Tucker Hill
65 Marble Hill Rd., Waitsfield, 802-496-3983, 800-543-7841; www.tuckerhill.com
American menu. Breakfast, dinner. Bar. Children's menu. Outdoor seating. Closed Sunday-Monday. $$

WARREN

This northern Vermont town is close to two ski areas, Sugarbush and Mad River Glen. The town has several small bed and breakfasts and quaint restaurants that feed and house skiers at the end of a day on the mountain.
Information: Sugarbush Chamber of Commerce, Waitsfield, 802-496-3409, 800-828-4748; www.sugarbushchamber.org

WHAT TO SEE AND DO

Sugarbush Resort

1840 Sugarbush Access Rd., Warren,
802-583-6300, 800-583-7669;
www.sugarbush.com

Area has seven quad, three triple and six double chairlifts, four surface lifts, patrol, school, rentals, concession area, cafeteria, restaurant, bar, nursery. More than 100 runs, longest run more than two miles, vertical drop 2,650 feet. Early November-late April: daily.

HOTELS

★★★Sugarbush Inn

1840 Sugarbush Access Rd., Warren,
802-583-6114, 800-537-8427;
www.sugarbush.com

Surrounded by slopes, hills and trails, this activity-oriented inn is between the towns of Waitsfield and Warren. Snowshoeing, snow tubing, ice skating and horse-drawn sleigh rides are available on the property. 143 rooms. Complimentary full breakfast. Three restaurants, bar. Children's activity center. Fitness room. Indoor pool, outdoor pool, whirlpool. Golf, 18 holes. Tennis. Ski in/ski out. **$$**

★★★The Pitcher Inn

275 Main St., Warren,
802-496-6350, 800-735-2478;
www.pitcherinn.com

Perfect for skiers, this inn accommodates them with a locker room for ski storage and a boot and glove warmer. Rustic, yet rich and elegant guest accommodations in the main house capture Vermont's colonial history, while two suites in the adjacent barn are perfect for families. The inn's restaurant serves breakfast and dinner and boasts a 6,500-bottle wine cellar.
11 rooms. Complimentary full breakfast. Wireless Internet access. Restaurant. Bar. **$$$$**

SPECIALTY LODGINGS

Sugartree Inn

2440 Sugarbush Access Rd., Warren,
802-583-3211, 800-666-8907;
www.sugartree.com

9 rooms. Pets accepted, some restrictions, Children over 12 years only. Complimentary full breakfast. Restaurant. Closed three weeks in April. **$**

RESTAURANTS

★★★The Common Man

3209 German Flats Rd., Warren,
802-583-2800;
www.commonmanrestaurant.com

Located in Vermont's Mad River Valley, this 1880s restored barn houses a casual dining spot.
American menu. Dinner. Bar. Children's menu. Casual attire. Reservations recommended. Closed Sunday-Monday; two-four weeks in spring and November. **$$**

WATERBURY

Close to many outstanding ski resorts, including Stowe, Mad River Valley and Bolton Valley, this area is also popular in the summer for hiking, backpacking and bicycling.
Information: Central Vermont Chamber of Commerce, Barre, 802-229-5711

WHAT TO SEE AND DO

Ben & Jerry's Ice Cream Factory Tour

Route 100, Waterbury, 866-258-6877;
www.benjerry.com

This half-hour guided tour, offered every 30 minutes (and even more frequently in summer, spring and fall), takes visitors through the ice cream factory that cranks out such beloved flavors as Cherry Garcia and Chunky Monkey. The tour includes a seven-minute "moovie," views of the production line (except on weekends) and free samples in the FlavoRoom. There's also a gift shop, where you can pick up one of those famous tie-dyed cow T-shirts and a few pints to take home. Daily.

270

VERMONT

Camel's Hump Mountain

Long Trail, Waterbury, 802-244-7037
State's third-highest mountain, the trail is quite challenging. Weather permitting, Canada can be seen from the top.

Cold Hollow Cider Mill

3600 Waterbury-Stowe Rd.,
Waterbury Center, 802-244-8771,
800-327-7537; www.coldhollow.com
One of the largest cider mills in New England features a 43-inch rack-and-cloth press capable of producing 500 gallons of cider an hour. Also, jelly-making operations (fall). Samples are served.

Long Trail

802-244-7037;
www.greenmountainclub.org
A 22-mile segment of backpacking trail connects Camel's Hump with Mount Mansfield, the state's highest peak. Primitive camping is allowed on both mountains. Recommended for the experienced hiker.

HOTELS

★★Best Western Waterbury-Stowe

45 Blush Hill Rd., Waterbury,
802-244-7822, 800-621-7822;
www.bestwesternwaterburystowe.com
79 rooms. Restaurant. Bar. Fitness room. Indoor pool. Tennis. **$**

SPECIALTY LODGINGS

Birds Nest Inn

5088 Waterbury-Stowe Rd.,
Waterbury Center,
802-244-7490, 800-366-5592;
www.birdsnestinn.com
Surrounded by black locust trees, this restored 1832 farmhouse has rooms with private baths and down comforters. A hearty three-course breakfast made with local produce is served daily. In the evening, complimentary wines and hot and cold hors d'oeuvres are offered. The inn is close to all major ski areas.
   5 rooms. Children over 15 years only. Complimentary full breakfast. **$**

Thatcher Brook Inn

1017 Waterbury Stowe Rd., Waterbury,
802-244-5911, 800-292-5911;
www.thatcherbrook.com
Built in 1899; twin gazebos with front porch. 22 rooms. Complimentary full breakfast. Restaurant. **$**

WEST DOVER

A south central Vermont village, West Dover is located in the Green Mountains and near several ski resorts.
Information: Mount Snow Valley Region Chamber of Commerce, W. Main St., Wilmington, 802-464-8092, 877-887-6884; www.visitvermont.com

WHAT TO SEE AND DO

Mount Snow Ski Area

12 Pisgah Rd., West Dover,
802-464-2151, 800-498-0479;
www.mountsnow.com
Area has two quad, six triple and nine double chairlifts, patrol, school, rentals, snowmaking, cafeterias, restaurant, bars, entertainment and nursery. More than 100 trails spread over five interconnected mountain areas. Longest run is 2 1/2 miles, with a vertical drop of 1,700 feet. Half-day rates. November-early May: daily.

SPECIAL EVENTS

Oktoberfest & Craft Show

Mount Snow Resort, 12 Pisgah Rd.,
West Dover, 802-464-2151, 800-498-0479;
www.mountsnow.com
New England artisans exhibit pottery, jewelry, glass, graphics, weaving and other crafts; German-style entertainment. Chairlift rides and foliage. Columbus Day weekend.

Shimano NORBA National Mountain Bike Series Finals

Mount Snow Ski Area, 12 Pisgah Rd.,

West Dover, 802-464-4191, 800-451-4211;
www.mountsnow.com/summer/norba
More than 1,500 cyclists from throughout the world compete in downhill, dual slalom and circuit racing events. Late August.

HOTELS

★★West Dover Inn
108 Highway 100, West Dover,
802-464-5207; www.westdoverinn.com
Built in 1846, this inn was once a stagecoach stop and a general store.
12 rooms. Children over 12 years only. Complimentary full breakfast. Restaurant. Bar. $$

★★★The Inn at Sawmill Farm
Highway 100 and 7 Crosstown Rd.,
West Dover, 802-464-8131, 800-493-1133;
www.theinnatsawmillfarm.com
This inn is housed in a converted barn, and the location is perfect for skiers looking to hit the slopes of nearby Mount Snow. Weathered floors and hand-hewn posts and beams hint at the original construction, yet this inn has a decidedly polished flair. The restaurant offers haute cuisine that rivals many of its city competitors.

21 rooms. Restaurant. Bar. Fitness room. Outdoor pool. Tennis. Closed April-May. $$$$

★★★Four Seasons Inn
145 Route 100, West Dover, 802-464-8303;
www.thefourseasonsinn.com
18 rooms. No children allowed. Complimentary full breakfast. Wireless Internet access. Restaurant. Bar. Spa. Outdoor pool. $$

RESTAURANTS

★★★The Inn at Sawmill Farm
Highway 100 and Crosstown Rd.,
West Dover, 802-464-8131, 800-493-1133;
www.theinnatsawmillfarm.com
This restaurant's exposed beams and chandeliers create a perfect place to relax and enjoy delicious home-style cooking. The restaurant features a seasonal American menu specializing in locally farmed game such as quail, pheasant, rabbit and venison. The impressive wine list offers a selection of 1,285 wines in the 30,000-bottle cellar.
American menu. Breakfast, dinner. Bar. Business casual attire. Reservations recommended. Closed April-May. $$$

VERMONT

WILMINGTON
This town is located in central Vermont's Green Mountains and is close to several area ski resorts.
Information: Mount Snow Valley Region Chamber of Commerce, W. Main St.
802-464-8092, 877-887-6884; www.visitvermont.com

WHAT TO SEE AND DO

Molly Stark State Park
705 Highway 9 E., Wilmington,
802-464-5460
A 158-acre park named for the wife of General John Stark, hero of the Battle of Bennington (1777); on west slope of Mount Olga (2,438 feet). Fishing in nearby lake, hiking trails, tent and trailer sites (dump station). Fire tower with excellent views. Standard fees. Memorial Day-Columbus Day.

HOTELS

★★Horizon Inn
861 Hwy. 9 E., Wilmington,
802-464-2131, 800-336-5513;
www.horizoninn.com
28 rooms. Complimentary continental breakfast. Wireless Internet access. Restaurant. Bar. Fitness room. Indoor pool, whirlpool. $

★★★White House of Wilmington
178 Hwy. 9 E., Wilmington,
802-464-2135, 800-541-2135;
www.whitehouseinn.com

This historic inn offers an indoor and out-door pool, steam room and sauna. Built in 1915 as a summer home for a wealthy lumber baron, the inn was restored in 1978, but many of its original details were left intact (including a secret staircase, a favorite of guests). The original house has nine guest rooms, some with fireplaces and some with both fireplaces and whirlpool tubs An adjoining guest house has eight additional rooms designed to accommodate families. 25 rooms. Children over 8 years only. Complimentary full breakfast. Restaurant. Bar. Fitness room. Indoor pool, outdoor pool. Ski in/ski out. Closed April. **$$**

SPECIALTY LODGINGS
Trail's End - A Country Inn
5 Trail's End Lane, Wilmington,
802-464-2727, 800-859-2585;
www.trailsendvt.com
Located near Mount Snow ski resort, this country inn has rooms with four poster beds.

5 rooms. Complimentary full breakfast. Outdoor pool. Tennis. **$**

RESTAURANTS
★★White House
178 Hwy. 9 E., Wilmington,
802-464-2135, 800-541-2135;
www.whitehouseinn.com
Dine in one of the three dining rooms of this 1915 mansion. The menu changes seasonally and includes local Vermont cheeses and entrees such as roasted Vermont duckling and Wiener schnitzel. A wine list with a 100-plus selection is also offered. Located in the White House of Wilmington, the restaurant is easily accessible from Routes 9 and 100.
American menu. Dinner. Bar. Casual attire. Reservations recommended. Closed Monday-Tuesday; April; first two weeks in May. **$$$**

WINDSOR

Situated on the Connecticut River in the shadow of Mount Ascutney, Windsor was once the political center of the Connecticut Valley towns. The name "Vermont" was adopted, and its constitution was drawn up here. Many notable inventors (and inventions) were developed here in the 19th century, including the hydraulic pump, sewing machine, coffee percolator and various refinements in firearms.
Information: White River Area Chamber of Commerce, White River Junction, 802-295-6200

WHAT TO SEE AND DO
Constitution House
16 N. Main St., Windsor, 802-672-3773;
www.historicvermont.org
An 18th-century tavern where the constitution of the Republic of Vermont was signed on July 8, 1777. Museum. Late May-mid-October: Wednesday-Sunday 11 a.m.-5 p.m.

Mount Ascutney State Park
Hwy. 44A, Brownsville, 802-674-2060
This 1,984-acre park has a paved road to the summit of Mount Ascutney (3,144 feet). Hiking trails, picnicking, tent and trailer sites (dump station). Memorial Day-Columbus Day.

Vermont State Craft Center at Windsor House
54 Main St., Windsor, 802-674-6729
Restored building features works of more than 250 Vermont craftspeople. January-May: Thursday-Saturday 10 a.m.-6 p.m., Sunday 11 a.m.-5 p.m.; June-December: Monday-Saturday 10 a.m.-6 p.m., Sunday 11 a.m.-5 p.m.

HOTELS
★★★Juniper Hill Inn
153 Pembroke Rd., Windsor,
802-674-5273, 800-359-2541;
www.juniperhillinn.com

This 1902 Classical Revival mansion is perched atop 14 acres of hillside. A 30-by 40-foot Great Hall features a floor-to-ceiling fireplace, and the library in the west wing of the inn, offers a great place to read or play board games. Past visitors include Teddy Roosevelt.

16 rooms. Children over 12 years only. Complimentary full breakfast. Restaurant. Outdoor pool. Closed two weeks in November; three weeks in late March-early April. $$

WOODSTOCK

The historic charm of Woodstock has been preserved, at least in part, by determination. Properties held for generations by descendants of original owners provided built-in zoning long before historic district status was achieved. When the iron bridge that crosses the Ottauquechee River at Union Street was condemned in 1968, it was replaced by a covered wooden bridge. The nearby town of Queechee is equally charming and is home to the famed Simon Pearce glass and pottery studio and restaurant.
Information: Chamber of Commerce, 18 Central St., 802-457-3555; www.woodstockvt.com

WHAT TO SEE AND DO

Kedron Valley Stables
Hwy. 106 S., South Woodstock, 802-457-1480, 800-225-6301; www.kedron.com
Hayrides, sleigh rides, picnic trail rides, indoor ring, riding lessons by appointment. $$$$

Marsh-Billings-Rockefeller National Historic Park
54 Elm St., Woodstock, 802-457-3368; www.nps.gov/mabi
Includes Marsh-Billings-Rockefeller mansion, which contains an extensive collection of American landscape paintings. Mansion is surrounded by 550-acre Mount Tom forest. Interpretive tours are available. Reservations recommended. Park also offers hiking, nature study and cross-country skiing. Memorial Day-October: daily 10 a.m.-5 p.m.

Suicide Six Ski Area
S. Pomfret Rd., Woodstock, 802-457-1100; www.skivermont.com
Area has two double chairlifts, J-Bar, patrol, PSIA school, rentals, snowmaking, cafeteria, wine and beer bar, lodge. Twenty-two runs, longest run is one mile, with a vertical drop of 650 feet. Site of the first ski tow in the United States (1934). Early December-late March: daily.

Vermont Institute of Natural Science
Route 4, Quechee, 802-359-5000; www.vinsweb.org
Property includes a 47-acre mixed habitat site with trails. VINS Nature Center includes the Raptor Museum, which has 26 species of hawks, owls and eagles May-October: daily 9 a.m.-5:30 p.m.; November-April: daily 10 a.m.-4 p.m.

Woodstock Country Club
14 The Green, Woodstock, 802-457-1100, 800-448-7900; www.woodstockinn.com
An 18-hole championship golf course, 10 tennis courts, paddle tennis, cross-country skiing center with more than 35 miles of trails, rentals, instruction, tours. Restaurant, lounge. Fee for activities. Daily; closed April and November.

Woodstock Historical Society
26 Elm St., Woodstock
Dana House (1807) has 11 rooms spanning 1750-1900, including a children's room; also silver, glass, paintings, costumes, furniture and research library; Woodstock-related artifacts, photographs. Farm and textile equipment. Gift shop. Late May-late

★
★
★
★
★

October: Monday-Saturday 10 a.m.-4 p.m.,
Sunday noon-4 p.m.

HOTELS
★Pond Ridge Motel
506 Hwy. 4 W., Woodstock, 802-457-1667;
www.pondridgemotel.com
20 rooms. $

★The Shire Riverview
46 Pleasant St., Woodstock, 802-457-2211;
www.shiremotel.com
42 rooms. Wireless Internet access. $

★★★Woodstock Inn & Resort
14 The Green, Woodstock,
802-457-1100, 800-448-7900;
www.woodstockinn.com
The centerpiece of Woodstock, the Woodstock Inn & Restaurant and has been around since the 18th century. The rooms and suites capture traditional Vermont style, with handmade quilts, built-in alcoves and original prints, while technology is represented with 29" flat-screen TVs and CD/MP3 players. Downhill and cross-country skiing are two of the resort's most popular winter activities, while the Woodstock Country Club's prestigious course attracts golfers. Biking, canoeing, fishing, horseback riding and nature walks are some of the activities available, and the town's shops are within walking distance. Three restaurants serve everything from gourmet cuisine to casual fare and traditional tavern-style food. 142 rooms. High-speed Internet access, wireless Internet access. Restaurant. Bar. Fitness room, fitness classes available, spa. Indoor pool, outdoor pool, whirlpool. Golf, 18 holes. Tennis. Ski in/ski out. Business center. $$$

★★★Kedron Valley Inn
10671 South Rd., South Woodstock,
802-457-1473, 800-836-1193;
www.kedronvalleyinn.com
Located five miles outside Woodstock, this small historic inn is a great home base for guests focused on antique shopping or checking out the local shops.

26 rooms. Pets accepted, some restrictions. Restaurant. Bar. Closed April. $$

★★★Quechee Inn at Marshland Farm
1119 Quechee Main St., Quechee,
802-295-3133, 800-235-3133;
www.quecheeinn.com
This inn was built in 1793 and has simply decorated rooms, complete with many modern conveniences.
24 rooms. Complimentary full breakfast. Restaurant. Bar. $$

★★★★★Twin Farms
452 Royalton Turnpike, Barnard,
802-234-9999, 800-894-6327;
www.twinfarms.com
This secluded, exclusive hideaway in central Vermont offers one of the most uniquely sybaritic lodging experiences to be had in America. With 10 private cottages and 10 sumptuous guest rooms, Twin Farms is designed to cater to the individual experience. Meals are made to order and can be taken in the main dining room or the privacy of your cottage. Each was decorated to reflect a different theme by renowned interior designer Jed Johnson—the Moroccan-influenced Meadow has Persian rugs and a mosaic-tiled fireplace while the Scandinavian Barn has bleached pine floors, walls and rafters and crisp white and blue fabrics and upholstery. The cost is all-inclusive. 16 rooms. No children allowed. Complimentary full breakfast. High-speed Internet access, wireless Internet access. Restaurant (guests only). Two bars. Fitness room, spa. Tennis. Ski in/ski out. Airport transportation available.

SPECIALTY LODGINGS
Applebutter Inn
Happy Valley Rd., Woodstock,
802-457-4158; www.applebutterinn.com
Built in 1846, this inn used to be a stagecoach stop and a general store.
6 rooms. Complimentary full breakfast. $

Canterbury House Bed and Breakfast
43 Pleasant St., Woodstock,

275

VERMONT

★
★
★
★
★

802-457-3077, 800-390-3077;
www.thecanterburyhouse.com
Victorian home built in 1880; antiques.
7 rooms. No children allowed. Complimentary full breakfast. Restaurant. **$**

Charleston House
21 Pleasant St., Woodstock,
802-457-3843; www.charlestonhouse.com
Greek Revival house built in 1835.
9 rooms. Complimentary full breakfast. **$$**

The Lincoln Inn at the Covered Bridge
530 Woodstock Rd., Woodstock,
802-457-3312; www.lincolninn.com
This renovated farmhouse's property (circa 1869) is bordered by the Ottauquechee River and a covered bridge.
6 rooms. Complimentary full breakfast. Restaurant. **$**

Maple Leaf Inn
Hwy. 12, Barnard, 802-234-5342,
800-516-2753; www.mapleleafinn.com
This property is located on 16 acres of maple and birch trees near the quaint town of Woodstock, where antique stores, unique shops and outdoor recreations abound.
7 rooms. **$$**

Parker House Inn
1792 Quechee Main St., Quechee,
802-295-6077;
www.theparkerhouseinn.com
Victorian house (1857); former senator's residence.
7 rooms. Pets accepted, some restrictions; fee. Complimentary full breakfast. Restaurant. **$**

Woodstocker Bed and Breakfast
61 River St., Woodstock,
802-457-3896, 866-662-1439;
www.woodstockervt.com
Built in 1830.
9 rooms. Complimentary full breakfast. Whirlpool. **$**

276

VERMONT

RESTAURANTS
★★★Barnard Inn
5518 Hwy. 12, Barnard, 802-234-9961;
www.barnardinnrestaurant.com
Built in 1796, this inn is quaint and simple in a charming New England way. The restaurant serves dishes prepared with French technique, such as steamed mussels with saffron and garlic.
French menu. Dinner. Bar. Children's menu. Closed Sunday-Monday. **$$**

★★★Kedron Valley Inn
Highway 106, South Woodstock,
802-457-1473, 800-836-1193;
www.kedronvalleyinn.com
This inn, located just outside Woodstock, is a local favorite for its cheerful rooms and reasonable prices. The menu at the inn's restaurant features Vermont-raised produce and meat.
American menu. Breakfast, dinner. Bar. Children's menu. Closed Tuesday-Wednesday, November-July, week of December 25. **$$**

★★★Prince and the Pauper
24 Elm St., Woodstock, 802-457-1818;
www.princeandpauper.com
Chef and owner Chris Balce offers a menu that changes seasonally. The house specialty is boneless rack of lamb in puff pastry with spinach and mushroom duxelles.
American menu. Dinner. Bar. Business casual attire. Reservations recommended. **$$$**

★★★Quechee Inn at Marshland Farm
1119 Quechee Main St., Quechee,
802-295-3133, 800-235-3133;
www.quecheeinn.com
The restaurant is in the main house of this inn, which dates back to 1793 and overlooks the Ottauquechee River. The cuisine is served in a casual, but sophisticated setting, with a wine list to match.
American menu. Breakfast, dinner. Bar. Children's menu. Business casual attire. Reservations recommended. Outdoor seating. **$$**

★★★**Simon Pearce**
1761 Main St., Quechee, 802-295-1470;
www.simonpearce.com
Part of the glass-blowing and pottery complex that has become an emblem of Vermont, this spacious, contemporary restaurant has beautiful, forested views of the Ottauquechee River and a covered bridge. The cuisine is innovative American with Asian accents, and the breads and soups are homemade.
American menu. Lunch, dinner. Bar. Casual attire. Reservations recommended. Outdoor seating. **$$$**

★★★**Woodstock Inn**
14 The Green, Woodstock,
802-457-1100, 800-448-7900;
www.woodstockinn.com
Nightly piano entertainment perfectly suits the romantic atmosphere at this quaint restaurant in the Woodstock Inn. The kitchen makes full use of local and seasonal produce with offerings like organic field greens with Vermont chevre, raspberries and maple mustard vinaigrette and char-grilled black Angus filet mignon with a Vermont gorgonzola crust and a cider reduction.
American menu. Dinner, Sunday brunch. Bar. Children's menu. Business casual attire. Reservations recommended. Valet parking. **$$$**

VERMONT

INDEX

279

281

INDEX

★
★
★
★
★

282

INDEX

★
★
★
★
★

285

INDEX

★
★
★
★
★

INDEX

★
★
★
★
✩

289

INDEX

★
★
★
★

INDEX

★

★

★

☆

★
★
★
★
★

293

INDEX

★
★
★
★
★
✩

295

INDEX

★

★

★

★

298

INDEX

299

INDEX

300

INDEX

★
★
★
★
★

NOTES

★
★
★
★
★

NOTES

★
★
★
★
★

NOTES

★
★
★
★
★

NOTES

★
★
★
★
★

NOTES

★
★
★
★
★

NOTES

NOTES

307

INDEX

★
★
★
★
★

mobiltravelguide.com

NOTES

INDEX

★
★
★
★
★

NOTES

★
★
★
★
★

NOTES

★
★
★
★
★

NOTES

NOTES

★
★
★
★
★

NOTES

★
★
★
★
★

NOTES

★
★
★
★
★

NOTES

★
★
★
★
★

NOTES

INDEX

★
★
★
★
★

NOTES

★
★
★
★
★

NOTES

INDEX

★
★
★
★
★

NOTES

319

INDEX

★
★
★
★
★

NOTES

★
★
★
★
★